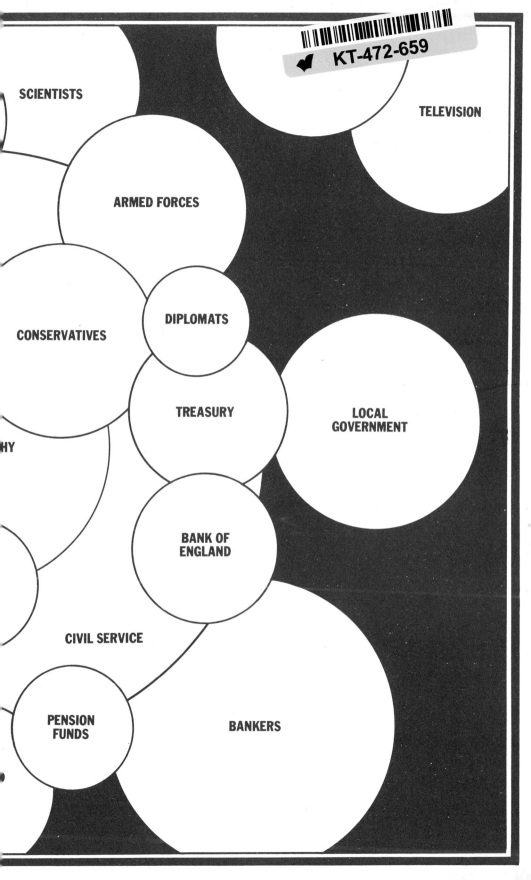

SCIENTISTS

TELEVISION

ARMED FORCES

DIPLOMATS

CONSERVATIVES

TREASURY

LOCAL
GOVERNMENT

HY

BANK OF
ENGLAND

CIVIL SERVICE

PENSION
FUNDS

BANKERS

KT-472-659

The Changing Anatomy of Britain

By the same author

The Changing Anatomy of Britain

Anthony Sampson

HODDER AND STOUGHTON
LONDON SYDNEY AUCKLAND TORONTO

The chart on p. 343 is reproduced with the kind permission of Times Books Ltd from *The Times 1000, 1981-82*, published by Times Books in 1981.

British Library Cataloguing in Publication Data
Sampson, Anthony
  The changing anatomy of Britain
  1. Great Britain—Social conditions
  I. Title
  941.085¹8   HN385.5

ISBN 0 340 20964 X

FOR ROBIN DENNISTON

(who really invented it)

Acknowledgments

In this book as in my previous *Anatomies* I have been helped by hundreds of people inside different institutions and professions, many of whom would prefer not to be publicly thanked. I am grateful for the hospitality of the many people in top positions who have agreed to talk to me, from the prime minister to the Prince of Wales, and from Moss Evans to Lord Denning. Among those to whom I have applied only two have been unwilling to see me: Rupert Murdoch, owner of *The Times*, and 'Tiny' Rowland, owner of the *Observer*.

In the arduous task of organising the whole book, seeing it through every stage, draft and crisis I have been totally dependent on my assistant Alexa Wilson who has helped me with five of my previous books. For loyal support and encouragement from the beginning, I owe much to Hodder and Stoughton who published my first *Anatomy* twenty years ago and my seven books since: I am specially grateful to Michael Attenborough, Eric Major, Alan Gordon-Walker and particularly to Morag Robinson who has tirelessly and thoughtfully edited the complicated typescript. For advice as well as negotiation I am as usual indebted to my agents at A. D. Peters in London, Michael Sissons and Pat Kavanagh and Norman North; to Anthony Gornall of the Intercontinental Literary Agency; and to my old friend Sterling Lord in New York. For research assistance concerning parliament I am indebted to Carol Howard; and I owe a great deal to Emma Duncan, who helped me extensively both with research and interviewing for the chapters on Pensions, the Treasury, Local Government, Scientists, Farmers and Television. For the thorough and rapid index I am very grateful to Douglas Matthews of the London Library. For advice, support and ideas I owe much as always to my wife Sally.

The mistakes are my own, and I will be grateful to any readers who point them out, however angrily, so that they can be put right in subsequent printings.

Contents

Introduction

Change and Decay

Anatomy is Destiny.

Sigmund Freud

I don't think that whatever qualities we have as British people come from the blood or from race. They come from the historic continuity of our institutions, which themselves form our identity as long as we remember them.

Professor Hugh Trevor-Roper, 1975

'WHAT have you changed?' Margaret Thatcher was asked when she became prime minister, and replied: 'I have changed everything.' There was nothing new about the claim, which successive prime ministers had made over the past twenty years, each painting their own picture of the new Britain.

Harold Macmillan portrayed himself as stealthily navigating the retreat from empire, to make Britons face up to a new era of commercial adventure. 'It's exciting living on the edge of bankruptcy,' he said to me in 1961. 'People don't realise that the Victorian age was simply an interruption in Britain's history.' Harold Wilson depicted himself as harnessing the forces of the 'white-hot technological revolution' to British government: 'I think we produced in forty-eight hours the biggest revolution in Whitehall since Lloyd George,' he assured me in 1965. 'You've got to appeal to the Dunkirk spirit.' Edward Heath wanted above all to teach people to 'stand on their own feet': 'We have to get back to the traditional British attitude of independence from the state,' he told me in 1971. 'Already people's attitudes are beginning to change.'

Margaret Thatcher was even more emphatic about the need for individual responsibility: 'I've always regarded the Conservatives,' she told me in 1977, 'as the party of the individual.' She was more dogged and articulate than Heath, and she took over when Britain was much more disillusioned with trade unions and the welfare state, and when all Western countries were reacting against state bureaucracies. Her crusade to revive capitalist enterprise and to reverse Britain's long decline was acclaimed not only by British Tories but by conservatives across the Western world.

For Britain, the first industrial nation, was the first to show many ominous signs of the running-down of an advanced capitalist society, and other countries were watching anxiously for their own symptoms of 'the English disease', including over-powerful unions and too-easy welfare. There was nothing new about Britain's industrial decline, and many historians traced it to the mid-nineteenth century, when Britain was already becoming technologically backward compared to Germany or the United States. Some blamed the economic forces which weakened Britain's competitive advantage; others blamed Britain's ruling class who retreated from industry and trade and failed to respond to the new challenges. Whatever the causes Britain's economic decline had become far more evident over the past twenty years, as Western Europe overtook her standard of living and Japan loomed as a more formidable competitor. But other countries were beginning to encounter some of Britain's difficulties, and they watched the British experiments all the more anxiously. Was Britain the forerunner of every late industrial state?

Britain has the extra interest of a country which has not only been the world's greatest industrial power with an empire across five continents, but which has maintained ancient institutions which in the past have survived and adapted to new challenges and threats. The problem of achieving change through conservative institutions has confronted successive prime ministers. 'It is a very difficult country to move, Mr Hyndman,' Disraeli, just before he died in 1881, warned the socialist leader, 'a very difficult country indeed, and one in which there is more disappointment to be looked for than success.'[1] In the following century Britain's entrenched institutions and countervailing powers have put up higher obstacles against any government which wants to change their direction, whatever their mandate from the electors. 'I want Number Ten to be a powerhouse, not a monastery,' Harold Wilson told me (like many others) in 1964. 'This place is like a tremendous organ,' he went on, 'anything you play comes out at the other end.' But was the power-house plugged in to the grid? What happened to the organ-music? Each reforming prime minister was confronted with the limitations of his power as the bureaucracies, unions, and autonomous institutions closed their ranks against innovation. 'Power? It's like a dead sea fruit,' said Harold Macmillan. 'When you achieve it, there's nothing there.'

It is still early to assess how far Margaret Thatcher has succeeded in changing Britain's direction or attitudes, as she vowed to do. But

---

[1] As Disraeli's conservative biographer remarks, 'it does not follow that Disraeli wanted to move it'. (Robert Blake: *Disraeli*, Eyre and Spottiswood, 1966, p. 764.)

certainly her resolute policies at a time of world recession have shed a
harsh light on British institutions and their leaders, compelling them
to justify themselves. Overconfident trade unionists or paternal
company chairmen, index-linked civil servants or embattled local
councillors—none of them has looked as secure in the age of the Iron
Lady. She has insisted that the Falklands expedition, which proved
her own firmness, has marked a turning-point in Britain's self-
confidence.

In this book I look back on the twenty years since I wrote the first
Anatomy of Britain, during which both parties made bold promises of
change and reform, and try to reflect what happened to the promises,
and why. As in my previous *Anatomies* I try to conduct the reader
through the institutional labyrinth, and to show Britain's workings
not so much in terms of mechanical levers, as of people and attitudes.
I have tried to avoid forcing my subjects into any preconceived
pattern or theory, and to let them speak for themselves about their
attitudes, motives and drive. But in this tour I give more attention to
the special characteristics of British institutions, their self-
deceptions and resistance to change, the loyalties to tribal groups
and the reassertion of old patterns of behaviour. I take note of
Murphy's law ('if something can go wrong it will go wrong'), to
Howard's law ('every change achieves the opposite of what was
intended') to Monnet's law ('it is more useful to *do* something than to
be someone'), to Russell's law ('resistance to new ideas increases as
the square of their importance').

It is a deliberately personal and informal tour of a single country,
but it has an epic theme which is more universal. Throughout these
twenty years the more serious politicians have realised the unique
dangers of a nation in the aftermath of empire: they had to steer it
from the wider seas of world domination into the narrower waters of
national competition and co-operation with neighbours. They knew
the parallels with other post-imperial nations from Egypt to Spain,
though they kept their real fears private. When I asked Iain Macleod
in 1961 what would happen to Britain if she did not enter Europe, he
only replied when the tape recorder stopped: then said, 'No question—we'll just be like Portugal.'

But the problems of retreat and adjustment now also face other
nations including the United States, while Britain's industrial predicament looks less unique as younger industrial countries in East Asia
with their extreme flexibility and drive are challenging all Western
nations. The tensions between old and new institutions, between
national traditions and international competition, between conser-
vation and development are now evident in all Western countries,
while Britain has some advantages which others envy—above all a

tradition of political stability which looks more precious to countries afflicted by terrorism.

Journalism has changed over twenty years along with other institutions, and a succession of books, articles and reports have offered their own dissections and investigations into the state of the nation. Some obscure regions, including industrial corporations, the Treasury and even the Bank of England, have been opened up to let in a few chinks of light. Chairmen of corporations, who two decades ago were wary of any journalist, are now well accustomed to the arts of being interviewed. Diaries and memoirs by ex-cabinet ministers which used to be rarities are now commonplace, and the four volumes of Richard Crossman's diaries provide an invaluable source-book for anyone interested in the workings of political power. Sociologists and political scientists have given their own analyses of the machinery of government. But there is still scope I believe for a journalist to add flesh and blood to these pictures, and to try to convey the atmospheres, pressures and tensions which cannot be measured but which help to explain the operations of power. And it may be easier for an outsider to trace the connections and relationships between the circles of power, and to put them in a larger context.

In the meantime my own perspective and techniques, like those of others, have changed. Watching top people come and go, making their large claims while concealing many of their real problems, I have become more sceptical about interviews, and more interested in the historical perspective and the repetitions of old patterns. Having travelled widely over twenty years and having lived for a year in the United States, I have become more interested in the parallels with other countries and in Britain's interdependence with the rest of the world. This *Anatomy*, I hope, is presented in a larger context, of both time and place.

No doubt the author has himself changed in ways that he cannot judge himself. Twenty years older, it is doubtless harder to maintain indignation about mistakes in high places—or to take seriously men of power with whom one has been at school. The game of toppling father-figures loses some of its attractions in middle age, while the study of the more subtle corruptions of power becomes more interesting. No doubt I have developed my own deep prejudices as a self-employed individual confronting a world of intricate bureaucracies; but I hope this may qualify me to guide other outsiders through the institutional maze which is Britain.

This is a book about the people who are responsible for running the country and its institutions, not the other millions at the receiving end of their decisions. It is not therefore about minorities, about the unemployed or about inner cities, which are subjects for books on their own. Nor is it concerned with Northern Ireland, except as it impinges on political and military problems; this is an Anatomy of Britain, not of the United Kingdom, and the power-structure of Ulster requires a separate expertise. Nor is it about the spiritual side of the British, or questions of private or social morality: I have not attempted to write about the Churches, which have influenced many other areas of power. It is not a book about how Britain *should* be, about new policies or possibilities; but about how it is—or at least how it looks to an individual journalist who remains curious about its unique and odd institutions.

London, July 1982

PART

ONE

———

Politics

1

Monarchy: the Surviving Tribe

A family on the throne is an interesting idea also. It brings down the pride of sovereignty to the level of petty life. No feeling could seem more childish than the enthusiasm of the English at the marriage of the Prince of Wales. They treated as a great political event, what, looked at as a matter of pure business, was very small indeed. But no feeling could be more like common human nature as it is, and as it is likely to be.

Walter Bagehot: The English Constitution, 1867

IT is still useful to start a tour of British institutions at Buckingham Palace. Not just because the monarchy is the oldest of them all, the central totem of a continuous tribal system which is Britain's most obvious distinction; or because the Queen is the formal head of many institutions which follow including parliament, the civil service, the Commonwealth, and the Guards. But also because the monarchy is not a bureaucracy or a hierarchy but a family whose values and attitudes are more personal and comprehensible than those of most other institutions.

It is a family that has become more expert than any other institution in one critical art—the art of survival. In spite of the magic and sentimentality that surrounds it, the family has to be more realistic and less fooled by its mystique than its admirers; the view from the palace is like looking at Britain from backstage, where sets, floodlights and props are seen as part of the illusion. While most other monarchies have been toppled or cut down, the British royal family have developed skills which have enabled them so far to survive each new republican threat. And the more Britain worries about her own survival and future, and the more her other institutions become discredited, the more interesting and reassuring is the continuity of the institution that pre-dates them all.

THE QUEEN

Queen Elizabeth's thirty-year reign itself provides a useful yardstick to measure Britain's progress in the post-imperial age. Her
accession in 1952 coincided with the full flood of Britain's decolon-
isation: and the rituals of kingship, anthropologists remind us, have
much to do with the ordering of time. Her three decades have been
marked not only by the disappearance of the rest of the empire, but
by some of the most rapid social changes in the island's history,
including the doubling of the standard of living, the proliferation of
cars, television sets and home gadgets, the transformation of city
centres and the extension of air travel across the world.

In the midst of these upheavals the Queen's own life has remained
almost uniquely unchanged. She still pursues her timeless progress
between her palaces and country estates, surrounded by the rituals
of nineteenth-century rural life, concerned with racehorses, forestry
or corgis. She is still accompanied by friends from landed or military
backgrounds, with a strong hereditary emphasis. The Mistress of the
Robes is the Duchess of Grafton; the Ladies of the Bed Chamber are
the Marchioness of Abergavenny and the Countess of Airlie. The
Prince of Wales' private secretary is the son of the Queen's former
private secretary, Lord Adeane, who was himself the grandson of
King Edward VII's private secretary, Lord Stamfordham.

Behind this unchanging style the Queen is more concerned with
contemporary Britain than might appear. She watches politics carefully and reads the boxes she is sent by her government. She is
interested in industry, critical of British management, and impressed by Japanese methods. She knows more about world affairs
than most diplomats who visit her, and she has complained to her
Foreign Office about its elementary briefings. She has brought some
newcomers into the palace, including her private secretary, Sir
Philip Moore, who once worked for Denis Healey, and her press
secretary, Michael Shea, a Scottish ex-diplomat who writes thrillers.
She is not formally well-educated, but she has the best sources of
information and her remarks can be sharp. As one American diplomat described her: 'I've learnt a lot from her. She's what we'd
call—if you'll excuse the expression—"street smart".'

Her husband Prince Philip enjoys criticising the complacency and
self-inflicted wounds of the British, the wrecking of the environment,
the narrowness of education and the rheumatism, as he describes it,
that afflicts Britain's anatomy. He particularly likes to champion the
cause of the individual against bureaucracy and potential
totalitarianism. As he said in 1981: 'Once a determined government
begins the process of eroding human rights and liberties—always

with the very best possible intentions—it is very difficult for individuals or for individual groups to stand against it.'

But the life-style of the Queen and Prince Philip still does not have much connection with the urban, industrial lives of most of their subjects; and from time to time Prince Philip drops a brick which suggests that he does not begin to comprehend the gulf that separates him from other working (or non-working) men. 'A few years ago everybody was saying we must have much more leisure,' he said in June 1981. 'Now that everybody has got so much leisure—it may be involuntary, but they have got it—they are complaining they are unemployed. People don't seem to be able to make up their minds what they want, do they?'

While the Queen's life-style and social surroundings have come in for periodic ridicule and political attack, the institution of monarchy has been almost unscathed, and has even increased its prestige as her reign continued. For it was one of the few British institutions whose reputation was not battered by the humiliations of economic decline, the retreat from empire, and the divisions within the nation. While trade unions, universities, civil servants, industrialists or politicians came under heavy fire for their incompetence or irrelevance the monarchy—which might appear the most irrelevant of all—was the most obviously popular and (in its own terms) the most efficient. The British car industry collapsed, corporations went bankrupt and public services went on strike, but the Palace still worked like clockwork. Royal patronage—whether of the royal parks, crown estates, royal colleges or the Royal Opera House—still provided some guarantee of standards. Royal visits still ensured a measure of discipline, so that an architect who wanted to get his building finished on time would try to arrange for a royal to open it. The immaculate timing of the great royal events—whether the trooping of the colour, Lord Mountbatten's funeral, or a royal wedding—reminded the British that they could still do some things better than anyone else. While foreigners mocked Britain's declining standards and industry they conceded that they could not compete with British ceremonial. As the *Boston Globe* put it after the royal wedding: 'The Royal Family of England pulls off ceremonies the way the army of Israel pulls off commando raids.'

As British governments came and went, promising their opposite cures and institutional upheavals, so the continuity of the Queen, who has seen seven prime ministers come and go, became more reassuring. The Queen showed herself able to come to terms with each new lurch of the political system. When Harold Wilson came to power in 1964 the palace was apprehensive about the Labour revolutionaries, and some ministers even refused to wear formal dress for court occasions. But the Queen was soon having friendly talks every Tuesday with Wilson, who later paid tribute to her helpfulness and commonsense; and she later confided in James Callaghan whose company she particularly enjoyed. Michael Foot first kept himself carefully aloof, but can now charm the royal family with his literary talk (though Tony Benn is careful not to be seen with them in public). It was with recent Tories that the Queen had a stickier time—all the more since they were less interested than Labour in the Commonwealth. Ted Heath never established a rapport with his monarch; and the weekly meetings between the Queen and Mrs Thatcher—both of the same age—are dreaded by at least one of them. The relationship is the more difficult because their roles seem confused; the Queen's style is more matter-of-fact and domestic, while it is Mrs Thatcher (who is taller) who bears herself like a queen.

As foreign republics went through upheavals the institution of monarchy could still show some advantages. The Shah was a bad advertisement for kingship, but the new King of Spain suggested that monarchy could still give stability to a divided state. In Washington during the Watergate crisis, Richard Nixon could deploy all the panoply of the 'imperial presidency' to cast his spell over Congress and the media. In Paris, President Giscard could exploit the regal mystique of the Elysée, to the fury of his socialist enemies. But the English prime minister still has no grandeur to compare with the monarchy's; and it was this argument that had swayed many British radicals in its favour in the past. 'It is at any rate possible,' said George Orwell in 1944, 'that while this division of functions exists, a Hitler or a Stalin cannot come to power.' Or as Antony Jay expressed it in the film *The Royal Family*: 'The strength of the monarchy does not lie in the power it has, but in the power that it denies to others.'

And by a remarkable turnabout it was in the former empire, where the monarchy had been most associated with domination and oppression, that the Queen came to play a historic role which took full advantage of her continuity. Under the formula which Nehru and Mountbatten had devised for India she was accepted as 'Head of the Commonwealth' even after most of the new nations had become republics, which enabled her to be much more than a figurehead; and countries which had seen the royal family as instruments of hegemony began to recognise the Queen as a useful ally in their links with the West. While the British public and politicians were becoming bored or disillusioned with developing countries in the late seventies the Queen was becoming increasingly well-informed about them, taking great care with her briefings about their cocoa-crops or sisal exports, surprising their diplomats by her curiosity, and discreetly lobbying for their interests, such as concessions for overseas students. While her Foreign Office was becoming obsessed with Europe, she was much more interested in the Commonwealth. She took a personal interest in the Commonwealth Secretariat (which inhabits her grandmother's old palace, Marlborough House, in the Mall); she gave special access to the Secretary-General, Sonny Ramphal; she agreed to become patron of the Centre for World Development Education; and every March she attended the Commonwealth Day party, where the steel band echoed through Marlborough House.

As black governments were overthrown and regimes toppled, so the Queen's continuity in the Commonwealth became more valuable. Since she held no political power she could forge her personal links without being accused of paternalism or political opportunism, and as a woman she enjoyed a kind of neutrality in this club of men. She became the unifying element at the conferences of Commonwealth prime ministers, even though she took no formal part in the proceedings, and however anti-British the mood, the premiers were always glad to have their separate audiences. When Ted Heath as prime minister in 1973 was most resentful of the Commonwealth, the Queen still insisted on attending the conference of prime ministers at Ottawa. Her most historic role was at the 1979 conference in Lusaka, just after Mrs Thatcher had become prime minister—to the alarm of many African leaders. The government, abetted by the *Daily Telegraph*, had warned the Queen against going to Zambia while the civil war was raging in next-door Rhodesia, and advised switching the conference to Kenya. But the Queen stuck to her plans, paying special attention to the president of Zambia, Kenneth Kaunda, providing a relaxed family atmosphere before Thatcher's arrival and de-fusing some of the political tensions. The deadlock had been averted, and the Queen had made up for her prime minister's tactlessness. The Lusaka Conference agreed to begin the critical negotiations which eventually brought about the independence of Rhodesia-Zimbabwe and the end of the civil war; and while Mrs Thatcher and Lord Carrington took most of the credit, the Queen had undoubtedly played an indispensable role.

THE COST OF FAIRYLAND

The rich, old-fashioned and mildly eccentric life-style of the royal family, carefully screened from close public scrutiny, helped to preserve its mystique as a kind of fairyland in the midst of workaday realities. The courtiers had followed the precept of Walter Bagehot,

'We must not let in daylight upon magic', allowing enough light to fascinate, but not so much as to reveal the family's basic ordinariness. The Queen had agreed to allow the BBC to televise some of her activities in the film *Royal Family* in 1969: but then the doors closed again, and she and her husband returned to their habitual aloofness and dislike of the media. While the Scandinavians and the Dutch monarchy (which is even richer then the British) cultivated a commonsensical and accessible image, the courtiers in Buckingham Palace were acutely conscious of the magical element, enhanced by the British cult of secrecy. The more exposed and publicity-conscious other British institutions became, the more mysterious was this secretive palace—the best-known yet the least-known of all buildings.

The attraction was enhanced by the continuous family saga. The family had become more tattered at the edges after the divorces of Princess Margaret and the Earl of Harewood, but this only added sub-plots to the long soap opera, in which glittering ceremonies were mixed up with an extended family—including the bachelor heir, the bad-tempered sister, the naughty aunt, the adored granny and a succession of babies—which could rival *Dallas* in its range of situations. 'You can't separate the private and public functions of the Queen,' one of her chief courtiers once explained to me; 'that's the main difference between a monarchy and a republic. In a republic you know that the president's life is arranged by the state, and that eventually he'll retire back to his own home. What most impresses the visitors to Windsor or the royal yacht is the feeling that they're in a private home—that it's part of family life.'

The Queen has always insisted on living a family life on her own terms, elaborately protected by her courtiers, and this domestic priority has defied every change of government and political mood. However powerful or radical the visitors to her palaces, they find themselves inside a self-contained world with the Queen at the centre, from which the world outside looks irrelevant or transitory. When in May 1977 the seven leaders of the Western world were invited to dinner at Buckingham Palace, the Queen sat between President Carter and President Giscard; but the Japanese prime minister, Fukuda, found himself next to the Duchess of Grafton, the Mistress of the Robes; the British prime minister, James Callaghan, was next to the Queen's sister, Princess Margaret; and Mr Blumenthal, the American minister, sat next to an obscure equerry, Lieutenant-Colonel Blair Stewart-Wilson.

Richard Crossman, the most overtly republican of Harold Wilson's ministers, was infuriated when he had to travel up to the Queen's castle in Scotland to take part for a few minutes in some trivial ritual, kneeling on one knee and walking backwards, in the midst of a government crisis. 'I don't suppose anything more dull, pretentious or plain silly has ever been invented,' he complained after one ceremony. 'It would be far simpler for the Queen to come down to Buckingham Palace,' he wrote later, 'but it's *lèse-majesté* to suggest it.'[1] Yet Crossman could not conceal his own fascination with the private life of the royal family, and his satisfaction when he established a personal relationship with the Queen.

The monarchy still retains its ability to make other people behave in comical ways, as if it filled some gap in their subconscious. When the Queen arrives at a party her presence can still transform the most cynical subjects: the path is cleared before her, conversations are distracted and necks are strained towards the small woman in blue surrounded by aides. When the Queen came to a gathering of authors in March 1982 she faced an eccentric array ranging from Harry Secombe to Lord Longford, from Alan Whicker to Arthur Bryant, from Margaret Drabble to John Mortimer; yet the whole assembly agreed to be shepherded to stand meekly in rows, to bow low or curtsey and say 'ma'am'; and even the Australian owner of *The Times*, Rupert Murdoch, often suspected of being a republican, was observed to bow lower than most and to beam long after his brief royal conversation was over. An autocrat paying homage to a monarch has always had a special anthropological interest: and Bagehot observed how Lord Chatham, the most dictatorial of English statesmen, bowed so low to George III 'that you could see the tip of his hooked nose between his legs . . . There was a kind of mystic enchantment in vicinity to the monarch which divested him of his ordinary nature.'[2]

The magic has always been more contrived than it looked, and behind it lies a realistic commercial bargain: the taxpayers and their governments are prepared to subsidise the royal family, provided that they show themselves sufficiently frequently, and do not over-step their political limits. The bargain became more open in 1971 when a select committee of parliament investigated the royal budget after complaints about the effects of inflation. ('We go into the red next year,' Prince Philip explained in 1969, '. . . we may have to move into smaller premises, who knows?') The committee, sup-ported by the Heath government, agreed to double the Queen's civil list to £980,000 and to adjust it in line with inflation—so that it amounted to £4.2 million in 1982—while the government paid the heavy costs of maintaining the royal palaces, the royal yacht

[1] Richard Crossman: *The Diaries of a Cabinet Minister*, vol 2, Jonathan Cape, London, 1976, p. 44.
[2] Walter Bagehot: *The English Constitution*, 1867, chapter 2.

Britannia, the Queen's flight and other royal services which between them cost over £12 million a year.

The Queen's entire income remains tax-free, which distinguishes her from all her subjects, and her shareholdings and private wealth remain secret. (The monarchy is a kind of caricature of Britain's mixed economy: on the one side it is a thoroughly nationalised industry, on the other a very free enterprise, free of tax or disclosure.) The total cost of the monarchy might be reckoned at £20 million a year—a sum which does not look exorbitant compared to the £42 million which Unilever spent on advertising in 1981—but is enough to raise angry questions from Tony Benn or the Militant Tendency. The royal family realise that they must provide their money's worth in terms of public exposure, and the Queen's Jubilee and her son's wedding have for the time being allayed most of the criticism; but as one of the royal family put it: 'There are quite a few people over in Westminster who are waiting to attack us again.'

Behind the great pageant of ritual and magic-making the monarchy has remained, in the Hanoverian tradition, a down-to-earth, middle-class, rather philistine family with whom many other English people can identify. In spite of their great estates and aristocratic friends they keep their distance from the ducal world or the House of Lords, and they take care to project a sense of classlessness and to communicate with ordinary people, which they know is essential to their survival. 'The monarchy,' Norman St John-Stevas, the former Tory cabinet minister, said in 1982, 'has become our only truly popular institution at a time when the House of Commons has declined in public esteem and the Lords is a matter of controversy. The monarchy is, in a real sense, underpinning the other two estates of the realm.'[3]

It was the royal wedding which provided the climax to what Professor Edmund Leach calls 'the irrational theatre of monarchy'. It could combine all the old power of ritual with a contemporary love story, the more interesting because an English bride was now being inducted into the magic circle. No laws of political science, psephology or economics could explain its magical effects, which spread far beyond Britain (when I watched it at a dawn wedding party in America the American guests seemed more afflicted than the British). The openness of the monarchy was all the more spectacular when so many world leaders were taking to bullet-proof cars, and Prince Charles had personally insisted on open coaches and the use of St Paul's rather than Westminster. For the Prince, the tumultuous reception gave a new reassurance that feelings for the monarchy could transcend all the classes, and all parties.

[3] *The Times*, February 1, 1982.

But the very success of the wedding, coinciding as it did with a deepening recession and the outbreak of unprecedented riots at Toxteth and elsewhere, raised awkward questions for the British. Would they ever be able to devote the same energies and enthusiasm to the challenges of the future as they did to the rituals of the past? Was the fascination of the monarchy linked to the evasion of industrial realities? And could the monarchy retain its popularity and neutrality in the face of a much angrier new generation?

THE PRINCE OF WALES

The heir to the throne, the Prince of Wales, is fully aware of the implications and difficulties of his inheritance. He was brought up with the fair certainty—'It dawned on me with a ghastly inexorability'—that he would some day be king. He was trained by his parents in all the necessary disciplines; he was sent to his father's old school, the spartan Gordonstoun in Scotland, and to Geelong in Australia; and at Cambridge he studied two subjects very relevant to kingship, history and anthropology. His reading of anthropology made him realise that people, after all, did not change all that much: he was fascinated by ancient Indian writings about kingship, and the way that the modern monarchy could still reveal unexpected yearnings among ordinary people, as if some spiritual element had been neglected. His reading of history gave him a powerful sense of the insecurity as well as the continuity of monarchy; and he has no illusions about the fickleness of public attitudes to the crown.

He is conscious of his descent from the Hanoverians, who first came to Britain as suspect foreigners subject to much ridicule, and he has a soft spot for George III, the much-abused monarch who was the butt of cartoonists and pamphleteers. He knows very well the traditional difficulties of rebellious Princes of Wales as they waited to become monarch—whether of his great-uncle who became King Edward VIII, or of his great-great-grandfather who was fifty-nine when he became King Edward VII. 'All the world and all the glory of it,' as Walter Bagehot wrote of him, 'whatever is most seductive, has always been offered to the Prince of Wales of the day, and always will be. It is not rational to expect the best virtue when temptation is applied in the most trying form at the frailest time of life.'[4]

Prince Charles emphasised to me the limitations of his position, as a man with little formal authority of his own, the junior member of the 'family firm' whose important decisions are all taken by his mother the monarch. As a shy man, concerned with his own private life, he faces the strains of having to be seen and having to confront

[4] Bagehot: *op cit*.

the media, while trying to maintain his own privacy. But his uncle Mountbatten—whose portrait hangs in his study—told him that 'In this business you can't afford to be a shrinking violet,' and he has always taken trouble to get out and about. He realises that the monarchy cannot survive without publicity: 'If the photographers *weren't* interested, that would be the time to start worrying.' He has tried to like the Press; but he has found the frontier between publicity and privacy very hard to protect. He knows that his influence is what he makes of it, depending on the effort he puts into it.

He sees his own role in modest terms, as an individual who may be able to have some effect on human attitudes and values. He is concerned with the importance of individuals and smaller units as opposed to big impersonal institutions: 'For our prosperity in the future we must look far more to human psychology.' He has been especially impressed by the big companies such as Sainsbury and Marks and Spencer—those other 'family firms'—which can make all their staff feel personally involved. He has been influenced by the ideas of Kurt Schumacher and other proponents of *Small is Beautiful*: 'We need to provide small businesses, where people can use their skills far more imaginatively.' In his own private life he prefers, like his mother, country pursuits ('I'm a countryman—I can't stand cities'); and he has tried to encourage small business activities in his own Duchy of Cornwall (the surplus revenue of which he inherited at twenty-one) and at Highgrove. But he has learnt like his father to take an interest in management and industry, and he spends much time visiting factories and discussing industrial psychology.

In conversation he gives a strong impression of an independent and questioning person, living within a family, looking out across a world of anonymous institutions, speculating about what role he can play among them. Surrounded by all the myths and exploitations of monarchy, he is determined not to be misled, as some of his ancestors have been. The modern monarchy is more realistic than most people who gaze at it: it is the emperor who realises that he has no clothes.

Like his mother, he is very conscious of the importance of the Commonwealth, all the more since his tour of India, where he received a rapturous reception in Calcutta, which has a communist government. He has tried to encourage investment abroad through the Commonwealth Development Corporation of whose board he is a member; and he feels himself much more at home in the Commonwealth than on the Continent. But he has no constitutional position: it is the Queen who is Head of the Commonwealth, and it is not even altogether clear whether the position is hereditary or not.

His more immediate interest is in race relations within Britain, where he feels very strongly the need to make immigrants feel part of the community: he has insisted on visiting immigrant areas including Brixton, where warnings of hostile demonstrations were disproved; and he has made a point of praising the achievements of Asian businessmen, a recognition which politicians have shied away from. ('Many of them come here without a bean, and they end up as millionaires. They know what the customers want and they seek them out. Surely we should follow their example.') When the English complain that Asians keep too much to themselves, he likes to remind them that many English families living abroad have the same reputation. The Prince has a black girl secretary on his private staff, but many people concerned with race relations think that the Palace should go further by appointing a black aide or equerry who could more visibly demonstrate that the monarchy has no racial bias.

It is implicit in the Prince's upbringing and experience that he has had to think more carefully than any politician about his relationship with the country and its institutions, and what they really mean. He is conscious that the monarchy is always in danger of becoming pompous and getting out of touch with the people; but he is impressed by the advantages of constitutional monarchy. He realises that the monarchy can never compete with the democratic process, which allows electors to take their choice; but he finds some benefits in never having to be elected. 'Something as curious as the monarchy,' he said to me, 'won't survive unless you take account of people's attitudes. I think it can be a kind of elective institution. After all, if people don't want it, they won't have it.'

Parliament: the Faltering Pendulum

> The English people believes itself to be free; it is gravely mistaken; it is free only during election of members of parliament; as soon as the members are elected, the people is enslaved; it is nothing. In the brief moment of its freedom, the English people makes such a use of that freedom that it deserves to lose it.
>
> *Jean-Jacques Rousseau*

ONCE a year the monarchy makes contact with democracy in the extraordinary ritual of the state opening of parliament, where officials parade in fancy dress, leaders of the opposition process two-by-two with government ministers, and the Queen reads out the speech which the government has written for her. It can still amaze foreign visitors and infuriate radical members of parliament: 'It's like the *Prisoner of Zenda*,' complained Richard Crossman in 1967, 'but not nearly as smart or well done as it would be at Hollywood. It's more what a real Ruritania would look like—far more comic, more untidy, more homely, less grand.'[1]

But the ritual still illustrates the basis of the British constitution: that the sovereignty of monarchs has passed to the sovereignty of parliament, leaving the monarchy with the trappings of power, while prime ministers are still denied the kind of pomp that is accorded to American and French presidents. The 'dignified' role of the crown in the constitution (as Walter Bagehot described it a century ago) mingles with the 'efficient' role of parliament and the executive. Parliament is the obvious starting point for pursuing what Aneurin Bevan called 'the will o' the wisp of power'. But does parliament still belong to the efficient part, or has it (as Crossman suggested in 1959) joined the monarchy as 'merely one piece of the dignified part'[2] leaving the real power to be wielded in Whitehall or elsewhere?

It is the intimacy and clubbiness of the British parliament which

---

[1] Crossman: *op cit*, vol 2, p. 544.
[2] *The Backbench Diaries of Richard Crossman*, Jonathan Cape, London, 1981, p. 737.

remains its most striking characteristic, going back to its origins as a body which, as its name suggests, ruled the country by talk. The small chamber, with a floor only sixty-eight feet long, still has the atmosphere of a drawing-room: it is a quarter of the size of the House of Representatives in Washington, which has fewer members.[3] The members crowded on their green leather benches—baying, giggling or sleeping—seem unaware of the public galleries above them. They are not supposed to read their speeches, and their impromptu debates are much more intimate than the speechifying in Washington or Paris. They dawdle in and out of the chamber, bowing to the Speaker and whispering to their colleagues, while in the lobbies, bars and restaurants they pick up their information and gossip. They can all feel the 'mood of the House', which no prime minister can altogether ignore: even Churchill at the height of his wartime power remained (as Attlee described him) 'a good House of Commons man'. And during a crisis such as Suez or the Falklands it is the mood of the House which is ruling the nation.

All the ritual still revolves round the Speaker, elected by members at the beginning of each parliament, personifying the independence and autonomy for which parliament fought in the seventeenth century. The present Speaker, George Thomas, a Methodist lay preacher and the son of a Welsh miner, rose from the Labour benches to be Secretary of State for Wales, and now like all Speakers forswears his party allegiance. He sits on the Australian-made throne, wearing his full-bottomed wig, intoning 'Order, Order' in his sonorous Welsh voice and occasionally intervening to prevent a brawl or to 'name' or expel a member. His special privileges emphasise the dignity of parliament. He lives as a bachelor in a huge house inside the Palace of Westminster; takes precedence over every commoner except the two archbishops, the Lord Chancellor, the prime minister and the Lord President of the Council; and becomes a peer on retirement. Thus detached, the Speaker can preside impartially over parliament, maintaining good manners in the heat of argument: 'We have one of the most robust and lively parliaments in the world,' Speaker Thomas insists. 'It is a living, vibrant democracy.'

The continuity of parliament remains its historic achievement, replacing an erratic monarchy with a self-regulating club, and it is still the critical link in the democratic process. But all ancient institutions and rituals carry the danger that their members lose sight of their real purpose, and become removed from the lives and understanding of ordinary people; that stability turns into immobility. And parliament is the most self-regarding and resistant of all.

[3] Kenneth Bradshaw and David Pring: *Parliament and Congress*, Quartet Books (revised edition), London, 1981, p. 124.

As both sides of parliament have pressed almost every other British institution to reform, parliament itself has been the most reluctant to contemplate change, while in the last two decades its critics have questioned some of its most-loved assumptions.

Even the architecture is now called in question. The wide rectangle, with the rows of members facing each other and the Speaker in the middle, provides the natural stage for two parties competing on the adversary system, seeing every argument as a contest between prosecution and defence. The heroic encounters between Disraeli and Gladstone, Attlee and Churchill, Thatcher and Foot, have become part of Britain's political psychology, accepting that the opposition may suddenly find itself changing sides and becoming the government; and the same two-sided pattern is common to many other British institutions, from football and the law courts to negotiations between 'two sides of industry'. But the confrontations in parliament began to look less attractive in the last half of the twentieth century, as they appeared more clearly to represent not just the two parties but the two classes—workers and trade unionists on one side, bosses and managers on the other. The assumptions of fair play or football could easily be transposed into the setting for class warfare, in which every member was pressed on to one side or the other.

Most Continental parliaments are very different, laid out like an amphitheatre or semicircle, with deputies facing the President of the Assembly, while each speaker orates from the platform below the President. A British spectator is instantly aware of the difference of atmosphere: it is not so much like a club or a law-court as like a spacious theatre. This was the setting for the French assembly just before the revolution in 1789, when the nobles took up their position of honour on the President's right while the 'third estate' of commoners sat on his left. This ceremonial seating-plan came to symbolise the political differences between conservatives and radicals, with moderates occupying the centre; and by the 1920s British politicians were beginning to call each other 'left' and 'right', even though the words bore no relation to their own seating, and were little understood by ordinary voters.[4]

The French pattern could be said to reflect a more respectful attitude to the state, represented by the President's podium; and Continental deputies did not face the same ordeal of addressing their enemies at close quarters. But the amphitheatres can represent a more flexible system, allowing changing coalitions to show themselves in the seating, or the centre to remain unaligned, while the

[4] For a discussion of the emotional confusions of left and right see Sam Brittan: *Left or Right, the Bogus Dilemma*, Secker and Warburg, London, 1968, pp. 29–31.

arguments are not necessarily between opposites and adversaries. Many British critics of the two-party system, including Liberals and Social Democrats, complained that the design of the House of Commons was encouraging out-of-date divisions and arguments: 'The first thing I'd do about parliamentary reform,' said one Social Democrat leader, 'is to call in the carpenters.'

THE MEMBERS

The individual member of parliament has found himself caught between contradictory pressures. He was first selected as a candidate by his constituency committee to represent their views; he belongs to a party pledged to its own election manifesto; yet his self-respect depends on following his own principles and judgment. Most members would like to agree with Edmund Burke who told the electors of Bristol, 'Your representative owes you not his industry only, but his judgment; and he betrays instead of serving you if he sacrifices it to your opinion.' But MPs have become much more aware that pursuing their own judgment may exclude them from the House, if their local committee withdraws its support. Tory MPs are very mindful of the example of Nigel Nicolson, who lost his seat in Bournemouth after he criticised the Suez adventure, while Labour constituencies now insist on reselecting their members every two years—making MPs more like American congressmen in their anxiety to please their electors. The tension between a delegate and his local committee (which very inadequately represents his constituency) is inevitable in any democratic system; but for the British MPs, with their tradition of independent members, it has become increasingly painful.

The British MP is much more isolated than a German deputy or an American congressman with his large staff and suite of offices. The House still resists bureaucratic organisation, and vaguely assumes that the member is an amateur politician with a job and an income elsewhere. It still operates for only about thirty-two weeks a year, with a break of twelve weeks from August until mid-October—longer holidays than any other profession except dons. It was not until 1963 that the House of Commons recognised that any members with no outside income were seriously deprived, and the salary was put up to £3,250. By 1981 members were receiving £13,950 a year together with £8,480 a year for secretarial expenses, up to £4,900 a year for travel expenses, free telephone calls within London and unlimited crested writing paper (at least one member has written an entire book on it).

The House has gradually provided some kind of office for each member—in the towers or courtyards of the Gothic palace itself, in draughty corridors or up winding staircases, or in the cavernous Norman Shaw building across the road. But members never know whether they should be amateurs or professionals, and probably never will. The compactness and the club atmosphere depend on the presence of fairly leisurely individuals with interests outside, while the complexity of government demands specialised committees, time and resources. Without professional resources a member is ill-equipped to question the workings of departments; and he is an easy prey for pressure groups, foreign governments and corporate lobbyists, luring him with retainers, meals and free trips. A member for a constituency may gradually turn into a member for Vickers, South Africa or the Falklands and the appearance of individualism can become a façade, with much manipulation behind the scenes.

Members have always come from very limited backgrounds, partly dictated by the financial needs. After the Second Reform Act of 1868 first gave votes to householders in the boroughs, two-thirds of the members were still landowners, and middle-class or working-class voters were only gradually represented by their own kind. The members on both sides of the House are still very unrepresentative of their voters. In the last twenty years the numbers of barristers has diminished on both sides, and the numbers of Tory farmers and Labour journalists have also gone down. But there are still too many Conservative company directors and farmers, too many Labour teachers and trade unionists, and far too many lawyers on both sides (though not so many as in Washington, where fifty-seven of the hundred senators are lawyers). These were the leading occupations of members after the general elections in 1959 and 1979:[5]

	1959	1979
CONSERVATIVE		
Barristers	72	51
Solicitors	14	19
Farmers	38	22
Armed forces	37	20
Journalists	26	31
Businessmen	113	115
LABOUR		
Teachers	36	66
Miners	34	21
Barristers	27	15
Journalists	25	13
Skilled workers	22	40

[5] *The Times Guide to the House of Commons*, 1959 and 1979.

The most obviously obligated group of MPs are those sponsored by trade unions, who in 1979 made up 133 out of the 268 Labour MPs—almost half, and the biggest proportion since 1935—including twenty-one from the engineers' union, twenty from the Transport and General Workers' Union and sixteen from the National Union of Mineworkers. The 'Tumps' have long been resented by other members, as they spend their days sitting in the tea-room, looking into the chamber only briefly to listen to questions. But they have become less significant since the forties and fifties when they more genuinely represented workers' interests. Frank Cousins, the head of the Transport and General Workers' Union, began sponsoring sitting MPs, and after the 1979 election a fifth of the Tumps were university-educated, many with no real experience of the unions: among them was the only remaining Old Etonian in the Labour party, Tam Dalyell, and one of the only two Wykehamists, Giles Radice, sponsored by the railwaymen.

The union leaders may still mobilise their sponsored MPs in bargaining with Labour governments and Sid Weighell, the railwaymen's leader, will sometimes threaten to deploy his twelve 'Nurmps'. But they cannot bind their members: Bill Rodgers (sponsored by the General and Municipal Workers) and John Horam (sponsored by the Transport and General) both became founder-members of the Social Democrat party. Trade unions provide useful benefits for candidates, paying for agents and expenses for elections and conferences; but the trade unionists in parliament are not as high-powered as they were when they included the railwaymen's leader J. H. Thomas in the twenties, or even Ray Gunter in the sixties. Trade unions nowadays send their second-class men or pensioners into parliament, and keep their best men for their own organisations. The other MPs complain not so much that they wield decisive power, as that they are lobby-fodder with few original views.

It is whom the House of Commons does *not* include that is more striking; and among the members are no blacks and Asians, and only a few representatives of half the population, women. Since women over thirty first got the vote in 1918 they have encouraged much wider subjects for parliamentary debate, including welfare, health, social services, abortion and divorce; but they have had much less effect on the make-up of the House. After Nancy Astor became the first woman member in 1919 the numbers increased rapidly, but more recently they have fallen again, with only nineteen women in the House in 1979, the lowest since 1951, even though two of its most prominent members are women. This is largely due to their difficulties in taking the job; as Shirley Williams has complained: 'Look back on the women MPs of a generation ago; a very high proportion were single or widowed, some succeeding their deceased husbands for the same constituency. Of today's women MPs and candidates, many are trying to keep a family and a job going at the same time. Parliament's timetable ensures that any reasonably responsible parent will live in a perpetual state of mild guilt . . .'[6]

Many male MPs still owe much to the long-suffering of their wives – the 'St Stephens Widows' who endure long evenings alone and sit loyally beside their husbands at meetings. But this kind of partnership is now much less certain. Divorce is an occupational hazard of politics, and problem children and suicides provide warnings of the dangers of combining politics with family life. The most spectacular example of a loyal consort today is not a wife, but the prime minister's husband.

With all its humiliations and discomforts the House of Commons can still attract very able people. The new members in 1979, though less distinguished than in such vintage years as 1945 or 1959, none the less included enough first-class brains to maintain a high standard. As the college from which any future government will be chosen, the House still offers the basic lure of political power; and to achieve this ambition members will put up with a long and boring apprenticeship. But it is the backbench MP who may never come to power who is the soul of the House, and his self-respect has been steadily undermined, for he can be much less confident that he is contributing, as Burke insisted he must, his own judgment. And his influence has been increasingly eclipsed by the influence of Whitehall.

COMMITTEES AND CHAMBER

Gradually members have tried to grapple with the details of policy-making inside Whitehall by questioning ministers and civil servants. There is nothing new about parliamentary committees. The first one, the Public Accounts Committee, was established by Gladstone in 1861 to scrutinise government accounts; it is still the most prestigious, under a chairman who is always a prominent member of the opposition—at present Joel Barnett, the Labour tax expert who was Chief Secretary of the Treasury in the last Labour government. The PAC has as its instrument the huge department headed by the Auditor-General, now Gordon Downey, an ex-Treasury man who presides over a staff of civil servants, checking government spending. But the PAC is not concerned with policies

---

[6] The *Guardian*, October 30, 1979.

and their execution, which have increasingly interested MPs, and it is only in the last three years that more effectively wide-ranging committees have been formed.

It was under the new Tory government that the Leader of the House, Norman St John-Stevas, introduced what he called 'the greatest constitutional change of the century', which set up fourteen new select committees to examine the spending, administration and policy of the chief government departments. They were each given three or four permanent staff, unlike the earlier committees, and their membership was deliberately made independent of party leadership, excluding both ministers and shadow ministers. The new committees were soon able to make some impression, questioning the Home Office or Foreign Office, for instance, with much more persistence and less partisan attitudes. The most important of them is the Select Committee on the Treasury and the Civil Service, headed by the Tory financier Edward du Cann—who once hoped to be the Tory leader and now relishes the job of questioning ministers.

The Select Committee provides a much subtler and less publicised spectator sport than the histrionics in the debating chamber, and it is much more instructive. In an upstairs room in the House of Commons, looking over the river, a row of MPs sit round an improvised horseshoe of tables, facing the Chancellor of the Exchequer who is flanked by senior Treasury men, while a row of journalists and observers sit along one wall. It is more like a university seminar than a political debate. Du Cann thanks the Chancellor for coming and the members politely ask questions, led by Jeremy Bray, the Labour MP who is most concerned with the Treasury. The Chancellor tries to explain his monetary controls, consulting carefully with his advisers, and only occasionally protesting—'It should not be allowed to imply any such thing . . . I'd rather not give an ill-considered response to that'—while the members try to uncover contradictions between policies and their execution. The discussion reveals much more about how the Treasury works than any debate in the chamber; but, du Cann insisted to me: 'The real name of the game is controlling the money: it's not until we get our hands on the annual estimates that they'll really take note of us.'

Members still face great difficulties in grappling with the government departments and nationalised industries. In theory they have sovereignty over them, but in practice they know little about how to control them, and they are up against bureaucrats and ministers who often do not *want* them to know. The chief ambition of most members (unlike congressmen's) is to become part of the government, so that they never want to appear too rebellious; and it is the traditional debating between the parties which still stimulates many members, including Michael Foot or even Dennis Skinner, much more than uncovering the details of bureaucracy and policy-making. But the select committees have undoubtedly brought a new vigour and purpose to the House of Commons, providing a much more serious enquiry into how the country is run, while members with their own offices and secretaries can take their job more professionally than was possible twenty years ago.

So it is hardly surprising that the central arena of parliament, the chamber itself, has become emptier and emptier. There are still great occasions, such as the budget, when there will be standing room only—there are only 437 places for 635 members—but for many debates the chamber will contain only a handful. It is in the evening that it appears most desolate, when members drone on to the deserted benches opposite with a few men lying sideways or lounging back asleep, while the Speaker in his wig remains immobile. The secret of the empty chamber is well-kept: the newspapers will still report a debate as if it were a thrilling combat in a packed arena, without mentioning that only a tiny band of MPs may be listening. Though there is a quorum of thirty for a vote, the minimum required for an actual debate is only four—the opposition member, the minister, a government whip and the Speaker—and there have been times when only four have been present.

The influence of parliament has depended as much on communicating as on legislating—on the 'educative function' which Walter Bagehot saw as among its chief purposes. When Attlee was asked how Churchill won the war he replied, 'He talked about it'; and the best speakers, such as Enoch Powell and Tony Benn, still put their faith in the spoken word. 'Through talk,' Benn explains, 'we tamed kings, restrained tyrants, averted revolution.' Contemporary political scientists, including Professor Beer and Professor Crick, have seen parliament's function less in terms of control than of 'mobilising consent' through communication and debate.

But the House has been increasingly eclipsed as the chief means of political communication ever since the 1740s when the *Gentleman's Magazine* employed a memory man to record the speeches, which were then put into formal English by Dr Samuel Johnson, and publicised to the world. By the nineteenth century newspapers were the dominant form of communication, and by the 1930s politicians could broadcast by radio direct to their voters; but members of parliament always remained jealous of the intimacy of their debates, and it was not until 1977 that they allowed the microphones in.

However the broadcasting of parliament turned out to be an anti-climax; for television, a much more powerful intruder, had already taken over the role of eavesdropper and chief political educator. TV commentators had long pressed for the cameras to be admitted: 'Parliament,' complained Robin Day, 'should not be as blind and stubborn towards the television as it was in the unhappy struggle with the Press.' But the House of Commons—alone among Western democracies except Ireland—has still refused to admit the cameras, in a succession of debates and votes on the issue. In 1981 Jack Ashley, the deaf Labour MP, brought up the question again, warning members that parliament was becoming more remote from the people, and was no longer affecting opinion, as television pushed it aside. But another Labour MP, Joe Ashton, warned parliament that the cameras would make it like a party conference, presenting pictures rather than words, belittling serious issues and encouraging terrorists. The members, by 176 votes to 156, once again decided to keep out the cameras.

The competition of television was only part of the public's diminishing interest in parliament during the sixties and seventies. The self-important behaviour of members looked much less attractive to a younger generation facing dole queues and a declining standard of living. The rituals of parliament, from the state opening to the endless arguments about privilege, projected a self-contained and secure world of mutual admiration and widened the gap between the members and the people. The clubby character of the House of Commons, through which members could attack each other across the chamber and then retire to the bar to drink together, could easily appear as mere shadow-boxing, a national game which looked more fatuous as the economic crisis worsened. And while parliament was engrossed with rival political and economic theories, with majorities, abstentions and divisions, a new left-wing generation was growing up with a much more immediate attitude to protest and a professional awareness of how to attract the attention of the television cameras.

There is nothing new in complaints about the weakening influence of parliament, or about 'extra-parliamentary protests': riots, demonstrations and petitions formed the background to Victorian parliaments, and the suffragettes were expert at 'media events'. Yet most observers would probably agree that the House of Commons over the last two decades has lost more influence than over previous periods, as its powers have been diminished from different directions—with civil servants taking more of the responsibility of government, with the media taking over more of the education and debate, with constituencies and trade unions controlling members more closely, and with some critical areas of policy-making moving towards Brussels.

It is now only in rare national crises that parliament again becomes the dramatic heart of the nation which can influence events, change policies and hold the public's attention; when the debating-room is suddenly no longer formal and lethargic, but an emotional hot-house, as it was during the Suez and Falklands wars. When the news of the Argentinian invasion of the Falklands came through on Friday April 2 many MPs could only with some difficulty summon up a sense of outrage (I was at a conference in Cambridge at the time, attended by several members); but when they were called to Westminster for a special sitting of parliament the next day—the first for twenty-six years on a Saturday—they soon took on a much more excitable and militant mood, as the intensity of the chamber exerted itself. The most forceful speakers, including Michael Foot, Margaret Thatcher and David Owen, all showed their form; the less adept, such as John Nott, were booed; the members returned to their constituencies with a new sense of purpose; and for the next weeks the radio broadcasts were listened to as never before. The chamber still faced stiff opposition from other means of communication, including the *Jimmy Young Show* and *Panorama*, but it was parliament which provided the test of the government's ability to carry the nation. The debates about the armada and the army attracted the kind of rapt attention which was never given to the debates on industry or science. It was magnificent, but what did it have to do with Britain's long-term problems?

HOUSE OF LORDS

The most ancient element of parliament, the House of Lords, has remained the most baffling obstacle to reform over the last two decades, confusing almost everyone with its blend of fact and fantasy, romance and exploitation, comedy and dignity. The whole style of the high Victorian building was calculated to play on past glories. Stained-glass windows shed a red light, while the barons of the Magna Carta look down like saints from the walls, conveying the atmosphere of a grand private chapel which sanctifies the most banal interventions. On the red sofas a few old men fiddle with their deaf-aids, whisper and sometimes sleep, and sitting on a big red pouf stuffed with wool, called 'the Woolsack', is a muttering old man in a wig who turns out to be the Lord Chancellor of England, Lord Hailsham, the holder of the most ancient lay office in the kingdom, older than the Norman Conquest.

The attempts to modernise the world's oldest legislative assembly have met with repeated frustrations. The most drastic recent reform came from the Tories, when Macmillan in 1958 created life peerages.

No prime minister since 1964 has created hereditary peers and only one of the last five prime ministers (Douglas Home) has accepted a peerage for himself. The prestige of hereditary peers was further undermined in 1963, when they were allowed to renounce their titles and sit in the Commons: Lord Stansgate (who had instigated the bill) became Tony Benn and Lord Home became Sir Alec Douglas-Home, thus enabling him to become prime minister.

In 1968 Harold Wilson, in cahoots with Ted Heath, tried to reform the Lords further by proposing a new Parliament Bill which would introduce a 'two-tier' system, drastically reducing the number of hereditary peers who were allowed to vote, to provide a more balanced chamber. But Wilson fumbled the bill, and provoked furious opposition from both the far left, led by Michael Foot, and the far right, led by Enoch Powell. Foot was in favour of abolishing the Lords altogether and Powell for keeping it intact, but they both revealed a mystical attachment to the traditional House, and a common interest which came together again in opposing the entry to Europe in 1972. ('If one wipes away the hereditary varnish,' protested Michael Foot, 'all one is left with is a Bill establishing a crude, vulgar, nominated chamber.') After facing angry debates and ingenious time-wasting, Wilson gave up the attempt at reform, and the fiasco seemed to bear out the theory that (as Lord Campbell of Eskan put it to me): 'The only justification of the Lords is its irrationality: once you try to make it rational, you satisfy no one.'

By 1980 the Labour party was again promising to abolish the House of Lords, and at the party conference Tony Benn threatened to create a thousand new Labour peers to ensure that the bill for abolition would be passed. But legal experts, including Lord Denning, raised great doubts as to whether the Lords could be abolished without the consent of the Law Lords; and a Labour government with this programme would soon find itself faced with a constitutional crisis.

So the Lords remain for the time being with their irrational membership. In two decades the hereditary peerage has declined rather more rapidly than expected, as ancient titles disappear through lack of heirs. The dukedom of Leeds has become extinct and two more dukedoms, Atholl and Portland, are now without heirs. There are nine fewer Marquesses since 1961, and two more (Cambridge, and Dufferin and Ava) have no heirs. Forty-six earldoms have gone, and six more are unlikely to survive the next decade.

The links between the old aristocracy and politics are much more tenuous than they were two decades ago when Macmillan, himself the son-in-law of a duke, surrounded himself with interrelated aris-

TITLE	CREATED	CURRENT HOLDER	EDUCATION	HOME
NORFOLK 17th	1483	Miles Fitzalan-Howard	Ampleforth; Oxford	Arundel Castle, Sussex
SOMERSET 18th	1546	Percy Seymour	Blundell's; Cambridge	Maiden Bradley, Wiltshire
HAMILTON and BRANDON 15th and 12th	1643 1711	Angus Douglas-Hamilton	Eton; Oxford	Lennoxlove, East Lothian
BUCCLEUCH and QUEENSBERRY 9th and 11th	1663 1684	Walter Montagu-Douglas-Scott	Eton; Oxford	Bowhill, Selkirk
GRAFTON 11th	1675	Hugh FitzRoy	Eton; Cambridge	Euston Hall, Norfolk
RICHMOND and GORDON 9th and 4th	1675 1876	Frederick Gordon-Lennox	Eton; Oxford	Carne's Seat, Sussex
BEAUFORT 10th	1682	Henry Somerset	Eton; Sandhurst	Badminton, Gloucestershire
ST ALBANS 13th	1684	Charles Beauclerk	Eton; Cambridge	Monte Carlo
DEVONSHIRE 11th	1694	Andrew Cavendish	Eton; Cambridge	Chatsworth, Derbyshire
BEDFORD 13th	1694	John Russell	Privately	Woburn Abbey, Bedfordshire
ARGYLL 12th	1701	Ian Campbell	Le Rosey; Glenalmond; McGill University, Canada	Inverary Castle, Argyll
MARLBOROUGH 11th	1702	John Spencer-Churchill	Eton	Blenheim Palace, Oxfordshire
ATHOLL 10th	1703	George Murray	Eton; Oxford	Blair Castle, Perthshire

RUTLAND 10th	1703	Charles Manners	Eton; Cambridge	Belvoir Castle, Grantham
MONTROSE 7th	1707	James Graham	Eton; Oxford	Pietermaritzburg, South Africa
ROXBURGHE 10th	1707	Guy Innes-Ker	Eton; Sandhurst; Cambridge	Floors Castle, Kelso
PORTLAND 9th	1716	William Cavendish-Bentinck	Wellington	London
MANCHESTER 11th	1719	Sidney Montagu		Nairobi, Kenya
NEWCASTLE (Under Lyme) 9th	1756	Henry Pelham-Clinton-Hope	Eton; Cambridge	Lymington, Hants
LEINSTER 8th	1766	Gerald FitzGerald	Eton; Sandhurst	Langston House, Oxford
NORTHUMBERLAND 10th	1766	Hugh Percy	Eton; Oxford	Alnwick Castle, Northumberland
WELLINGTON 8th	1814	Arthur Wellesley	Eton; Oxford	Stratfield Saye House, Berkshire
SUTHERLAND 6th	1833	John Egerton		Mertoun, Roxburghshire
ABERCORN 5th	1868	James Hamilton	Eton; Cirencester	Barons Court, Omagh, Northern Ireland
WESTMINSTER 6th	1874	Gerald Grosvenor	Harrow	Eaton Hall, Cheshire
FIFE 3rd	1900	James Carnegie	Gordonstoun; Cirencester	Elsick House, Kincardineshire

tocrats—many of whom could be placed in the same extended family tree, branching out from either the Duke of Abercorn or the Duke of Marlborough. Macmillan's network was itself a kind of throwback which reflected his own snobbery more than the real basis of power . It is true that the British landed aristocracy still has a formidable network of interrelationships; and that the huge increase in values of land, antiques or old masters has made many rich families much richer. The Duke of Devonshire still presides like a second monarch over Chatsworth in Derbyshire; the Duke of Norfolk, the premier duke, has his own Catholic community around Arundel Castle in Sussex; the young Duke of Westminster's estates in Belgravia bring in several million pounds a year. The richest landowners have their own discreet lobbying methods which help to safeguard the big estates and landed incomes.

HOUSE OF LORDS		
	1961	1981
Royal Dukes	5	3
Dukes	27	25
Marquesses	38	29
Earls	203	157
Viscounts	138	103
Barons	523	474
Bishops	26	24
New Lords	18	18
Life Peers	43	345

But few bother to spend much time in the Lords except for the occasional debates about forestry, salmon-fishing or game. Margaret Thatcher is not tempted by country-house life, and she showed no qualms in her purge of 1981 when she sacked the son-in-law of a duke, Sir Ian Gilmour, and the son-in-law of Winston Churchill, Lord Soames. There was no political convulsion when the Duke of Devonshire, who had been a junior Tory minister under Harold Macmillan, announced in March 1982 that he had joined the Social Democrat party. The dukes are now a race apart, pursuing their own path from Eton to Christ Church, Oxford, to their country estates: the table on p. 26 suggests a similarity of life-style.

In the meantime the life peers have multiplied so that by 1981 (together with the bishops) they make up 345 of the 1,178 members of the House of Lords. Every prime minister since Macmillan has found life peerages an invaluable means to reward their political friends, party benefactors or personal cronies. Harold Wilson made 183 peers, more than anyone, and his patronage provoked a scandal by including dubious enterpreneurs and showbiz tycoons who had performed no obvious public service—one of whom, Lord Kagan, later went to jail for fraud (he could be stripped of his knighthood but not of his peerage). Callaghan was more circumspect, creating only a handful of political peers including the trade unionist, Lord Scanlon; but Jack Jones, the outstanding union leader of his generation, was one of the very few men to refuse a peerage. Mrs Thatcher has been prompter than any prime minister in rewarding political allies, giving peerages not only to Tory tycoons such as Lord Sieff, Lord McAlpine, Lord Forte and Lord Weinstock, historians such as Lord Thomas and Lord Dacre (formerly Hugh Trevor-Roper), but also to the new owner of the *Daily Express*, Lord Matthews.

The life peers, who include academics, trade unionists, scientists and actors (Olivier and Miles), undoubtedly brought some new blood to the Lords; but they have not made it much more relevant to modern Britain. The debates, it is true, are often more thoughtful and better-informed than those in the Commons, with fewer rules and formalities: most of the hereditary 'backwoodsmen' never bother to turn up, and only about three hundred peers attend regularly, collecting £11.65 for each day they sign in plus £10.60 for secretarial help, plus hotel and travel expenses: it adds up. But few active tycoons spare the time to speak in debates, and most life peers are already in their sixties, becoming more aloof from practical problems. The House of Lords now looks even more like an old folk's home, as the average age creeps relentlessly up (though three of the nonagenarians—Lord Shinwell, Lord Brockway and Lord Noel-Baker—are more active than many peers in their sixties); and the younger Lords, such as Melchett or Gowrie, are inevitably hereditary. Nor can life peerages ever give the House of Lords a political balance like that of the Commons: not just because the hereditary peers are overwhelmingly Tory, but because many Labour life peers have defected to the Conservative benches as they got older. Thus overwhelmingly conservative and elderly, the Lords are an easy prey for any radical critic; but they still defy any practical scheme for reform.

THE PENDULUM

The British are often proud and thankful that their electoral process is almost uniquely short and sharp: after the prime minister decides to go to the country the campaign may take only three weeks. The political atmosphere is transformed. Members of parliament hurry back to their constituencies, and cabinet ministers surrounded by power are suddenly transformed into representatives pleading for votes. Posters are stuck up on house windows, pollsters roam the country, newspapers examine the mood of constituencies, bookmakers take bets. The country is infected with the spirit, not only of politics, but of the race-course. On the last Thursday the polling-booths open, the count is taken, and next morning the new government is known. The departing prime minister calls on the Queen, the removal vans arrive at Downing Street, and the new prime minister moves into the house on the same day, with the suddenness of a *coup d'état*.

The British process is far quicker and cheaper than the American presidential elections which cast their shadow over more than a year, with no 'lame-duck' period between the defeat of one leader and the arrival of the next. And the British voters, who choose a party rather than a single leader, have more opportunity to consider policies rather than personalities. Television and the Press, it is true, have magnified the role of party leaders, and political theorists argue that British elections have become more presidential, and less parliamentary. Party policies are often blurred and incomplete, avoiding contentious issues (such as the police or Northern Ireland) which embarrass both sides. But the issues are still more clearly defined than in American contests. And the polls show that the voters still distinguish between the leader and the party, and may vote for the policy of one party even though they prefer the leader of the other.

Compared to Western Europe, the results of most British elections appear very decisive. They usually give a clear lead to a single party, which does not need any parliamentary manoeuvrings to maintain its majority—partly because the British system of a simple majority with a single ballot discriminates against the small parties much more than European systems of proportional representation. There have been only a few periods when British governments have depended on uneasy coalitions, as the Labour government depended on Liberals in the late seventies.

The workings of democracy have come to depend on what the Victorian prime minister, Lord Salisbury, called 'the great law of the pendulum'. The opposition has often worried that the pendulum has stuck. Since 1884 when universal household suffrage began the Conservative party has been in office much longer than Liberals or Labour; and between 1951 and 1964, under four successive Tory prime ministers, they retained power for so long that many socialists feared they might never get back. But the pendulum swung again in 1964, again in 1970, again in 1974 and again in 1979. In spite of sporadic victories by Liberals and regional parties, parliament was still dominated by the two giants.

After the Labour victory in 1974 both the big parties became worried by the by-election successes of the Liberals and the Scottish and Welsh Nationalists, while many nationalists were prophesying

LIBERAL, LABOUR & ALLIES | CONSERVATIVE & ALLIES

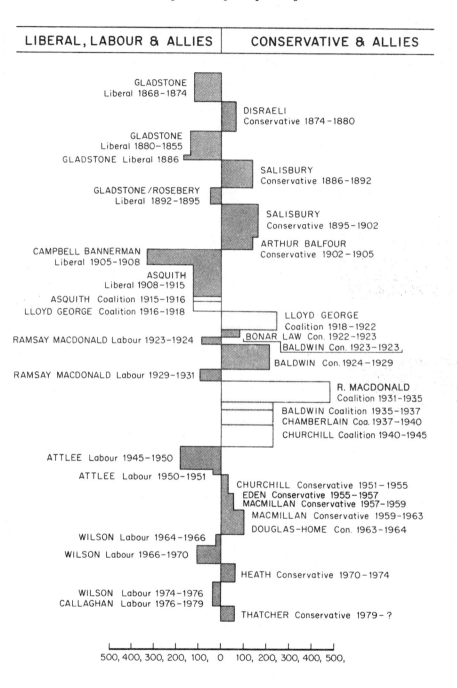

GLADSTONE
Liberal 1868–1874

DISRAELI
Conservative 1874–1880

GLADSTONE
Liberal 1880–1855
GLADSTONE Liberal 1886

SALISBURY
Conservative 1886–1892

GLADSTONE/ROSEBERY
Liberal 1892–1895

SALISBURY
Conservative 1895–1902

CAMPBELL BANNERMAN
Liberal 1905–1908

ARTHUR BALFOUR
Conservative 1902–1905

ASQUITH
Liberal 1908–1915
ASQUITH Coalition 1915–1916
LLOYD GEORGE Coalition 1916–1918

LLOYD GEORGE
Coalition 1918–1922
BONAR LAW Con. 1922–1923
BALDWIN Con. 1923–1923

RAMSAY MACDONALD Labour 1923–1924

BALDWIN Con. 1924–1929

RAMSAY MACDONALD Labour 1929–1931

R. MACDONALD
Coalition 1931–1935
BALDWIN Coalition 1935–1937
CHAMBERLAIN Coa. 1937–1940
CHURCHILL Coalition 1940–1945

ATTLEE Labour 1945–1950

ATTLEE Labour 1950–1951

CHURCHILL Conservative 1951–1955
EDEN Conservative 1955–1957
MACMILLAN Conservative 1957–1959
MACMILLAN Conservative 1959–1963
DOUGLAS-HOME Con. 1963–1964

WILSON Labour 1964–1966

WILSON Labour 1966–1970

HEATH Conservative 1970–1974

WILSON Labour 1974–1976
CALLAGHAN Labour 1976–1979

THATCHER Conservative 1979–?

500, 400, 300, 200, 100, 0 100, 200, 300, 400, 500,

that the United Kingdom could not stay united. The Labour government wooed the Scots with concessions and promises of devolution and eventually had to make a pact with the Liberals to ensure its survival; when the Liberals withdrew, they were soon defeated. During the election campaign in 1979 the smaller parties still hoped to hold the balance. But the Conservatives swept back with a majority over Labour of seventy-one. The Liberals, though they won 4.3 million votes, won only eleven seats in the new parliament, while the Scottish Nationalists fell from fourteen seats to four. The two big parties were not as strong as they looked: only 61 per cent of the electorate had turned out to vote for Labour or Conservative, the lowest proportion in any post-war election except the two in 1974; and the British voters were showing themselves more volatile than ever, with some constituencies having swings of over 10 per cent.[7] But the two parties seemed once again to share out the whole kingdom; and the pendulum was still swinging from left to right.

Many European observers were impressed by these bold assertions of the will of the people: 'This is real democracy!' an Italian visitor said to me after Callaghan's fall. 'The people are fed up with him—so he goes!' But the British have paid a heavy price for these dramas over the past two decades; after each swing Labour or Conservatives carried out the promises of their manifesto, reversed policies, dismantled institutions and tried new experiments. The two parties were becoming more polarised in their policies, while many more voters were becoming less committed to either, some floating towards the smaller parties, others disillusioned with all parliamentary politics.

After all the promises of reform there were few signs of remedying Britain's most obvious shortcomings—its antiquated industry and lack of investment, its technological backwardness, its class divisions and bitter labour relations. Some politicians were beginning to suspect that their own system must be blamed for some of Britain's failings. As Roy Jenkins put it in November 1979: 'We cannot successfully survive unless we can make our society more adaptable; and an unadaptable political system works heavily against this. Politicians cannot cling defensively to their present somewhat ossified party and political system while convincingly advocating the acceptance of change everywhere else in industry and society. "Everybody change but us" is never a good slogan.'[8]

The people, in their brief moment of freedom described by Rousseau, had chosen. The new government moved into Whitehall

---

[7] See Ivor Crewe's essay, 'The Voting Surveyed', in *The Times Guide to the House of Commons*, 1979.
[8] The Dimbleby Lecture, the *Listener*, November 29, 1979.

to carry out their mandate. But what was the extent of the people's choice, and their subsequent control over government decisions? Could individual members of parliament influence the government? Could the government itself impose its wishes on the bureaucracies and corporate powers that surround it? Was the two-party system really as entrenched as it looked?

3

Conservatives: Consensus and the Iron Lady

*In politics, if you want anything said, ask a man; if you want anything
done, ask a woman.*

Margaret Thatcher, 1965

I am a woman. When I think, I must speak.

Rosalind in As you Like It (III, ii)

BOTH the major political parties were facing changes in the post-war
decades which had many similarities with the rest of Western
Europe. The working class was becoming more fragmented and
more prosperous in the post-war boom, while the old ideologies were
losing their appeal: capitalism and socialism were finding some
common ground in the mixed economies and expanding welfare
states. But British politicians faced the especially dangerous predicament of a period of industrial decline, when people were looking
back on the past glories of empire and a heroic world war, reluctant
to face up to Britain's diminishing and more workaday role. To
navigate either party from the wider sea into narrower waters called
for exceptional skills, involving some deception and cunning. Political leaders were well aware of the fates of previous post-imperial
nations, such as Spain and Portugal in the sixteenth centuries,
trapped and confused by the hierarchies and values of an earlier age.

For the Conservatives, with their respect for traditions, the aftermath of empire was a critical challenge. In the century of elections
since the Second Reform Bill of 1867 they had shown a remarkable
ability to reassert themselves as 'the natural party of government',
adapting to new voters and circumstances. The great post-war
landslide to Labour in 1945 seemed to many Tories at the time to
mark an irreversible trend. But a group of liberal Conservatives
under R. A. Butler set out to 'Make change our ally' and to re-occupy
the middle ground of British politics; and they devised policies for
'enterprise without selfishness', or 'humanised capitalism', as Butler

called it, which prepared the way for the return of Churchill in 1951. The Suez disaster seemed to mark a new dead-end for the Tories, but when Harold Macmillan took over the premiership in 1956 he knew that his future depended on regaining the middle ground and appealing to workers as well as the middle classes. Building on Butler's foundations and much helped by relatively high economic growth, he was able to satisfy the unions' wage demands while increasing the standard of living. There were a few rebellions, as when Peter Thorneycroft and Enoch Powell resigned over inflationary policies; but there was no serious revolt, and no convincing alternative leader. Macmillan was able to befuddle his own right wing by sounding like an imperialist while retreating from the empire, and his theatrical style enabled him, as he privately explained, to juggle with five balls in the air.

Macmillan could maintain an aristocratic and paternalist style in the midst of great social changes. As the son-in-law of a duke, the grandson of a Scottish crofter and a former MP for Stockton he presented himself as bridging the class divide, while spurning the 'suburban' middle classes whom he so disliked. ('I'm always rather depressed by the rootlessness of modern Britain,' he told me in 1958, 'particularly in the south. To think that within twenty miles of this room there are eight million people living suburban lives.') For most of his prime ministership he could reconcile the two conflicting elements of conservatism, benign paternalism and aggressive free enterprise, but it was the paternalism which was dominant, conducted in a lofty style. 'The Tory party is run by about five people,' Oliver Poole, the former party chairman, told me in 1961, 'who all treat their followers with disdain. They're mostly Etonians, and Eton is good for disdain.'

After his victory in 1959 Macmillan had few new political ideas except to take Britain into Europe. He looked to the European Community, more than he dared publicly admit, as the means to resolve many British problems which he had otherwise evaded: to infuse more competition into industry, to dilute the power of the unions, and above all to give the British a new challenge in a wider identity which broke with nostalgia for the past. 'It is a cold shower that we enter,' he warned, 'not a Turkish bath.' Other Tories such as Macleod and Heath shared his view that Europe was essential to Britain's revival; but Macmillan was also still wedded to Churchill's old idea that Britain was at the intersection of three circles—Europe, America and the Commonwealth: 'Making our ties with Europe closer and stronger,' he told me in 1962, 'doesn't mean weakening the others.' So when Macmillan tried to get into Europe de Gaulle was still able to depict Britain as a potential Trojan Horse within

Europe, who would always look to the open sea rather than the Continent. And when de Gaulle's veto wrecked Macmillan's European policy in early 1963, Macmillan was left with no real view of the future. The right wingers were already impatient with his 'pink' policies and appeasement of the unions; the Profumo scandal, against the background of Harold Wilson's aggressive opposition, marked the end of his era, leaving the Conservatives with a crisis of identity from which they never fully recovered.

The three elections for the leader over the next twelve years brought into the open all the doubts about what Tories should be. Was the party paternalist or aggressive, aristocratic or upstart, traditional or radical? The different ingredients seemed to separate when Macmillan, with all his ambiguities, departed.

The first testing-ground was the extraordinary autumn conference in Blackpool in 1963, when Macmillan announced that he would resign. His own favourite was Lord Hailsham whom he saw (with Iain Mcleod) as one of 'the true inheritors of the Disraeli tradition of Tory radicalism'. But Hailsham, having hastily renounced his title, became over-excited in front of the television cameras. Butler, who represented the liberal reformist tradition, was not trusted by the old guard. Reginald Maudling, though much favoured by younger MPs, failed to rise to the challenge. While the three contenders damaged each other's prospects, the Earl of Home was waiting in the wings, and Macmillan from his sick-bed was invoking the 'customary processes', taking soundings from each section of the party, which showed Home as the most likely choice. In a last-minute counter-attack Powell and Macleod tried to press Butler to refuse to serve under Home, but Butler would not take up the challenge; and the leadership thus went to the man representing the least dynamic element in the party. Iain Macleod, his most effective critic, angrily revealed how the 'magic circle' of Old Etonians had planned the succession, while he and Maudling were kept in the dark. The Tory party in its time of crisis had reverted to its secretive old roots, and turned its back against change.

Sir Alec Douglas-Home (as Lord Home became) looked like a caricature of Macmillan's paternalism, with none of his radicalism, and in parliament he was the ideal foil for Harold Wilson. When the Tories lost the 1964 election they inevitably looked for someone with an almost opposite style, to compete with Labour's modernising image; and when Sir Alec was eased out after only two years as leader the Tory field was almost unrecognisable from its appearance two years earlier. Hailsham and Butler were out of the running, Macleod was dying, and only Maudling was standing again, while Enoch Powell was a right-wing outsider.

A brand-new candidate, Ted Heath, was now presented as the Tories' answer to Harold Wilson, with the same working-class background and technocratic command. The old guard suppressed their misgivings at Heath's abrasive style, and the election for the leader was much more open and systematic than the old customary processes. Heath's campaign was efficiently master-minded by the young financier, Peter Walker, and he won by 150 votes to Maudling's 133. Maudling, who had expected his great ability to be naturally recognised, retreated into disappointment and money-making.

Ted Heath had his own paternalist tendencies, but after he led his party to a second defeat in 1966 he was more determined to sharpen the attack on socialism. He played down his old liberal sympathies for welfare, the unemployed or the Third World, and advocated a much more self-interested and commercialised nation, in the tradition of Palmerston, which could reverse the trend of decline. His domestic slogan was 'stand on your own feet' and with the help of eager colleagues such as Sir Keith Joseph and Anthony Barber he put together a whole network of policies to make industry more competitive and government leaner and more efficient. The old guard made fun of his bleak crusade and were pessimistic about his prospects, but when he won the election in 1970, to the surprise of many of them, his position was all the more powerful; he dominated the young technocrats in his cabinet and only Lord Carrington and William Whitelaw felt able to argue with him on general issues.

As prime minister Heath appeared determined to reject the Macmillan inheritance: he was embarking, he promised the Tory conference, on 'a change so radical, a revolution so quiet and yet so total, that it will go beyond the programme for a parliament'. He kept trade unionists at arms' length and showed his ruthlessness to his own allies by allowing Rolls Royce to go bankrupt, while he and his Chancellor, Anthony Barber, encouraged a stock-market boom by liberating bank lending. He was set against Macmillan's policy of consensus: 'There never *was* a consensus in the sense of a deliberate effort of will,' he told me crossly in March 1971. 'The parties never came together in their policies. Even the idea of "Butskellism" was sloppy and inaccurate.'

But Heath was soon caught up in new problems of economic stagnation with rising inflation. Although unemployment was increasing it was not modifying the unions' demands, and after he failed to settle with the miners in February 1972 the wage-claims became more reckless. Heath could not countenance causing still higher unemployment as a means to discipline the unions. ('No one of Mr Heath's background and generation,' his political adviser

Douglas Hurd later commented, 'could easily dismiss rising unemployment as a statistical fiction or as unimportant.') Heath was showing himself a less than whole-hearted capitalist, as he observed the excesses of profit-making and the 'unacceptable face of capitalism' without much corresponding industrial improvement: the stock-market boom was producing a host of property speculators, but few industrial entrepreneurs.

Heath was stubborn but still open to persuasion, and by 1972 he was convinced that government must intervene to revive industry, and that only an incomes policy could stem the tide of inflation. In his historic U-turn he passed the new Industry Act which provided large funds to the Department of Trade and Industry, and constructed a statutory incomes policy, reviving the old instrument of national consensus, Neddy (the National Economic Development Council). The two changes marked an emphatic reversal of the previous policy, but the cabinet, which included Keith Joseph and Margaret Thatcher, did not oppose them. As Minister of Education, Thatcher (as Heath later lovingly recalled) was the keenest of the big spenders, while Joseph was enthusiastically enlarging the social services, adding an expensive tier of administrators to the hospitals.

Heath's lasting achievement was to succeed where Macmillan had failed, in getting Britain into Europe. It seemed to mark a decisive change of perspective, an indication that Britain had finally discarded her imperial past, and was prepared to limit her sovereignty. But his victory showed no immediate rewards: it meant heavy payments to Brussels and gave less scope for national swash-buckling, while it made him many enemies inside the party. Britain paid a heavy price for her long aloofness from the Continent and when she finally entered, she was (as Willy Brandt put it) either too late or too soon. 'If you had come in fifteen years earlier' (said Robert Marjolin who was one of the framers of the Treaty of Rome), 'you would have got the benefits of the long European boom, and your people would have accepted Europe.' The timing, it turned out, could hardly have been worse.

Heath's wage restraint only lasted a year, and by the end of 1973 the militancy of the miners, much encouraged by the new energy crisis, provided a deadly new confrontation. The right wingers in the cabinet, led by Lord Carrington, pressed for a showdown and Heath took up the challenge, imposing a three-day week, inducing a sense of national crisis and calling a general election in February 1974. But the Tory confrontation was muddled and bungled by misleading statistics; the Labour party could now present itself as the peacemaker; and by a majority of five seats Harold Wilson defeated the Tories and was back as prime minister. Wilson could now promise a social contract with the unions to restore stability, and in his second general election in October he came back with an increased majority of forty-three.

After two defeats in one year the Tories were once again in a crisis of identity, and they lost little time in turning against their leader, as they had done ten years earlier. Heath remained embattled, taking his friends for granted, and apparently confident that he could deploy the party machinery. But the right wing felt betrayed by his U-turn—all the more since they had assented to it—while many younger MPs were disenchanted by Heath's autocratic style. There was no obvious challenger. Maudling was now partly discredited by his rash financial adventures. Jim Prior and William Whitelaw, who had served in Heath's cabinet, lacked aggression in opposition. The most popular right-wing candidate was Keith Joseph, in spite of his past involvement with Heath; but Joseph was showing some signs of being 'unsound', and he made a disastrous speech at Edgbaston referring with apparent callousness to deprived children 'in socio-economic classes four and five' which caused political fury. He decided with much anguish to withdraw from the contest. Immediately a new surprise candidate entered the ring as Joseph's substitute and special protégée: Margaret Thatcher. She was little known in the country, and she had never held any of the great offices of state. But she offered what Tories were desperately looking for after the past confusion: a conviction that they still had a special mission and a special solution to Britain's decline.

Sir Alec Douglas-Home had devised a new system for elections allowing for three ballots, making the leader more vulnerable (the MPs called it 'Alec's revenge'). Heath had the votes of most of his former cabinet, but he had made many enemies among those whom he had left out, and Thatcher's militant approach appealed to a new generation of Tory MPs who were much more determined to stand no nonsense from trade unions and nationalised monopolies, and who had much less sense of guilt—or social conscience—than their elders. While Peter Walker was again Heath's campaign manager, Thatcher's crusade was run by a heroic old Tory Airey Neave who had been her patron as a young barrister twenty years before. She was backed not only by Keith Joseph but by other old Tory mentors including Peter Thorneycroft and Angus Maude. 'I am trying to represent,' she said in Finchley just before the first ballot, 'the deep feelings of those many rank and file Tories in the country—and

potential Conservative voters too—who feel let down by our party
and find themselves unrepresented in a political vacuum.'

Heath was inevitably vulnerable to this mood of bitter resentment, and the first ballot in February 1975 produced a decisive
defeat: Margaret Thatcher had 130 votes, Heath had only 119 (the
maverick third candidate, Hugh Fraser, took sixteen). When
Heath promptly resigned, four new rivals emerged for the second
ballot—Jim Prior, Geoffrey Howe, John Peyton, and William
Whitelaw, the former party chairman. Whitelaw was the obvious
conciliator, and the most likely alternative: he and Thatcher provided the classic contrast between the two historic elements of
Conservatism—the benign paternalist against the aggressive self-
helper. But Thatcher was now acquiring the aura of the 'Iron
Maiden' (as the *Daily Mirror* called her) which made Whitelaw look
flabby, and the second ballot was a pushover, giving Thatcher 146
votes compared to seventy-nine for Whitelaw. The Tory party was
as surprised as the country by the speed with which they had
chosen, for the first time in their history, a woman. 'It wasn't an
election,' exclaimed her ecstatic Catholic supporter Norman St
John-Stevas, 'it was an assumption.'

It was a misleading romanticism, for during the contest Margaret
Thatcher had already shown herself tougher than her male rivals; as
Lord Shinwell, the old Labour ex-minister, put it: 'She stood
because she was the only man among 'em.' It was characteristic of
the Tories, as their historian Lord Blake explained, that they turned
to extraordinary leaders such as Disraeli or Bonar Law in times of
crisis. Now, in this special crisis, they turned to the most extraordinary leader of all.

The choice of Thatcher was in some ways more like the choice of
Heath ten years before than her supporters cared to admit. Like the
earlier Heath, she promised to cut back the role of the state in favour
of self-reliance and free enterprise; like Heath (and like Wilson and
Callaghan) she came from a lower-middle-class home—her father
was a grocer in Grantham, Heath's father was a builder in Broad-
stairs—dedicated to the virtues of thrift and self-help. Like Heath
she was a loner and a newcomer to the political heights, isolated
from her shadow cabinet colleagues. Intellectually she was less
thorough than Heath: she had thought less deeply about her Conservatism, she was ignorant of foreign affairs, and she never produced
elaborate blue-prints for policy-making. But she was far more articulate and less inhibited, and better able to project herself to the
nation and her colleagues, with the appearance of moral conviction.
Heath had, like most prime ministers, neglected Conservative
theory during his years in government: 'There was a great deal of

policy,' as Douglas Hurd admitted, 'but by 1970 not much philosophy.' By 1975 his one great achievement of entering Europe was already looking less attractive.

And Mrs Thatcher in 1975 had one overwhelming advantage over Heath in 1965: she arrived at a time of far greater disillusion with the unions and the welfare state, when the right was reasserting itself more confidently throughout the West.

THATCHER'S CONSERVATISM

She was always a less complicated character than Heath without his internal tensions and suppressed liberalism. 'I'm a plain straightforward provincial,' she told me in 1977. 'I've got no hang-ups about my background, like you intellectual commentators in the south-east. When you're actually *doing* things you don't have time for hang-ups.' She was brought up in the bleak Lincolnshire town of Grantham, strongly influenced by her father, who was an alderman and local worthy. 'Papa was a pretty unusual corner grocer,' she recalled. 'I remember him saying at a Rotary meeting that Hitler and communism would crush the religious and human spirit of the individual. I've always regarded individualism as a Christian mission. I always regarded the Conservatives as the party of the individual, as Hogg explained it in his book in 1945; I was astounded when later on the Tories were attacked as the party of the establishment.'

When she went up to Oxford in the bulging post-war generation, she joined the Oxford Tories alongside aristocrats such as Edward Boyle and John Grigg, though she never, she insists, felt they were the privileged party: 'If it was privileged, what was I doing there?' She could not afford a political career, and she concentrated on science, believing that it held new opportunities. But her friend Airey Neave, a barrister and independent-minded backbench MP, persuaded her that the law was essential for a grasp of politics, and helped her to get into his chambers; in the following years Neave's views of patriotism and freedom (including his distrust of the Foreign Office) were often echoed by Thatcher. 'Science and law both taught me to find out the facts,' she told me, 'and then deduce the hypothesis.' She was asked to stand as the Tory candidate for Dartford, where she met and married a rich industrialist, Denis Thatcher, who had inherited a paint firm. She now had no cause to worry about money, and she always had a nanny for her children. But her marriage never affected her self-image as a woman who had climbed up the hard way.

Her career in politics was swift and self-assured: 'Since I first stood for parliament in 1950 when I was twenty-three I haven't doubted I could cope with whatever I was doing.' By 1959 she was elected to parliament as the member for Finchley; by 1967 she was in the shadow cabinet. By 1969 she was appointed shadow Minister of Education, defending the Tory policy against socialist critics—particularly the education correspondents—which she later saw as her most testing experience: 'They gave me a lunch which was one of the most disagreeable experiences I have ever had. But I am glad I had that experience: steel is tempered by going through fire. I knew that nothing worse could be done to me.' By the time she was Minister of Education under Ted Heath in 1970 she was able to withstand any attacks. She watched Heath's turnabout with some disillusion and she began to look for a tougher kind of conservatism. She knew that as a woman she could be more forceful and direct than her male rivals, and she talked with the bossy heartiness of a governess or games mistress, full of phrases like 'come along, then', which men found it hard to contradict. When in talking to her I had to admit that I had not read an early book by Dr Hayek, she told me: 'Well, go away and read it.' She opposed legislation for equal rights for women, partly on the grounds of Socrates: 'Woman once made equal to man becomes his superior.' Nor did she have much sympathy for the women's lib movement: 'What has it done for me?' she once asked. 'Some of us were making it,' she told an audience in Chicago, 'long before women's lib was ever thought of.'

Her Tory beliefs gained greater conviction in the new political climate. The leftward movement of the Labour party gave more edge to the Conservative insistence on freedom of choice and individual liberty, while all Western democracies were worried about the costs and bureaucracies of their welfare states. In the United States, though Carter had won the election of 1976, the conservatives were becoming fiercer and more effective, as they showed when they cut property taxes in California. Thatcher and Joseph (who remained her mentor) were naturally attracted to the economic theories of Milton Friedman, who had been gaining influence since he first published *Capitalism and Freedom* in 1962.

Friedman liked to cite the British case history, to show how socialist bureaucracy can destroy enterprise and freedom, and looked back to the golden age of British economic expansion before the First World War: he looked to Thatcher as the forerunner of the economic revival of the West. Moreover his insistence on limiting the money supply gave the Tories a mechanism for imposing stern discipline in the most impersonal way, without the embarrassment of confronting trade unionists or workers. Previous Chancellors, particularly Denis Healey, had already been making more use of monetarist controls; but Thatcher and her chancellor Sir Geoffrey Howe were able to embrace Friedman as a philosopher as well as a practitioner.

For her deeper Tory support Thatcher looked to Professor Friedrich Hayek, the old Austrian philosopher who had written his attack on socialism, *The Road to Serfdom*, forty years earlier; as Tories had used Hayek to attack the Labour fellow-travellers in the late forties, so they used him against the new left in the late seventies. 'Few are ready to recognise,' he warned in his introduction, in Mrs Thatcher's favourite passage, 'that the rise of Fascism and Nazism was not a reaction against the socialist trends of the preceding period, but a necessary outcome to those tendencies.' And for more detailed economic ammunition for attacking the welfare state Thatcher could look to the invaluable British Institute of Economic Affairs, the most effective lobby for free enterprise. The Institute's surveys had revealed how Labour voters as well as Tories were becoming dissatisfied with the welfare state, thus giving further support for right-wing policies.

For more polemical thoughts she was helped by her exotic friend Alfred Sherman, the leader-writer on the *Daily Telegraph*, who had once fought as a communist in the Spanish Civil War. For historical support she turned to Professor Hugh Thomas (whom she later made Lord Thomas), a former Labour supporter who defected to the Tories, who could reassure her that 'there is no instance of political liberty existing without free enterprise';[1] and that democracy, invention and economic growth had always depended on capitalism. Supported by her advisers, Mrs Thatcher made much of the fact that the 'tide of collectivism' was now turning, all over the West. 'We are sustained by the knowledge that we ride on the crest of a philosophical tide,' she said at Cambridge in July 1979.[2] She implicitly rejected the Macmillan era as a diversion from the true Tory tradition, and she harked back continually to earlier ages of enterprise, under Churchill, Disraeli or Queen Elizabeth I. In a succession of philosophical speeches she presented herself at home and abroad, much more romantically than the earlier Heath, as carrying the capitalist banner against the armies of socialism and bureaucracy. She was applauded by American republicans, Swiss bankers and Australian graziers, and she was very conscious of becoming an international heroine of the right.

[1] Hugh Thomas: *History, Capitalism and Freedom*, Centre for Policy Studies, 1979, p. 7 (Introduction by Margaret Thatcher).
[2] Swinton Lecture, July 6, 1979.

THATCHER'S PEOPLE

Thatcher's chief guru was still Sir Keith Joseph, the anguished Tory intellectual who provided a personification of U-turns. He had served in Macmillan's cabinet, and had then gone along with most of Heath's policies and reversals: he had ardently attacked government bureaucracy before 1970, then greatly added to the social service bureaucracy, and was now reverting to his previous viewpoint. When I visited him in December 1975 in his new Centre for Policy Studies—the brain-box of the new Conservatism—I found him in a new mood of disarming self-criticism about his intellectual predicament. 'I was misled in government because I was obsessed with squalor and avoidable misery, which a minister never should be,' he told me. 'So I was inclined to avoid the question of whether universal benefits do more harm than good . . . After two defeats I find it hard to find any decision by politicians or civil servants which was correct . . . we concentrated on symptoms not on men and women. Of course in 1969 I was singing the same tune as now: but I am more humbled by experience and more sure that it's the right tune. But I admit we are still too fresh from our last mistakes to be convincing as anti-bureaucrats.'

For her shadow cabinet Mrs Thatcher brought back two veterans whom she seemed to see as father-figures from an earlier tradition—Angus Maude, the right-wing intellectual, and Lord Thorneycroft, Macmillan's old critic and colleague. She brought in her own supporters, such as Airey Neave and Norman St John-Stevas and she promoted the obedient Sir Geoffrey Howe as her shadow Chancellor. But she also included old Heath allies, and she knew that most of the shadow cabinet had voted against her. She represented a minority among her colleagues, who did not conceal their scepticism. Maudling, who was one of them, said to me: 'We're not a very convincing crowd, are we?' Many of the aristocrats looked down on her narrow zeal; Sir Ian Gilmour warned that the Tories must not 'retire behind a privet hedge'; and Harold Macmillan was heard to complain that 'they're a rather suburban lot'.

But she knew she had been elected because she was more resolute and combative than her rivals; and as she projected herself to the country on television she became more confident of her supremacy. Her moral passion was unleashed against the Labour government, and during the disastrous winter of strikes she gained full advantage from this 'reversion to barbarism' as she called it. 'Our society was sick—morally, socially, and economically. Children were locked out of school; patients were prevented from having hospital treatment; the old were left unattended in their wheelchairs; the dead were not buried; and flying pickets patrolled the motorways.' The Iron Lady appeared more desirable in the midst of the chaos caused by the strikes; and when Callaghan's government fell in April 1979 the Conservatives were ready for their crusading campaign. When they won the election with a majority of forty-three, they knew that they owed their victory to Thatcher; like Heath before her, she became prime minister from a position of lonely strength.

A WOMAN IN POWER

Once she was voted into office the magic of power soon took effect. She became more assured, less strident and more convinced of her special relationship with the British people. She began communicating more instinctively on television and in public speeches, which allowed her to by-pass and defy her more weak-willed colleagues. The adrenalin of power made her more forceful and—some colleagues thought—more attractive. She saw her challenge in more personal terms than her recent predecessors, and she had a straightforward attitude to patronage, speedily rewarding those who helped her, and using the honours list to recompense short-term political services, while civil servants who went on strike for more pay were threatened with having their honours withheld. She was determined to use her power to weaken the influence of the left, as she saw it, on the media. She approved the purchase of *The Times* by the right-wing Australian, Rupert Murdoch, and she approved the appointment of the Conservative ex-editor, Sir William Rees-Mogg, to be both vice-chairman of the BBC *and* chairman of the Arts Council.

She was in a position to construct the kind of cabinet she wanted, owing few political debts, but she did not make very bold choices. The first Thatcher cabinet included several old Heath followers such as Whitelaw, Walker, Prior and Carrington (who had used all his charm to try vainly to reconcile Thatcher and Heath). There were seven Old Etonians—one more than in Macmillan's cabinet—including Lord Hailsham and Lord Soames who had served under Macmillan. There were no members of the Monday Club, the far-right group of MPs, many of whom had backed Thatcher. Only Norman St John-Stevas had been a close supporter, and within two years he had been sacked. It was soon clear that Thatcher's cabinet was more disloyal and leaky than any Tory cabinet since the war (except perhaps Macmillan's during his last year); they quickly revealed to journalists the secret arguments over trade union policy or public expenditure, and made jokes about her like schoolboys after the teacher has left.

Each prime minister has a different relationship with a cabinet, giving political scientists the opportunity to construct new theories every few years about cabinet government, presidential government or prime ministerial government. Thatcher's relationships fitted into no existing theory and her system of government, like Harold Wilson's before her, probably had a closer resemblance to a political farce such as *Anyone for Denis?* than to the explanations of political scientists. She did not much enjoy presiding over this group of men, with their public-school jokes and giggles, and she was glad it only happened once a week: she preferred seeing them in smaller groups, or alone. She described her cabinet as *them*, or sometimes 'my blue bunnies', and treated them as if they were quite separate from her, like a parliament, constantly trying to stop her doing things. She was frequently in a minority in cabinet; and when they frustrated her she would sometimes resort to television.

She looked outside the cabinet for much of her influence. To impose her monetary policies she looked to her shock troops in the Treasury—Sir Geoffrey Howe, Nigel Lawson and John Biffen—who were establishing a unique political beachhead (see chapter 11). To fortify her authority she looked to her own small staff in Ten Downing Street, whom she had brought in from outside Whitehall: they included a computer tycoon, John Hoskyns, an enterprising old Wykehamist who liked to depict all problems in terms of neat diagrams and boxes; and David Wolfson, the elegant nephew of Lord Wolfson the entrepreneur, who had advised Tory Central Office on computers and who now served as a factotum and general lubricant in the Downing Street office. Later she introduced her own economic adviser, Alan Walters, the ardent monetarist whom she brought back from a professorship in Washington. To try to cut back spending in Whitehall she hired Sir Derek Rayner, the anti-waste expert from Marks and Spencer (see chapter 10) to whom she gave her full personal support. 'If Derek can't do it,' she explained, 'nobody can.'

But her changes in Number Ten were much less far-reaching than those of her Labour predecessors. In spite of her complaints about Whitehall she worked happily with the young civil servants from the Treasury and the Foreign Office who served as her private secretaries, and who could influence her through sheer proximity, retaining control over access through the Diary—the critical key to power. She leant heavily on the Secretary of the Cabinet, Sir Robert Armstrong, who presided over the Cabinet Office beyond the green baize door; he had been the loyal private secretary to Heath ten years earlier but he was soon indispensable to Thatcher too. She was quite friendly with individual senior civil servants including Sir Douglas Wass and Peter Middleton at the Treasury. To some more radical people around her, she seemed to like civil servants rather too much. Her Press secretary, Bernard Ingham, was a civil servant who had once been a labour correspondent on the *Guardian*. Her original political adviser, Adam Ridley, was soon eased out of Number Ten, and she had no real political adviser to compare with Bernard Donoughue who had advised both Wilson and Callaghan and had run Callaghan's election campaign.

Her sense of isolation was reinforced by being a woman. 'She appears more like a second queen surrounded by courtiers than like a prime minister,' said Shirley Williams, who watched her from the opposite benches. With confidence her bearing became still more queenly, and the contrast between herself and the real queen in the background became more marked. When she appeared in the House of Commons for question time she could have an electric effect. Her cabinet ministers would be reclining on the front bench with feet forward and arms stretched back, until she strode in from behind the Speaker's throne, brisk and immaculate, clutching her papers like a weapon, to sit among them. They would pull themselves up, adjust their legs and turn towards her: it was like the entrance of a matron or a headmistress. When the first question came up—'Is the prime minister aware . . .?' she would stiffen as if ready to pounce, stand up by the dispatch box, and reply with a withering phrase: 'The right honourable member *really* should know the difference between . . .' The Labour members would cat-call and jeer, but her high voice would ring above the baying like a flute playing descant over horns. She loved the challenge of attack, and made no bones about it: 'The adrenalin flows,' she explained. 'They really come out fighting me, and I fight back. I stand there and I know: "Now come on Maggie, you are wholly on your own. No one can help you." And I love it. '

THE THATCHER REVOLUTION

Mrs Thatcher was always determined to change Britain's attitudes more drastically than Heath or Macmillan, through her own sense of moral purpose. Britain's greatest failure, she insisted, was a failure of nerve like that of Athens in the fourth century. 'The mission of this government,' she said in 1979, 'is much more than the promotion of economic progress. It is to renew the spirit and the solidarity of the nation . . . At the heart of a new mood in the nation must be a recovery of our self-confidence and our self-respect.'

She was soon able to exhibit her own combativeness. She took up an uncompromising stand against the Soviet Union, insisted on more military spending, and, in a public confrontation, she demanded large cuts in Britain's contribution to the European Community. In Whitehall she wanted to cut down the numbers of civil servants and tried, without success, to cancel their index-linked pensions. In the Treasury she insisted, against some opposition from Sir Geoffrey Howe, that the highest tax-rate should go down from 83 to 60 per cent, making the rich much richer. And she gave inflation the highest priority, undeterred by rising unemployment: unlike Macmillan, or even Heath, she had no searing personal memories of pre-war unemployment, and no sense of guilt.

She was not as intransigent as she looked. Her cabinet forced her to moderate her opposition to the trade unions, and she postponed drastic legislation: she knew that the unions had brought down Ted Heath. ('If you want to persuade Margaret to do something,' as one of her cabinet explained to me, 'you only have to say that Ted Heath would do the opposite.') When the miners in 1981 threatened to strike over pit closures she quickly agreed to settle. She could not avoid subsidising some nationalised industries, and the government still paid huge subsidies to British Leyland, British Steel and British Rail; nor could she denationalise British Airways as she had promised, for no one would buy it. Her fierce rhetoric never quite fitted with her more deliberate actions. 'Machiavelli said you should either annihilate or conciliate,' Harold Macmillan observed at a lunch party, 'but these people don't seem to be doing either.'

In the meantime the world recession, with high interest rates and high unemployment, was inducing a harsher climate than most Conservatives had dreamt of and Britain could not easily protect herself from the fierce global competition—still less since she was a member of the European Community. The cold shower that Macmillan had prescribed twenty years earlier had turned into an icy bath. The numbers of jobless were unprecedented since the thirties, and by late 1981 they topped three million. Thatcher's policies looked much more ruthless as Britain faced the full fury of international competition, with the high value of the pound making British exports much more expensive; but she still refused to relax her monetary controls and her stand against inflation. Some big industrialists, whether grudgingly or admiringly, admitted that they had needed their workforce to become 'leaner and fitter' (see chapter 23). But many smaller companies went bankrupt or deeply into debt through paying penal interest. Much of the commercial hardship and unemployment would have happened with or without Thatcher and monetarism, in this harsh global climate of 1980 and 1981. But it is part of the vanity of prime ministers that they cannot admit how much they are at the mercy of world forces; and Thatcher (though she passionately denied it) was vainer than most.

As the recession bit deeper Mrs Thatcher's intransigence became more damaging to the party's prospects, and opinion polls showed a drastic decline in popular support. Her forceful style, still rejecting the old Tory paternalism, prevented her from offering reassurance or taking credit for any measures to mitigate hardship. Her government was in fact moderating some of its policies, giving more subsidies to industry and allowing some reflation. But she held firm, refusing to countenance any U-turns, and she still insisted: 'There is no alternative.' She was stuck with the image of the Iron Lady, who could not be seen to be made of rubber. 'It's very difficult to change her mind,' said one very senior civil servant. 'Ted Heath was stubborn, but he could recognise the national interest. Margaret seems to panic if you challenge any part of her policy: she's afraid that if one piece goes, it will all go.'

Ted Heath was now her angriest critic. He had little hope of getting back into power, but he was spurred on by a kind of negative ambition which made him furious to see someone else mishandling his old job; while he was widening his own perspective as a roving world statesman. He constructed careful speeches to demolish her grand design, attacking her for wrecking the economy, making the Tories the party of unemployment, and turning Britain's back to the world. The man who had been so caustic about consensus politics now attacked her for destroying the consensus, to which she delivered a ferocious reply from Australia: 'To me, consensus seems to be the process of abandoning all beliefs, principles, values and policies . . . It is the process of avoiding the very issues that have got to be solved merely to get people to come to an agreement on the way ahead.'

The word consensus always made her see red: it struck at the heart of her belief that achievement rests on personal responsibility, on saying what you think, on leadership rather than 'followership'. She saw herself battling against the forces of consensus, like the early Christians against the Romans; and she insisted that democracy was based on consent, not consensus. She hated the consensus which Britain had to reach within the meetings of the European Community, agreeing to a lowest common denominator between Schmidt and Mitterrand: it meant a weakening of national resolve and confusion of purpose, abetted by the European fanatics at the Foreign Office, whom she never really trusted. She maintained a spiky relationship with the European leaders, particularly the French. Mitterrand she found charming, but dangerously ignorant of economics and rash in his policies. With President Giscard there had been almost total non-communication between their two vanities; they made speeches at each other without trying to respond, and Giscard once remarked of her: *'Je ne l'aime, ni comme homme, ni comme femme.'*

In Downing Street she seemed—at least to this writer—even more the crusading moralist than she had been in opposition, much more of a loner, with a greater detachment than any of her predecessors from the politicking around her: striding round her study, with her eyes bulging, turning every question into a moral issue, exploding with indignation about wetness or consensus or inflation—gosh! poof! my goodness me! Her indignant and exclamatory moral style made it difficult for anyone to reply without sounding immoral, though her own political morality was very limited. She appeared not so much at the top of an organisation as free-floating around it, sending out her own shock waves. She seemed to her staff genuinely uninterested in the more mechanical side of politics, the vote-counting and manoeuvring. She was contemptuous of the full-time politicians who were obsessed with getting themselves re-elected, practising followership not leadership; she hated the tendency for election policies to become a set of conditions which voters would accept. She insisted that politicians should have something to say, and say it. She saw her crusade in very personal terms. She presided over Number Ten as a private house, sometimes lunching upstairs with a secretary, and maintaining a kindly relationship with her staff. When she appeared on television with signs of weeping when her son Mark was missing on a car rally in the Sahara one of her secretaries said, 'That's the human side that we've all got to know.'

THE REVOLT OF THE WETS

As she stuck to her economic policies the moderates in her cabinet—the 'Wets' as the Monday Club first called them—became more exasperated by her obstinacy, more indiscreet and disloyal. Sir Ian Gilmour, the languid aristocrat with a Macmillanish style who shared the Foreign Office with Lord Carrington, was the chief intellectual critic and had already offered his own Tory philosophy in his book, *Inside Right*, which stressed that Tories must retain the middle ground and avoid the traps of ideology and dogma. After only a few months in office he was publicly warning that Hayek's version of economic liberalism could undermine Britain's sense of community and political freedom, and that monetarism alone could not work.

Jim Prior, the Minister of Employment, had always opposed Thatcher's plans to legislate against the unions, and he was now much more worried about the desolation caused by joblessness and disintegrating inner cities. A rubicund farmer with an easy-going style, Prior was the model of a modern Tory paternalist, and he now feared that his party were digging themselves a deep hole which they could not climb out of. Lord Soames, the Minister for the Civil Service, had some sympathy with the civil servants' demands when they struck for higher pay in 1981, and he did not conceal his worries about the party's future. Francis Pym, the Minister of Defence, resisted the heavy cuts that Thatcher called for until he was replaced by the more obedient John Nott, when he allied himself more closely with Prior. The divide between the Wets and Drys in cabinet was becoming unbridgeable.

In July 1981 a sudden social crisis focused all their arguments. A succession of riots broke out in inner cities—first in Brixton, then in Liverpool, then in Manchester—with looting, violence and open hatred of the police. Many Wets in the cabinet saw the riots as revealing the ultimate danger of impersonal monetarism, a warning that government could not turn its back on the needs of communities. The extreme economic policy was being met with an extreme protest, as if it were in the early nineteenth century. In the following weeks the balance in cabinet seemed to be moving towards the Wets, and the Minister for the Environment, Michael Heseltine, was sent up to Liverpool to work out an emergency programme to revitalise the inner city. By the autumn the Wets were becoming more openly rebellious, as the Tories' electoral prospects looked still weaker; and even Lord Thorneycroft, the loyal chairman of the party, having vainly tried to soften Thatcher, publicly expressed his concern about the economic policies.

But already in July the prime minister had decided that she could dispense with the Wets, and that she needed a more resolute cabinet. In September she purged her cabinet more ruthlessly even than Macmillan in his 'night of the long knives' in 1962: while Macmillan had brought in younger men from the left, Thatcher was moving further to the right. She fired Soames, Gilmour and Thorneycroft—all Old Etonians associated with the suspect paternalism. She exiled Prior to Northern Ireland. She bought in a young new chairman, Cecil Parkinson, who seemed made in her own mould: the son of a railwayman, a successful self-made industrialist, a dedicated MP and party worker, with a clean upstanding style and old-fashioned rhetoric. And she promoted Norman Tebbit, the hardest of the hard men, to Prior's job as Minister for Employment. A former British airline pilot and son of a shop manager, Tebbit represented the anti-union wing and was a master of invective in parliament: 'a semi-house-trained polecat', Michael Foot called him. But he was invaluable to his prime minister as a man who could beat the unions

CONSERVATIVE CABINET June 1982

Post	Holder	Age	Education
Prime Minister	Margaret Thatcher	56	Kesteven & Grantham Girls'; Oxford
Home Secretary	William Whitelaw	64	Winchester; Cambridge
Lord Chancellor	Lord Hailsham	74	Eton; Oxford
Foreign Secretary	Francis Pym	60	Eton; Cambridge
Chancellor of the Exchequer	Sir Geoffrey Howe	55	Winchester; Cambridge
Secretary for Education and Science	Sir Keith Joseph	64	Harrow; Oxford
Leader of the House of Commons	John Biffen	51	Bridgewater GS; Cambridge
Secretary for Northern Ireland	James Prior	54	Charterhouse; Cambridge
Secretary for Defence	John Nott	50	Bradfield; Cambridge
Minister of Agriculture	Peter Walker	50	Latymer
Secretary for the Environment	Michael Heseltine	49	Shrewsbury; Oxford
Secretary for Scotland	George Younger	50	Winchester; Oxford
Secretary for Wales	Nicholas Edwards	48	Westminster; Cambridge
Secretary for Industry	Patrick Jenkin	55	Clifton; Cambridge
Secretary for Trade	Lord Cockfield	65	Dover County; London School of Economics
Secretary for Transport	David Howell	46	Eton; Cambridge
Secretary for Social Services	Norman Fowler	44	King Edward VI School, Chelmsford; Cambridge
Chief Secretary to the Treasury	Leon Brittan	42	Haberdashers' Aske's; Cambridge; Yale
Leader of the House of Lords	Lady Young	55	Headington; Oxford
Secretary for Energy	Nigel Lawson	50	Westminster; Oxford
Secretary for Employment	Norman Tebbit	51	Edmonton County GS
Chairman of the Conservative Party (attending cabinet)	Cecil Parkinson	50	Royal Lancaster GS; Cambridge

at their own game, and could lay into the Labour benches with the same toughness that they applied to the Tories.

Mrs Thatcher's cabinet is now much more in her own image. The twenty-two members, it is true, still include three Old Etonians; four or five are farmers; all but seven have been to public schools, and only three have never been to Oxbridge. But key positions—in the Treasury, in Employment, in Trade and in Energy—together with chairmanship of the party, are all held by people in tune with her views. There are no real grandees with independent power bases, as in Macmillan's day, who might challenge her leadership; Lord Hailsham, who remains Lord Chancellor, is loyal to his prime minister. Peter Walker, who had carefully befriended the farmers at the Ministry of Agriculture, is the only Wet with a convincing power base, but he also has many enemies. The rest of the Wets had shown after the purge that they were, after all, wet. Ian Gilmour who said when he was sacked that the party was 'heading for the rocks', was now suggesting that the Tories need not change their leadership since the collective will of the cabinet was forcing her to moderate her policies; but so long as she remained leader she seemed likely to alarm the electorate.

FLEXIBILITY AND THE FALKLANDS

Unlike previous prime ministers at mid-term, Mrs Thatcher showed few signs of returning to the middle ground to prepare for electoral victory. She was increasing spending and borrowing, and talking about flexibility; but that did not have much political impact while she could not acknowledge her U-turn, and the image of a flexible Iron Lady was blatantly contradictory. The gap between rhetoric and actions was confusing not only the public but the government itself. The Tory party had now broken with its paternalist tradition, while the middle ground was being contested by a new party which was determined to settle there without the ideological baggage of Labour. This gave the Tories another difficulty: for the appeal of their philosophy, whether defined by Thatcher or Gilmour, rested on defending personal freedoms against state ownership and socialist centralisation; but the new Social Democrat party was just as opposed to the extreme left, and much harder to attack. The true role of conservatism seemed more disputed and confused than at any time over the post-war decades.

No one who was worried about Britain's decline and encroaching bureaucracy could withhold all admiration for Thatcher's crusade. After three years in power she was proud of having changed the mood of the country, diminished the power of the unions, cut back the nationalised monopolies, and compelled big business to become more efficient: and certainly she had played a role in these changes. She had projected her personal leadership more effectively than any of her five predecessors. Her championing of outspoken individualism against stuffy institutions was always refreshing: surely no one who hated the Foreign Office *and* the Bank of England could be all bad?

But her rhetoric and her outlook revealed some obvious flaws, for she remained oddly two-dimensional as her personal morality refused to come to terms with the real responsibilities of a wider society. Her promotion of self-help and enterprise meant little to the three million unemployed or the inhabitants of desolate inner cities. Her encouragement for small business looked increasingly hollow as high interest rates bankrupted enterprising small companies while lazy giant corporations survived. With her insistence on diminishing the role of government she could never work out the relationship with the millions who would always depend on government. She insisted that her party was offering both incentives and security, 'the ladder and the safety net', as Churchill called it; but her style as well as her policies increased people's insecurity. Her view of Britain's challenge remained in many ways old-fashioned and insular; she could not take in or convey the global dimension, as unemployment and inflation were sweeping through the West; and her individualist philosophy made no contribution to the problem of competing with the highly organised forces of international trade.

By late March 1982, when the Conservatives lost the by-election at Hillhead in Glasgow to the Social Democrats, Mrs Thatcher's future looked more uncertain than ever. And then, by a totally unexpected political accident, a crisis eight thousand miles away transformed the entire Westminster scene. The Argentines' invasion of the Falklands provided the kind of challenge that might have been especially devised to suit the prime minister's temperament: a challenge which immediately detached her from economic or social problems and put all the Wets and appeasers in parliament or the Foreign Office at a disadvantage. It was a challenge to all her notions of pure resolution and will-power. 'Now we will see of what metal she is made,' Enoch Powell told the House of Commons at the beginning of the crisis, and she was observed to be quietly nodding as if to show that she was after all made of solid iron.

In the first days of the crisis the Conservatives looked very vulnerable to criticism, having failed either to reach a settlement with the Argentines or to anticipate the invasion of the Falklands. But after Thatcher had replaced Lord Carrington with Francis Pym, and after John Nott had shown himself more resolute as Minister of Defence, the government soon appeared firmly in control. When the fleet set sail the opposition was committed to support it, and Foot was tied to Thatcher's mast. The prime minister presided over a 'war cabinet' which included the party chairman Cecil Parkinson to support her firmness; and while other ministers expected that the fleet would serve as a deterrent, to bring pressure on Argentina in the negotiations, Thatcher was always fully prepared for the use of force. Or as President Reagan was reported to have said to his Secretary of State, Alexander Haig: 'Maggie wants a skirmish.'

While Pym and Nott looked increasingly strained and exhausted, Thatcher seemed to thrive on the crisis, concentrating all her mind on the details and excelling herself in the successive emergency debates. While most women did not share the male enthusiasm for the operation, she emerged as a more confident war leader than any of her colleagues could have been; and when South Georgia was recaptured by British troops she appeared in Downing Street to tell her people to 'rejoice' in a style that none of the men could have used. She established much closer relations with the admirals and generals than with the diplomats, and talked about 'our boys' with a possessive emotion. She saw the challenge as an intensely personal one—'I am asking the invader to withdraw'—and she put herself firmly in the context of heroic British military victories: 'Just as our forefathers did not flinch . . .'. She fitted naturally into the role of war-queen, while the monarch—whose son Prince Andrew was part of the expedition—sounded much more maternal.

Her popularity leapt ahead with the mounting crisis, and poll after poll showed the rise in the Tory fortunes. The local elections in May were dominated by the Falklands factor, showing a striking Tory success, and the Conservatives swung back in two parliamentary by-elections. The British firmness in defence of a principle seemed to merge completely with her own combative personality and moral certitude; and her insistence on renewing the nation's self-confidence seemed to be symbolised by the armada achieving what many had said was impossible, sailing eight thousand miles to recapture well-defended islands close to hostile shores. And her own decisiveness weakened the impact of right-wing critics who wanted to bomb the Argentine mainland, including Winston Churchill and Julian Amery, a relic of the old 'Suez Group' who had been criticising Tory moderation since the fifties.

But how far did this military sense of purpose, self-confidence and unity help the British to work together to solve their more difficult economic problems about industry, technology or unemployment? How far did the patriotic fervour help to strengthen Britain's position in an interdependent world? Could Margaret Thatcher give Britain a new image of herself, as Charles de Gaulle gave France? The questions will recur.

4

Trade Unions: Politics, Wages and the Dole

The trade union movement has lost its way, its sense of mission. The sense of brotherhood has no meaning. The powerful get what they can, and they leave the weak to get what they can.

Les Cannon, 1970

We are very good at stopping what we do not like, but not at starting anything.

Len Murray, 1976[1]

WHO are the real opposition confronting the Conservatives? Are they the Labour party, or the Liberals and Social Democrats, who all face them across the parliamentary benches? Are they the left-wing organisations outside parliament? Or are they the trade unionists who first brought the Labour party into being? The doubts have grown over two decades, as the future of Labour has become more uncertain; and before looking at the Labour party it is important to survey the trade unionists who play a large role in its policies, but whose own position in the country is constantly disputed. Are they an indispensable part of the corporate system, a 'fifth estate' of the realm, 'essentially part of the fabric of our national life' as Harold Wilson described them in 1968? Or are they a passing phenomenon, a relic of an earlier age of full employment and class solidarity? Are they part of the anatomy, or of the pathology of Britain?

Under each government the unions appeared in a different light. Macmillan depicted them as the responsible partners of industry, to be appeased and befriended by his Ministers of Labour. Harold Wilson soon became exasperated by them, as forces which were frustrating Britain's revival and tried unsuccessfully to cut back their powers. Ted Heath saw them first as the enemies of Tory progress, then as necessary collaborators in restraining wages, and

[1] Robert Taylor: *The Fifth Estate*, Routledge, London, 1978, p. xii.

then again as his antagonists in the election battle fought over the issue: Who Governs Britain? Then Wilson, back in office, portrayed them as the responsible co-authors of the social contract, given new privileges in return for supporting his government, until his successor, Callaghan, seemed so inseparable from the unions during the bitter strikes of the 'winter of discontent' in 1978–79 that they lost him the election.

Then Margaret Thatcher largely ignored them. Their bargaining power was undermined by the vastly increasing unemployment while their unpopularity with voters damaged both themselves and the Labour party. The union leaders who had appeared as the co-rulers of Britain now seemed powerless to protect jobs, while the recession cut back their membership. The proportion of unionised workers had gone up during the seventies from 44 per cent to 53 per cent, while it was declining in many other countries: but in 1981 alone the Trades Union Congress lost half a million members. Many Conservatives such as Thatcher could congratulate themselves that they had shown up the unions as paper tigers. But others such as Prior insisted that no real industrial recovery could be achieved without collaboration from the union leaders. Where did the real future lie?

TRADES UNION CONGRESS

Certainly the unions still represent a formidable array of organised labour when they come together for the annual meeting of the Trades Union Congress, where 1,200 delegates representing nearly twelve million workers assemble at the seaside in the first week in September. It has been meeting for the last 114 years, the oldest such organisation in the world—thirty-five years older than the Labour party which it set up—and it includes trades such as printers and weavers whose organisations go back several centuries. It has all the established ritual of a fixed institution, still with a strong proletarian character.

The meetings alternate between Blackpool and Brighton, but it is in Blackpool, the faded yet exuberant Lancashire resort, that the TUC feels most thoroughly at home. The town, with the old-fashioned jollity of seaside postcards, has become more uncompromisingly working-class over the years. The elegant Victorian terraces and hotels have been covered over with hoardings and plastic façades, and the front has been filled up with boarding-houses, funfairs and beer-halls. The Metropole Hotel is now a Butlin's camp, and the old Winter Gardens is surrounded with pin-ball machines and refurbished with plastic facsimiles of baronial halls. And in the old opera house the trade union delegates assemble for their conference every other year.

The Trades Union Congress shows a wider cross-section of Britain's life than any other assembly—ranging from farm-workers to doctors, from the 1.8 million members of the Transport and General Workers' Union to the twenty-five cloth pressers and the twenty-six wool shear workers. Unlike meetings of managers or politicians, it represents people at the receiving end of decisions; in a nation separated by class and the two 'sides', it shows how the other side thinks. The meetings are full of distractions: the speeches are emotional, with a whole range of accents and intonations; the rigmarole is long-winded and legalistic; the elaborate compromises concealed by 'composite motions' are confusing and frequently misunderstood. Television cameras have encouraged the congress to become a formalised pageant; and the real divisions and decisions are concealed by sentimental references to unity and the 'movement', ending with the singing of 'Auld Lang Syne'. But the congress still gives a voice to interests which it would be unwise to ignore. It is here—much more than in parliament—that the raw stuff of leadership shows itself, where an orator can sway his audience with almost palpable power. And this congress gives a more convincing indication than parliament of what the British people can, or cannot, take.

What does the power of the congress really amount to? Every year the commentators who try to assess it are faced with the paradoxes. The British unions have been among the strongest in the world, yet powerless to prevent the headlong increase in unemployment. More people joined them, yet they became more and more unpopular. The unions are linked still more closely to the Labour party; yet a third of their members voted Tory in 1979. The leaders are too powerful, but they are not powerful enough. The British trade union movement is strong enough to bring down the whole edifice (as the miners' leader, Arthur Horner, used to say), but it would be crushed by the fall.

Yet no one could doubt the extent of the unions' negative power; and it is this that has exasperated successive governments, and the public at large. The language of the congress reveals all the pessimistic assumptions of a movement that was brought up with the deepest distrust of owners and management through years of slump and depression. Most of their leaders have come to assume that higher productivity will mean higher unemployment, that higher profits will not mean higher wages, and that therefore their most important power is the power to prevent change. Politicians and journalists (including this one) have been slow to accept or detect the extent of this power. The head of any organisation, whether a school or a nationalised industry, likes to present himself as being wholly in charge: he prefers not to admit how far his powers are circumscribed. Lawyers or doctors who have built up their own elaborate restrictive practices like to think of them as quite different from union restrictions. Journalists or TV producers who are hamstrung by their own unions are in a weak position to criticise overmanning elsewhere. Only belatedly has the real extent of the unions' negative power been revealed.

All the limitations of the TUC are personified in the thankless job of its general secretary, who presides over the headquarters near the British Museum. The central organisation is much weaker and relatively poorer than in most other countries, and in 1981 the annual income of the TUC was less than £4 million, while the headquarters' staff numbered only forty. The general council, which controls the TUC, who meet once a month round the horseshoe table, consists of forty-one general secretaries of individual unions, many of them much richer than the TUC. The general secretary is the only full-time member who acts as the co-ordinator and chief spokesman of trade unions' policy.

But his position is constantly frustrating. He has no vote on the council; he cannot order a strike, or call it off; he can only mediate, cajole, and bring pressure on the council. He cannot interfere with the unions' organisations: 'I'm welcome in anybody's backyard,' as Vic Feather, the former general secretary put it, 'but I'm not going to dig up their dahlias.'[2] From outside he may appear as the embodiment of union power, but inside he is only a secretary to the secretaries. Many general secretaries have tried to strengthen and reform their headquarters, but none has really succeeded. As the TUC admitted in their own report on reform in 1970: 'A propensity not to offend, and not to appear to be interfering with union autonomy, has historically often led the TUC to eschew taking initiatives.'

The headquarters has acquired its own bureaucratic character, its team of graduates removed from the more earthy style of the individual unions. General secretaries are succeeded by their deputies, who are trained up inside the office. In 1960 Vincent Tewson was succeeded by his deputy George Woodcock; nine years later Woodcock was succeeded by Len Murray, whom Woodcock had recruited. Each of them has developed some sense of irony and resignation which goes with the job, as they sit up on the dais at the annual conference, listening to demagogues and wondering where their movement is going. 'What are we here for?' asked Woodcock in

[2] Taylor: *op cit.*

1962. 'When we know, then we can talk about the kind of structure that will enable us to do what we are here for.'

Len Murray has a hyperactive style which is almost opposite to that of his old master, Woodcock. He chops the air with his gestures, talking tirelessly: but over eight years he has developed his own sense of irony. He likes to reminisce about his idealistic youth. He was born in Shropshire, and went to grammar school, influenced more by books than actions. He consumed Upton Sinclair and American radical writers, and sang American labour songs: 'I was a Sunday-afternoon Joad socialist.' He became a wartime army officer, took a degree at Oxford, and then joined the TUC. Like Woodcock he thought wages were more important than politics: 'We'd fought man and boy in 1945 to get Labour into power: we didn't think enough about wages,' he told me. 'I got on well with Woodcock: we shared a pluralist view of society; we both realised it was easier to bargain with business monopolies which could control prices.' When he took over as secretary in 1973 he was determined to initiate more ideas and research and to co-ordinate the unions more closely; but he became increasingly impatient with the exorbitant wage-claims of individual unions, and more discouraged about reforming his organisation. 'We need to have pressure from the government to reform ourselves,' he told me in 1975, 'whether from Labour or Tories.' After a heart attack he seemed more resigned and aloof, and still more sceptical, as he tried without success to hold the unions together.

GENERAL SECRETARIES

'What are we here for?' might be inscribed above the entrance to Congress House: none of the recent secretaries of the TUC has given a confident answer. While they wanted to concern themselves primarily with wages and economic recovery, individual union leaders were more interested in their political battle against the Tories, their influence over the Labour party, or with their inter-union rivalry for members, which became more intense as the total membership went down. 'We spend so much time comparing ourselves with other unions,' one major union leader said to me in 1982, 'we lose sight of our real interests.'

The general secretaries of the biggest unions, as they sit up on the dais year after year, have appeared more permanent and unchallenged than any comparable group of British leaders. Their enduring and unaccountable power has been compared to that of medieval bishops or eighteenth-century dukes, and certainly they are almost impossible to displace. The cheeky smile of Frank Chapple, secretary of the EETU since 1966; the sly grin of Clive Jenkins, secretary of ASTMS since 1968; the twirled moustache of Tom Jackson, secretary of the communications workers from 1967 to 1982; they have all been part of the stage army of national celebrities for most of two decades, watching prime ministers and company chairmen come and go. They are not only the fixed heads of their unions but universal committeemen, serving on more and more boards, commissions and councils, travelling the world as fraternal delegates, appearing on television as instant commentators on everything, to represent the views of their armies of workers.

When they first emerge at the top, popping up from obscure union offices like jack-in-the-boxes, they are surrounded by myths and fears. When Jack Jones and Hugh Scanlon, with very left-wing records, were elected to run the two biggest unions in 1967–68, the 'terrible twins' were seen as agents of a new revolutionary era. Twelve years later they appeared as the guardians of moderation: Jack Jones was the saviour of the Labour party, and Scanlon was Lord Scanlon.

Once at the top the general secretaries move in the heart of the committee-country which has stretched out from Whitehall, where no major committee is complete without a trade unionist. Before 1939 governments hardly bothered to talk to them; but during the war Beveridge consulted the TUC for his plan for social insurance and Keynes talked to them when he planned the post-war economic reconstruction. The post-war Labour government invited the TUC on to a whole range of committees, and the union bosses soon began insisting on these sinecures. 'We never knew what they were doing,' George Woodcock later complained. 'In fact they did damn all.'[3] Committees could give retired trade unionists a kind of pension and a sense of busyness, and the multiplication of 'quangos' was later mocked and attacked by Conservatives.

A few committees gave them scope for real influence and patronage, as part of Britain's 'secret constitution': senior civil servants consulting with senior trade unionists and industrialists constituted a new network of patronage, which extended the unions' negative power in the emerging corporate state. At the heart of the network was Neddy (see chapter 11) set up by Macmillan in 1963, which Woodcock insisted must include six union members chosen by the TUC. These 'Neddy Six' or 'gold-plated six' came to represent the inner circle of trade union policy-makers: in 1982 they were Len Murray, David Basnett, Moss Evans, Terry Duffy, Frank Chapple and Geoffrey Drain.

The general secretaries remain men of two worlds: sitting round

[3] Taylor: *op cit*, p. 153.

tables with the mandarins one moment, addressing angry shop stewards the next. They are less rugged and individualist than two decades ago, when they included such massive shapes as Ted Hill or Dan McGarvey of the boilermakers (whose voice was so loud, it was said, that he could *spit* the rivets in). But they are still quite different from any other British elite, still predominantly non-graduates, still preserving working-class attitudes, or 'proletarian hobbies'. They are not guilt-bound or inhibited from using their power, arguing with a down-to-earth language which makes managers and bureaucrats sound prissy and mealy-mouthed. Unlike other elites—civil servants, businessmen or politicians, for example, who have all become more alike—most of them could never be impersonated by the same actor.

The picture of union leaders wielding the autocratic powers of eighteenth-century dukes remains thoroughly misleading. Their influence varies according to their unions' varied and intricate constitutions, which were lovingly drawn up to express different ideals of democracy. But they are all circumscribed by their councils, sitting in secret, which are among the last conclaves which have resisted the encroachments of publicity: cabinet leaks are commonplace compared to leaks from the railwaymen or miners. From outside the general secretaries may look like unchallenged bosses, but from inside the unions—and from the factory floors—they often look irrelevant compared to the day-to-day bargaining powers of shop stewards. The heads of the big unions have had to become much more sensitive to the complaints from the shop floor, and many politicians, dealing with union leaders who cannot deliver their members, complain, as did Ted Heath in 1967: 'The trouble is not that the trade unions are too strong. It is that they are too weak.' Opposite are the biggest unions in 1981 with their general secretaries and members, and their membership twenty years earlier.

They may look studiously united at their annual conference as they dutifully refer to their brethren in the movement, but for most of the year they are engrossed in their unions' affairs, competing with others for members or votes. In the suburban offices of NUPE in Blackheath, of the GMWU in Surrey, or of ASLEF in Hampstead each has its own powerful political atmosphere. The headquarters of the older unions, decorated with faded photographs and banners, conjure up all their romantic history of battle and protest over successive stages of the industrial revolution. They have a more vivid sense of the past than the headquarters of big corporations: for while investors and managers have moved on to new activities and sources of profit, the older industrial unions such as the boilermakers, rail-

UNION	MEMBERSHIP thousands		HEAD
	1981	1961	
Transport and General Workers (TGWU)	1,887	1,302	Moss Evans
Amalgamated Union of Engineering Workers (AUEW)	1,100	973 (AEU)	Terry Duffy
General and Municipal Workers (GMWU)	916	796	David Basnett
National and Local Government Officers' Association (NALGO)	782	285	Geoffrey Drain
National Union of Public Employees (NUPE)	699	200	Rodney Bickerstaffe
Association of Scientific, Technical and Managerial Staff (ASTMS)	491	25 (ASSET)	Clive Jenkins
Union of Shop, Distributive and Allied Workers (USDAW)	450	355	Bill Whatley
Electrical, Electronic Telecommunication and Plumbing Union (EETPU)	405	243 (ETU)	Frank Chapple
Union of Construction Allied Trades and Technicians (UCATT)	312	192 (ASW)	Les Wood
National Union of Mineworkers (NUM)	257	586	Arthur Scargill

waymen or steelworkers have been left with all the problems of a declining and defensive workforce, overshadowed by their past. Looking back on their history, it is not altogether surprising that their attitudes are negative.

But it is more misleading than ever to generalise about disparate unions in a time of recession and high unemployment. They have their own industrial and regional traditions and their own constitutions which can be as different as the constitutions of countries; and now they are faced with varying degrees of challenge and retrenchment, according to the vulnerability of their industry. Each of the old industrial groups—whether railwaymen, engineers, miners or ordinary manual workers—had to fight its own battles in a time of diminishing jobs and opportunities.

RAILWAYMEN

The most visible and exposed of the old unions is the National Union of Railwaymen, based on Unity House near Euston Station, which traces its origins back to 1871. It was then that the Amalgamated Society of Railway Servants was set up as a defence against the railway owners, and it was their general secretary, Richard Bell, who moved the proposal in 1899 which was to give birth to the Labour party. Now the railwaymen's union has seen its membership halve in the past twenty years, to less than 170,000, while it vies unhappily with two rival unions, the locomotive engineers and firemen (ASLEF), and the Transport Salaried Staff Association (TSSA). The general secretary of the NUR, Sid Weighell, a cautious Yorkshireman, fights doggedly to defend the railways against road transport, with the help of his twelve 'Nurmps' (see chapter 2) in the House of Commons. But his lobby is no match for the power of the giant Transport and General Workers, which includes the lorry-drivers, and which has defeated any attempts to extend railway sidings to compete with road traffic.

The railwaymen form one leg of the new 'triple alliance' of old industrial unions, with the miners and the steelworkers. 'If anybody doubts the ability of this triple alliance,' Sid Weighell boasted in 1981, 'to stop things dead in Britain, you test it.' But the next year Weighell was made bitterly aware that his union could be damaged by a still more negative power, the engine-drivers' union, ASLEF, which has only 27,000 members, with a dwindling future, though having a disproportionate influence in the TUC. Its general secretary, Ray Buckton, is a left-wing militant who fights more fiercely because his old 'craft union' is in decline, and takes his orders from a determined council which sometimes even meets without him. When British Rail in 1982 tried to insist that 'flexible rostering' was a condition of a pay increase for ASLEF, Buckton organised a succession of strikes to disrupt the railways, which incurred as much anger in the NUR as among the public. Ray Buckton claimed a victory after the findings of the negotiator, and Sid Weighell later protested that the 'unnecessary and crazily expensive confrontation' might have cost the railways £150 million, and to call it a victory, he said, was like 'cheering at your own execution'. But in the next months both ASLEF and the NUR led strikes which induced a new level of public resentment.

ENGINEERS

The exact relationship between a general secretary and his council is determined by each union's constitution; and the most intricate rules are those of the second biggest union, the Amalgamated Union of Engineering Workers (AUEW). Its Victorian constitution was meant to democratise every post in the union, but actually provides the greatest scope for manipulation and confusion. The president, who is the chief spokesman, is re-elected every three years, so members can achieve sudden switches in the leadership. For eleven years the president was Bill Carron, the Catholic turner from Hull, who was passionately anti-communist and doggedly loyal to Labour leaders—first Gaitskell, then Wilson—and exploited his union's block vote to the limit. In 1967 he was superseded by Hugh Scanlon, the militant ex-communist from Manchester, who reigned for the next ten years, fighting each government's attempts to limit his union's scope, but failing to stem the decline in the engineers' wages relative to other workers.

In 1978 up came another jack-in-the-box, with almost opposite ideas: Terry Duffy (like Carron), a Catholic imbued with a hatred of communism. He was toughened by serving as a union official in the Midlands, surrounded by left-wing militants ('I came out of the jungle')—and he rose with unusual speed; he is a simple man, a former boxing champion who can sound embarrassingly naive. But much of the real influence in the union has come from its general secretary for the past seven years, Sir John Boyd, a right-wing Scotsman with a shrewder grasp of political in-fighting. In future much will depend on his successor, Gavin Laird, a more radical leader from Clydeside who has an unusual grasp of the international problems of his industries.

GENERAL AND MUNICIPAL

The most steadily conservative union has been the General and Municipal Workers (GMWU), which represents many low-paid workers such as dustmen and roadmenders. Its roots go back to the militant gasworkers' union founded by Will Thorne in 1889, but after the amalgamation in 1924 it became a pillar of working-class conservatism, under a succession of respectable leaders: Charles Dukes (later Lord Dukeston), Tom Williamson (later Lord Williamson), and Jack Cooper (Lord Dukeston's brother-in-law, later Lord Cooper). 'Thirty years ago their job was on the street corner,' said Dukes in 1941, 'today it is in the conference room.' The present general secretary, David Basnett, comes from the same hereditary tradition, as the son of an official in the same union. ('There wasn't much choice for me: I was brought up with trade unionists,' he told me.')

Basnett is now the elder statesman among the big union leaders. He presides over 'Ruxley Towers', the union's suburban headquarters in the stockbroker belt of Surrey, with the urbane and reasonable style of a corporate manager, like a businessman's idea of what a union leader *should* be. In private he is realistic and pessimistic about the unions' predicament, and knows that he cannot maintain the autocratic command of his predecessors. He is wryly critical of his militant colleagues on the TUC, and not convinced by their anti-European, anti-nuclear policies. But he could not afford to remain on the moderate sidelines. He saw himself as a bridge between the union movement and the Labour party as the divide became still wider.

The miners have always been a race apart, living in their own self-contained communities, with their own values and pride—all the more since the collapse of the General Strike in 1926 left them to be starved into submission. Their numbers declined from 800,000 in 1945 to 240,000 in 1980, but they increased their political leverage, particularly after the energy crisis of 1973. The National Union of Mineworkers (NUM) commands a unique loyalty, even though it is the most decentralised union: the forty-one organisations did not combine until 1945, and each branch controls its own large funds, providing generous salaries, cars and expenses for its union leaders. The most militant branch is now the South Yorkshire coalfield ('the Yorkshire Soviet') based on Barnsley; and it was Barnsley which produced the new president in 1982.

Arthur Scargill is the most vocal of the trade union revolutionaries, a small neatly-dressed figure with bright eyes and a high-pitched Yorkshire voice. The son of a communist, he joined the Young Communist League at the age of fifteen, inspired by reading Jack London and by visiting Moscow where he met Khrushchev. As a young miner he led a counter-attack against the right-wing domination of the Yorkshire coalfield: he was fighting a class war, he insisted, with any tools at his disposal. When Ted Heath came to power he saw his enemy and his opportunity. When the miners struck in 1972 after an overtime ban, Scargill (who was then only a rank and file member in Barnsley) organised pickets with military zeal, sending busloads of miners to docks, coke depots and factory gates round Britain. 'We weren't playing cricket on the village green, like they did in 1926,' he explained. 'We had to declare *war* on them, attack the vulnerable points.' When the police were forced to close the Birmingham coke depot, Scargill could boast: 'The working class had only to flex its muscles and it could bring government, employers, society, to a total standstill.' And two years later in the next miners' strike he claimed some credit for forcing Ted Heath to declare an election, thus causing his downfall.

Scargill has built up his own legend, and the miners' victories actually owed much to other trade unions, whose leaders resent Scargill's cockiness. 'He's really very right-wing,' one of them complained privately. 'He has a completely selfish view of the miners' interests.' But his heady experiences made him more confident that his version of socialism will achieve ultimate victory: 'My position is perfectly clear: I want to take into common ownership everything in Britain.' He does not conform with more orthodox Marxists: he does not believe in workers' control; he believes in proportional representation as a democratic necessity even when it does not favour Labour; and he has some worries about Soviet persecution of dissidents. But he has few doubts about centralised state ownership, including—as he likes to emphasise to radical journalists —nationalising all newspapers. He has complained that Tony Benn 'hasn't got the revolutionary ideas that I would like to see',[4] but he is close to Benn, and plays a major part in his campaigns. He insists that the Labour party should be a 'broad church'—which means expelling anyone who does not subscribe to Clause Four, proclaiming total nationalisation.

Scargill began his presidency in 1982 determined to safeguard his miners' jobs and to prevent the closing of pits which had become uneconomic; and Mrs Thatcher knew that he was a formidable opponent. But even the miners were less solidly united than before, and sometimes attracted by offers of redundancy money instead of backbreaking work in out-of-date pits; while other unions became more resentful of the miners' special immunity, and the resulting high price of coal. Scargill's personal power remained the most critical question in the future of the trade union movement.

RECESSION

All the big industrial unions faced far more troubled waters after the 1979 election. Their government had been defeated, to be followed by a prime minister who was determined to cut down their powers; and the gathering recession was soon sending hundreds of thousands of their workers on to the dole, rapidly reducing their membership and income, which they were powerless to prevent. The most shattered union of all was the steelworkers, who had long seen themselves as the aristocrats of labour on the commanding heights providing an indispensable product, led by their very civilised general secretary from Hartlepool, Bill Sirs. But when the steelworkers struck in 1979 Sirs was tragically unaware of the realities of world steel, which were soon rammed home with the arrival of Ian McGregor, the tough new chairman of British Steel (see chapter 25). The whole union movement felt shivers as the extent of the miscalculation became clear, and tens of thousands of steelworkers lost their jobs. As McGregor described it to me:

[4] See *New Left Review*: Interview with Arthur Scargill, September 1975.

The steel strike was traumatic—it was ill-timed, ill-conceived and proved that the British didn't need British Steel. It was a great trauma. Bill Sirs doesn't realise it: he painted himself into a corner and expected people to do handsprings to get out of it. In forty-five years on the labour front it was the most poorly-judged position I've seen. The Europeans were desperate to sell steel and Sirs gave them their chance: they flooded Britain with surplus steel. It was a gadarene rush and the price structure collapsed. Europe was selling steel that was better and cheaper while sterling was escalating. The moon and stars and everything were against the poor people here.

None of the industrial unions escaped the ravages of the recession. The union leaders saw not only their membership falling, but their whole influence and dignity dwindling; having joined committees and consulted with cabinets, having abandoned the street-corner for the committee-room, they now faced a government which showed no interest in their views. When the new Conservative Minister of Employment, Norman Tebbit, put forward his bill in 1982 to regulate the unions' powers, he did so without consulting them, and framed it more ingeniously than Heath's bill ten years earlier, so that it was much harder for them to attack. Having been seen as a third leg of the state, they were now treated like an appendix. It was the unions' greatest crisis since the thirties, or even before, for they lacked the solidarity of the movement in those days: and while they pinned their hopes on the return of the Labour party, that prospect was looking still more distant. 'They're really sleepwalking now,' as one of the general secretaries put it. 'They're pretending to be in control, when they aren't.'

The three million unemployed not only revealed the weakness of the unions to prevent a massive loss of jobs, and a rapid fall in their own membership. It also made their leaders less convincing when they spoke on behalf of all working-class people. The unemployed had no union, and without their job their old union was likely to lose contact with them; the phrase the 'doler's union' was used in the north with the bitter implication that they had no representation. The gap between those with jobs and those without them was getting wider—made wider by the bias of employers against immigrants and school-leavers. The big unions were too preoccupied with their own growing problems to have much time to involve themselves with their non-members or ex-members.

WHITE COLLARS

In the meantime the industrial unions had been rapidly losing ground within the trade union movement to the inrush of white-collar trade unionists—not just clerks, but highly-paid workers, such as airline pilots, doctors and actors. 'The teachers were the real break into the professions,' Alan Fisher, the leader of the National Union of Public Employees told me in 1975, 'and the ultimate were the doctors: all we want now is the clergymen.' The table on page 63 gives some idea of the rapid change of balance between unions in twenty years.

Many middle-class observers, such as *The Times*, predicted that these professional people would bring a more responsible and sophisticated attitude to the trade union movement, helping to bridge the old class divisions. Certainly the white collars came closer to the manual workers or 'blue collars', and by 1975 they had abolished their own 'non-manual conference'; when Len Murray asked the congress to vote with their hands he said: 'I think you won't tell the difference between manual and non-manual hands.' But the white collars soon brought more militancy than responsibility, and they were more subtle and effective in their claims. 'They used the force of argument,' as Alan Fisher put it, 'rather than the argument of force.'

They became more demanding as they felt more insecure in their jobs. As Len Murray said to me in 1975: 'They're much more numerate, more used to hierarchies, and they've got managerial competence: in those unions if you press a button, something comes up. But they're often more militant than the others. They first came into unions because they were frightened by changing conditions, and the size of companies: they felt they no longer 'knew the gaffer'—who might be in Detroit. When they first organised themselves they managed to get big increases—perhaps 25 per cent—and that made them want to keep up the pace. They're also politically more naive, so they're an easy target for the Trots. Provided they get their salary increases, they don't mind much about their political leadership.'

The white-collar leaders were undoubtedly more politicised and left wing than most of their followers; their revolutionary speeches could make a comic contrast with the stuffiness of civil servants or bank clerks. But they knew that they would be judged on their ability to push up wages and salaries. The office workers insisted on maintaining their differentials compared to manual workers and in many cases widening them; during the great inflation of 1975 the white-collar leaders were emphatic in voting against the flat-rate increase of £6 a week. Many of the white-collar union members were more visible to the public than those of the industrial unions, so that when they went on strike they could easily exasperate ordinary consumers. The 216,000 members of the Confederation of Health Service

Employees (COHSE) under Albert Spanswick could refuse to admit patients to hospitals; the 232,000 members of the National Union of Teachers (NUT) under Fred Jarvis could close the schools; the three civil service unions could bring chaos to Whitehall; the 700,000 members of the public employees (NUPE) under Alan Fisher could threaten large areas of public service. It was these white-collar unions which made the unions more unpopular at least as much as the manual workers; but while the middle classes attacked unions in general, they supported their own. 'It's a paradox isn't it?' said Clive Jenkins in 1982. 'Nobody is in favour of somebody else's strike, but they're always in favour of their own. And I fear that's a very human reaction.' They were reluctant to draw the conclusion: 'We have seen the enemy. The enemy is us.'

The growing white-collar militancy has been brilliantly expressed over the last two decades by the ingenious personality of Clive Jenkins, the most articulate of all the left-wing radicals. His career was dazzling: the son of a Glamorgan railway clerk (whose other son Tom runs a railway union, the TSSA), he left school at fourteen and began as a lab worker; at twenty he was the youngest union official in British history, already learning how to mobilise white collars. In 1968 his union ASSET was merged into ASTMS (the Association of Scientific, Technical and Managerial Staffs), which in the next ten years sextupled its membership from 75,000 to 450,000. Jenkins recruited from the 'ant-heaps' as he called them—the banks, insurance companies and down-trodden bureaucracies—with the help of provocative advertising: 'The boss doesn't like the colour of your eyes.' His own life-style was unashamedly *haut bourgeois*, with a house in Regent's Park, a cabin cruiser, and endless cocktail parties. 'I'm a round peg,' he once said, 'in a round, velvet-lined hole.' As he grew older he became less interested in aggro and more involved in committees and councils as an elder statesman of the TUC. But he remained publicly left wing, and the contrast between his policies and his members' showed all the limitations of '5 per cent democracy': most of his members were moderate conservatives, who paid no political levy to Labour and were only militant in their wage-claims. But provided Jenkins got them more money, they were content to let him play his own part on the national stage.

As more white-collar delegates came to the annual congress they became more resentful of the big industrial unions which dominated the general council up on the dais; by 1981 they were demanding more representation, led by Tom Jackson of the Communications Workers, and Roy Grantham of the clerical union, APEX. They succeeded in passing new rules which automatically gave a seat on the council to any union with more than 100,000 members—thus favouring white collars. The moderates in the movement hailed it as a victory, but the white-collar leaders were not all like Jackson and Grantham; they included many militants, such as Clive Jenkins or Alan Sapper, the leader of ACTT, the chief television union, who were already on the council.

Sapper, as it happened, was soon given an extra voice by becoming the TUC's annual chairman in 1981; and he expressed all the spirit of white-collar militancy, ruthlessly exacting high wages for his cameramen and technicians while his brother Laurie (the secretary of the Association of University Teachers) bargained more discreetly for lecturers and dons. Alan Sapper was a loyal supporter of Tony Benn, and a 'passionate advocate' of free collective bargaining, and he enjoyed a special leverage on the media: for the television producers knew that if they criticised his union, he would make sure that they went off the air. (Anyone being filmed on television who makes a blunder need only quickly mention the name Alan Sapper, it is said, to make sure that the sentence will never be heard.)

What did the real political power of the union leaders amount to? During the seventies the 'barons' (as they were called like so many other British bosses) were publicised as legendary figures, whether as the wielders of unaccountable power or as the guardians of the true spirit of socialism. But the moment when power is most proclaimed is often when it has passed its peak, and when institutions become self-important they are often crumbling within. The leaders of the big unions were all facing problems in holding their components together; and while they occupied the middle of the political stage, their following was being undermined—first by revolts from the factory floors, and then by the massive increase in unemployment. They were also increasingly unsure of their political relationships with the Labour party. And all these problems were very evident in the biggest of all, the Transport and General Workers'.

TRANSPORT AND GENERAL

For the last sixty years the T and G has played a dominant role in the TUC and the Labour party; and it is its general secretary, rather than the TUC's, who is proclaimed as the most powerful union leader. His union, with nearly two million members, is still the biggest in Europe, and it makes up a fifth of all union membership in Britain including such intimidating groups as lorry-drivers and dockers. When Ernest Bevin first created the amalgamation in 1922 he insisted on giving himself as general secretary exceptional powers: like the president of the United States, he was the only man elected by all the members, surrounded by his appointees; and unlike the president he could stay there for life. Since Bevin left the job in 1940 there have been only five occupants—Arthur Deakin, Jock Tiffin, Frank Cousins, Jack Jones and Moss Evans—all of whom, except Tiffin (who died after a few months), were prominent on the national political stage. But the general secretary's power is often misunderstood, and has recently been drastically modified.

Jack Jones, the Liverpool dock worker who ran the union for nine years from 1969, was certainly one of the most impressive leaders of men. In the mid-seventies, when exorbitant wage-claims were undermining the Labour government and the country, it was Jones who initiated the scheme to limit wage increases to £6 a week, which began to reduce inflation; while Harold Wilson took the credit as prime minister, Jones reckoned (as he put it to me) that ''Arold had nothing to do with it'. Jones held back his militants by the force of his rhetoric and personality until by the summer of 1977 he faced a much angrier mood at the union's conference at the Isle of Man. It was a historic encounter to watch, an insight into the real relationship between the leader and his union: Jones' lean and tense figure confronted his bitter delegates, warning them that unleashing wages would generate a new wave of inflation and bring down the Labour government. He was met with heckling and boos, and the head of the union for the first time in its history was defeated by his own delegates. The pay revolt soon spread through the unions; the Labour cabinet under Callaghan could not control it; and by 1979 the Labour government—as Jones had warned—was out of office.

The strength of Jones' personality had partly concealed the fact that the structure and character of the T and G was basically changing, partly through Jones' own policies. The autocratic tradition of Ernest Bevin was fading, and both Jones and his predecessor Frank Cousins had insisted that it should become more democratic. 'Please don't call me a trade union boss,' Jones said after taking office, 'I'm not a boss and don't want to be one . . . We aim to make the TGWU the most democratic union in the world.' He spent much time trying to open up communications with shop stewards, and to make his headquarters at Transport House more sensitive to the provincial branches. It was not easy: 'Democracy is not something which happens naturally,' one official remarked. 'Bureaucracy is.' But while the public saw Jones as the man with the two-million block vote, he saw himself as struggling to hold his scattered branches together.

It was only when Jones retired in 1978 that the dissolution of power became clearer. His successor, Moss Evans, had seen how his predecessor had been defeated, and had climbed up with narrower political horizons. He had made his name as an expert negotiator—'with a smile like a razor blade' as he liked to boast; but his political attitudes were never sophisticated. He had come up from the Welsh valleys through a route which seemed infinitely remote from the world of London politics, as he described it to me before he took office in 1978:

> My father was a miner and he was on the dole for nearly fourteen years. I never had a pair of shoes until I was about sixteen, when the war was on; I always wore boots that were studded. We had one room downstairs and one upstairs, which was divided by a wood partition built by my father, with three beds—we children would sleep at the top of the bed. I never had a full cup of tea until I had a paper round, when we moved to Birmingham. Before that, if we had a cup of tea my brother used to get the saucer and I'd get the cup.

His mother had worked in a brick yard when she was twelve and her first husband was killed in the First World War; later she worked in a brick yard at nights and as a postwoman during the day to bring up her twelve children. She took Moss to political meetings near Merthyr when he was five: she did not know much about Marxism, but she wanted to see a complete change in society. It was not until Moss was released from the Forces that he became politically aware: he became a shop steward in 1947, and an avid reader of books such as *My Life's Battles* by Will Thorne, *The History of Trade Unions* by the Webbs, and political writers including Marx.

Moss Evans took over his union while its scope was dwindling: it was unpopular with the public, losing members to the dole, and harder to discipline after Jones' democratising process. He seemed bewildered by the political confusion, less worldly-wise than David Basnett of the GMWU, and ineffective in controlling his union. When Evans had to take several months off in 1981 for surgical treatment his place was taken by his deputy, Alex Kitson, a rugged ex-lorry-driver with a thick Scottish accent, who was much more overtly political. Kitson visited the Soviet Union once a year, and saw his battle with Mrs Thatcher in very personal terms, all the more so when his union was defeated in the British Leyland strike. ('She broke us with that 3.8 per cent,' he said afterwards. 'I've got to prove that we can get what's there.') But neither Kitson nor Evans were as much in command of their unions as they sounded. It was the executive council drawn from the different regions who now made the major decisions; and the general secretary could not necessarily control their votes.

The T and G can still muster a formidable array of organised labour. It has three members on the general council of the TUC; it sponsors twenty-five members of parliament; it pays £350,000 a year to the Labour party. For sixty years it had played a central role in Labour politics. But as it developed the process of consultation and democracy its political scope was becoming more uncertain: the block vote had always concealed a wide variety of political views, and the disagreements were more embarrassing when discussions were more open, while a third of its members were voting Tory. 'And many of them aren't just Tories,' one of their leaders said to me. 'They're Alf Garnett Tories, real racialists. It's not for nothing that Johnny Speight who invented Alf Garnett spent some time at Transport House.' These Tory voters and other dissidents lurking in the heart of the Labour party, behind the façade of the block vote, were a growing embarrassment as the divisions within the party became fiercer. And while most unions' members were preoccupied with their wages, the leaders were more concerned with the future of the Labour party.

5

Labour: the Widening Rift

There is a cracking sound in the political atmosphere: the sound of the consensus breaking up.

Richard Crossman, December 1970

THE Trades Union Congress had existed for thirty-five years before the birth of the Labour party, when trade unionists had already had a long involvement with parliament. As early as 1874 Thomas Burt from the Northumberland miners had been elected as Radical member of parliament for Morpeth; and it was not until 1903 that the TUC's 'Labour Representation Committee' set up a constitution and a political fund which created the Labour party. Its rise was then rapid. By the 1906 election the new party was able to sponsor fifty candidates of whom thirty were elected compared to 400 Liberals; and by 1924 it had 151 members compared to forty Liberals and formed the first Labour government. In only two decades trade unionists had broken the two-party pattern of British politics, eclipsing the Liberals and producing a more emphatic two-party system divided by class, money and employment.

The successive Labour governments, working through parliament, faced inevitable tensions with the trade union leaders who naturally wanted the party they paid for to answer to them; and tensions increased in the post-war years, as Labour ministers became accustomed to power. Many moderate trade unionists now hoped that the unions would now concern themselves more with wages, and less with politics. As George Woodcock said to me in 1961: 'We created the Labour party to get what we wanted. Now we've got it, we don't need it in the same way. The Labour party's job is to get votes. Our job is to get wages.' But Woodcock's hopes were disappointed as most union leaders proved more interested in changing Britain's political structure than in putting up wages. Only Britain, among Western democracies, had its main party of the left so interlocked and so dependent on trade unions. The awkward triangle between union leaders, MPs and Labour governments was increasingly strained as the conflicts came to a head in the Labour crisis of the early eighties.

The social differences between the unions and the party have always been displayed at the annual Labour party conference, held a month after the TUC's, where the delegates from the trade unions and the constituencies represent different strands of the party. There are the union bosses, sitting among their delegates, holding up their card votes on behalf of their millions. There are the representatives from all the 634 constituency parties, younger, more middle-class and more fiery than the trade unionists. And there are the Labour members of parliament trying, sometimes uneasily, to mingle with the other groups. There is still a wide range of accents and styles at the conference, with some religious overtones. There are the non-conformists from Wales and the north, still with some of the old fervour of the chapel; the Scotsmen with uncompromising accents and hints of the old Calvinist hell-fire; the groups of Marxists and Trotskyists with their bookstalls of revolutionary pamphlets; the cranky fringe groups of pacifists, vegetarians or special crusaders. There are still a few smooth London lawyers and professional men with public-school voices. But over two decades the language of conference has become much more radical and strident, and the more moderate members more ill-at-ease.

THE WORSENING RELATIONSHIP

The long connection between Labour and the trade unions was not necessarily accompanied by mutual understanding. After 1964, when Labour ministers came to power after thirteen years in opposition, their relations with union leaders were much less close than they looked from outside. They kept in touch through the National Executive Council and joint government bodies such as Neddy, while the former head of the biggest union, Frank Cousins, was in the cabinet; but most ministers had few personal links. When George Brown and his staff at the Department of Economic Affairs needed union support for their national plan, they were soon aware of the gulf between themselves and the unions: 'We realised that we didn't even have their private telephone numbers,' one minister recalled. Dick Crossman and Barbara Castle, both left-wing ministers sympathetic to the unions, revealed in their memoirs how little social time they spent with union leaders, and how little they really understood them.

The escalating strikes increased the tensions. Already in 1965 Harold Wilson had set up a royal commission under Lord Donovan to consider changing the law to limit the immunity of unions; but the commissioners (excepting the economist Andrew Shonfield) would not recommend the bold remedies that Wilson had hoped for. By 1967, after more damaging strikes, Wilson was privately wishing that the Labour party could break away from the unions. But, he reflected: 'We shan't be like the Americans; we shall be like that miserable French socialist party.'[1] When Wilson and Castle rashly put forward their plan to make unions more responsible, *In Place of Strife*, the union leaders mobilised all their supporters; the pro-union MPs, including Callaghan and Foot, revolted; and Wilson was compelled to climb down, with only face-saving promises from the TUC to give a 'solemn and binding undertaking' to discipline strikers. Ted Heath taunted Wilson's government: 'Although they may still wear the trappings of power, the power resides elsewhere.' And many Labour politicians, including Barbara Castle, blamed the unions for their party's defeat in 1970.

When he came back to power in 1974 Wilson was determined to conciliate the unions, promising them new privileges in return for supporting the social contract. But the Labour party had made promises to the unions, including the repeal of the Tories' Industrial Relations Act, without exacting any serious promises from the unions to co-operate in wage restraint. 'The terms represented the most complete capitulation by the Labour party to the industrial movement,' wrote the contemporary historian Keith Middlemas.[2] 'They failed to realise,' the Labour MP Giles Radice wrote afterwards, 'that they were dealing with bargainers.'[3] For a party so closely linked with the unions, it was a staggering failure. As the wage-claims fuelled inflation many Labour ministers were soon privately disillusioned, as they later revealed. 'The only give and take in the contract,' said Joel Barnett, the Chief Secretary of the Treasury, 'was that the government gave and the unions took.'[4] Barbara Castle began with some hope: 'If there is an answer to this country's problems,' she told her diary in January 1975, 'it lies in this inchoate union between our government and the unions. I have always believed that our only hope is to make the unions *more*, not less political.' But four months later she was already disillusioned with the unions' response to the inflationary crisis: 'We have heaped goodies on them, but they have delivered nothing in return.' Tony Benn still insisted that 'Our first job is to defend the trade union movement,' and Castle still hoped to reform them: 'Our job is to *make* them exercise positive power.'[5] But many in the cabinet began to

[1] Crossman: *Diaries of a Cabinet Minister*, vol 1, p. 287.
[2] Keith Middlemas: *Politics in Industrial Society*, André Deutsch, London, 1979, p. 446.
[3] Essay in *The Socialist Agenda*, Jonathan Cape, London, 1981, p. 123.
[4] Joel Barnett: *Inside the Treasury*, André Deutsch, London, 1982, p. 49.
[5] Barbara Castle: *The Castle Diaries*, Weidenfeld and Nicolson, London, 1980, pp. 386, 424.

despair of the unions' irresponsibility. 'No government in history,' the Chancellor, Denis Healey told them, 'has ever taken the labour movement so much into its confidence as this one . . . you can't have special treatment without accepting responsibility.'[6]

The Labour government, it was true, could be grateful to Jack Jones, who by sheer force of leadership had got agreement in 1975 for his £6-a-week formula: this pay restraint lasted with diminishing effectiveness for two years. But by the 'winter of discontent' in 1978–79 Jones had retired, the social contract was in ruins, and the strikes in crucial services, from hospital workers to gravediggers, had destroyed any public confidence that a Labour government had special influence over the unions. Callaghan showed his own lack of awareness when he was asked about the crisis on his return from the summit at Guadeloupe, and replied: 'What crisis?' He was soon conscious of the political dangers; and he told the cabinet in February that he 'had never in fifty years been so depressed as a trade unionist'; but he still refused publicly to criticise the unions, and his only response was to propose a new joint 'concordat' with the TUC.

Other cabinet ministers were conscious that the trade unions had never been so unpopular. 'The trade union leaders had worked hard to earn the high degree of unpopularity they had now achieved,' said Joel Barnett. 'At conference after conference throughout the previous summer, they had led a campaign, not only for free collective bargaining, but for pay claims they must have known would only be attainable with rising prices and unemployment.' But Barnett, like many others, believed there was no alternative to fighting the next election side by side with the unions. 'We in the Labour party could never part from the institution that gave birth to us. We were stuck with each other, and had to make the best of it.'[7]

THE PARTY AND THE VOTERS

With all this intense public unpopularity, there were few doubts that the unions played a major part in the defeat of the Labour government in 1979—the third government they had helped to bring down in twenty years. The Labour party's tension with the unions was only one part of a confusion of identity which had been growing over the previous decades. From its origins Labour had been essentially a class party with working-men's unions as its bedrock and a small group of middle-class intellectuals mingling at the top. But the affluence of the fifties was already eating away at this class solidarity.

[6] *Ibid*, p. 658.
[7] Barnett: *op cit*, pp. 172–5.

'The new social pattern has certainly created problems for the Labour party,' Hugh Gaitskell told me in 1961. 'A combination of great fluidity and a more self-regarding and less community-conscious attitude has made difficulties for us.' Gaitskell was facing all the problems of dwindling party loyalty and solidarity, which were exacerbated by his left-wing critics, led by Harold Wilson and Frank Cousins, who insisted on further nationalisation and on nuclear disarmament, while Gaitskell could never bring himself to evade these serious issues by blurring them.

Harold Wilson was soon able to unify his party behind the panoply of power, and he had learnt about the arts of deception from watching Harold Macmillan. He could conceal the party's splits by his hectic improvisation and a sense of excitement. 'This party is a bit like an old stage-coach,' he loved to explained. 'If you drive it along at a rapid rate, everyone aboard is either so exhilarated or so seasick that your don't have a lot of difficulty.' He could easily confuse his critics, whether about Vietnam, nationalisation or Rhodesia: when he undertook not to use force in Rhodesia and promised that sanctions would become effective in weeks he was at the peak of his national popularity, leading what he now called the 'natural party of government'.

Perhaps the deception and blurring of issues was the inevitable price which Wilson paid, like Macmillan before him, for governing a country which was in retreat from empire and grandeur. Perhaps the voters could not take the truth, and demanded to be deceived. But Wilson (like Macmillan) paid a higher price than appeared at the time in terms of party loyalty. As the stage-coach jogged along he became easily contemptuous of his radical critics: 'You don't need to worry about the outside left,' he said, 'they've got nowhere else to go.' He was equally dismissive of his backbenchers in parliament, with their 'dog licences'. Wilson's manoeuvres and compromises held little appeal for idealists, and the younger left were already beginning to look outside parliament for their come-back.

The resentments against Wilson's first government were not eased by the heavy overloading of Oxford dons in the cabinet, particularly economists whose links with the unions were tenuous. The old Gaitskell coterie, including Roy Jenkins, Anthony Crosland, and Douglas Jay, became firmly entrenched under Wilson, and the cabinet looked even more rarified after 1968 when George Brown and Ray Gunter had left the government (to return, as Gunter put it, to the folk 'from whence I came'). At first this donnish government did not appear to worry the trade union leaders, and it often suited them to work through their parliamentary spokesmen, such as Dick Crossman and Barbara Castle. 'We didn't want the unions' power to be too visible in a place like the West Midlands,' one union leader explained to me. 'It served us better to have an MP like Dick Crossman who did what we asked.'

But the donnishness of the Labour cabinets gave them limitations. Most of them had never had to manage any kind of concern, except perhaps troops in the army, and many were far too confident about the effects of their policies. 'I'm the only one who's actually had to run a business,' Crossman explained to me in 1967, although his own farming business had been effectively delegated. The cabinet were inclined to take the trade unions at their face value—as 'an estate of the realm' as Wilson called them in 1968—without much knowledge of what lay behind them. The middle-class ministers felt themselves vulnerable to any charge of not understanding the problems of the workers or the unemployed, which became more evident after Labour's return to power in 1974. 'There was a sort of collective guilt complex round the cabinet table,' complained Joel Barnett of the later cabinet of 1974, 'which led to expenditure on "employment measures" that were far from cost-effective.' And Denis Healey eventually burst out: 'We should not allow middle-class guilt to blind us to what's going on.'[8]

When Wilson returned as prime minister in 1974 after a four-year interval he was less hectic in driving his stage-coach, and more prepared to delegate to his cabinet, while allowing the trade unions a greater say in the policies. Most of the reforming zeal had gone out of Labour as the earlier reforms had turned sour, and the government was preoccupied with crisis as they faced the full effects of inflation, recession and mounting debt. In the meantime the intellectual basis of the Labour moderates' arguments was under heavy fire. In the years after 1956 Anthony Crosland's book, *The Future of Socialism*, became the revisionists' bible, spelling out the merits of the mixed economy, the limits of nationalisation and the need for higher growth-rates to finance more welfare. Twenty years later the high growth had not been achieved, economic disasters had set back every expectation and the welfare state had become more unmanageable and expensive.

The face of Labour government was looking much less human, more bureaucratic and centralised, like some kind of corporate state, while the Labour revisionists had run out of ideas. In the new age of inflation and unemployment other reformist parties in the West were also coming to the end of an ideological road; but Labour in Britain was facing an angrier left, and even less industrial growth. The two-year premiership of Callaghan, like the brief rule of Douglas-Home, provided a kind of spluttering end to his predecessor's long

[8] Barnett: *op cit*, pp. 50, 175.

ride, with no new ideas or identity. Callaghan, like Sir Alec, having lost the election, left his party in shambles. And the old arguments about nationalisation and nuclear disarmament which had split the party twenty years earlier were burning more fiercely than ever.

Over twenty years the Labour party had seen much of its earlier support falling off. Since 1951, when Labour had won 48.8 per cent of the popular vote (though it lost the election) its share had strikingly diminished: by February 1974 it was 37.2 per cent, by October 1974 it had gone up to 39.2 per cent, but by 1979 it was down to 36.9 per cent. The old working-class loyalty was beginning to dissolve, and voting experts at Essex University, under Professor Anthony King, showed clearly how even Labour voters were becoming less attracted by the party's chief policies—including nationalising more industries, spending more on social services and keeping close ties with the unions.

By 1979 traditional Labour voters were showing sympathy for many Tory aims including tougher action against strikers, and selling off council houses. 'Seldom can a major party have penetrated so deeply,' wrote King, 'into the political thinking of the other side's staunchest supporters.'[9] While the unions had become an increasing liability to the Labour party at elections, the Tories were becoming more associated with personal freedom and liberty than Labour. 'Our opponents,' complained Professor Maurice Preston, 'have been able to capture the motto of liberty for their banner and have tried to depict Labour as the party of restraint.'[10] But while the polls showed clearly enough the causes of Labour's unpopularity, the party was now turning in a direction likely to make it still less popular.

THE NEW LEFT

The new leaders on the left were separate from the trade unions, though they overlapped with them, and very different from the old-style Moscow communists. In the fifties many members of parliament and trade unionists were still 'fellow travellers' who maintained close links with Moscow, but the invasions of Hungary and Czechoslovakia had cut many of those links. By 1980 the British Communist party had only 20,600 members compared to 34,300 in 1964: its daily newspaper, the *Morning Star*, sold only 32,000 copies compared to 123,000 sold by its predecessor, the *Daily Worker*, in 1974. The British Communist party and its paper were not completely unswerving in their loyalty to Moscow: at their annual

[9] The *Observer*, April 22, 1979.
[10] Lipsey and Leonard: *The Socialist Agenda*, Jonathan Cape, London, 1981, p. 188.

congress in November 1981 they condemned, like other European communist parties, the Soviet intervention in Afghanistan. But they were more loyal than most.

During the seventies, encouraged by the mood of detente, left-wing leaders were visiting the Soviet Union more frequently, and in 1973 the Labour party lifted its old ban on CP organisations. Some influential trade unionists are still members of the Communist party, including Ken Gill, the leader of the TASS section of the engineers' union, and Mick McGahey of the miners' union; Alex Kitson of the T and G is a regular, though critical, visitor to Russia. In 1981 the general secretary of the British Communist party, Gordon McLennan, proposed that communists should unite with the Labour party and have representatives on its committees and councils. Right-wing politicians continue to depict the British communists as a threat to the nation's security; but the links between Labour and Moscow are much weaker than thirty years ago.

It was another version of Marxism which extended its influence—the Trotskyists and their allies who believed in a 'permanent revolution' spreading through the bourgeois world. Ever since the Bolshevik revolution lost its first idealism, many intellectuals were attracted by the promise of an ultimate world revolution—which had the extra advantage that, being not easily attainable, it would not soon disturb their own bourgeois lives. The European Trotskyist parties gained a new impetus from the chain reaction of students' revolts in 1968: the brilliant rhetoric and sloganeering of Cohn-Bendit and his colleagues in Paris was directed against 'obsolete communism' as much as capitalism, and for a few days they even appeared to bridge the gap between workers and students. The immediate British student revolt was much less sensational, as Cohn-Bendit found when he came to the London School of Economics. But the intellectual fireworks had lit a slow time-fuse even in Britain, which inspired a new generation with the scope for revolutionary activity.

The new radicalism was certainly encouraged, as elsewhere in Europe, by the rapid expansion of universities and polytechnics (see chapter 8). The new graduates in sociology and political science emerged into an unwelcoming world, feeling very separate from the traditional university elites. The rapid expansion of higher education, followed by recession, contraction and graduate unemployment, provided the classic conditions for intellectual revolt: the armies of young post-graduates and teachers had the time and the zeal to spend long evenings in local Labour party organisation, outlasting their more moderate rivals. But this new intelligentsia —the 'polyocracy', or 'lumpenpolytariat' as Peter Jenkins called them—were only the catalysts of the leftward movement, and there is no need to look to conspiracy theories to explain the trend. The rising unemployment, the continuing and widening inequality between rich and poor, the end of the long Western boom and the rush of inflation after 1973 had all helped to disillusion Labour voters with the mixed economy, and the younger generation had good reason to be less optimistic and confident of social improvements than their elders.

Yet the new men on the left faced their own confusions of political philosophy, caught between reformism and revolution without any convincing mould for a socialist state, whether in Russia, Eastern Europe or China. In 1981 several left-wing writers, led by the Marxist historian Eric Hobsbawm, discussed their predicament candidly in the book *The Forward March of Labour Halted?* They revealed not only that capitalism was in crisis but that the left also was in confusion about what they wanted to put in its place. How could they reconcile equality with efficiency, industrial democracy with capitalist control, nationalisation of the media with freedom of speech, protection of British industry with support for the Third World? 'The truth is,' wrote the sociologist W. G. Runciman about the book, 'that it is no longer possible to formulate a "radical alternative" which can coherently reconcile the traditional set of socialist but still democratic objectives.'[11]

Within parliament itself, Wilson's cynicism and contempt for backbenchers during his long government had encouraged revolt. The membership of the 'Tribune group' of left-wing MPs (named after the weekly paper launched by Stafford Cripps in 1937 with Nye Bevan as its parliamentary writer and Michael Foot as dogsbody) had grown with each parliament, reaching eighty by 1974, reflecting the growing impatience with revisionist doctrines. When Wilson came back to power in 1974 the left-wing members were already much stronger: their veteran Ian Mikardo was elected chairman of the Parliamentary Labour Party, and they dominated the national executive. The setbacks to the mixed economy and the disillusion with the 'future of socialism' encouraged the left to demand more nationalisation. Britain's dependence on foreign bankers and markets, dramatised by the humiliating IMF loan in 1976, encouraged a more extreme and insular left, demanding import controls and the retreat from the Common Market.

Most of the new radical groups were much more interested in operating outside parliament. The Trotskyists, as always in their quarrelsome history, kept on splitting off from each other, so that they now include at least twenty-five separate organisations. But the

[11] *London Review of Books*, December 1981.

biggest groups—the Workers Revolutionary party, the Socialist Workers Revolutionary party, the Socialist Workers party and the Militant Tendency—named after the Trotskyist newspaper *Militant*—were attracting many new members and improving their organisation. They could collaborate in joint movements for popular causes, such as the Anti-Nazi League and the Campaign for Nuclear Disarmament; and the mounting clashes between the police and protestors or militant strikers provided a new theatre for television, which attracted much more public attention than speeches in parliament.

But the left wing were also rapidly penetrating the Labour constituency parties, which were decaying and easily undermined. By 1977 there were only eighty-six full-time Labour agents in Britain, compared to 225 in 1960,[12] and the Labour moderates had few local activists. The complacency of the Wilson years had produced a 'lost generation', disillusioned with the leadership, and the left-wing activists could fill part of the vacuum; they could spend successive evenings in political debate, bringing their thermoses and sandwiches and wearing out moderate opponents who lacked their spare time and motivation. They were pursuing their new policy of 'entryism', surreptitiously infiltrating the Labour party. By about 1970 the Militant Tendency had abolished its list of members, and was creating its own groups within the Labour party, to enable them to capture the power in constituency parties. The Militant Tendency, with its creepy membership and revolutionary rhetoric, became a sinister enemy of the Labour moderates over the next decades; but it distracted attention from the more serious threat of other apparently more democratic groups which were preparing to subvert the existing structure of Labour.[13]

By 1973 the tension between Wilson and the broader left had come to a head when Wilson rejected the new radical policy statement prepared by the national executive; and as a result a group of left-wing MPs met in the House of Commons to set up a new Campaign for Labour Party Democracy (CLPD), to promote the policies of the left within the Labour party. The secretary and chief organiser was a Czech émigré, Vladimir Derer, who set up the headquarters in his house in Golders Green with his wife Vera, a polytechnic lecturer. With tiny resources he began systematically lobbying the local parties, sending out 'model resolutions' and building up a team of activists, including Victor Schonfield, the jazz critic, Peter Willsman from NUPE, Andy Harris, a councillor

[12] Stephen Haseler: *The Tragedy of Labour*, Blackwell, Oxford, 1980, p. 142.
[13] See David and Maurice Kogan: *The Battle for the Labour Party*, Fontana, London, 1982 (to which I am indebted in this section).

from Putney, and Jon Lansman, an unemployed young Cambridge graduate.

Over the next eight years the small band of the CLPD played a disproportionate part in winning over to the left the constituency parties, and it later became interlocked with other new activist organisations, such as the Labour Co-ordinating Committee (LCC), which was formed in 1978 and run by Nigel Stanley, devoting itself to policy issues with the help of MPs including Stuart Holland, Michael Meacher and Bob Cryer. And in 1980, in the first year of Labour opposition, ten separate left-wing organisations, including the LCC, the CLPD, the Militant Tendency and the Institute for Workers' Control, agreed to form a joint organisation to press for change in the Labour constitution, which was called the Rank and File Mobilising Committee (RFMC). It was this co-ordinating group which was to transform the character of the party.

The committees on the left were pledged not only to commit the Labour party to radical policies, but to make the leadership and the MPs more responsive to the rank and file. They had been pressing since 1974 for MPs to be subject to 'mandatory reselection' which required them to come before their constituency parties every two years, thus undermining their Burkean independence. They had convincing democratic arguments, and the big unions had become increasingly disillusioned with MPs since Reg Prentice, the Labour MP for Newham who was sponsored by the Transport and General, revealed himself as a Conservative whom they could not dislodge, which disgusted even moderate union leaders such as Harry Urwin of the T and G. The movement to reselect MPs quickly gathered momentum but it was never as truly democratic as it pretended; for it would shift power from an unrepresentative MP to a still less representative group of party activists with little contact with any real 'rank and file'.

It was only belatedly that the ramifications of these left-wing networks became more publicly known. The Labour party itself preferred not to reveal them, and when the national agent, Reg Underhill, produced a report in 1979 on 'entryism' the NEC refused to publish it. Journalists tended to play down the left-wing activists, partly because they seemed rather absurd, partly because they followed the old rule, 'No enemies to the left', and partly because right-wing Conservatives had so often exaggerated and oversimplified the Red Menace, putting Trotskyists in the same category as Moscow communists. So when the campaigners began moving more effectively to exert their influence, few people predicted the extent of their success.

Were the new left-wing groups more or less dangerous than the pro-Moscow communists thirty years earlier? The old fellow-travellers, with their suspected allegiance to a foreign power, provided a more obvious danger to national security; the new Marxists had no obvious foreign connections—except perhaps with Libya—and the interests of many of them were strikingly insular. Behind their theatre it was never easy to know how seriously the extremists really believed in revolution, and the different components disagreed constantly about the meaning of socialism, as they showed in periodicals such as *New Socialist* and *Marxism Today*. The left wing could see very clearly how the revisionists had failed over the last twenty years, but they were reluctant to examine the greater dangers of alternative states elsewhere. By penetrating the Labour party and championing party democracy they became spectacularly successful in hounding the moderates, and undermining the parliamentary party; but they showed a few signs of knowing what to put in its place. They were a less obvious bogey than the old fellow-travellers, but they presented a greater danger to parliamentary democracy.

TONY BENN

The left had no single leader or prophet and when they found a figurehead he seemed an odd choice: not an intellectual, not from the polyocracy or the factory floor, but a very British ex-public schoolboy, the son of a Labour peer who came from five generations of well-to-do non-conformists. Tony Benn led the left, not through any rigorous intellectual approach, but through dazzling rhetoric and an instinctive populism, owing much of his appeal to his ability to always appear thoroughly English, reasonable and Christian.

In spite of his contradictions his career had a strong thread of continuity. At Westminster School—where I first met him forty years ago—he was never academically successful, but he already had the gift of the gab; when he incessantly spoke up in class he would be greeted with cries of 'Oh Benn!' He was always quite puritanical, though not godly. At Oxford he reacted against his hard-drinking contemporaries by becoming a lifelong teetotaller; and he married Carol De Camp, a forceful egalitarian from a rich and right-wing Cincinnati family who soon became a stern political force in her own right, becoming chairman of her local comprehensive school, Holland Park. The Benn family in their dingy house in an elegant avenue was close and all-of-a-piece, dedicated to the political battle. In the basement Benn's office was full of elaborate home-made filing systems, gadgets and papers hanging from clips on the ceiling.

When he went into parliament at the age of twenty-five he appeared almost a caricature of the boy scout politician, with his hearty style and square jaw, and he was much influenced by his father, a worthy Labour ex-minister who became Lord Stansgate, known as 'Big Benn' compared to 'Little Benn'. The more sophisticated Labour intellectuals did not conceal their contempt for his naive ideas, but he was always much more popular with the party outside parliament, elected year after year to the NEC, talking eagerly to meetings of trade unionists and activists, and much keener to confront workers than were his donnish colleagues. (Once when I invited the Benns to a party, they replied, 'Don't you *know* that's the day of the Durham Miners' Gala?')

Benn was neither obviously very radical, nor insular: he was at first enthusiastic about the European Community and when he became Minister of Technology in 1966 he was thrilled by the opportunities for still bigger business, forcing through the ill-fated merger between Leyland and the British Motor Corporation, and feeding ambitious technological ventures. ('I've been trying to work out,' said one of his civil servants, 'which has cost Britain more, the Second World War or Tony Benn.') He got on well with civil servants, protected their discretion, worked closely with businessmen and never allowed populism to interfere with his exercise of power. It was not until much later that he insisted that this corporatist policy was a disaster: 'It wasn't efficient, it didn't improve our rate of growth. It wasn't egalitarian, it wasn't democratic, it was very secretive and it was accompanied by a steady and continuing decline of British industry.'[14]

It was only when he came back into government in 1974 that he emerged more seriously as a leader of the left and a bogeyman of the right. The collapse of British companies after 1974 gave him, as Minister for Industry, a new image as the champion of nationalisation and workers' control, until Wilson took fright and moved him to Energy where he publicised the dangers of nuclear power and insisted that only the people could decide. The intervention of the International Monetary Fund gave Benn a new bogey, and he was now building up the evils of centralised power and international capitalism. 'I discovered,' he wrote later, 'how the immense power of the bankers and the industrialists in Britain, and world-wide, could be used to bring direct and indirect pressure, again backed by the media, first to halt, and then to reverse, the policy of a Labour government that both the electors and the House of Commons had accepted.'[15]

[14] Interview with Robert Mackenzie, the *Listener*, May 21, 1981.
[15] Tony Benn: *Arguments for Socialism*, Jonathan Cape, London 1979, p. 17.

Back in opposition in 1979, Benn was now poised for his greatest crusade, to capture the leadership of his party, climbing up from the left as Harold Wilson had done twenty years earlier. Thatcher's extreme policies stimulated the extremism on the left, and Benn admired the courage of her convictions. 'She defends the class she represents with great vigour,' he explained in 1981. 'This had the good effect of making *our* people feel that we should work as hard for the class *we* represent.'[16] Benn had now developed a phenomenal skill in public speaking, second only to Enoch Powell, able to sway audiences ranging from Texan oilmen to Yorkshire strikers at factory gates. He was no longer the hearty public schoolboy, but the gaunt prophet of doom and radical remedies, with fierce eyes, a thin smile and a mirthless laugh. In *Who's Who* he had first excised all reference to his education or parentage, becoming plain Mr Benn, and then disappeared from the book altogether.

He was building up a vivid picture of the capitalist establishment, interlocked with multinational corporations, the IMF and the media (like Spiro Agnew he knew that the more he attacked the media, the more they would build him up). In speeches and books he presented himself as the heir to the ancient British traditions of liberty and equality going back to Cromwell and the Levellers, combating the evil influences of centralised power, now on a world scale, which had reduced Britain to the condition of a colony. 'The people of Britain,' he wrote in 1981, 'have much less control over their destiny than they are led to believe: far less than they are entitled to expect and demand; and a great deal less than they had a generation ago.'[17]

With great clarity he presented important elements of truth. Both Tory and Labour governments (and notably Benn himself) had been far too little aware of the dangers of centralised power. The ruthless movements of international capital, in an age of high inflation, high interest rates and unemployment, had made many Englishmen feel bitterly helpless in the face of external forces, and the faceless men of Brussels, Washington and the IMF were the scapegoats. Benn's political antennae now sensed this wave of resentment. His eloquent speeches, with their sweeping simplifications and old-fashioned morality, recalled the American populists of the late nineteenth century who found followers likewise bewildered by the relentless centralisation of the time.

But when Benn put forward his remedies—more nationalisation, more protectionism, more workers' control—he never faced up to the real problems which he had himself seen at close quarters. He never discussed how state ownership could avoid still further

[16] To John Mortimer, *Sunday Times*, September 6, 1981.
[17] Benn: *op cit*, p. 4.

bureaucratic centralisation and infringements of liberty, as in Eastern Europe. He never explained how Britain, as a trading nation, could become more prosperous by extending protection. He never analysed the democratic problems behind his seductive slogan, 'Let The People Decide'. He was never a Marxist, but he advocated closer relationships with Marxists: 'A reconciliation of Marxism and political democracy,' he said in March 1982, 'is possible, necessary and urgent.' In his impatience for power he never looked too closely at the alliances he was making with groups on the left, and his political attitudes seemed to be becoming still more naive. 'I've always said about Tony,' said Wilson in 1981, 'that he immatures with age.'

Benn had been through wavering relationships with both the left-wing activists and the trade unions, and the overall label 'Bennite' was very misleading. He was only recently associated with the Tribune group in parliament, while the more conservative union leaders were suspicious of his radical rhetoric and Marxist friends. But Benn and his new allies understood what many other Labour leaders had ignored; that the real roots of power in the party now lay not in parliament or in the TUC, but among the rank-and-file of both the party and the unions; and that the decisive arena was the annual conference. Benn had a loyal band of energetic organisers, including his former parliamentary secretary, Brian Sedgemore, his former economic advisers, Frances Morrell and Stuart Holland, and his ghost-writer Chris Mullin, now editor of *Tribune*. His own brand of populism could find common ground with Marxists, local activists and union shop stewards. And they were all determined, whatever the electoral cost, to move the Labour party to the left.

THE LABOUR LEADERSHIP

By the end of the government in 1979 the Labour leadership was almost unrecognisable from fifteen years earlier. Most of the pre-war Oxford intellectuals had now vanished. Gordon-Walker, Jay, Castle and Longford had retired from government; Roy Jenkins was in Brussels; Tony Crosland, the guardian of its intellectual integrity, had died. The moderates of the party had less intellectual confidence and fire, and the new men at the top had come up through a more professionalised route. Roy Hattersley, who became Secretary for Prices in the cabinet, had begun as a city councillor in Sheffield: he was an instinctive politician and a sensitive writer, very conscious of his Yorkshire roots, but it was never very clear what he stood for. John Smith, who became Secretary for Trade, was a barrister from Glasgow, from a middle-class background. Eric Varley, the miner's

son from Merseyside, was an engineer's turner before joining parliament, rising to be Secretary for Industry, but he lacked the robust
earthiness of the old sons of toil. Only Roy Mason, who had risen to
be Minister of Defence and then Secretary for Northern Ireland,
belonged to the tougher proletarian tradition: he could boast that he
went underground at fourteen.

The ordeals of the last Labour government had left deep scars and
ideological confusion—from the great inflation of 1974 to the split
over Europe to the bitter arguments about the IMF loan in 1976,
which, some said, broke the heart of the Labour party. The last
months of government had brought the conflicts with the unions to a
head, and the party was still in a state of uncertainty when
Callaghan stood down in 1980, and four contenders stood for the
leadership.

Of the four Denis Healey was the most obviously qualified, as the
'iron Chancellor' for five years, and Minister of Defence for six years
before that. His wide experience spanned the post-war history of
Labour; his origins were earthy, his education intellectual. The son
of a technical school principal, he had gone to Bradford Grammar
School, and took a first in classics at Oxford, where he overlapped
with Jenkins and Crosland. As an anti-Nazi he joined the Communist party for two years, but after the war Major Healey emerged as an
uncompromising anti-communist. His talents were formidable: he
could master economics, nuclear strategy and political in-fighting;
he was cultured and well-read, but he could bully like an Irish thug.
('If I were you, Tony,' he once told me when I was arguing at a
dinner party against selling arms to South Africa, 'I'd keep your
bloody trap shut.')

As Chancellor he had pursued monetarist policies against inflation, infuriating the left and the unions. In opposition he presented
himself as a pragmatist determined to humanise government: 'The
only proper approach for a democratic socialist is that of a gardener,'
he said in September 1981. 'You have to respect the nature of the
soil.' But the left saw him as a personification of the compromises
and corruptions of power, who had been involved in all the turnabouts of twenty years: first defending British bases in the Far East,
then abandoning them; first urging the selling of arms to South
Africa, then repenting; and facing both ways on the European
Community. But he remained completely loyal to NATO and to the
Atlantic Alliance, and did not conceal his contempt for the new
insular left.

Peter Shore had long been Healey's rival. He had resisted
Healey's acceptance of the IMF terms, and his lean frame and
passionate oratory had become identified with patriotic attacks on

the European Community. He was seven years younger than Healey, with a narrower experience: the son of a merchant navy captain, he had gone to Cambridge via Quarry Bank School in Liverpool. He joined Labour's research department, helped to write the 1964 manifesto and reached the cabinet three years later. He was mocked as Wilson's lapdog, but soon made his own reputation campaigning against Europe with his own image of patriotism. 'You can see why I'm an anti-marketeer,' he said in 1978. 'I can't conceive of us ever having the kind of revival of morale and effort and achievement except within the concept of being the British nation.'

The least-known contender was John Silkin, offering himself as an anti-European from the left who could reconcile the party behind him. He is a rich, easy-going lawyer from a Labour family—his grandfather was a Lithuanian refugee, his father was a Labour minister, his brother had been Attorney-General. He had made his own name as Minister of Agriculture by well-publicised attacks on European farmers; and he had turned towards unilateralism as his party turned left. But in his anxiety to please he never revealed a very consistent picture of himself or of Britain's role.

Perhaps the most unexpected contender in 1980 was the romantic veteran of the Labour left, Michael Foot. For thirty years he had been a backbench MP, the scourge of both Labour and Tory ministers, rallying the left with his acrobatic oratory—arms flailing, hair scattering, sentences abruptly stopping and starting. He conjured up all the idealism of pre-war Labour, harking back to hunger marches and his hero Aneurin Bevan, whose biography he wrote and whose Welsh seat he inherited. He seemed made for the role of perpetual critic. His background was cultured and Liberal: he was bored by economics, and preferred literary models such as Hazlitt and Swift. He was a brilliant journalist, who admired Beaverbrook almost as much as Bevan, and a delightful friend.

Then in 1974 Wilson invited him to become Minister for Employment and he stayed in the cabinet for five years, using all his powers to persuade the unions to accept wage restraint. He was totally committed to the alliance with the unions, and when Callaghan stood down in 1980 his wife and his political friends—including Moss Evans and David Basnett, the two most powerful union leaders—convinced him that only he could unite the rival forces. Some Labour MPs supported him as a caretaker who could later pass on his votes to Shore. One or two right-wingers hoped that his election would precipitate the final split that they wanted. But most members hoped he would bring a new longed-for unity to the party. In the second ballot he defeated Healey by 139 votes to 129 and became leader of the Labour party at the age of sixty-seven. The personalities were crucial, for as David Owen said two years later: 'If either Tony Crosland or Denis Healey had become leader of the Labour party, perhaps there might not have been a Social Democratic party.'

Foot's election was the prelude not to a new era of unity, but to a rift that could not be bridged; and over the next two years he presided over the most agonising period of the party's history. As he put it:

> If the Labour party were to lose the next parliamentary election, it would be the most fateful loss since the party was founded in 1900. More peremptorily than ever before, if in a new form, R. H. Tawney's fundamental question is presented to us: who is to be master? If democratic socialists cannot secure the right answer at the next parliamentary opportunity, we may not be asked again, or rather this old famous socialist stream could perish in sectarian bogs and sands.

WHO RUNS LABOUR?

Who was now really in charge of the party? Was it the trade unions, the constituency parties, or (when in power) the prime minister and cabinet? Labour was always determined, in contrast to the Tories, to organise itself 'from the bottom up' and the party had a dual leadership under two rival committees. Each year the conference passed its resolutions or approved the election manifesto, which the cabinet or shadow cabinet would then partly adopt, and partly ignore. Each year the party elected its National Executive Committee (NEC), which arranged the conference itself; its twenty-eight members were chosen by different groups—among them twelve by the unions, seven by the constituency parties, one by the professional organisations, and five women elected by the whole party. The trade unions choose men from the biggest unions—usually not the leaders—to represent them, while the votes of the constituencies provide a kind of annual popularity poll, led by well-known figures, most of them on the left, many of whom have never been in government. At the top of this hit parade in 1981 stood:

> Tony Benn
> Eric Heffer
> Denis Skinner
> Frank Allaun
> Neil Kinnock
> Jo Richardson
> Joan Lestor

The unions control the majority of the NEC and wield an overwhelming majority of the votes at the annual conference—80 per cent against 20 per cent from the constituency parties and none from members of parliament. After 1974 the unions' influence was still greater, increased by the need for funds: in spite of complaints from party leaders such as George Brown the unions' funds became more dominant as the money from individuals and constituencies dwindled, and the unions now provide 80 per cent of Labour's income. 'With the decline of individual membership,' wrote Keith Middlemas in 1979, 'the trade unions established practical as well as policy-making hegemony.'[18] And the unions dominate the party's organisation with the major say in choosing the party's general secretary, usually preferring a man near the end of a career of loyal party work. The last incumbent, Ronald Hayward, had been the national agent, and in 1982 he was succeeded by Jim Mortimer, a former ship fitter who had spent most of his career as a trade union organiser.

Transport House had long been notorious for its slow-moving bureaucracy, shortage of funds, and 'penny-farthing' methods, as Harold Wilson called them. But during the seventies the party structure was decaying all over the country—which the leaders were slow to notice but which Tony Benn was quick to exploit. 'Much of the present wave of anxiety, disenchantment and discontent,' he said in 1972, 'is actually directed at the party structure. Many people do not think it is responding quickly enough to the mounting pressure of events or the individual or collective aspirations of the community.' The crumbling local parties offered easy opportunities for left-wing activists, while the only real alternative networks were the trade unions' own organisations: with all their faults, the unions were still the most convincing representatives of British working men. The moderate Labour MPs disliked both alternatives; but they had no confident power base of their own, and were becoming increasingly lonely.

A month after the elections for the NEC, the Labour MPs (the Parliamentary Labour Party or PLP) cast their own votes for the shadow cabinet which, though they do not bind the leader, do influence his choice. The shadow cabinet normally has more moderate and established members than the NEC, reflecting the more cautious views of the MPs. The twelve members elected in November 1981 included several veteran ministers from Callaghan's cabinet, but with an infusion of more radical members—including Eric Heffer, the rugged war-horse from Liverpool, and Neil Kinnock, the Welsh labourer's son and fiery opponent of private education. These were the twelve with their votes:

[18] Middlemas: *op cit*, p. 456.

Peter Shore	147
Gerald Kaufman	142
Roy Hattersley	135
John Silkin	132
Eric Varley	131
Merlyn Rees	128
Neil Kinnock	118
Albert Booth	114
John Smith	111
Brynmor John	105
Stan Orme	104
Bruce Millan	92
Eric Heffer	84
Peter Archer	83
Gwyneth Dunwoody	82

The Labour MPs had also always elected their leader and deputy leader, as they elected Michael Foot and his deputy Denis Healey. But the national executive and the constituency parties had increasingly been demanding their own say in the choice. They had strong arguments. The Labour prime ministers, from Ramsay MacDonald to Callaghan, had remained aloof from the party, and had never been dislodged by their own MPs as Chamberlain or Heath had been. The Labour system was not very democratic, and most other European socialist leaders were chosen outside parliament; but the British equation was distorted by the entrenched power of the unions with their very incomplete democracy.

By the last years of the Labour government the left was clamouring for a new system with an 'electoral college' to appoint the leader, made up of union leaders and constituencies as well as MPs, in addition to their proposals for mandatory reselection of the MPs themselves. By October 1979 they had scored a striking victory, when the annual conference agreed both to reselection and to appoint a special commission on electing the leader. By October 1980 the left-wing groups, mobilised by the RFMC, had gained more support for an electoral college; and by January 1981 the party delegates had to decide on the voting system at a special conference at Wembley. Michael Foot and the NEC wanted to give equal votes to MPs, unions and constituencies; but the left wing—led by Clive Jenkins, Tony Benn and the Militant Tendency—skilfully manoeuvred a humiliating defeat for the official leadership, which gave 40 per cent of the votes to the unions, and 30 per cent to each of the other two groups.

It was a remarkable outcome, when the unions were so unpopular with the mass voters, and when many of their leaders were anxious to play down their power, that they now should emerge much more openly as the controllers of the Labour party. And the victory of the left produced immediate and far-reaching convulsions.

6

Social Democrats and Liberals: Capturing the Middle Ground?

In a confrontation with the politics of power, the soft centre has always melted away.

Lord Hailsham, October 1981

THROUGHOUT the post-war decades the two big parties continued to dominate parliament. There were many signs of growing disaffection with both: the 'floating voters' increased, with fewer Tory 'deference' votes and dwindling working-class loyalty to Labour. By-elections between general elections often showed sensational protest votes against both the big parties. But at general elections most voters rallied behind one or the other.

General elections provided agonising disappointments for the Liberal party. Ever since the Lloyd George coalition had lost power in 1922, Liberals had been eclipsed by the new Labour party with its solid working-class base, but they still looked forward to a future in a less class-ridden Britain, and when Jo Grimond became their leader in 1956 he gave them a new glamour and ambition. Grimond was not exactly classless himself: the son of a Scots laird, he was married to Asquith's granddaughter and moved in rich Tory circles. His radicalism was limited, but his breezy rhetoric appealed to the young and to the media, and by the 1959 election the Liberals were fielding an array of young media candidates including Robin Day, Ludovic Kennedy and John Arlott. They only achieved 6 per cent of the vote, which gave them only six members of parliament, but as Macmillan's government lost its appeal they won the famous Orpington by-election in suburban London in 1962. After that some polls showed the Liberals getting over 50 per cent of the poll: and 'Orpington Man' was hailed as the prototype of the new socially-mobile elector.

Grimond now hoped 'that the full-blooded socialists would split off to the left leaving a radical party on the left centre of British politics, but free of socialist dogma'[1]; the Liberals would thus be the nucleus of a party committed to entering Europe, retreating from East of Suez and delegating power to the regions. But Labour never quite split, and the 1964 election brought a more bitter disappointment: the Liberals had almost doubled their support, with 11 per cent of the votes, but they still only had nine MPs. The full ruthlessness of the British electoral system was showing itself.

Grimond now hoped to make an agreement with Harold Wilson to share a radical programme and keep out the Conservatives: 'We must mobilise the great central body of opinion,' he said, 'for a long campaign of reform.' But Wilson was not responsive and after he increased his majority in 1966 he did not need the Liberals. The next year Grimond was succeeded by a less serious leader, Jeremy Thorpe, a superb showman with a defiant exhibitionism and lack of judgment which were to be his downfall. In 1970 the Liberals put up 332 candidates but only got six members of parliament; but the troubles of the Heath government soon gave them a new opportunity to catch disillusioned Tories who could not stand socialism. In February 1974 they won 19.3 per cent of the total vote—but still got only fourteen MPs. They now campaigned more indignantly for a system of proportional representation which would give them a fairer share, and PR looked more convincing since Britain had joined the European Parliament, to which other countries elected their members by PR. But the two big parties had no intention of undermining their duopoly.

The Liberals remained an odd mixture. There were rich country whigs who looked back to Asquith and saw freedom in terms of escape from bureaucracy and high taxation. There were individualists and windbags who could not submit to the discipline of the big parties. There were leaders in the traditional liberal regions of the 'Celtic fringe'—Scotland, Wales and the West Country—who resented the London hegemony. And there were radical young Liberals who regarded Labour as too hidebound for their crusades against apartheid or pollution. In some ways the Liberals were actually more class-based than the other two: they had proportionately more public-school candidates and a fruitier style. Some of them, standing repeatedly for hopeless seats, seemed actually to *prefer* losing. But the Liberals also included many original and dedicated politicians who were determined to maintain their concern for individual liberties and human rights against the encroachments of bureaucracy and corporate politics.

[1] Jo Grimond: *Memoirs*, Heinemann, London, 1979, p. 216. See also Ian Bradley: *Breaking the Mould*, Macmillan, London, 1981, p. 24.

The party looked still less credible by 1976 when Thorpe was being accused of taking part in a conspiracy to kill his friend Norman Scott. After successive revelations and pressures he finally agreed to resign and was succeeded by a new leader of unquestionable uprightness. David Steel had seemed too good to be in politics. The son of a Scots minister (who later became Moderator of the Church of Scotland), he was the youngest MP when he was elected in 1964 at the age of twenty-six. He took up worthy causes including anti-apartheid, the UN and the reform of the abortion laws, and among his noisy colleagues he looked a rather priggish boy scout. But he showed his mettle when he outplayed his rival, John Pardoe, in the fight for the leadership, and his patient handling of the prolonged Thorpe scandal, earned his party's gratitude. Steel was convinced that the Liberals could not hope for success on their own, and that after forty years in the wilderness they could only become credible if they were seen to share power. As Labour's majority dwindled in 1977 he saw his first chance, and agreed to a pact with Labour which postponed their downfall. Many Liberals criticised him for damaging their party's image by upholding a Socialist government; but he saw his role as strengthening Labour's right wing, which he hoped would split away from the left.

Steel's strategy showed no easy rewards. When the Labour government fell, after he had withdrawn his support, the Liberals got only 13.8 per cent of the vote in the 1979 election—the lowest share since 1931—which gave them only eleven MPs, while they were soon battered by the sensational trial of their former leader. But Steel was now beginning to see the crack which he and Grimond had both longed for: both parties were moving towards more extreme positions and Labour was splitting at last. Steel shrewdly reckoned that a link with a breakaway party from Labour would be much more useful than a bigger Liberal party; and when Roy Jenkins began talking about his own centre party he did not encourage him to join the Liberals.

LABOUR REVOLT

The revolt within the Labour party had been brewing for years, as the right wing became more exasperated with the unions, the left-wing activists and the anti-Europeans. But in 1964 the party was united by the experience of power, and it was not until Labour returned to opposition that the split seriously widened again, reaching a new crisis in 1972 when Wilson and Benn insisted on holding a referendum on pulling out of Europe. Roy Jenkins resigned as deputy leader and David Owen left the shadow cabinet in protest.

Labour right-wingers were now uniting on the issue of Europe, and when the referendum was held in 1975 they fought vigorously and successfully, working with Liberals and even Conservatives. But they lost their potential leader when Roy Jenkins became President of the European Commission in Brussels the next year; and his image of grand statesmanship, high living and foreign friends threw doubt on his political future.

But many members of the Labour government were becoming much more worried by the growing influence of both the unions and the left-wing 'entryists', to which the leadership of Wilson and Callaghan provided no effective antidote. Labour policy was, as David Marquand (who was Jenkins' aide in Brussels) saw it, 'a furtive mixture of corporatism and monetarism, disguised by increasingly hollow appeals to class solidarity and buttressed by an increasingly unreliable trade union vote'.[2] Already by 1975 a group of fervent Labour anti-communists, led by Stephen Haseler who had close American links, had formed their own Social Democratic Alliance (SDA) which launched uncompromising attacks on the left. Two years later a much broader group set up the Campaign for Labour Victory (CLV), which included three members of the cabinet—Shirley Williams, David Owen and William Rodgers. These three came closer together as they battled against the left and their worst fears were realised after the 1979 election, when the party took a sharp turn to the left, against Europe and for unilateral disarmament and nationalisation, while opinion polls showed a rapid erosion of support for Labour policies. 'Increasingly the electorate is footloose and up for the grabs,' as Rodgers put it.

In the meantime Roy Jenkins was pursuing his own ideas from the detachment of Brussels in his Dimbleby Lecture on BBC Television in November 1979. He described the dangerous rigidity of the two-party system and proposed a much stronger 'radical centre' which (he explained with prescience) 'could bring into political commitment the energies of many people of talent and goodwill who, although perhaps active in many other voluntary ways, are at present alienated from the business of government, whether national or local, by the sterility and formalism of much of the political game'.[3] He did not actually mention a new party; but privately he was talking with Labour dissidents about launching a new 'Social Democrat' party.

During 1980 the tide moved much faster. After the special Wembley conference reinforced Labour's anti-European policy, the 'Gang of Three' insisted that they would leave the party if it was committed

[2] *London Review of Books*, October 1–14, 1981.
[3] The *Listener*, November 29, 1979.

to leaving the European Community, and by the autumn conference they were much more embattled. The election of Michael Foot as leader against Denis Healey was the last straw. The Gang of Three tried in vain to persuade Healey to join their rebellion, and then moved without him. David Owen took the first step, resigning from the shadow cabinet; Shirley Williams, who had lost her seat in 1979, said she would not now stand as a Labour candidate.

Roy Jenkins in Brussels appeared aloof, while his band of followers impatiently awaited his return at the beginning of 1981. Back in England he quickly reached agreement with the Three, who now became the 'Gang of Four'; and the second Wembley conference in January, which gave trade unions the biggest say in electing the leader, precipitated the final breakaway. The Gang of Four issued their 'Limehouse Declaration' from David Owen's house which officially launched a 'Council for Social Democracy' supported by nine Labour MPs; and they hastily got together a hundred public names (including mine) to proclaim their support in the *Guardian*. Most Labour supporters still ridiculed the prospects of a breakaway party. But the advertisement produced a response which suggested a stronger tide of public support than even the Gang had predicted. It was only a question of time before they launched a new party.

THE FOUR

Roy Jenkins was the eldest and most improbable rebel. He had been through a political career of apparently effortless success, moving from the Welsh valleys to Oxford, with an easy road to parliament as the son of a former miner and Labour MP, rising through government to become a respected Chancellor of the Exchequer. In Brussels he seemed like a patrician Liberal: he was always fascinated by Asquith, the Liberal prime minister whose biography he wrote, and he admired David Steel. He surrounded himself with like-minded intellectuals, and did not conceal his taste for high living. He seemed reluctant to revert to the political hurly-burly, and looked forward to writing books in retirement. But from his European vantage-point he had become still more convinced of the need to make British society more adaptable: compared to Germany, Japan or America, he found, 'modern Britain has been sluggish, uninventive and resistant to voluntary change, not merely economically but socially and politically as well'. And he believed that the political system was at least partly to blame.[4]

David Owen was another Welshman—more Welsh than he sounded—but of the more fiery kind; he seemed to play Lloyd

[4] BBC Dimbleby Lecture, 1979.

George to Jenkins' Asquith. His rise had been even more rapid: a doctor's son from Devon, he practised medicine before moving into politics; by 1966 he was an MP for Plymouth, by 1968 he was a junior minister, and by 1977 he was Foreign Secretary. He combined an analytical mind with exceptional combativeness which he enjoyed practising against the stuffier diplomats. He had brushes with Jenkins in Brussels, but he was determined that Europe and the Atlantic Alliance were the keys to Britain's security. He detested the flabbiness of Labour's 'soft left', and it was when John Silkin supported nuclear disarmament that he decided he could stand the party no longer. But he was equally angered by the clamour for more nationalisation, and he now advocated a 'decentralised social market' which could harness the drive of capitalism with much tougher control of monopoly power: 'Socialist revisionism has often unwittingly emasculated the private sector by constraining its driving force, profits . . .'[5] He was in many ways the most radical of the four, determined to base the party on 'one man, one vote', and often impatient of Jenkins' more conservative attitudes.

Bill Rodgers was the least known, the last to reach the cabinet, but the toughest: though he went to Oxford his roots were in working-class Liverpool, and he represented many former Labour supporters in the North Country who were outraged by the left's take-over of the party. He was relentless at street-corner meetings, inviting arguments with hecklers and mastering the mike like a fairground showman. Like Owen he had apparently limitless aggression, which he directed against nuclear disarmers and anti-Europeans; but he was equally infuriated by right-wing rhetoric. (Once when he was listening to an extravagantly anti-communist speech by Harold Macmillan at a banquet he was observed bending his spoon in suppressed fury until it broke.) He had helped to organise the successive campaigns against the left, and he became more convinced, as he put it, that 'Politicians have failed largely because they have been prisoners—sometimes willing prisoners—of a political divide which is itself based on outworn assumptions.'[6]

Of the four, Shirley Williams was the most obviously indispensable, with the appeal of a candid and intimate friend who could share and sympathise with individuals' problems. The contrast between the two women politicians, Thatcher and Williams, at the top of this male profession was continually striking: Williams representing the compassionate, motherly side of womanhood, Thatcher standing for the more dominating headmistress side, and both talking more directly than most men. When Thatcher was first elected Tory

[5] University of Strathclyde: Fourth Hoover Address, 1981.
[6] William Rodgers: *The Politics of Change*, Secker and Warburg, London, 1982, p. 164.

leader Williams thought that her chances of leading Labour were finished, since the House of Commons would not stand for two women protagonists. But Thatcher's obduracy soon emphasised Williams' attractions: 'Politics isn't all made up of Mrs Thatchers and Richard Nixons,' she insisted. 'I don't believe in macho struttings and high noons.'

Shirley Williams had begun as a Labour favourite, with a chummy style and a Fabian mind. She inherited some of her politics from her mother, the novelist Vera Brittain, and as a child in America she was excited by the possibilities of reform. As a Catholic she was interested in both Europe and the Third World, with which she saw Britain's future interlocked. She was popular with the mass Labour party as well as in parliament; but she was never all politician. She valued her privacy and outside friendships—all the more after the break-up of her marriage—and always resented the male stronghold in Westminster. She never presented politics in purely economic and structural terms, but instead on the human dimension.

By 1974 she was in the cabinet as Secretary for Prices, and then for Education; but the left's anti-European campaign increased her doubts about Labour, and she seriously thought of leaving politics for academia. Her political star was still high, and in 1979 Wilson was predicting that either she or Bob Mellish would succeed to the leadership. Then she lost her seat in the Tory landslide, and with a mixture of shock and relief she found herself outside parliament, writing, broadcasting and studying unemployment: she was now coming to think that the Western nations must re-think their belief that they should substitute capital for labour wherever possible. Her political career seemed finished and she was in no hurry to find a new seat, but she remained on Labour's national executive, caught up in the bitter arguments about the party's constitution. With her common touch she was now the person on whom a new party would most depend.

THE NEW PARTY

Each of the Gang had suffered their own doubts as if they were leaving a Church. They had watched past rebels fail and disappear, as traitors to the party: timing in politics was everything, and if they got it wrong, they too could vanish through the trap door. They were now individuals with no tradition or organisation to reassure them: a new party without a defined power base or class loyalty challenged all the assumptions behind the law of the pendulum, and Jenkins and Williams had both publicly attacked the idea of a centre party in the past. No new major party had succeeded since Labour eighty years earlier: Oswald Mosley's 'New Party' in 1931 and Richard Acland's 'Common Wealth Party' in the forties had both come to ignominious ends.

But once the Gang had broken their links with Labour they were pressed ineluctably towards a new leap in the dark. The interim before the new party was launched was an extraordinary experience (I watched it as a member of two of its committees). The name of the party, the slogans, the colours, the headquarters and interim constitution, all had to be settled in a few weeks. Roy Jenkins used the phrase (invented by David Marquand) 'breaking the mould of British politics', but there was no model for a new mould, no historical precedent, no parallel with Europe or America, and no business support except for two members of the Sainsbury family and part of a merchant bank, Morgan Grenfell. The Four were determined to be independent of commercial interests, and to raise the money from members: they hired a bank's computer (with quite the wrong programme), arranged for payments by credit cards, and advertised for members in newspapers, led by the *Guardian* and the *Observer*.

Only seven weeks after the 'Declaration of a Hundred' the Gang of Four formally launched the new Social Democrat party at the Connaught Rooms in London, arrayed on the platform with twelve other MPs including one former Tory, Christopher Brocklebank-Fowler. It was, Roy Jenkins claimed, 'the biggest break in English politics for two generations' and it was reported by five hundred journalists, with television coverage which was reckoned to be worth £20 million in advertising time. The Social Democrats were soon attacked as the 'media party', though most political commentators were very sceptical. The Tory Press mocked them, the *Mirror* and the *Observer* were loyal to Labour, and only the *Guardian* was consistently sympathetic. But opinion polls soon registered much greater public support than even the leaders had expected. Their polling experts were soon emphasising that the support would be far greater if the SDP and the Liberals could share the same candidates. Already within two months there were strong pressures to form some kind of alliance.

The Four were prepared for bitter confrontations with ex-Labour colleagues, but the old party seemed too busy tearing itself apart. A week after the SDP launching Tony Benn announced he would stand against Healey for the deputy leadership under the new rules of the electoral college, thus re-opening all the old arguments. For the next six months the left-wing groups, co-ordinated by the Rank and File Mobilising Committee, devoted all their energies to championing Benn, who toured the seaside conferences of the individual unions to recruit support, compelling Healey to compete with the same kind of American-style campaign.

The Social Democrats had only vaguely spelt out their policy in 'Ten Tasks for Social Democrats'—quickly extended to twelve to include 'a better environment' and 'equality for women'. They began with the need for 'a reformed and liberated political system', 'a sensible system of proportional representation in which every vote really counts', an investment programme with a flexible incomes policy and a programme for training and apprenticeships to create new jobs. When they began analysing the tasks more rigorously, in a policy meeting at the Charing Cross Hotel, they came up against the practical disagreements. Should they legislate against trade unions, tax independent schools, abolish tax relief on mortgages? Nevertheless the basic policy planks—including the commitment to the European Community, to NATO and the nuclear deterrent—remained more defined than those of the two big parties. And many Social Democrats felt stimulated by the escape from the constraints and deceptions that had been the heavy price of the trade unions' support for Labour, and by the opportunity to work out policies which were in the interests of a wider range of people than the TUC and other pressure groups.

BY-ELECTIONS AND CONFERENCES

The Social Democrats were pledged, with the Liberals, to fight every by-election that came up, and they waited with trepidation for their first test. The party inevitably looked middle-class compared to the earthy roots of Labour: it had few trade unionists and many members in bourgeois enclaves such as Hampstead and Kensington who were mocked by socialists for being guilt-ridden intellectuals, drinking claret or driving Volvos, while Roy Jenkins still carried the stigma of Brussels. So they were specially apprehensive when a by-election was announced in the industrial town of Warrington in Lancashire, a seat with a Labour majority of 10,274. Shirley Williams, after consulting the psephologists, did not stand; but Jenkins unexpectedly said yes. The Liberals agreed to help, while the Labour left mobilised to support their candidate, Doug Hoyle from the ASTMS union, whose leader Clive Jenkins soon went up to Warrington to campaign against the middle-class traitors. There were endless jokes about this lisping grandee arriving in Wawwington: what would the workers make of this devotion to Europe and NATO?

Roy Jenkins knew it was his critical challenge to re-establish himself with a British electorate after his exile. He campaigned tirelessly, without attempting a downmarket style, offering an escape from class warfare and ding-dong politics, supported by the other leaders and a Liberal team. Like other northern towns, Warrington was not the rugged proletarian stronghold of southern clichés: it was lively and socially mobile, with an attractive new town whose electors seemed quite intrigued by this odd caravan arriving from London. By the eve of the poll, when Jenkins led a cavalcade through the town, he had apparently broken through class barriers: grannies waved from back-to-back houses where SDP posters were stuck up alongside Labour's. The next day the count showed that Jenkins had gained 12,521 votes, within some 1,700 of winning: it was the first time he had been defeated in an election, he said, but it was his greatest victory.

By the time of the autumn conferences the Social Democrats knew that they could not do without the Liberals, however irritating they found each other, and many of their policies were remarkably similar. At the Liberal conference at Llandudno the two parties formalised their link to create 'the Alliance'. The Liberals were becoming more disciplined with the apparent prospect of power, and David Steel was the first Liberal leader for half a century (he said) who could tell them to go back and prepare themselves for government.

The Labour conference at Brighton provided the dramatic climax to the battle between Healey and Benn for the deputy leadership, which many Social Democrats hoped would cause a new lurch to the left and throw more MPs into their arms. But though 83 per cent of the constituency parties voted for Benn the unions were not united behind him. The Transport and General felt impelled to consult their regional branches and after embarrassing chops and changes they did not support Benn, who then lost the total vote by a tiny margin. Michael Foot appeared to rally the party with his emotional appeal as a 'peacemonger' while the National Executive Committee, pressed by the engineers' union, showed a shift to the right. The unions and the party leaders tried to patch up their differences, and three months later they met at Bishop's Stortford where they announced broad agreement to fight together against the Conservatives. But they shirked the policy differences; and a succession of Labour MPs, disillusioned by the rifts or the ordeals of reselection, were still going over to the Social Democrats.

For their own autumn get-together the Gang of Four had gambled on a 'rolling conference', with a special train taking members from Perth to Bradford to London. The provincial meetings would expose the leaders for the first time to the brand-new members who were the backbone of the new party, and who could eventually out-vote them.

As the speakers came up to the platforms many turned out to be 'political virgins' speaking for the first time; mostly middle-class though from a wide range of occupations. Some were more radical than the leadership, whether anti-nuclear, anti-public schools or anti-Liberal; but most, to the leaders' relief, were broadly in sympathy with the party's basic principles—for Europe, NATO and the mixed economy. The members were all-important not only because their views would determine the party's policies, but because they financed it. By the time of the conference 60,000 people had joined, bringing with them £600,000, and the party was determined to depend neither on big business nor on big unions.

But only by-elections could provide the real test of the SDP's popularity, and these uniquely British rituals now acquired an unprecedented significance as the indicators of whether British voters would accept the break in the two-party system. Bewildered voters suddenly became regarded as the arbiters of Britain's future political structure, and were polled, canvassed and knocked-up as never before. Some mass meetings attracted audiences of over a thousand, confounding all earlier theories of the all-powerful appeal of television, and American journalists were astonished to observe that personal encounters could still play a pivotal role in politics. With each by-election the stakes became higher, as all parties realised the full dangers and threw more celebrities and more promises into the battle. But for the Social Democrat leaders the by-elections were make or break: one moment they would be working on long-term policy documents, the next they would have to move their troops to a distant battleground where a defeat could mean an end to the party's credibility.

Two more difficult by-elections came up after Warrington. In the London suburb of Croydon the little-known Liberal candidate, William Pitt, was a three-time loser who refused to stand down. But the electoral magic of the new Alliance worked all the same: Croydon suburbia was alarmed by Thatcher and fearful of Labour. When Pitt was elected with a majority of 3,254 he showed that the tide was consistent, and forced sceptics to take the Alliance more seriously. 'After Croydon,' Harold Wilson admitted, 'I and many like me are being compelled to think again.'[7]

In Crosby, a row of suburbs in Liverpool, Shirley Williams quickly agreed to stand before she knew much about it, except its Tory majority of 19,272. But the new party, she insisted, had to 'scale unscalable heights'. Crosby looked the least promising kind of peak—an entrenched Tory seat with three public schools and networks of rich old families. But a stubborn local organisation could

[7] *News of the World*, October 25, 1981.

also be a liability, and the Crosby Tories had chosen as candidate a naive Chelsea accountant, while the Social Democrats could field their best candidate with a full supporting cast. Williams whirled through the constituency, addressing overflow meetings in a caring style which emphasised the contrast with Thatcher. The Labour candidate was a young Bennite schoolteacher, whose prospects looked so poor that many anti-Tory voters switched their votes to the SDP; and the Tory Central Office soon virtually forsook their unfortunate candidate. By polling-day the result was a foregone conclusion, and Shirley Williams became MP for Crosby with a majority of 5,289, two years after she had been turned out of parliament. The result was as damaging to Labour as to the Tories: 'When we won four general elections out of five I called the Labour party "the natural party of government",' Harold Wilson now lamented. 'Now we are not even the natural party of opposition.'

After Crosby the polls showed a new surge of public support for the Alliance, reaching a brief peak of 50 per cent, as both Tories and Labour became still more unpopular. But by early 1982 some of the first enthusiasm was fading. The Liberals and Social Democrats were arguing bitterly over the carve-up of seats, until Bill Rodgers threatened to break off the negotiations, which brought complaints that this was like the old politics. The SDP MPs could not agree about anti-union legislation on which they voted three ways. And the question of the party leadership was still not resolved. The collective leadership had the advantages of a four-sided appeal, with strong emphasis on individualism. But there were obvious strains: Williams and Owen were more radical and egalitarian, convinced of the need for drastic social reforms, and worried that Jenkins would become increasingly Asquithian, more concerned with personal freedom and sound management than with equality and poverty. Jenkins was the most obviously convincing future prime minister, and Owen and Williams were quite prepared to serve under him; but they wanted the leader to be elected by all the members rather than only by MPs, to ensure more radical pressure on him. In the meantime Jenkins was not even in parliament and the confusion of leadership was worrying the public and undermining party discipline, for if any SDP leader pursued a wild line of his own there was no single leader who could gently warn him that he might not get a job in a future government.

Some public support was slipping away when a new by-election came up in Hillhead, the traditional Tory seat in Glasgow. Roy Jenkins was advised not to stand by Steel and Williams, who saw dangers in a four-cornered contest including the Scottish Nationalists, who would pre-empt some of the discontent. But Jenkins insisted on taking the gamble, remembering how his hero Asquith had stood triumphantly for another Glasgow seat, Paisley, at the age of sixty-seven in 1920—though the parallel was tricky. ('Paisley was a false dawn, both for Asquith and for the Liberal party,' had written Jenkins, 'at best it was the equivalent of some later winter daybreak on the fringes of the Arctic Circle.'[8])

Jenkins soon found himself in a tougher fight than he had expected, as an obvious Southerner competing with three residents in Scotland. Mrs Thatcher made no secret of the fact that she saw it as a test of approval of her policies, which looked less doctrinaire after the budget—while many Tory Wets privately hoped that a Jenkins victory would give them more leverage against her. Tony Benn threw his full support behind the left-wing Labour candidate, with a mass meeting in Glasgow; and the Scottish Nationalists looked more plausible than the SDP as a decentralising party. The national popularity of the SDP was slipping further and the local polls predicted failure for Jenkins, who trudged the consti-tuency—from the grand terraces near the university at the top to the shipyards at the bottom—with some signs of despondency. He knew it could be his last chance to re-enter parliament, and hence to lead the party, while a defeat in Hillhead could spell disaster for the alliance with the Liberals.

Hillhead was beginning to look like a watershed for the entire British political system, and the polling-day of March 25 coincided, as it happened, with the anniversary of the founding of the new party. The Social Democrats threw everything into the fight and Jenkins himself (according to one poll) personally met 18 per cent of the constitutents—twice as many as the Labour candidate. In the last three days the swing towards the SDP, which had underlain the three previous contests, at last began to show itself, until the final vote showed Jenkins with a clear 2,000 lead, with Labour in third place and the Scottish Nationalists (having less than 10 per cent of the vote) losing their deposit. Roy Jenkins was back in parliament after five years, and was soon offering himself as the leader of the new party which he had outlined three years earlier. 'You can't start a movement as I have done,' he said after his election at Hillhead, 'and then say, "No, I'll have nothing to do with it".'

Then only a week after Hillhead the balance of British politics was suddenly transformed by the Falklands crisis which temporarily put all other issues in the shade. The Conservatives shot up in the popularity polls as the patriotic fervour took over the country, and unemployment, welfare and budgets were forgotten in the preoccu-pation with the armada and the recapture of the islands. The

[8] Roy Jenkins: *Asquith*, Collins, London, 1964, p. 489.

highly-charged debates had their own impact on the Social Democrats so that David Owen, with decisive speeches and a record of firmness as Foreign Secretary, became a more convincing candidate for the leadership. But the SDP, as the party of Europeans and internationalists, was at a disadvantage in an atmosphere of national preoccupation. The Falklands factor overshadowed all the SDP campaigns in the local elections in May 1982, when the new party did not achieve the breakthrough they had hoped for, while the Liberals were relatively successful. The next two parliamentary by-elections, in the midst of the war fever, showed only half the electorate voting, and disappointing results for the SDP. At Beaconsfield the Conservatives retained their safe seat, while at Merton, Mitcham and Morden the ex-Labour member Bruce Douglas-Mann who was standing for re-election as a Social Democrat was ignominiously defeated by a fighting Conservative, Angela Rumbold. In both seats the Labour party suffered still more serious setbacks, and the Conservative morale seemed to be restored. The whole country seemed to have reverted to an earlier context of politics, and the language of war and national rivalries took over from the language of economics and international co-operation.

NEW SOLUTIONS?

The future of the Alliance remains in the balance. But the trend towards a third party had been much more significant than the sporadic Liberal victories over the last two decades, and these new voters seemed to see the new Alliance not just as a scourge of the two other parties but as a potential alternative government. For some years the pollsters had found growing evidence of a changing political landscape as the Labour vote had declined and the Tory identity became more confused. Both parties had become trapped in more extreme adversary politics, each encouraged by their financial supporters—whether corporations or unions—whose interests were not those of mass voters. Between the two there was now a wider middle ground where the Alliance had set up their tents, hoping to build settlements before the two armies reoccupied it. But the middle ground could not mean more cautious policies. The problems that Britain faced were extreme, and they called for radical solutions.

The leaders of the Alliance would face all the problems familiar to earlier governments: the problems of an ex-imperial nation with a declining industry, deep class divisions and profound resistance to change. The problems were made more serious by the global recession and fiercer world competition which was decimating old industries and throwing hundreds of thousands out of their jobs. Rising unemployment, exorbitant interest rates and high inflation had more to do with the world markets and economic climate than with British government policies. The most emphatic government response would be to put up barriers against imports, as Tony Benn and his group of economists advocated; but the Social Democrats were more committed than anyone to free trade and international- ism. The sense of helplessness against foreign capitalists was constantly encouraging the new left-wing populists, but both Social Democrats and Liberals were convinced that Britain as a major trading nation could only be prosperous within the framework of Europe and the international community. They had to accept Britain's dangerous dependence on world trade, and they refused to make specific economic promises against such a changeable back- ground. But they could not agree with Thatcher that government should play only a minimal role in the recovery of industry and jobs. They were determined to produce changes that would enable Britain to become both a fairer society and a more effective industrial competitor with the rest of the world.

The leaders of all the political parties could look back on a long history of governments intervening but failing to stop the decline. Over twenty years both Labour and Tories had zealously set about trying to reform almost every area of administration to make Britain more efficient and equitable. Yet nearly all of these bold endeavours had ended in disillusion, if not fiasco, as the next chapters will suggest. Were British institutions so old and ossified that any tam- pering, like breaking into a tomb, would now be for the worst? Had the recurring contradictions between the two sides—between mana- gers and workers, right and left, capital and labour—led to a dead- lock of immobility which could not be broken? Was government powerless to grapple with ancient and self-contained professions and hierarchies? Or were the politicians, lacking serious political will and good faith, more interested in the appearance of change than the realities? Could the recollection of mistakes be turned into lessons for future success?

PART

TWO

Government

7

Schools: The Private Resurgence

We really cannot go on with a system in which wealthy parents are able to buy what they and most people believe to be a better education for their children. The system is wrong and must be changed.

Hugh Gaitskell, 1953

Politicians shy away from the question of what makes a good school because they prefer to explain things in terms of systems. It makes reform so much simpler. *Shirley Williams, 1981*

THE sixties and seventies in Britain constituted a new age of reform which could be compared to that extraordinary period a century earlier when the Victorians within a few years reorganised much of the structure of their administration. In 1867 the Second Reform Bill gave the vote to householders in towns; in 1868 the TUC held its first regular meeting in Manchester; and 1870 saw a rapid succession of reforms. The army was reconstructed with the modern system of regiments; the professional civil service was established with competitive examinations; and perhaps most important of all, the first great education bill was passed, providing the basis of universal education. 'Upon the speedy provision of elementary education,' said William Forster who carried the bill, 'depends our industrial prosperity.'

A hundred years later, British governments from both sides were bent on reforms which were intended to be equally far-reaching, as we will see in following chapters; and the most ambitious plans were once again in the field of education. Why did this second age of reform lead to such rapid disillusion? Were the politicians not really serious, or limited by short periods of office? Were the public too impatient for results? Or had the bureaucracies and structures of a century earlier become so hardened and so full of vested interests that they could not be adapted? The next chapters will follow some of the reformers through the central strongholds of Whitehall—

beginning with the reform on which so much else would depend.

During the 1960s and 1970s British political leaders gave more emphasis to education and training than ever before. A succession of reports—from Crowther, Robbins, Newsom, Plowden, or Donnison—reiterated the same need to escape from class patterns, to create new institutions, to mobilise the nation's talent. Educationalists became the prophets of change, and politicians, including Anthony Crosland, Margaret Thatcher and Shirley Williams, rose to fame or notoriety as Ministers of Education. The proportion of the gross national product that the British spent on education went up from 3.2 per cent in 1954 to 6.5 per cent in 1970. For the first time in history Britain spent more on education than on defence.

Yet nowhere was there more disillusion. The state system of comprehensive schools which had been the object of so many hopes became the butt of increasingly bitter complaints. The old grammar schools, the ladders up which so many politicians (including Thatcher, Heath and Wilson) had climbed to the universities, were abolished or turned into fee-paying schools. The old fee-paying public schools, whose future seemed so shaky two decades earlier, had more pupils than ever before. Many parents who longed to see British class divisions eroded at this formative stage now watched the reforms apparently widen the divide, without the traditional bridge of the grammar schools. 'My general rule,' one headmaster observed with pleasure, 'is that most reforms achieve the opposite of what they intended.'

COMPREHENSIVES

The chief objects of the discontent were the comprehensive schools which had spread through the country in the sixties; but they had been the result of irresistible political pressures. It was no longer politically possible to maintain the ruthless segregation of children at the time of adolescence, through the 'eleven plus' examination which sorted out children into grammar schools or secondary moderns—the 'submerged three-quarters'. Most countries in Europe were revolting against this segregation, not just because of its unfairness but because they wanted to make full use of the nation's brains for industrial efficiency.

Comprehensive schools had already been invented in the fifties by local authorities who were being pressed by parents to abolish segregation, but during the late fifties and sixties they became national symbols of the new opportunities. With their wide choice of subjects—from Latin to typing, from mathematics to carpentry—

they aimed to break down the old British barriers between academic and vocational schooling; and cheerful new buildings and spacious sites emphasised the prevailing confidence in 'social engineering'. Many Tories as well as socialists agreed that new educational systems could begin to break down the class barriers which were holding back Britain's performance.

Behind the enthusiasm in Britain and elsewhere, there was a widespread exaggeration and confusion about the social role of schools. 'It was the age of dumping every conceivable problem on schools,' said David Maland, High Master of Manchester Grammar School. 'I certainly did think that schools could compensate for family deprivation. There was an over-inflated expectation of what schools could do. In the fifties and up to the mid-sixties there was a coherence and a sense of purpose in education that was lost afterwards. But between 1965 and 1972 the rigid hierarchy of school life was shattered, and we just wondered what had hit us. Those who had had twenty years of unchallenged despotism retired early, and were often broken people. The teachers had to open themselves up to their pupils, and while the good teachers got better, the bad ones got worse. The parents insisted on involving the teachers in their children's problems, as they would never have expected in the fifties. Home was putting the squeeze on school.'[1]

It was only gradually that politicians and educationalists faced up publicly to the limitations of these brave new institutions. The huge schools with big classes easily got out of control without a strong head. The teachers, whose numbers were swelling, were changing too rapidly, with too few qualifications and too much freedom to do their own thing, ignoring the essentials of the three R's; while the powerful National Union of Teachers protected them from being sacked for incompetence. The new schools needed stability and time to build up their standards and confidence, but the hectic changes and turnover of teachers—particularly in the big cities—constantly demoralised them. The role of comprehensive teachers as the engineers of a classless society became much less certain, and research soon suggested that schools were much less important than family background or social environment in providing incentives and opportunities. It was not until James Callaghan and Shirley Williams launched the 'great debate' on education in 1977 that the Labour party began to face up to the need for more rigorous curricula and standards for ordinary schooling.

The characters of comprehensives were always more local and variable than national arguments and statistics suggested. It is the local authorities (the 'partners' as the Department of Education

[1] Interview with Emma Duncan, March 1982.

hopefully called them) who have the biggest say in their development, so that the expression 'state schools' is really misleading; in
addition, headmasters and headmistresses have greater powers than
their counterparts in, for example, France. Many comprehensives in
country areas stream their children into clever and less clever
classes, almost as thoroughly as before the 'eleven plus' was
abolished. There are some schools in rich suburbs, such as Camden
School for Girls in Hampstead, where middle-class children compete for Oxbridge as if they were at an old grammar school. And
there are many schools in impoverished inner cities which contend
with all the problems of poverty, immigrants and indiscipline.
Schools are now the most visible examples of the recurring political
problem: how to maintain standards while allowing decentralisation? The more independent the local authorities, the more unequal
the schools are likely to be. The prosperous areas, as in America, can
provide better schools which attract more prosperous parents; while
the poorer areas face their own vicious circle. Yet all the schools
needed an individual attention and local awareness which could not
be supplied by a central authority.

Politicians on both sides, most of them educated in schools with
long and proud academic traditions, organised and reorganised the
state system without thinking much about the continuity of the
individual schools. 'The factors which have made the world of the
comprehensives peculiarly difficult,' wrote the educationalist Auriol
Stevens, 'are constant organisational change, both in schools and
local authorities.' The comprehensives face the added difficulty of
'living with an unresolved, and possibly unresolvable, conflict between egalitarianism and elitism. It is a conflict which divides
members of staff as much as it divides outsiders.' [2] Individual headmasters and headmistresses play a crucial role in forging the character of the comprehensives, and strong heads have maintained
remarkable academic standards—for example Philip Slater at
Finham Park, Coventry; Lawrence Norcross at Highbury Grove,
London; or Keith Marsh at Magdalen College School in Northamp-
tonshire, which was first a public school, then a grammar school,
and is now a comprehensive with a continuing university record.
The most remarkable heads are those who take over the more
turbulent inner-city schools with bad reputations and impose
discipline and standards, such as David Kelly who took over Acland
Burleigh School in London in 1979. 'Education is a pretty simple
business,' Kelly maintains. 'You have to get the discipline right.' He
stresses, however, that discipline doesn't mean crushing people, but
making them responsible by trusting them. He has

[2] Auriol Stevens: *Clever Children in Comprehensive Schools*, London, Penguin, 1980.

kept his teachers together, he tries to persuade pupils that their chances of good jobs depend on the school's reputation, and he insists on maintaining the bedrock: 'that a child can go into a classroom and can learn'.[3]

Several factors are now improving the prospects for the big comprehensives. After the turmoil of the early seventies the teachers are more stable, the classes smaller, and the supervision more ordered. Determined and highly-educated parents can form very effective pressure groups to insist on higher standards and discipline. The heads of the comprehensives can make the difference between self-respect and cynicism, between continuity and chaos; but their effectiveness depends on maintaining a stable system, and on being rewarded with respect. They remain underpaid and unrecognised compared to their French or German equivalents; and while protected civil servants who take few personal risks are automatically honoured and promoted, headmasters who take the full brunt of public criticism and exposure remain in the shadows.

Comprehensive schools have resisted classification. They vary as much as the communities they serve or the hundred local authorities which run them: each has its own specialities, weaknesses and values, and their headmasters oppose any attempts to compare them. Much of their interest is in individual self-expression, and no one can reliably measure the results of their varied activities, from orchestras and art classes to theatre and sport; though the surge of interest in music, drama and art in two decades must owe much to schools as well as to families. But this book must concentrate on the ladders by which people reach the positions of power in Britain, rather than happiness or creativity.

The restless reorganisations of schools in the sixties and seventies left great confusions, and their academic achievements are still hard to assess compared to those of the old grammar schools. 'There is evidence that a massive and dramatic disruption has so far done nothing to raise academic attainment at the top levels,' Auriol Stevens reckoned in 1980, 'but has coincided with growing measured attainment at the middle-ability levels.' [4] No one can happily contemplate a future in which state schools are not competing for the highest academic places which lead on to positions of power: it would create a wider class division at the top than anything in the past. But excellence in any individual school cannot be achieved immediately, and the results of the reforms of the sixties are only now beginning to emerge. After Forster's Education Act was passed a century ago many Conservatives believed, like Lord Salisbury, that

[3] Interview with Emma Duncan, March 23, 1982.
[4] Stevens: *op cit*, p. 158.

universal education was 'pumping learning into louts'; and many years passed before the need was generally accepted.

The original arguments for comprehensive schools are still hard to refute. No ambitious parent who pays taxes within a democracy can readily tolerate the demotion of a child at the age of eleven, which is wasteful as well as inequitable. Yet the nation's efficiency and survival still depends on maintaining some kind of elite—which can only be tolerated by a democracy if it is seen to be selected fairly and effectively, without privilege. The French elite, the most formidable in Europe, has been tolerated in spite of its arrogance and visibility, because it emerges from a rigorous and reasonably democratic state system, where selection is based on brains and hard work. But Britain, having never undergone a revolution, retains a very different traditional elite, still based on a tiny group of fee-paying boarding schools beyond the range of most parents, whose influence on the country now appears greater than ever. And in the meantime the alternative route to the top, via the grammar schools, has disappeared.

GRAMMAR SCHOOLS

As soon as comprehensive schools began to spread in the sixties, they inevitably threatened the future of their neighbouring grammar schools which creamed off the cleverer children; but it took some time to sink in. The grammar schools, after all, included some of the oldest in the country; and the 174 'direct-grant' schools (financed by the Department of Education, as opposed to the 'maintained' schools financed by the local authorities) had educated many prominent British leaders, particularly in the north (forty-six such schools were in Lancashire). The proud city schools sent a large proportion of their pupils on to university and into wide areas of achievement. Bradford Grammar School had produced Delius, Humbert Wolfe, Denis Healey and David Hockney. Quarry Bank in Liverpool, run by an ambitious Old Etonian headmaster, had produced Bill Rodgers (Social Democrat), Peter Shore (Labour) and David Basnett, the trade union leader. Nottingham High School produced both the present Governor of the Bank of England, Gordon Richardson, *and* the Permanent Secretary of the Treasury, Douglas Wass. Grammar schools had provided the route to the top for many politicians including Margaret Thatcher from Grantham and Harold Wilson from Wirral Grammar School, who had promised that they would be abolished 'over my dead body'.

The grammar school children had long been in rivalry with the products of public schools when they converged at university or elsewhere. The public school boys liked to depict them as conformist swots, while they liked to regard public school boys as arrogant amateurs. The attitudes of north and south, of day schools and boarding schools, differed widely but they were coming closer together: public school boys became more competitive and serious while grammar school boys became more confident and broadly cultured. The best grammar schools seemed to point towards a more promising future elite, more numerate and technological, while public school headmasters began to make common cause with them as they faced the common threat of comprehensives. 'The expansion of comprehensives,' warned Peter Mason, the former High Master of Manchester Grammar School, 'will at the end of the day break down the bridge between the private and maintained sectors.'

But the battle to save the grammar schools was doomed as politicians could no longer justify subsidising this kind of elite, and the movement towards comprehensives gathered weight. 'Grammar schools of the traditional kind cannot be combined with a comprehensive system of education,' the Donnison Report to the Labour government concluded in 1970. 'We must choose what we want. Fee-paying is not compatible with comprehensive education.'

The heads of the grammar schools observed bitterly that the Labour cabinet, many of whom had risen up through them, were now presiding over their dissolution; but the pressure towards comprehensives came not just from Labour; in every constituency parents were furious when their children were not selected. As one headmaster put it: 'No one wants to agree to a set of standards which they know excludes their own child.' And even Finchley, Margaret Thatcher's constituency, was pressing for comprehensives. The Conservatives could delay the process but not reverse it; and when Labour returned to power the big grammar schools were finally faced in 1976 with the withdrawal of their direct grants. They had to choose whether to convert themselves into comprehensives or to become full fee-paying schools: 119 of them chose the second course, and so followed the most ironic consequence of reform: there were now more fee-paying schools than ever, while the ladders by which poorer children had climbed to success had been kicked away.

As the Labour party went on to press for the abolition of all private schools, there were some bitter critics from their own ranks, including Lord Lever, the former Labour cabinet minister. At a prize-giving in 1981 at Manchester Grammar School, where he had been a pupil, he pointed out that the independent schools had provided Labour leaders from Attlee and Gaitskell to Benn, Foot and Silkin. 'All wisdom demands that we should preserve and enhance these great schools and, with the aid of public funds, continue to ensure ever-widening opportunities for entry into them.'

Manchester Grammar School, which had been founded by the Bishop of Exeter in 1515, had few doubts that it must continue to be selective, and thus had to become independent. It maintains one of the most impressive academic records: 85 per cent of its boys now go on to university, and a third go to Oxbridge. Old Mancunians achieve worldly success in many different fields; they now include six judges, a clutch of permanent secretaries and ambassadors, the pianist Richard Ogden, the playwright Robert Bolt, three Sieffs from Marks and Spencer, and politicians as different as Lord Lever and Frank Allaun. Ten years before becoming independent, MGS was already changing socially: when the boroughs in northern Manchester went Labour and cancelled their subsidies of free places, it became a more middle-class south Manchester school. Now, with a well-endowed bursary fund and some past help from the previous Tory Greater Manchester Council, it claims to have changed neither its social structure nor its academic standards since it became independent. Its present High Master, David Maland, is an enthusiastic and open-minded man, who worked in both state and independent schools before coming to Manchester. But he firmly defends the present educational system, insisting that the independent schools can survive financially; and warning that 'Adolf Hitler is the only man in Western Europe ever to have banned private schools'. He is proud of his school's role in producing future engineers and industrialists as well as administrators, and stresses that it is now more interested in universities other than Oxbridge. 'Fifteen years ago we would have had a script about the benefits of Oxbridge—which most of us would choke on now.'

PUBLIC SCHOOLS

With the disillusion over comprehensives, the old public schools looked stronger than ever, surviving every attempt to reform or abolish them. When the Fleming Committee reported on them in 1944, at the end of the Second World War, the members were very conscious that all classes had contributed to the war effort, and worried that public schools were hardening social distinctions. 'It may almost be said that nothing could have been better devised to perpetuate them [social distinctions] than this educational development.' Fleming proposed that public schools should allocate a quarter of their places free to the state primary schools; but this 'guinea-pig' plan was soon frustrated by both the public and grammar schools. Twenty years later in 1965 the Labour government appointed the Newsom Committee which recommended that local authorities should assist half the pupils going to public schools; but local authorities as well as headmasters resisted the scheme. With heavy taxation under Labour many people now assumed that middle-class penury and the competition from grammar schools would gradually cause the public schools to wither away. But parents and grandparents still found capital to pay the mounting fees, and the expansion of comprehensives increased the attractions.

The public school headmasters were beginning to unite for the first time with a counter-revolutionary zeal which was to transform, if not reform, their schools over two decades. Already in 1962 they had appointed a PR consultant who soon warned them that they would face an emotional bombardment in the coming election. The next year the Headmasters' Conference, the club of 200 heads, started up their own magazine, *Conference*, to combat (it said) the damaging impressions given by critics, including the *Anatomy of Britain*. The two public school headmasters on the Newsom Commission, the progressive John Dancy of Marlborough and the right-wing Tom Howarth of St Pauls, collaborated to divert the Labour attack. By 1967 the headmasters had hired a full-time PR firm, and by 1972 they had formed the Independent Schools Information Service (ISIS) which became their lobbying organisation. A new threat came in 1973 when Roy Hattersley, Labour's shadow Minister of Education, frankly told the headmasters that his party would abolish them. The headmasters now formed their own joint committee, carefully not calling themselves 'public schools', with the associations of snobbery and privilege, but 'independent schools' which sounded, like independent television, free and democratic.

In the meantime the public schools had been shaken by the sudden crisis of authority in the late sixties—which came not from national politics but from the contagious discontent and assertiveness which had swept through the West. The university student revolts in 1968 and 1969 were less spectacular in Britain than on the Continent or in America; but the schoolboys in Britain were often more ferocious, seeing their masters and prefects as hate-figures associated with military discipline in the last spasm of empire (dramatised by Lindsay Anderson's film *If*). Many masters felt themselves vulnerable. 'The pupils' questioning of authority exposed the adults' unresolved adolescence,' as John Rae put it. 'That is to say the teachers—in common with other adults—retained from their own adolescence uncertainty about identity and an unresolved ambivalence about their own worth as individuals.'[5] But this crisis of identity prepared the way for important changes: in the

[5] John Rae: *The Public School Revolution*, Faber, London, 1981, p. 104.

seventies nearly all schools abolished beating and most fagging, and many masters relaxed relationships with boys to the point of exchanging Christian names. Several headmasters, beginning with John Dancy at Marlborough, actually introduced girls into their sixth forms, which Dancy saw partly as a way to 'consolidate the liberal position so that the changes were irreversible'.[6] The girls soon helped to civilise the boys as Dancy had hoped, but the change threatened the headmistresses of established girls' schools. The schoolboys' revolt had indirectly done more than headmasters or governments to reform the old public schools—and to strengthen them for the competition to come.

When most of the old grammar schools disappeared in 1976 the public schools found a new vacuum to fill, just when many of them were coming close to bankruptcy. 'Sixty per cent of the public schools would have gone under,' said Eric Anderson who was then headmaster of Shrewsbury, 'if the grammar schools had remained.' In spite of high taxes applications for entry to public schools abruptly increased, while 119 former grammar schools joined their ranks as full fee-paying schools. By the mid-seventies, when the Labour party was failing to abolish their charity status, the public schools were becoming more confident. The top schools were competing more ruthlessly, both to attract clever pupils and to get them into their traditional citadels of Oxford and Cambridge: they would no longer admit the children of any old boy—not even the son of a Tory cabinet minister. They still looked for some means to bend to the political wind, and in 1976 several headmasters persuaded the Conservatives to accept a new plan for 'assisted places' to enable poorer boys to go into public schools. But many other headmasters complained that it would waste money while insulting the state schools, and it looked embarrassingly like the old 'guinea-pig' scheme thirty years earlier. The plans to reform the public schools seemed to be ending up where they started, and when the Conservatives came back in 1979, bringing down the high tax-rates, the schools looked for the time being secure against change.

Whatever had happened to the idea of the meritocracy? When Michael Young first coined the word in 1958, in his prophecy *The Rise of the Meritocracy*, he foresaw the state effectively squeezing the public schools by a capital levy; improving the grammar schools beyond recognition, with ruthless selection by intelligence tests; and governments abandoning the democratic ideal of comprehensive schools as inefficient, until 'the workshop of the world became the grammar school of the world'. He foresaw this new meritocratic elite ruling the country while the lower classes were left with rudimentary

[6]*Ibid*, p. 132.

education, until in the year 2033 the populace rebelled, burning down the Ministry of Education and trying to assassinate the chairman of the TUC.[7]

But Britain changed otherwise in the twenty-four years since Michael Young (now Lord Young) wrote his book. The grammar schools' elite was eclipsed by the comprehensives which became the only roads to the top for most children. It was the public schools which became the new meritocracy, competing much more systematically for Oxbridge. But would this elite, combining privilege with more intensive education, be any less likely to provoke eventual revolution?

The older public schools are among the most striking examples of continuous British institutions. In 1861, in that previous age of reform, the British government had appointed the Clarendon Commission to report on the nine prominent ancient schools, all founded before 1612. A few newer schools, such as Marlborough, Wellington or Stowe, have since rivalled them, but the nine 'Clarendon Schools' still retain a disproportionate influence. These are they, in order of foundation:

FOUNDA-TION	SCHOOL	BOYS	BOARDING FEES 1981	HEADMASTER
1382	Winchester	630	£4,200	John Thorn
1440	Eton	1250	£3,780	Eric Anderson
1509	St Paul's	720	£3,387	James Hale
1552	Shrewsbury	650	£3,990	Simon Langdale
1560	Westminster	306	£4,050	John Rae
1561	Merchant Taylors'	800	£4,148	Dr Johnston-Jones
1567	Rugby	749	£4,050	Brian Rees
1571	Harrow	750	£4,050	Ian Beer
1611	Charterhouse	666	£4,380	Peter Attenborough

The best public schools have undoubtedly adapted, realising that they must justify themselves both to politicians, parents and the public. They are less philistine and more artistic, less preoccupied with classics, more interested in science and engineering (19 per cent of public schoolboys going on to university now study technology). They have become much more competitive with each other, comparing their scholarships and entries into Oxbridge and other universities, and concentrating more than ever on the rigours of A-level examinations which are the keys to university entry, and which cast their shadows down the schools. The intensive training for A-levels and university entrance adds to their attractions to parents, but it provides a narrower concept of excellence and

[7] Michael Young: *The Rise of the Meritocracy 1870–2033*, Thames and Hudson, London, 1958.

success, and cuts them off still further from the rest of the school system. 'The public schools used to be anti-elite,' as John Rae put it to me, 'but they're now quite elitist. The basic problem is social justice—yet you need injustice to achieve long-term ends. The biggest damage we do is to perpetuate a class division. But it may be the price we have to pay for excellence.'

The co-existence of independent and state schools—like that of the BBC and commercial television, or of nationalised and private industry—has been part of the British mixed economy over the post-war decades; and many politicians defend the right to choose between them. But the growing elitism of the independent schools, which still cater for only 6 per cent of the school population, makes the dual system harder to defend. Labour leaders are again committed to abolishing public schools, while many Social Democrats also advocate drastic reform. 'It is with reluctance,' wrote Shirley Williams, the former Minister of Education, in 1981, 'that I for one conclude that the freedom to send one's children to an independent school is bought at too high a price for the rest of society.'[8]

WINCHESTER AND ETON

The upper reaches of many British institutions, from banking and industry to politics and government, are still largely populated by the products of a handful of old schools, who crop up in later chapters; and more than ever by two of the oldest medieval foundations—both over five centuries old. Far from weakening their hold, they have extended their influence into new areas over the last twenty years.

Winchester College, founded by William of Wykeham in 1382, has long been famous for its rigorous academic standards. Wykehamists invite caricature: intellectually highly-developed and emotionally under-developed; articulate and analytical, trained to argue with clipped precise sentences which leave little room for imagination or speculation. Their famous motto is 'Manners Makyth Man', but they lack the tact and easy charm of Etonians and their confident rationality is more reminiscent of the icier products of French lycées.

It is said of Wykehamists that, once given a ladder, they will climb to the top of it without questioning its purpose. Certainly their record of worldly success is second only to Eton's although it has only half its school population. During the sixties Wykehamists reached a new peak of influence, ranging from Hugh Gaitskell, Richard Crossman and Douglas Jay on the Labour benches to David

[8] Shirley Williams: *Politics is for People*, Penguin, London, 1981, p. 158.

Eccles in the Tory cabinet, from Cecil King of the *Daily Mirror* to Lord Carver, the head of the army. They lost some ground in the seventies but by the eighties they were more pervasive than ever, their numbers including the present Chancellor of the Exchequer and the Home Secretary, two of the five chairmen of the big banks and a bevy of television men, including Alasdair Milne, the head of the BBC, and Peter Jay, the chairman of breakfast television. Winchester has been above all a factory for the legal profession—the most solid ladder of all—and it has produced nine current judges. The senior of them, Lord Wilberforce, described their special burdens at a ceremony at Winchester in July 1981:

> They have to fix the sentences knowing that if they are too short people will say that crime does pay, knowing that if they are too long another Wykehamist, the Home Secretary, will say that there is no room in the prisons, and that if he tries to build more, another Wykehamist, the Chancellor, will say that there is no more money, and that if the Chancellor tries to go to the banks other Wykehamists, chairmen of banks, will say that they have better use for their cash.

The headmaster of Winchester, John Thorn, is a bouncy historian who first became widely known when he was thrown out of a public inquiry on a Winchester motorway. He is a tireless propagandist for public school freedom, and as chairman of the Headmasters' Conference in 1981 he launched a pre-emptive strike on the 'appalling and criminal lack of resources' in the state education system. 'The education of 94 per cent of the nation's children is being allowed to languish and decay.' Labour proposals to tax public schools, he complained, overthrew every principle of Western liberal democracy: 'Abolish the independent schools and you abolish some of the riches of European civilisation.' But he offered no real solution to bridging the gap or improving the situation of the other 94 per cent.

The national role of the most famous of all public schools, Eton College, is almost as powerful as ever. Etonians no longer infiltrate the Labour party as Hugh Dalton or Lord Longford did; and there has been no Etonian prime minister since Sir Alec (the twentieth) was defeated in 1964. Many of Mrs Thatcher's close colleagues, including Tebbit, Fowler and Parkinson, come from grammar schools; but her cabinet still had seven Etonians (including the party chairman) until she sacked three of them in 1981, and there are still fifty Etonian Tory MPs. Eton is still the chief nursery for merchant banking, diplomacy and the Guards; and there are always shrewd and flexible Etonians waiting in the wings to chair the BBC or a bank, to take over the Foreign Office or to edit *The Times*. Eton's influence can never be separated from that of the old families and wealth which contribute to its special political awareness and confidence. But the school constitutes not only an educational establishment but a political training-ground, a charm school and a unique national network.

Younger Etonians are certainly more qualified than their elders: over the last ten years, under Michael McCrum and Eric Anderson (the past and present headmasters) the school has selected its pupils much more strictly, turning down many sons of Old Etonians. Twenty years ago 60 per cent of the new boys were sons of old boys; now (Anderson told me in 1981) only 43 per cent are, and the number is still going down. The teaching is more rigorous, and boys find it harder to 'bump along the bottom'; they have to compete in A-level exams which they used to ignore altogether, and they are much more likely to get into university: in 1980, 66 per cent of Eton leavers went to university. The Provost and Fellows are now much more concerned with academic excellence; when they searched for a new headmaster in 1980 they looked for the 'best goods on offer', and found the former head of Shrewsbury, Eric Anderson, a down-to-earth Scotsman who was educated at George Watson's College in Edinburgh and at Balliol, Oxford. Anderson is preoccupied with the educational standards—which are what, he insists, parents pay for—and his open, boyish enthusiasm seems out of keeping with the arrogance of some of the boys. Like Thorn of Winchester, he insists that independent schools are essential 'if you consider what a mess governments have made of the educational system'. But he is less aggressive than Thorn, and concerned that there may be a new upsurge of class arrogance in the public schools and Oxbridge: 'the Brideshead syndrome'. He would like to have closer exchanges with other schools and to break down Eton's reputation as a snob school. 'All public school headmasters would welcome some links with the state system,' he claims, 'if they can keep their freedom.'

What gives Etonians their special record of success—on a broader front than Winchester's? The school is no longer quite so closely linked to old wealth and inheritance as it was when Macmillan cultivated his family tree. Certainly Etonians owe much to political skills which, as Anderson explains, the school's traditions help to encourage: the boys are constantly standing for election by their peers, to be prefects or members of 'Pop'; the style of the Eton houses, which are self-contained and loosely structured, puts a premium on persuasion; and the easy relations with masters, with a high pupil-teacher ratio, encourages adult communication. But the most obvious asset of Etonians remains social confidence, based on a fixed belief in their own superiority, which can quietly demoralise others. The combination of assurance and political awareness

equips Etonians to be power brokers who can be relied on to reconcile differences and hold things together, whether at British Steel or
the BBC; but the confidence is not necessarily closely related to
special qualifications.

The old charge against Etonians was that they were confident,
stupid and out of touch with the lives and needs of most of the
country. The new charge is that they are confident, clever—but still
out of touch. As Eton becomes both more expensive and more
intellectually competitive, combining the ambitions of Winchester
with its own political smoothness, so it is likely to become more
exposed to attack, as providing an elite which still owes much to
privilege. Eton and Winchester have both shown a capacity to
survive which seemed unimaginable in the mid-sixties. Who would
have thought that in 1982 they would between them have produced
the two top men of the BBC, all five chairmen of the banks, the editor
of *The Times*, the head of the home civil service *and* of the foreign
service? Can they, it might be asked, really effectively represent the
other 99.5 per cent of the people in this diverse country who went to
neither medieval foundation?

EDUCATION AND SURVIVAL

There are many who argue that the elitism of the public schools,
with all its social dangers, is the necessary price for national survival.
But many critics insist that they produce the wrong kind of elite
anyway. 'The Victorian public school,' wrote the historian Corelli
Barnett in 1975,[9] 'is one of the keys to our decline, turning out by
means of curriculum and the moulding influence of school life alike a
governing class ignorant of, and antipathetic towards, science, technology and industry . . .' The ignorance is less marked than it was.
Over the last twenty years headmasters, with some prodding from
industry, have encouraged boys towards science and engineering,
and many more public school boys now take engineering degrees.
Some headmasters looked forward to an ultimate breakdown of the
barriers between the arts and sciences. The headmaster of Eton in
1961, Robert Birley, told me: 'Our ambition is to have the head of
Harwell Research Station, an Old Etonian who learnt Greek at Eton
and reads the lesson at Harwell Parish Church.' But the gulf between arts graduates and scientists remains as wide as ever, and the
strands of politics and science remain very separate, even under a
scientist prime minister. 'Scientists are still narrowly educated,' said
John Rae. 'There's really a three-way split between scientists, technicians and the arts.'

[9] *The Times*, September 30, 1975.

Entrepreneurs have their own complaints about the public-school system: that it discourages enterprise, money-mindedness and personal ambition. In the words of Sir James Goldsmith, who left Eton early, already an entrepreneur:

> The public schools were meant to create a rather pleasant non-specialist gentleman who would hand on the British civilisation throughout the world. They weren't really trained for doing business and the standards they wanted to achieve. There are very few successful people in business who have come out of the public school mould, very few. When I was young people used to say that you had to look rather stupid to succeed. Clemenceau said the strength of the English is that if you take ten upper-middle-class Englishmen they all look the same; one is astoundingly intelligent but you can't tell which one. In England you find the open, naked kind of ambition among odd people, or among people like trade union leaders who have fought their way up.[10]

Complaints that the British elite has become too protective, too averse to risk-taking, will recur in the following tour of the administration and industry. But this aversion to risks has, of course, deeper roots than any system of schools; and the prejudice against entrepreneurs is more evident at the next stage in the education of Britain's rulers, in the old strongholds of Oxford and Cambridge.

The more fundamental criticism of the public school elite is the most obvious one: that it reinforces and perpetuates a class system whose divisions run through all British institutions, separating language, attitudes and motivations. The assumptions of trade unionists and most Labour party leaders become more separate from public-school attitudes as politics become more polarised; while the communications between boardrooms and the shop floor remain contorted, separated by different work-times, lunch-hours, canteens or dining-rooms. The failure to communicate is the product not just of class arrogance but of the compensation for it—the element of 'public school guilt' which refuses to face up to the rough tactics of working-class leaders, and which shows itself in Labour cabinets as well as boardrooms. It is no accident that most formidable industrialists in Britain come from right outside the public school system, and many from right outside Britain.

[10] Interview with author, June 23, 1981.

8

Universities: Expanding, Contracting

We are very good at killing tomorrow in order to save today.
Professor Tom Stonier (Bradford University), 1981

THE enthusiasm to expand universities was wider than the movement to reform schools, and shared by both parties and many other countries. In the boom of the late fifties nearly all European governments were bent on having more students, looking enviously towards the earlier university expansion in the United States. Britain had proportionately fewer students, according to some statistics, than any European country except Turkey; but British students were also more privileged and more separated from the rest of the population. Many of them were living in colleges or hostels, much more comfortably than the tens of thousands who milled round the Sorbonne or the German universities, and were much less likely to drop out before the end of their course. So multiplying the numbers of British students was both more significant and more expensive.

The first big move came from impeccably Conservative quarters, stimulated by the historic report in 1963 of Lord Robbins, who was then chairman of both the *Financial Times* and the London School of Economics. Robbins was an unashamed expansionist who was worried by the Oxbridge monopoly: 'It is not a good thing,' he complained, 'that Oxford and Cambridge should attract too high a proportion of the country's best brains and become more and more exclusively composed of a certain kind of intellectual elite.' And Macmillan's government, encouraged by its Minister of Education, Lord Hailsham, approved the implementation of the Robbins Report in forty-eight hours. 'I do not regret my enthusiasm,' Hailsham wrote twelve years later. 'Big decisions like this need to be taken with the heart rather than the head.' [1]

[1] Lord Hailsham: *The Door Wherein I Went*, Collins, London, 1975, p. 148.

The most visible expansion was the building of the eight new universities—an idea which itself seemed totally new. They seemed daring innovations at the time, but each of them was modelled on Oxbridge, cloistered and consciously stylish, each run by a vice-chancellor from Oxbridge. Sussex University rose up outside Brighton with its ecclesiastical arches designed by Sir Basil Spence. Kent had luxurious refectories with high windows looking down on Canterbury Cathedral. East Anglia had a row of ziggurat buildings designed by Sir Denys Lasdun in parkland outside Norwich. The eight were much publicised, but compared to the total expansion they were relatively tiny: there were many more new students in the old Redbrick centres which were spawning new buildings and faculties. London University increased from 16,000 in 1961 to 46,000 in 1981—more than all the new universities put together. The University of Wales based on Cardiff went up to 17,000. Manchester University stretched out along Oxford Road with a cluster of new laboratories and centres, like a city in itself.

The idea of a university became a national obsession and nearly everyone wanted to be a graduate. The colleges of advanced technology were soon promoted to universities by the Labour government in 1966. The word university, as in America, had ceased to be exclusive: the sixties were the decade of the degree which seemed to provide the magic key to every promising career, and by the end of it twice as many people were becoming graduates. Universities, rather than schools, were becoming the clearing houses for social change and advancement, and industrialists looked to graduates for wider perspectives: a student could enter a university with a diffident Lancashire accent and emerge as a confident recruit for a multinational corporation.

The magic wand which transformed the universities was not a government agency but one of those 'typically British' bodies which exist in the no-man's-land between government and different professions. The dons of the University Grants Committee (UGC) saw themselves as a benign buffer state between government and academia, who could accept more and more money while still promising the universities independence. It was a contradiction, but it partly worked; when students on the Continent or in America revolted in 1968 they could depict their professors as the tools of either government or capitalism; but British students faced a much fuzzier enemy in the form of this committee of dry old dons inhabiting their half-world between academia and Whitehall.

But the British system also added to the confusion as to what the expanded universities were really for: were they for 'the national interest', or for the personal self-expression of students, or for the dons' pursuit of pure truth or knowledge? The expansion soon generated new pressures which few people had predicted: the leaders of 'the student estate' became political powers in their own right, particularly in the peak years of full employment, who could drive bargains with vice-chancellors and intimidate politicians. Most students could study what they wanted, so that numbers in the faculties of sociology or psychology shot up, while practical subjects such as accountancy or engineering were still short of students. The British students remained more elitist and expensive than those on the Continent: they were 'the pampered darlings of society', complained Sir Michael Swann, the vice-chancellor of Edinburgh, 'showered with every advantage'.

The students were multiplying, but the dons were multiplying more irreversibly. The new demand had attracted an inrush of second-rate teachers who could secure their coveted 'tenure' more quickly and easily than their fellows in most other countries: after a few years they could not be sacked or moved or asked to adapt. The high-sounding principle of 'academic freedom' (like 'freedom of the Press') could easily be invoked to protect lazy or incompetent incumbents from any interference; and in the meantime the dons' unions were adept in discreetly pressing wage claims on governments. Dons who worked for thirty weeks in the year could lead far more leisurely lives than their equivalents in industry, who earned similar salaries with only four weeks' holiday.

Already by the early seventies governments and educationalists were worried about the results of university expansion and the extent of the 'pool of ability' from which they were fishing: by 1976 only 6.5 per cent of state school children were obtaining three A-levels—the standard set by the better universities—and the proportion only crept up thereafter. Many Redbrick universities were showing embarrassingly poor results, while industrialists and other employers were complaining that they were being offered the wrong kind of graduates. The bold plans for a new industrial university at Warwick—'the MIT of the Midlands', as Richard Crossman saw it—were effectively frustrated by the students' revolt of 1968; and the wave of student unrest made the universities still less popular with their local communities, who became even less willing to provide extra funds. In contrast to the United States, the expansion of universities remained almost entirely dependent on government funds. The new universities were losing much of their glamour as the dons became middle-aged: 'They all started fifteen years ago with academics aged between thirty-five and fifty; now they are all fifty to sixty-five,' as one vice-chancellor put it. 'They've got a very unpleasant age profile.'

As unemployment began to hit graduates more seriously in the late seventies the mis-matches were more evident: by 1981 many new universities—including Sussex, East Anglia and Kent—were finding that more than a fifth of their graduates could not get jobs. The universities with the highest ratio of jobs to students were often the most modest in their ambitions, such as Aston in Birmingham, Salford outside Manchester and City University in London. The gap between academia and industry yawned wider than ever.

By the time Mrs Thatcher came to power in 1979, determined to cut back public spending, the universities were already ripe for the chopper. Her Minister for Education, Mark Carlisle, warned the University Grants Committee that they must make drastic cuts, and over eighteen months they worked out a plan to prune the universities, under their chairman Edward Parkes, an unobtrusive professor of mechanical engineering and expert on braced frameworks. It had been relatively easy to hand out more money each year, but cutting down required much more definite and political decisions: these frameworks could not be braced. The committee supposedly decided on two yardsticks to measure achievement: the value of the research grants that universities received, and the numbers of A-levels of their new students. But these yardsticks imposed the most drastic cuts on some of the most practical and down-to-earth places, including Aston and Salford with their good record of graduate jobs; while Oxford and Cambridge, which were in the centre of the A-level contest, and which got large research projects, were relatively little affected. Some of the cuts were very understandable: universities such as Keele and Essex with many social science students suffered heavily, while a few technological universities such as Bath were well favoured. But the net result of the cuts, as the table on p. 138 suggests, was to favour old universities against new and to deal a body-blow to the more practical institutions.

TECHNOLOGISTS UNDER STRESS

It was the new technological universities that protested most angrily, for they had only fairly recently been promoted to universities in the expectation that they were secure; and they had good grounds for claiming that they were more valuable in the national interest than the arts-based universities. The lack of enough higher education in engineering and technology had been a familiar complaint in Britain ever since the mid-nineteenth century, when German and French institutions began training very effective technology managers. The British had built up three very formidable technical colleges in the three biggest cities: in Glasgow the famous old Royal College, which had been the pride of Scottish engineering, became the University of Strathclyde; in Manchester the old Tech, which had spread through the slums alongside the university, became UMIST, the University of Manchester Institute of Science and Technology, now run by a controversial chemist, Robert Haszeldine. The most famous of the trio was Imperial College, the huge complex of buildings in South Kensington which had become, along with Oxford and Cambridge, one of the chief nurseries of original research and Nobel prizewinners, now run by the outspoken nuclear physicist Lord Flowers (see chapters 14-15).

These three great institutions could hold their own with most European competitors, but British academics always tended to become increasingly removed from industry, all the more when they belonged to full universities; and while the British had a spectacular record of winning Nobel prizes, they were notoriously ineffective in translating research into practical applications. 'If you set something up as a technological university,' said Sir Denys Wilkinson of Sussex, 'in no time at all everyone will be wanting to win Nobel prizes.' In any assessment of the technological revolution, whether white-hot or luke-warm, the more humble colleges of technology were expected to play a critical role by improving industrial efficiency, and many of them had specialised in providing 'sandwich courses' which could be taken by technologists while working in companies. So it was hardly surprising that when these technological universities were faced with the most drastic cuts of all they responded with exceptional fury.

The noisiest reaction was from the vice-chancellor of Salford, Professor John Ashworth, a combative young professor of biology who had just been the chief scientist in the cabinet Think Tank. He let fly against the UGC's unaccountable judgment and pointed out that the universities which were represented on the Committee had got off relatively lightly. The kind of engineers that were being cut, he complained, 'were the middle managers, the good NCOs who see that goods are made properly and delivered on time. They didn't cut Cambridge, which produces officers.' At Bradford University, which was also drastically cut, the vice-chancellor, Professor John West, complained bitterly that the government was 'totally abdicating' from the problem of helping with redundancies, and Professor Tom Stonier, who lectures at Bradford on science and society, insisted that the cuts were simply a symptom of the 'British disease': as soon as systems come under stress they return to the old orthodoxies. 'The educational system is responding in the same way as industry does under stress, by cutting research and development . . .'

The uproar at least attracted unprecedented attention to these universities, and the vice-chancellors made the most of it. At Salford, Ashworth quickly launched a pressure group called CAMPUS (Campaign for the Promotion of the University of Salford) with support from numbers of industrialists, including Sir Robert Telford (the managing director of GEC-Marconi) who insisted that Salford was 'one of the few technological centres in the British university system focused on the needs of industry'. At Aston, the technological university in Birmingham which was the second worst hit by the cuts, the vice-chancellor, Frederick Crawford, was another battler—an expert on plasma who had spent his previous twenty years at Stanford University in California, working in 'Silicon Valley', the industrial electronics centre. He was full of zeal to bring American dynamism to Britain; and he went into partnership with the Birmingham City Council to establish a 'science park' at Aston to attract small technological companies to work near the university on the California pattern. It is possible that the new technological universities will be lighter on their feet than the old ones, and carve out their own niche with more advanced industrial researchers, as many American universities have. But the results of these collaborations will take many years to show themselves.

The UGC's cuts in technology were not quite as illogical as their critics complained: Salford had large overlaps with UMIST a few miles away, and among universities as a whole engineers were being treated better than most students. The challenge of the cuts had released new energies, and free-enterprise theorists could argue that if industrialists needed these technologists, they should help pay for them. But the effect of the cuts nevertheless was to deliver a brutal blow to the status and confidence of technologists, and (as Ashworth complained) to label these new universities as failures. It was a bitter outcome for colleges which had eagerly become universities a few years before, at the peak of the white-hot enthusiasm: 'If we had remained colleges of advanced technology,' said Professor West of Bradford, 'where we were at the top of the public sector list, we would not have been suffering now. We would have been expanding.'

ROBBINS IN REVERSE

The UGC was now attacked from all sides. The members were predominantly unpolitical academics who, although technically appointed by the Minister of Education, tended towards self-perpetuation. Other dons complained that the UGC was no longer an autonomous body, but an arm of government, with the worst of both worlds: they were telling vice-chancellors what to do, but with no attempt at long-term planning. Industrialists accused them of not going far enough, shirking the responsibility for national survival. What Britain needed, the *Economist* suggested, was to take the opportunity of contraction to cut out the dead wood, to provide a kind of Robbins in reverse, a Snibbor report. But contracting universities, left to themselves, were more likely to exclude young teachers than to dislodge the old dons who were protected by tenure—even though Britain desperately needed younger teachers in the new technologies. 'British universities' (said a report in 1981 headed by John Roberts, the vice-chancellor of Southampton), 'have had for many years a tradition of tolerating dead and dying wood.'

The chairman of the UGC, Edward Parkes, was now in an almost impossible position as the scapegoat for the government's cuts. 'The government has sheltered behind the UGC,' complained David Marquand from Salford University, 'and the UGC has sheltered behind the government.' Parkes was in touch with the government who were his paymasters but as a civil servant, he insisted to me, he could not disclose the nature of their discussions, so he had to take the full brunt of the rumpus. The UGC was as secretive as ever, 'a big black box', as one vice-chancellor called it, in the middle of the university system. Several members in fact had considered resigning, but decided that they would be wrong to desert the committee when times were bad. The UGC clearly had their own private assessments and calculations: 'They have secret formulae,' as one vice-chancellor put it, 'showing how much each student in each faculty should cost, and they give preference to universities with lowest costs per student.' They could force universities to cut back their spending, and they could favour scientific universities against arts ones, but they could not tell them how to discriminate: 'If you refuse to cut a department,' as another vice-chancellor explained, 'they can just go on cutting your grant until you do.' The autonomy of the UGC, according to some dons, had been eroded ever since the mid-sixties when it came under civil servants in the Department of Education rather than the Treasury; but in a contracting economy the pressure was bound to become greater. The real purpose of the universities was as ambiguous as ever, all the more since the national purpose was itself uncertain. 'You have to ask what higher education is *for*,' as Sir Denys Wilkinson the scientist vice-chancellor of Sussex put it. 'One side of the answer is educational, that it is a good thing that people should be educated. The other side is social: and our country is worse at making use of the people we've educated than other countries.'

Britain still, at the end of twenty years of expansion, had fewer students than most other Western countries: only seven out of a thousand people in Britain were studying for first degrees in 1978, compared to forty-one in the United States or twelve in France. But British universities taught their undergraduates much more intensively, with many fewer drop-outs than elsewhere, and the proportion of people who were actually *awarded* first degrees each year was higher than in most Western countries except North America and Japan. Robin Marris, the Professor of Economics at Birkbeck who compiled the table below, insists that British graduates provide the best value for money in the world, and that 'what matters to a modern society is the ultimate stock of graduates per head of population. Any country that allows that statistic to decline is allowing herself to decline.'[2]

1978 Figures	First degree students per thousand pop.	Percentage first degree annually	First degrees awarded per thousand pop.	Teachers per thousand university students
Belgium	10.9	17.5	1.91	—
Canada	21.7	18.8	4.08	57.9
Denmark	19.3	9.0	1.74	—
Finland	16.0	16.0	2.56	98.1
France	11.7	15.3	1.79	49.5
Germany	14.6	9.5	1.39	123.9
Italy	17.2	7.5	1.29	41.3
Japan	15.6	18.3	2.85	82.3
Netherlands	9.9	7.3	0.72	94.6
Sweden	13.3	12.3	1.64	—
Switzerland	8.7	10.7	0.93	71.1
UK	7.0	25.2	1.76	88.7
USA	40.8	13.9	5.67	54.9
Average	15.9	13.9	2.18	76.2

Sources: Unesco, EC (Eurostat) and author's calculations. First columns include degree-level students at non-university institutions and exclude university students on non-degree-level courses. Last column relates to all students and teachers at universities only.

For the early champions of the new universities, the cuts were shattering. 'With this sort of cuts operation,' said Lord Briggs, who was on the original subcommittee of the UGC which planned the new universities (and who later became vice-chancellor of Sussex), 'you lose the things that are really interesting . . . It is frightening to feel that the retreat has been so disorganised.' For Lord Robbins

[2] *The Times*, February 5, 1982.

himself the outcome was specially bitter, for he had become chancellor of the one new Scottish university at Stirling, which was intended to be the fine flower of the broad tradition of Scottish education, mingling disciplines and judging students by continuous assessment; but Stirling was now told to cut back by 22 per cent and to aim for a student population of only 2,000 instead of the 3,200 they had planned for the mid-eighties. Robbins was outraged by the 'utterly disgraceful treatment' of Stirling, all the more since the UGC had not visited it since 1975, and he was appalled by the general destruction of the ideals in his report two decades before. 'The government cuts were monstrous,' he said. 'Any self-respecting committee should have refused to impose them, and at least some of them should have resigned. What are they about?'

But behind all the academic complaints lay the stark political fact that both the main parties had become disillusioned with the consequences of new universities. 'Labour saw it as a means of useful social engineering,' said Geoffrey Lockwood, the present registrar of Sussex, 'but it was soon obvious that the new universities were being monopolised by the middle classes. The Conservatives looked on them as a means of providing people who could solve the country's economic problems. That didn't work either, so both parties were disenchanted.'[3]

NEW POLYS

The cuts in university spending were paralled by cuts in the polytechnics, the tail-end-charlies of British higher education. Like the universities they had been through a wave of optimism and expansion in the sixties; in 1967 the Labour Minister of Education, Anthony Crosland, had transformed an odd jumble of colleges of technology, commerce and art into thirty 'new polytechnics' which were to remain separate from the university system under Crosland's 'binary system', and more directly controlled by local authorities and government. Many of the new polys were old places with new names: the South Bank Polytechnic in London was made up of a marvellous mixture of the City of Westminster College of Commerce, the Borough Polytechnic, the Brixton School of Building and the National College for Heating, Ventilation, Refrigeration and Fan Engineering.

The new polys were meant to remain practical and down-to-earth, welcoming part-time students, and avoiding the more rarified university atmosphere; but in the mood of the time they inevitably aspired to become more like universities, and they attracted a new

[3] The *Guardian*, January 18–20, 1982.

FOUNDATION	UNIVERSITY	VICE-CHANCELLOR AND SUBJECT	STUDENTS IN 1981	% LOSS EXPECTED 1980-84[1]	% UNEMPLOYED OR IN TEMPORARY JOBS 1975-79[2]
1249	Oxford	G. J. Warnock (Philosopher)	9,429	-2.7	9.1
1284	Cambridge	Harry Hinsley (Historian)	9,378	-2.0	9.0
1411	St Andrews	J. S. Watson (Historian)	3,382	-7.4	14.6
1451	Glasgow	A. Williams (Geologist)	10,878	-3.2	7.3
1495	Aberdeen	G. P. McNicol (Medicine)	4,891	-3.9	8.7
1583	Edinburgh	J. H. Burnett (Botanist)	10,868	+0.1	13.3
1832	Durham	F. G. T. Holliday (Marine Biologist)	4,211	-3.8	11.8
1836	London	Randolph Quirk (Linguistics)	46,438 (internal) 29,679 (external)	-3.5	14.4
1851	Manchester	M. H. Richmond (Bacteriology)	15,311	+0.2	12.0
1852	Newcastle	L. W. Martin (International Studies)	7,638	-4.1	11.0
1880	Birmingham	E. A. Marsland (Oral Pathology)	8,687	+0.3	9.6
1893	Wales	C. W. L. Bevan (Chemist)	16,457	-6.9	15.3
1903	Liverpool	R. F. Whelan (Physiologist)	8,222	-2.1	8.0
1904	Leeds	Vacant (ex Lord Boyle—Politics)	10,401	-1.7	11.2
1905	Sheffield	G. D. Sims (Physicist)	7,566	same	10.4
1909	Bristol	Sir Alec Merrison (Nuclear Physicist)	6,992	-3.9	12.8
1926	Reading	E. S. Page (Computer Science and Data Processing)	5,819	-5.2	16.3
1948	Nottingham	B. C. L. Weedon (Research Chemist)	6,961	-3.6	14.7
1952	Southampton	J. M. Roberts (Historian)	6,131	-0.5	11.1
1954	Hull	Sir Roy Marshall (Lawyer)	5,457	-17.2	13.5

Year	University	Head			
		(Nuclear Physicist)			
1962	Keele	D. Harrison (Chemical Engineer)	2,852	−16.8	16.9
1963	East Anglia	M. W. Thompson (Experimental Physicist)	4,326	−3.2	25.6
1963	York	S. B. Saul (History of Economics)	2,690	−0.3	14.1
1964	Essex	A. E. Sloman (Linguistics, Spanish)	2,864	−4.0	17.2
1964	Lancaster	P. A. Reynolds (acting)	4,145	−6.9	18.0
1964	Strathclyde	G. J. Hills (Physical Chemistry)	6,491	−4.3	8.3
1965	Kent	D. J. E. Ingram (Physicist)	3,959	−7.3	19.3
1965	Warwick	J. B. Butterworth (Lawyer)	5,099	−1.1	20.0
1966	Aston	F. W. Crawford (Physicist)	5,720	−22.1	4.9
1966	Bath	P. T. Matthews (Theoretical Physicist)	3,592	−3.2	7.4
1966	Bradford	J. C. West (Electrical Engineer)	4,310	−19.0	10.0
1966	Brunel	R. E. D. Bishop (Mechanical Engineer)	4,009	+0.4	7.6
1966	City	R. N. Franklin (Engineer and Computer Science)	3,100	−5.2	7.5
1966	Heriot-Watt	T. L. Johnston (Economist)	3,074	−12.8	7.9
1966	Loughborough	C. C. Butler (Physicist)	5,961	−2.6	8.3
1966	Surrey	A. Kelly (Physical Sciences)	2,918	−14.2	9.4
1967	Dundee	A. M. Neville (Civil Engineer)	3,111	−0.4	8.7
1967	Salford	John Ashworth (Biochemist)	4,209	−30.2	7.5
1967	Stirling	Sir Kenneth Alexander (Economist)	2,850	−18.2	18.7

[1] Based on cuts announced by the University Grants Committee in 1981.

[2] The average share of each university's bachelor-level graduates who in 1975–79 ended their year of graduation with no more than a temporary job. See Michael Dixon in *Financial Times*, July 9, 1981.

generation of teachers who soon gave the polys a reputation as centres for left-wing activists and half-baked Marxist ideas. Much of the mockery of the 'polytariat' or the 'lumpenpolytariat' was unfair, for most of their courses continued to provide practical instruction in fan engineering, ventilation and so on; but their upgrading and enlargement made them more conscious of their second-class status, producing the kind of political seedbed which Crosland and his Minister of State, Shirley Williams, never anticipated, full of teachers and students who felt excluded from the more privileged university system.

Many educationalists hoped that the polys would widen their intake, admitting more mature students; but by the autumn of 1981 they were facing their own round of cuts, and arguing bitterly with local authorities and the government about how to carry them out: they got no central guidance about numbers of students, but the government threatened to claw back money from local authorities who spent more on students. And in the meantime the polys were more in demand among students who could not get into universities. In late 1981 most polys were taking in many more students: there were 38 per cent more at Teesside polytechnic and about a quarter more at Sheffield, Middlesex, Portsmouth, Sunderland and Kingston. The results of this new inrush of would-be undergraduates are still to be seen; but they may well politicise the polys still further, and move them further away from their practical roots.

OPEN UNIVERSITY

Among the twenty years of hopes and disillusions about higher education there was one undisputed success story, the Open University which was started to provide degrees for mature students by correspondence course and television. It is one of the very few brand-new institutions in Britain which has held its own and survived almost unscathed, and was the achievement of which Wilson was proudest when he resigned in 1976.[4] It was the original brain-child of Michael Young, the prophet of the meritocracy (see last chapter) and founder of the Consumers' Association, whose innovative mind had a rare capacity to translate ideas into action, through sustained and subtle persuasion (significantly he emerged not from a conventional public school but from the eccentric Dartington Hall, whose founders, the Elmhirsts, regarded him as their protégé, and where he now presides as deputy-chairman). Young's idea of a correspondence university was taken up by Harold Wilson and

[4] Castle: *op cit*, p. 699.

Jennie Lee in the mid-sixties; it had not started when the Tories returned in 1970, but the new Minister of Education, Margaret Thatcher, was dogged in defending her territory, and realised that the Open University could provide graduates much more cheaply than conventional ones.

So it was set up under a Tory government, in an appropriate brand-new setting, just off exit 14 on the M1, in open fields which eventually became the new town of Milton Keynes. The first crop of 25,000 students—more than Oxford and Cambridge together —were very middle class, and a third of them were teachers who would earn more money with degrees: once again the middle classes were the main beneficiaries of an originally socialist concept. But over ten years the numbers of teachers went down, and those of workers went up—to almost a third in 1981—while the proportion of women went up from 32 per cent to 45 per cent. Most students still prefer arts to science, but the numbers in social sciences have gone down over the last eight years while those in technology have gone up. The competition to join is still quite stiff, in spite of rising fees: in 1981 41,000 people applied for the 21,000 undergraduate places, which are allotted on a regional basis. But there are always more applicants from the south, while those from the north have dropped quite sharply; and the OU faces strong competition from the polytechnics which provide shorter and cheaper courses.

The Open University remains a remarkable achievement, having produced 45,000 graduates over ten years at an average age of thirty-eight, with about six thousand degrees a year; and among the teachers or housewives there have been outstanding working-class students (such as the Coventry milkman Eddie Dealtry, who having left school at fifteen took a five-year course at the OU, gained nine distinctions, and is now a computer analyst with Dunlop). Four out of five of its graduates say that they have benefited from their studies by better pay or improved skills. Its new headquarters at Milton Keynes has 400 full-time dons and 300 broadcasting staff who have evolved their own educational techniques: the text-books are models of careful communication, superbly produced and integrated with the courses. The OU is a unique achievement, which has not affected the complacency of other universities, although some radical dons complain that it has allowed governments too readily to neglect adult education elsewhere.

NEWNESS AND ANTIQUITY

The forty-two British universities represent their own history of British education through all its stages. There are the English medieval foundations, Oxford and Cambridge, and their four dour Scots equivalents, St Andrews, Glasgow, Edinburgh and Aberdeen. There is London University, which was set up in 1836 as a non-conformist rival to Oxford and Cambridge and which now has more students than both, including University College, King's and Birkbeck (for adult students). There are the big civic universities, such as Birmingham, Leeds, Manchester or Liverpool, which were set up in the late nineteenth century by mayors and corporations as part of their local pride. There are the smaller provincial universities, with cleaner air and quieter surroundings, such as Nottingham and Leicester, Bristol, Exeter and Southampton. There are the eight new universities—Sussex, Essex, Kent, Lancaster, East Anglia, Warwick, York and Stirling—which were established in the sixties during the enthusiasm for expansion. There are the three great engineering centres—Strathclyde, Imperial College and UMIST—with their own specialised high standards. And there are the promoted colleges of advanced technology, such as Bath, Brunel, Aston or Loughborough. Many of these universities have established their own high reputations in special fields: Bristol has very high standards for entry, and excels in drama and English; Lancaster is expert in systems analysis; Loughborough is well-equipped for engineering; Southampton is one of several which hopes to become a kind of miniature MIT.

Yet despite the great wave of expansion and expenditure none of the universities had achieved the kind of all-round reputation of the two oldest ones. Some of the big civics, such as Manchester and Leeds, expanded almost to the size of Oxford and Cambridge; but they did not rival them as centres of excellence, as the best state universities in America rival Harvard or Yale. Even in science Cambridge was still supreme, the Cavendish Laboratory being the biggest producer of Nobel prizewinners (see chapter 14). Many of the newer universities were still too small to provide the libraries, laboratories or concentration which could attract the best dons or students, and many educationalists now regretted that they had not built fewer universities with better resources. After two decades of ambitious innovation, there was still no substitute for antiquity and inherited wealth.

The road to most of the top jobs in Britain remains almost as narrow as ever. The only serious rival to Oxbridge as the nursery of power is the London School of Economics, which includes only about a thousand British undergraduates among its four thousand students, but which has extended its influence in the age of economics. Their alumni include twenty-seven members of parliament (including two prominent Tories, Rhodes Boyson and Reg

Prentice), Lord Weinstock, Lord Croham (the former head of the Treasury), John Sparrow (the head of the cabinet Think Tank), and a roll-call of world figures ranging from Pierre Trudeau to Wilfried Guth of the Deutsche Bank, from Norman Manley to Senator Patrick Moynihan. The LSE, which was founded by the first Fabian, Sidney Webb, has long since ceased to be particularly left wing. It was an ideological battlefield before and during the 1968 student revolt, when LSE students occupied the buildings, tore down the steel gates and persecuted the principal, Dr Walter Adams. But it has since become a more peaceful and hardworking centre for students who are now more interested in econometrics and systems analysis than in sociology and psychology. Its current director, Ralf Dahrendorf, who was a professor and minister in Germany, combines a radical curiosity with a broad authority—not least because the LSE now raises only 40 per cent of its funds from the government, compared to 80 per cent eight years ago: in two years' time, Dahrendorf claims, it will be as independent of government as the 'Independent University' of Buckingham. A few dons have refused to go into the senior common room of the LSE ever since the student revolts, but most of the atmosphere of confrontation and ideological fury has evaporated.

The university student revolts in Britain had much milder repercussions than on the Continent or in America. 'In Britain the institutions never crumbled,' Dahrendorf says, 'as they did in Germany and France where they were far more brittle. The British never ask "what did you do in 1968?".' But the British revolt against materialism and conformity did help to polarise a new student generation: some were permanently alienated from traditional hierarchies, while others took refuge in non-political specialisation. The student revolts, coming after the rapid expansion of universities and polytechnics and soon followed by recession and contraction, created new activists for the Labour left wing, which included a very high proportion of teachers.

OXBRIDGE

The two ancient universities still provide the chief route to the heights of power, twenty years after Lord Robbins complained about their monopoly, 'composed of a certain kind of intellectual elite'. Senior civil servants, barristers, diplomats, BBC executives and merchant bankers are still preponderantly from Oxbridge, as the following chapters will show. Labour cabinets have become much more proletarian since the extraordinary heyday of Oxford dons twenty years ago (see chapter 5); and the new 1979 parliament had only fifty-eight out of 268 Labour MPs from Oxbridge, compared to eighty-six out of 363 in 1966. But the Conservative cabinet after Thatcher's purge of 1981 still had ten members from Cambridge, six from Oxford and none from other universities; while the 339 Conservative MPs in June 1979 included ninety-four from Oxford, seventy-five from Cambridge and only eighty-seven from other universities (with eighty-three who had never been to university). And Oxbridge still catches a high proportion of the 'best brains' as Robbins called them—at least as judged by the rigid examination system: in 1980 83 per cent of the new undergraduates in Cambridge, and 72 per cent in Oxford, had gained A-levels consisting of at least two Bs and an A; compared to an average of 27 per cent in other universities.

Both universities are sensitive to criticisms from the left that they provide a class-based elite. In 1981 Oxford for the first time took more new undergraduates from state schools than from independents, while a fifth of its places went to pupils from schools which had been comprehensive for at least six years. The competition is not all that intense; in 1981 Oxford admitted two applicants out of five, and three-quarters of the classicists—who include fewer from state schools. But Oxford and Cambridge are both becoming more competitive as they try to scoop up more intelligence. 'Dons prowl the countryside like medieval friars searching for brains,' as Harry Judge, the director of educational studies at Oxford put it, 'while sixth-formers from comprehensive schools are welcome on visits and reassured of the accessibility and normality of the place.' It is the greatest social change, Judge claims, that Oxford has accomplished in its seven hundred years. 'A price has doubtless been paid, but the meritocracy has triumphed.'[5]

Future years may show some weakening of the Oxbridge influence in high places. The civil service recruiters (see chapter 10) have gradually managed to drum up more entrants from other universities. The multinational corporations, most of them foreign-owned and thus more immune to British snobberies, find their managers from a much wider mix of backgrounds. But Oxbridge graduates are still favourites in the 'verbalising' occupations where social confidence and smoothness are at a premium; and as jobs get scarcer they are competing in other fields. 'They're going into different things,' said Tom Snow of the Oxford University Appointments Board in 1982. 'Many more are going into accountancy, banking, insurance, computers or advertising. But Oxford isn't a particularly good place for industry to recruit from, since two-thirds are arts graduates.'

[5] *The Times*, February 24, 1982.

Oxford and Cambridge are both federations of individual colleges, each fortified by its own buildings, endowments, high tables and wine-cellars; and their close collegiate system still distinguishes them from most other universities. The colleges were forced to give up some of their jealous autonomy after Lord Robbins threatened a special enquiry into their anomalies, and they now co-operate in a fairer system of admissions. Some new colleges have sprung up alongside the medieval foundations—including Robinson in Cambridge, endowed by a shy tycoon; St Anthony's in Oxford, founded by a French trader; and two colleges endowed by Lord Wolfson ('the only man since Jesus to have colleges named after him in both universities'). The college traditions remain very distinctive and they have become socially more self-sufficient since they began to admit women, who spread from Cambridge to Oxford in the seventies. By 1974 five Oxford colleges were admitting women, and others quickly realised that they must 'grab the best girls for themselves'; by 1982 only Oriel was holding out. The prospect of girls in the quadrangles appalled many of the dons; but girls tended to make the colleges both less drunken and more self-contained, since men need not now leave their own college to find them. Even Christ Church reluctantly came to terms with the admission of women in 1980, not without a sad backward glance, hazarding the thought that 'the single-sex colleges, evolved first in the conditions of the Middle Ages and then of the 1870s, were a unique and successful venture'.

Many older colleges have their own long-standing relationships with outside professions, nurtured by their dons and generations of post-graduates. At Cambridge, Trinity has a special tradition of scientists and philosophers; Trinity Hall next door still specialises in judges; King's has its own proud tradition of homosexual intellectuals and spies; while Peterhouse cultivates right-wing historians. Oxford has always had closer links with London politics and power: Balliol College has been specially preoccupied with the worldly ambition fostered by its Victorian master, Benjamin Jowett, and continued by A. L. Smith, whose grandchildren are now scattered round the seats of power. The products of the Balliol forcing-ground are still very visible in this book, including politicians such as Denis Healey, Roy Jenkins, Jo Grimond and Ted Heath. But younger Balliol men show less evidence of driving ambition, and their academic superiority is now challenged by other colleges, for example University, Merton and St John's.

Christ Church, the traditional nursery of Tory politicians, bishops or bankers still pervades this book like no other college. It is true that it has produced no new prime minister since Sir Alec Douglas-Home (its thirteenth), and by 1982 it had only two members of the cabinet,

Lord Hailsham and Nigel Lawson; but it still has twenty-two members of parliament (all Tory apart from Fred Mulley)—more than any other college or establishment except the London School of Economics. Christ Church maintains its traditional disdain for twentieth-century activities, with an annual newsletter which reads like a parody of British snobberies, beginning with honours, Lords Lieutenants and royal service ('Mr D. H. B. Chesshyre, formerly Rouge Croix Pursuivant, aptly became Chester Herald of Arms'), and ending with vulgar achievements in business, journalism and sport.

The seductions of Oxford and Cambridge have probably increased over the last twenty years, as the climate elsewhere has become harsher. The old universities depend like others on the grants and cuts of the UGC, but their magnificent buildings, their endowments, libraries and new benefactions are immune from the axe, and the colleges can add to their incomes by renting themselves to business conventions during vacations. They can still attract many of the best dons to a way of life that can augment mere salaries with college houses, high tables and servants (who are more plentiful and long-suffering than elsewhere in Britain). The master of an Oxbridge college can still enjoy a life-style which has changed remarkably little since the nineteenth century, entertaining friends in elegant surroundings with a style few tycoons can achieve; civil servants, lawyers or scientists, not surprisingly, long for a mastership as their final haven, to bring their career full circle. The status of dons has increased as that of others has declined, and politicians have always been specially vulnerable to the lures and wiles of academe which—at least until the Thatcher era—in turn enhanced the lobbying-power of the dons.

Should these two old seducers be blamed for Britain's failure to face up to her economic predicament? Are they, as the Labour party complained in 1980, 'profoundly ignorant of and remote from the mainstream of British society'? They are certainly less contemptuous of industry, more worldly and realistic, than they were twenty years ago: there is much more to-ing and fro-ing between Oxbridge and London; and behind the more glittering surface of balls, debates and exhibitionists there is another Oxbridge of industrious and often penurious scientists and engineers who spend their afternoons in labs and their evenings at books. But the spells and enchantments which these universities cast on many of their graduates still (I believe) exact a high price. They encourage them to be preoccupied with the past, to assume that structures are permanent and unchanging, and they provide few links with the world of industry and the north. It is hardly surprising if they have produced no British entrepreneur (as Algy Cluff, the oil tycoon, claims): risk-taking, bold decisiveness or foreseeing new activities could hardly be more foreign to their assumptions. The classic route to fame and fortune, from public school to university to the Bar to the House of Commons, has involved moving through ancient institutions without ever having to hire, fire or manage other people; and a lack of interest in management compared to policy-making, whether among civil servants or politicians, contributed to many of the fiascos of failed reform which feature in the following pages.

The time-honoured Oxbridge structures—on top of the foundations of medieval schools—can easily encourage their inhabitants towards the most conventional kind of ambition, to climb up existing trees rather than plant new ones, while colleges love to honour alumni who perpetuate the familiar pattern. But at a time of challenge and innovation these traditional values are much less obviously useful. Jean Monnet, the father of the European Community, learnt from his American friend Dwight Morrow: 'There are two kinds of people—those who want to *be someone*, and those who want to *do something*,' and Monnet believed it was the second kind who forsook the limelight, who got things moving.[6] It would be absurd to blame Oxbridge alone for the British tendency to revere institutions and their formal hierarchies; but their formative influence still lurks behind many of the country's more complacent and unchangeable institutions.

The stability and continuity which Oxbridge represents—almost as prominently as the monarchy itself—had great benefits during the social and economic upheavals of the past. In Victorian times, when Oxford and Cambridge were modernised along with other professions, they fitted in with the ideal of the well-educated gentleman who looked specially desirable while Britain was seething with commercial and political change, providing stabilisers to a dynamic nation, like Confucian traditions in contemporary Japan. But in an ex-imperial country which is constantly tempted to take refuge in its past such institutions can become like ballast to an overloaded ship. Or as Roy Campbell put it:

> They use the snaffle and the curb all right
> But where's the bloody horse?

The Oxbridge influence would be less worrying if it were only one elite of many with different values and ambitions. The old American 'Ivy League' universities, led by Harvard and Yale, have similar charms and influences, fortified by rich benefactors and New Eng-

[6] Jean Monnet: *Memoirs*, Collins, London, 1978, p. 519.

land families. But they have not turned their backs on business and industry, and their elite is only one of several: the more rugged social hierarchies of Detroit, Los Angeles or Houston scarcely notice their seductions. Oxbridge, by contrast, still maintains its pervasive network and style which can easily demoralise Scots engineers or Yorkshire scientists; and no comparable elite is evident in the fields which follow this chapter.

9

The Law: Judges and Politics

The Law is the true embodiment
Of everything that's excellent
It has no kind of fault or flaw,
And I, my Lords, embody the Law.
The Lord Chancellor in Iolanthe
(Gilbert and Sullivan)

ALL the conservatism and exclusiveness of old institutions is to be found in the legal profession, which has grown up alongside the old universities, as part of the classic route to parliament and political power, with its roots deep in history and religion: 'that great Gothic structure of authority,' as John Mortimer calls it, 'with its stone buttresses of power and its ancient ecclesiastical ornaments'.[1] The law is the most extreme British example of a closed and self-regulating community, with all its strengths and weaknesses. Its proud traditions can enable judges to stand apart from the state apparatus, as the ultimate guarantors of human liberties; but they have also enabled lawyers to resist reforms more stubbornly than anyone, and to fortify their own privileges. Right-wing lawyers love to complain about the monopolies and restrictive practices of trade unions while they enjoy the most restrictive monopoly of all, protected by one of the oldest trade unions.

The chief theatre of English law is the gothic Royal Courts of Justice in the Strand, built in 1880 when the legal profession was at its height, with an atmosphere which makes the law seem part of religion. Barristers cover their ordinariness with gowns and horse-hair wigs, and judges surround themselves with ancient pomp. Anyone who enters the high, hushed law courts is conditioned to the notion of legal authority which appears as natural and unchanging as the architecture. But the legal profession often seems to have stood still since the nineteenth century. Since that heyday of private property, when lawyers advised and fought over rich men's estates, individuals have been overshadowed by industrial

[1] John Mortimer: *Clinging to the Wreckage*, Weidenfeld and Nicolson, London, 1982, p. 90.

corporations, trade unions and insurance companies, while the great apparatus of state administration has crept up on the old powers of the law. Most lawyers are now representing one institution against another—a trade union against an insurance company for example—and they have become increasingly cut off from the public, who fear and distrust them: only a few radical lawyers have set up neighbourhood law centres in poor districts, to bring their services close to ordinary people. But the law remains very distant from most people's grievances against the state, and the consumers' interests have had very little impact on the rituals and procedures which often seem designed to baffle the layman.

SOLICITORS

The legal monopoly is supported by the strict division between solicitors and barristers which was enforced in the late nineteenth century and which is found in only a few other countries including Sri Lanka and South Africa. Only a solicitor can deal directly with the public, only a barrister is allowed to plead in the higher courts; and the two branches of the profession sustain each other's monopolies. There have been many different justifications for the separation. Many solicitors defend it as a form of sub-contracting which provides a cheaper service: the barristers are specialists with minimal overheads who are skilled in court procedure and trusted by judges. 'The one is a man of business,' Lord Hailsham the Lord Chancellor has said, 'the other, to some extent, an artist and scholar.'[2] Lord Rawlinson, the former Attorney-General has even suggested that 'much of the liberty of the subject depends on the separate roles of private practitioners'.[3] When the chartered accountant Sir Henry Benson chaired a Royal Commission on Legal Services which reported in 1979 many barristers feared that he would recommend the 'fusion' of the two professions, but he did not. Even the American Chief Justice, Warren Burger, exasperated by inexpert lawyers pleading before the Supreme Court, has talked with admiration of the English specialisation. But the division has also helped to reinforce the rigidity of the English legal profession, and its object is not so much to meet the needs of the clients as to maintain the employment of lawyers.

The English have long prided themselves on being less lawyer-ridden than most countries: they have about 840 lawyers for every million people, compared to about 1,500 in the United States. But

---

[2] Hailsham: *op cit*, p. 265.

[3] See Michael Zander: 'Independence of the Legal Profession—What does it mean?' *Law Society's Gazette*, September 22, 1976.

English lawyers have been increasing rapidly: there were only 25,000 solicitors in England and Wales in 1960, but 41,000 in 1982. 'What will so many find to do?' asked the President of the Law Society, Jonathan Clarke, in 1980; but many clients were worried that they would find it all too easy to spin out their time, lovingly exchanging long-winded letters while the clock ticks up their fees. Solicitors have become increasingly defensive in maintaining a monopoly of many jobs which could be done by less qualified people: they even mounted an extravagant advertising campaign, paid for by a special solicitors' levy, to warn the public about the dangers of using a non-solicitor, 'Whatsisname'. They have fought hard to defend their most lucrative and leisurely business, the conveyancing of houses, which accounts for half their income and which employs expensive solicitors for work that can be done by secretaries or clerks. But the conservatism and defensiveness of the profession have also limited its future. The ablest solicitors have tended to gravitate towards the big law firms, such as Slaughter and May or Linklaters and Paines, which have huge scope in advising big corporations. The solicitor's profession has, however, been so engrossed in its past that it has allowed the upstart accountants to move into the most profitable corporate regions, advising on financial control and taxation. Only a few solicitors such as Lord Goodman or Lord Tangley have played a political and commercial role comparable to that of the great Washington legal partnerships.

There has been mounting public indignation against overcharging, delays or embezzlement by solicitors; for the chief means of redress is the Law Society which is also their powerful trade union. The Law Society has a compensation fund to reimburse clients who have been defrauded, but they are alarmed by the mounting claims, which amounted to £2 million in 1980. 'We must be more determined than we sometimes are,' said their president in 1980, 'to warn the Law Society when we see the telltale signs that all too often indicate that something is going wrong in another solicitor's practice.' Yet the Law Society is reluctant to investigate most complaints about incompetence, and usually advises an angry client to go to *another* solicitor to try to take action against the first one, which exasperates the client still further.

The public resentment of solicitors became so strong that three Labour MPs (Christopher Price, Michael English and Peter Archer) proposed to set up an independent enquirer, who was finally incorporated into the Solicitors Act of 1974: the Lord Chancellor now appoints a 'Lay Observer' who deals with about 300 complaints a year and issues an annual report. The present Lay Observer, Major-General John Allen, complained in 1980 about the long delays, particularly in administering estates which can take ten years to wind up, and about solicitors who too often take on cases which they cannot properly handle. But the Lay Observer cannot himself investigate complaints and he has pressed the Law Society to set up its own arbitration scheme and extend its independent investigations. 'There was a feeling,' he said, 'that as the solicitors' professional body they were both judge and jury in their own court.'[4]

BARRISTERS

It is the five thousand barristers who remain the 'senior branch' of the legal profession, and only they can reach the top of the pyramid—a high court judgeship. Of all British subgroups they remain the most arcane and segregated. More than half work in a tiny area of London half a mile across, in one of the four Inns of Court, where they can lunch at long wooden benches in hammer-beam halls, as in a public school or an Oxbridge college. 'You can recognise a law student at the end of the first year,' one experienced QC assured me, 'as much as a divinity student: they've already acquired a special respect for authority'. The oldest and richest Inn is the Inner Temple, alongside a round Saxon church, which has produced most judges, and is more exclusive than the Middle Temple next door. Across the road, Lincoln's Inn is frequented by Chancery lawyers: Gray's Inn, the newest, had a long decline after its heyday in the sixteenth century, but has more recently produced a good crop of judges. The Inns have retained more completely than Oxbridge colleges their ancient autonomy and privileges. Their constitution was described by Sir Frederick Pollock in 1922 as 'a survival of medieval republican oligarchy, the purest, I should think, to be found in Europe'; and it has not changed much since for the Inns have refused to delegate real power to the barristers' professional body, the Bar Council. During the heyday of Victorian reformers in the 1860s and 1870s they resisted pressures much more successfully than parliament, universities, the civil service or the army: they refused to change their constitutions and provide a system of legal education, and they remain today uncontrolled by any statute.[5] They are ruled by their 'benchers', the self-perpetuating senior lawyers who sit at high table, and their wealth remains secret, since they are (almost uniquely) exempted from publishing accounts.

[4] *The Times*, April 29, 1981.
[5] See Nicholas Warren's chapter on The Inns of Court, in *The Bar on Trial*, Quartet, London, 1978, p. 42.

Barristers—even more than parliamentarians—have been concerned with reforming everything except their own profession. They are protected from the modern world not only by their Inns but by their 'chambers', where groups of barristers work in a collegiate atmosphere, with sets of rooms round the courtyards approached by stone steps. A young barrister usually depends on finding a 'tenancy' in chambers to enable him to get briefs, and the patronage of the head of chambers, which can be crucial to future success, determines much of the social character of the Bar: some chambers still refuse to admit women, and most favour candidates from Oxbridge. Through their chambers, barristers remain grandly aloof—far more than solicitors—from matters of management or 'trade'; and they leave all commercial questions to the clerk of their chambers who is socially beneath them but who may often be richer than any, and who can make or break a young barrister by his shareout of briefs.

Against the background of this unchanging corporate life the barristers remain more individualist than any other profession, and by their own decree they cannot share their risks like doctors or solicitors: they make money only for themselves, and if they fall ill no one takes their place. Moving between their chambers and the courtroom, they can develop an odd mixture of scholarship and showmanship which cuts them off still further from ordinary people, and the Bar still has a fellow-feeling with the stage, which is visible at the Garrick Club which they share. The Lord Chancellor, Lord Hailsham, often appears like an actor manqué, and was once photographed with his stage counterpart in Gilbert and Sullivan's *Iolanthe*. 'I really went to the Bar,' said one of his predecessors, Lord Gardiner, 'because I thought it would be easier to go on to the stage after failing at the Bar than to the Bar after failing on the stage.' But barristers are coming to terms with a more humdrum age, and they are more likely to be recounting the details of a factory accident to a sceptical judge, than to be passionately urging the innocence of a murderer to a weeping jury. They can earn high fees as tax or legal advisers in the City or industry, and many of the cleverest have left the Bar for banks or business, such as Lord Shawcross, Mark Littman, Philip Shelbourne or Gordon Richardson (the Governor of the Bank of England). When a High Court judge, Sir Henry Fisher, left the bench for a bank in 1970 the former Lord Chancellor Lord Dilhorne complained it was 'unprecedented and unacceptable', but no disaster followed, and Fisher is now president of Wolfson College, Oxford.

MAGISTRATES

The average citizen is much more likely to appear before a magistrate than before a judge; and the great bulk of British justice is carried out not by professional lawyers but by unpaid magistrates who sit on the bench only one day a week or a fortnight. A magistrates' court provides a complete contrast to the pomp of a law court, with no wigs, no gowns and often no lawyers. The three justices sit below a modest lion-and-unicorn, only slightly removed from the courtroom, with a magistrates' clerk below who can advise them on points of law. The courtroom is often full of mothers, friends or relations and the atmosphere is far less male than the higher courts. The exchanges are brisk and matter-of-fact and only when lawyers appear are they caught up in legal rigmarole.

The origins of the Justices of the Peace go deep into the Middle Ages, before any legal bureaucracy existed. They were established in 1361—the first English institution set up by statute—to provide three or four people in each English county to keep the peace and punish offenders.[6] For several centuries they ran the whole of local government as the instruments of the monarchy, many of them serving both as justices and members of parliament. Arbitrary and eccentric JPs, who controlled local constables and dealt ruthlessly with local poachers or vagrants, were a recurring subject for protest and comedy, such as Justice Shallow in Shakespeare's *King Henry IV*.

But this undemocratic institution remarkably survived the Victorian reformers. Justices lost some duties to the police forces and the new county councils took over their local government powers in 1888; but they were now used much more to give summary jurisdiction at their courts, the 'Petty Sessions', and their work was swelled by matrimonial cases and by the separate juvenile courts which were set up in 1908. Eventually a few 'stipendiary' magistrates were set up in London and eleven other towns, who were professional lawyers working full-time, but in 1977 there were still only fifty-two 'stipes'.

After the Second World War the magistrates were still very unrepresentative and often eccentric: a quarter were aged over seventy and fourteen were over ninety. Nearly all were Tories. In the country many were large landowners, as they had been six hundred years earlier. In the towns mayors, ex-mayors and London aldermen automatically became magistrates, often autocratic ones. The Lord Chancellor selected the others through a secretive and elaborate old-boy network, and since magistrates dispensed licences for pubs

[6] Thomas Skyrme: *The Changing Face of the Magistracy*, Macmillan, London, 1979, p. 2 (to which I am indebted in this section).

and gaming (which they still do) they could sometimes have corrupt motives.

Many socialists expected the post-war Labour government to abolish amateur justices altogether in favour of a professional bench. But successive Lord Chancellors found it so convenient and flexible, compared to the legal bureaucracy, that they reformed it instead. They gradually changed the political balance: by 1977 34 per cent of magistrates were Conservative, 31 per cent Labour and 14 per cent Liberal. They brought in many more women, who now make up about a third of all magistrates. They insisted on compulsory retirement, first at seventy-two, then at seventy (or sixty-five in juvenile courts). And they tried, with much less success, to broaden the class basis. Lord Gardiner even tried to find some farm labourers to be JPs, but their trade union could only come up with two candidates. By 1962 the first black magistrate was appointed in Nottingham, but by 1977 there were still only seventy-nine immigrant JPs. Black magistrates were much needed as urban crime increased, but they were still hard to recruit.

Magistrates are still predominantly middle-class, selected by secretive local advisory committees, which sometimes tend to perpetuate organised groups such as Rotarians and Freemasons. Many emerge through the party political network, others are co-opted by their elders. This ancient institution, even after the reforms, was not easy to defend or explain in a modern democracy. Yet it was not under serious attack. The chief complaint against magistrates is that they are too influenced by police evidence, and the style of the courts encourages the suspicions: it was only after 1949 that the old 'police courts' were re-named 'magistrates courts' and many are still in the same building as the police station. But the part-time magistrates do not produce noticeably different verdicts from the 'stipes' and they include a much higher proportion of women than professional lawyers, which has a special value in the juvenile courts. Since the magistrates sit in twos or threes, with a clerk to advise them, their scope for eccentricity is limited.

Lord Chancellors have still found JPs very convenient: being unpaid, they have no formal hierarchy or bureaucracy and they can do extra work when needed. Many people are thankful for a legal system which includes so few lawyers. As even Lord Hailsham put it: 'We have an extraordinarily small legal profession, and I regard this as thoroughly beneficial to society . . . I would rather have too few lawyers than too many as in the United States. Lawyers are indispensable to any civilised society, but they have limitations and weaknesses and should not be too thick on the ground.'[7]

[7] Hailsham: *op cit*, p. 263.

JUDGES

The keystone of the rule of law in England has been the independence of judges. It is the only respect in which we make any real
separation of powers.

Lord Denning, 1981[8]

Because of the magistrates, England has far fewer professional
judges than most countries. When Lord Gardiner ordered a survey
in 1965, it showed that England and Wales had only eight judges per
million of population, compared to thirty-four in the United States;
while other countries outside the Anglo-Saxon legal system had as
many as 200 judges per million. English judges remain a small and
self-contained profession, as they have been for the past few centuries, carefully dignified by the 'majesty of the law'. All of them
except circuit judges (who can be solicitors) must be appointed from
the ranks of the barristers, in spite of repeated protests from solicitors; so that the isolation of the Bench is reinforced by the detachment of the Inns of Court and the ancient privileges of the Bar.

The transformation of a barrister into a judge is one of the oddest
of all British career-changes. A barrister who earns perhaps
£100,000 a year will have to cut down to £35,000 a year as a High
Court judge, but he leaves a highly-competitive and insecure business for a totally secure one; and he now becomes part of the ancient
fabric of justice. When I asked a newly-appointed High Court judge
how he felt he replied: 'Well, it's nice deciding who *wins*.' A man who
has spent his life in specialised pleading, taking up briefs to defend
murderers or swindlers and arguing with insistent one-sidedness, is
suddenly required to take the most balanced view, and to exercise
the mysterious faculty of judgment. The quick-talking advocate
suddenly becomes the silent and impartial upholder of justice.

The Lord Chancellor appoints judges through a centralised and
self-perpetuating system, consulting with senior judges and looking
through his card-index of barristers and references. A barrister after
about fifteen years may successfully apply to 'take silk' and become
one of four hundred Queen's Counsel when he earns higher fees and
becomes known as John Smith QC. Or he may be appointed one of a
hundred 'circuit judges', when he is known as His Honour Judge
Smith; or a prominent QC may be chosen for the High Court, where
he becomes known as 'The Hon Mr Justice Smith' or 'Sir John
Smith' (acquiring a knighthood automatically). From there he may
become one of thirteen judges in the Appeal Court, where he will
wear black robes, become a privy councillor, and be known (though

[8] Lord Denning: *The Family Story*, Butterworths, London, 1981, p. 191.

not a peer) as 'Lord Justice Smith', 'Smith, L.J.', or the 'Right Honourable Sir John Smith'. At the peak he may be made one of the ten Law Lords or 'Lords of Appeal in Ordinary' who sit in the House of Lords as life peers earning £41,000 a year (in 1981) and known as 'the Right Honourable Lord Smith'.

The competition to become a judge is less severe than it looks: an ambitious barrister can probably become some kind of judge by the age of fifty-five, and the recent inflation in judges has led to second-rate appointments. But once appointed, the judges are supported and protected by all the formal machinery of the law, in a life-style which is like no other. For two hundred and twenty-five days in the year they sit in their wigs listening to barristers arguing abstruse points of law. They move between an office in the Law Courts, the high table of an Inn of Court and occasionally the Reform or the Garrick clubs. They all take their long vacation in the same two months of the summer—to the fury of many litigators. They are more detached than American judges from society and social development, and left-wing critics complain with some reason about their narrow experience. Their social background has changed less than that of senior civil servants or even diplomats. A survey in 1968 found that out of 394 judges, 292 went to public schools and 273 went to Oxbridge; ten years later three-quarters of seventy-four High Court judges still came from public schools, and their later experience was largely limited to the Bar. 'Their attitude to the political and social problems of our time,' said the authors of the left-wing *Manifesto* in 1981, 'is shaped and determined by their class, their upbringing and their professional life . . . Their attitude is strongly conservative, respectful of property rights and highly authoritarian.'[9]

How far judges' backgrounds influence their verdicts and sentences is constantly disputed. Lord Hailsham, the Lord Chancellor, insists that 'it would be difficult to imagine young men and women who have a wider view of the causes of human unhappiness than those who go to the Common Law Bar at the present time'.[10] But many laymen are sceptical, and suspicions of class bias are periodically supported: as when in 1977 an Old Etonian judge, Mervyn Griffith-Jones, gave a suspended sentence to an Old Etonian who had raided two banks with a sawn-off shotgun. But the more serious charge against judges is that they underpin the class system with different attitudes towards the rich and the poor. Certainly the Bench has done less than other elites to try to widen its background, and as judges inevitably become more involved in political arguments, their narrowness will make them more suspect.

[9] *Manifesto: A Radical Strategy for Britain's Future*, Pan, London, 1981, p. 99.
[10] Hailsham: *op cit*, p. 258.

The Lord Chief Justice of England is the senior judge below the Lord Chancellor: he can decide which judge hears which case, he can make bold public statements, and he has the ear of the government. He earned £44,000 in 1981 and he need not retire until he is seventy-five. He presides in his own large green court, with chandeliers and velvet curtains, sitting with two of his colleagues in red robes and flapping white tabs, in front of a carved lion and unicorn. The present Lord Chief, Lord Lane, came up through a conventional route, beginning with Shrewsbury and Cambridge (with a First in Moral Philosophy), with a gallant interval in the wartime RAF. He was made a QC at forty-four, a High Court judge at forty-eight, an Appeal judge at fifty-six, Lord Chief at sixty-two. He is a congenial, well-liked conservative, who has outspokenly attacked the bureaucracy of law: he has complained that the administrative tail is 'apt to get above its station and wag the judicial dog', and he has tried to rescue the backlog of cases at the Court of Appeal. He has called for shorter sentences for petty offenders, and endorsed a move in 1981 to extend prisoners' paroles. But he is respectful of the established order; and when the Home Secretary wanted to deport the young American journalist Mark Hosenball in 1977 on grounds of national security, he granted a deportation order.

The supreme judiciary are the nine Law Lords (including two Scottish lords from the separate Scots hierarchy), who form the ultimate domestic court of appeal. Their backgrounds are even more limited than other judges: eight of the nine went to Oxford, all but two went to public schools; one of them, Lord Russell, is the son of a Law Lord and the grandson of both a Lord Chief Justice and (on his mother's side) a Chancellor of the Exchequer. The Law Lords sit not in wigs and robes in elaborate courtrooms, but in plain grey suits in a committee room of the House of Lords, listening to arguments which have become more abstruse and rarified as they have travelled up the courts. But in recent years Law Lords have also been asked more frequently to serve as wise men or commissioners to advise governments on controversial issues, which tests their impartiality to its limits.

The most popular of these trouble-shooters is Lord Scarman, whose benign style and patient investigation make him the favourite of both parties for defusing explosive conflicts: he investigated the riots in Ulster in 1969, the Grunwick dispute in 1977 and—most visibly—the Brixton riots in 1981. He took on the task at Brixton with a careful eye on publicity, which annoyed many of his colleagues: he was seen with black children, talked with people in the streets and joined the Brixton Domino and Social Club. It was an exercise in public relations as much as justice, and he produced a report which trod a careful middle path, defending the blacks while partly justifying the police. But Scarman's importance has gone further than enquiries: he spent seven years as chairman of the Law Commission, recommending new definitions which were made into statutes, after which he became more concerned about the need for a bill of rights and for an American-style Supreme Court, to protect citizens from the full power of parliament. 'When times are abnormally alive with fear and prejudice,' he said in a Hamlyn lecture, after anti-terrorist laws had been rushed through parliament, 'the common law is at a disadvantage: it cannot resist the will, however frightened and prejudiced it may be, of parliament.'

LAW LORDS

Name	Education	Age
Lord Wilberforce	Winchester; Oxford	74
Lord Diplock	Whitgift; Oxford	74
Lord Edmund-Davies	Mountain Ash Grammar School; London; Oxford	75
Lord Fraser	Repton; Oxford	70
Lord Scarman	Radley; Oxford	70
Lord Roskill	Winchester; Oxford	70
Lord Bridge	Marlborough; Army	64
Lord Russell	Beaumont; Oxford	73
Lord Keith	Edinburgh Academy; Oxford; Edinburgh	59

The most politically influential of the judges, however, has been the Master of the Rolls, Lord Denning, who until he retired in 1982 at the age of eighty-three saw himself as the champion of individual freedom against the bureaucracies. Sitting in his Dickensian office in the Law Courts, with his innocent smile and bright eyes, talking about de law and de people in his Hampshire accent, he portrayed himself as the common man who has strayed to the top, concealing his sharp mind with homely simplicity. He has lovingly described his childhood at Whitchurch, as the son of an unbusinesslike draper who loved books and music, and who produced five sons, including General Denning and Admiral Denning, the former head of naval intelligence.[11] Tom Denning won a scholarship from Andover Grammar School to Oxford, and moved from mathematics to law, where he soon showed his mastery. With his own modest roots he dismisses the attacks on a class-based judiciary: 'The youngsters believe that we come from a narrow background—it's nonsense—they get it from that man Griffith.[12] A lot has changed in

[11] Denning: *op cit*.
[12] Professor Griffith at the London School of Economics.

twenty years.' But much of Denning's courage and originality stems from his country roots which are very different from most of the Law Lords'. He has a basically simple, moral view of the law, and insists that law and religion are interlocked: 'Without religion there can be no morality; and without morality there can be no law.' 'A lot of judgment,' he said to me, 'is a feel for what you think is right: I may consider previous rulings, but really I've just done the job as it comes along.' 'So long as I did what I thought was just,' he wrote in his autobiography, 'I was content. I could sleep at night. But if I did what was unjust, I stayed awake worrying.'[13]

He made the most of his own independence, as an old judge whom no one can shut up. He enjoyed appearing on television, against the Lord Chancellor's wishes, and distancing himself from the administrators and legislators. His preoccupation has been with the problem of freedom under the law: 'What matters in England,' he said in his Hamlyn Lecture in 1949, 'is that each man should be free to develop his own personality to the full; and the only duties which should restrict this freedom are those which are necessary to enable everyone else to do the same.' His concern for the individual has brought him repeatedly up against the powers of the administration and trade unions: 'Properly exercised the new powers of the executive lead to the welfare state; but abused they lead to the totalitarian state.'

It is administrative law, he told me, which has shown the most important changes over the last two decades:

> We've been more critical of parliament and government; we've intervened much more—as we did when we overruled the minister over Freddie Laker's Sky Train. Fifty years ago judges were very reluctant to interfere with any power. Now they're much more concerned to prevent abuses. If parliament were to get too extreme some of us might not follow them. We can't help having political consequences, but we're not political. In the United States, the Supreme Court is far more political because they make policy, about schools, blacks, or debussing; but they're still held in the highest regard. You can't avoid being *thought* political except by being neutral or cold and analytical, discussing words, which is not like me.

LORD CHANCELLOR

At the top of the law the boundaries with politics are more muzzy, and the conflicts between legal impartiality and political expediency are very evident in the government's senior law officers—the Solicitor-General and the Attorney-General—who are chosen from

[13] Denning: *op cit.*

barrister MPs. Lawyers have often excelled in politics, but not often reached the peak. A few barristers such as Thatcher or Asquith have become prime ministers; the last (and only) solicitor was Lloyd George. Only one law officer ever became prime minister, Spencer Perceval in 1809, and he was shot dead two years later. In the past, politics has been the natural goal for successful barristers, who could combine a political career with their lucrative practice; but now that both careers are more specialised fewer barristers are interested in parliament. There are still seventy-five barristers in the House of Commons (compared to ninety-nine in 1959); and barristers are very prominent in the present government, particularly in the Treasury team (Sir Geoffrey Howe, Leon Brittan and Peter Rees). But the lawyers are few compared to the numbers in Congress in Washington.

At the highest peak between the law and politics sits the Lord Chancellor who combines three quite separate functions. As the head of the legal profession and senior judge he selects judges, QCs, magistrates and tribunals, and presides (if he wishes) over hearings of the Law Lords. As Speaker of the House of Lords, he periodically sits on the Woolsack and (theoretically) maintains discipline among the peers. As a member of the cabinet he is virtually the Minister of Justice, and the government's chief legal adviser. He is the only man in Britain who combines the powers of the legislature, the judiciary and the executive: he helps to make the laws, to carry them out, and to interpret them. He thus thoroughly contradicts the theory of the separation of powers which was put forward by Montesquieu and followed by the American founding fathers. As the present Lord Chancellor described the critical difference:

> If America is a monarchy with an elected King, Britain has become a republic with a hereditary head of state. Parliament is supreme, and no judge can declare an Act of Parliament void, not even, strictly speaking, under the 'Common Market' Act. The British cabinet is not, as in the United States, a collection of random characters assembled by the elective William III from outside Congress. It is a committee of leading members of the legislature chosen from the ruling party, and though they are selected by the prime minister, they remain in parliament even if they resign and cease to serve. No Haldemans, Deans, Ehrlichmans or Mitchells can exist here.
>
> On the other hand, the importance of an independent judiciary is not less but all the greater when judges have to serve under an all-powerful parliament dominated by a party cabinet, and concentrating all the power, and more than all the powers, of the executive and legislature combined in one coherent complex.[14]

[14] Hailsham: *op cit*, p. 245.

The Lord Chancellor's post is the most ancient in government, five centuries older than the prime minister's, dating back to Augmundus who became Chancellor in 605; his seniority is reflected in his salary of £55,640 a year, more than the prime minister, and in his precedence at formal occasions, when he walks in front of the prime minister. He lives in a Victorian house inside the Palace of Westminster, adjoining the House of Lords.

Lord Chancellors, who usually reach the job in their sixties, are not likely to be bold reformers and neither of the two recent Labour incumbents, Lord Gardiner and Lord Elwyn-Jones, were keen on drastic changes. Lord Gardiner achieved his main ambition of setting up a law commission to restructure the law, but he was loth to make changes in the legal profession and spent much time sitting unnecessarily on his Woolsack. The present Lord Chancellor, Lord Hailsham, was appointed by Heath in 1970 and was reappointed after a five-year gap by Thatcher in 1979. He was soaked in the law: his father had been Lord Chancellor before him—the only father-son team since the Bacons in the sixteenth century—and his son Douglas is now a barrister and Tory MP. Hailsham was always conservatively-minded. As a scholar at Eton, he travelled without much difficulty up the old road—Christ Church, the bar, a seat in the House at the age of thirty-one. His sense of superiority seemed to make him blithely indifferent to other people's thoughts, and he could easily lose his temper. He was a rather unnerving chairman of his party, and when Macmillan suddenly resigned in October 1963 he wrecked his chances as a possible successor by his demagogic antics on television. He is now the last relic of Macmillan's government which he first joined (as First Lord of the Admiralty) in 1956.

'My fundamental philosophy,' Hailsham explained when he first reached the Woolsack, 'is very akin to Lord Melbourne's—if it works, leave it alone. But sometimes a stage comes when things cannot be left alone any longer. Very often when that stage is reached the most conservatively-minded person turns out to be the most radical in practice.' He did not in fact make very radical changes. He got bored on the Woolsack, and appointed Deputy Speakers to sit there. He refused to be 'a sort of interdepartmental housemaid, sweeping up the debris after some kind of mess or scandal had occurred'. And he did not, like Lord Gardiner, assume formal responsibility for the law as such. He concentrated 'on being as good a Chancellor as I knew how.' Hailsham, like Denning, sees the law in terms of his own philosophy and religion: 'I believe there is a golden thread which alone gives meaning to the political history of the West,' he wrote in 1975, 'from Marathon to Alamein, from Solon to Winston Churchill and after. This I chose to call the doctrine of liberty under the law.' Like Denning and Scarman he believes that the independence of judges will loom larger as the powers of bureaucracy and the pressures of politics increase. When in opposition—though not when in power—he has advocated, like Scarman, a bill of rights to protect the citizen. But other judges insist that the pragmatist tradition of case-law must be allowed to develop without codified principles.

For all their high concerns with human liberties, and their ultimate defences against dictatorship and autocracy, the pronouncements of judges and the intricacies of English case-law have little obvious relevance to the ordinary citizen who is surrounded by the agents of the administration—by the police, by taxmen, by petty civil servants or town hall officials. The Law Courts, with all their Victorian style and exorbitant costs, have been overshadowed by the massive expansion of the national bureaucracy, which has its own impersonal rules, its own day-to-day powers and sanctions, which show no signs of diminution.

10

Civil Service: The Unloved Establishment

The most difficult thing in government is the attempt to view policy as a considered whole at any one given time.

Lord Hailsham, 1975

The imbalance between the negative forces in Britain and the positive one lies at the centre of our problems; and the civil service is the most effective of the negative ones.

Shirley Williams, 1980

THE reform of the national bureaucracy seemed almost as important in the early sixties as educational reforms, as civil servants extended their influence through industry as well as government.

The creation of a professional civil service, alongside new schools and a new army, had been the crowning achievement of the earlier age of reform a century before. The historic Northcote-Trevelyan report of 1853 had found that the public service was 'attracting the unambitious, and the indolent and incapable' and recommended that it should become a professional group recruited from the universities by a competitive examination, like the Indian civil service which had already been reformed. It was to be a profession of amateurs, in the sense described by Lord Macaulay, of having been educated in studies 'which have no immediate connection with the business of any profession'. The reformed civil service, which was established in 1870, was the first great British meritocracy, providing the 'administrative class' of graduates largely recruited from Oxford and Cambridge. They came to be seen as a model bureaucracy, envied by many other countries, uncorrupt, unpolitical and dedicated.

But in the years after the Second World War the admiration began to turn sour, and Macaulay's amateur principle became more suspect as civil servants multiplied twenty-fold, controlling huge specialised areas, building roads, running hospitals, supervising industries and scientific research. By the early sixties, as Richard Wilding of the Treasury put it, 'the belief that civil service organisation was a gently ossified muddle staffed by intelligent, urbane, but managerially innocent mandarins became the accepted wisdom of the day . . .'[1]

It was in this public mood that Harold Wilson in 1966 appointed a committee headed by the vice-chancellor of Sussex University, Lord Fulton, to investigate the civil service, with a fanfare of publicity. Its members included dons and politicians as well as civil servants, and the prime minister's views were supposed to be represented by Dr Norman Hunt (later Lord Crowther-Hunt). Two years later the Fulton Committee reported, with every appearance of radical intentions. 'The home civil service today,' the report boldly began, 'is still fundamentally the product of the nineteenth-century philosophy of the Northcote-Trevelyan Report. The tasks it faces are those of the second half of the twentieth century. This is what we have found; it is what we seek to remedy.'

They insisted that the cult of the amateur or 'generalist' was 'obsolete at all levels and in all parts of the Service'. They complained that engineers, scientists and other specialists were excluded from administration, and that civil servants were graded into 1,400 separate classes . And they proposed drastic reforms: all these classes should be abolished and replaced by a single grading structure; specialists should have more responsibility; a new college should train civil servants and undertake research; and a new Civil Service Department, independent from the Treasury, should supervise the reforms and run the service.

Wilson seemed genuinely determined to push through these proposals, with the co-operation of the new Head of the Civil Service, Sir William Armstrong, who was already something of a legend in Whitehall: six years earlier he had taken over the Treasury to implement changes which he had himself proposed. Armstrong had a fine analytical intellect and strong democratic instincts—his parents were both officers in the Salvation Army. He kept an open mind, and enjoyed sharing his thoughts with outsiders including journalists like myself. Sir William was the obvious man to run the new Civil Service Department and reform Whitehall, and his grey but friendly figure soon personified a public service which was opening itself up. He identified himself with the Fulton Report with personal publicity on television and in the Press unprecedented for a civil servant, and he gave welcome indications that civil servants were taking a larger view. 'We are not in business on our own account: we are not a debating society, a private army or a social

[1] Richard Wilding: 'The Post-Fulton Programme', lecture, March 9, 1970.

club', he told a conference of civil servants in 1968. 'We are the instruments through which our fellow countrymen seek to exercise their collective will—for their benefit, and only incidentally for ours.'

But Armstrong had his own reservations about breaking down the barriers between specialists and administrators: 'I'm with you on getting rid of unnecessary obstacles from bottom to top,' he told Harold Wilson. 'But it isn't on for doctors, laywers or engineers to become administrators. The traffic would be all one way.'[2] He knew that the two biggest Whitehall unions—the Society of Civil and Public Servants and the Civil and Public Servants' Association—would doggedly defend the barriers. And the task of reform was soon put in the hands of a cluster of committees of civil servants, most of them clearly resistant to specialists, who knew very well how to wield their main weapon, delay. 'We kept the nuggets,' as one of them put it to me, 'and left the dross.' Norman Hunt, as the prime minister's nominee, was committed to seeing the reforms through, but he soon saw himself as 'an academic with little experience of Whitehall in-fighting . . . engaged in an unequal struggle against the arch-mandarin, Sir William Armstrong'.[3] By the time Labour went into opposition in 1970 Hunt was convinced that Armstrong had no intention of abolishing the classes.

Fulton had laid much stress on the need for a college, to broaden the education of civil servants, with an eye on the French Ecole Nationale d'Administration; and a college was duly set up in Sunningdale, to provide specialised courses for the administrators and also to teach specialists about administration. But from the beginning Sunningdale lacked academic authority: it gave rather superficial lectures, full of buzz-words from American business schools, and its first principal, Eugene Grebenik, was an outspoken demographer who was soon at loggerheads with the mandarins who wanted to control it. The ambitious plans for administrative research were soon dropped; Grebenik retired early; the post of principal was promptly down-graded; and the college settled down into a humdrum existence, providing courses firmly controlled from Whitehall.

Four years after Fulton, most of its recommendations had been quietly forgotten. There was now, it was true, an 'open structure' among the seven hundred people at the top, with the rank of under-secretary or higher, who could move more freely horizontally. But most specialists were still kept at arm's length; the top bureaucrats were still trained in 'studies which have no immediate connection

---

[2] Peter Kellner and Lord Crowther-Hunt: *The Civil Servants*, Macdonald and Jane, London, 1980, p. 63.
[3] *Ibid*, p. 75.

with the business of any profession'; and they retreated thankfully back into their obscurity. Scientific advisers soon found themselves down-graded and denied direct access to ministers (see chapter 14), while industrialists were still exasperated by the civil servants' lack of interest in manufacture and salesmanship. 'Almost without exception,' complained Sir Alan Cottrell, the former Chief Scientific Adviser, in 1975, 'none of the civil servants has been in the front line of making and selling things. They totally underestimate the difficulty of these activities, so that when it comes to a conflict between commercial considerations and social and political ones, the commercial ones almost always go to the wall in the last resort.'

The picture of Whitehall professionalism was still confused by the bureaucrats' habit of giving themselves titles which appeared to be specialised. The 'Auditor-General' for instance, *sounded* highly-qualified but in fact had no professional training in auditing; while Whitehall's attitude to accountants was still amateurish. The Fulton Report had called for a 'strong force of highly-qualified professional accountants', and by 1975 the government had actually appointed a senior chartered accountant, Kenneth Sharp, with the rank of second permanent secretary. But by 1979 there were still only 364 accountants in the Government Accountancy Service, compared to 309 when Fulton reported; and civil servants still conducted their internal audits without using either auditors or modern techniques of control. In 1976 Sharp was asked by the Conservative MP Nicholas Ridley: 'Are you saying that apart from the Ministry of Defence, internal audit has not hitherto been done by auditors?' Sharp replied: 'Yes, I am saying that.' 'Is that not rather extraordinary?' asked Ridley. 'Extraordinary it may be,' replied Sharp, 'but it is a fact.'

The failure of Fulton was in sharp contrast to the success of the drastic reforms which had brought the civil service into being a century earlier. But that was hardly surprising; for in the meantime it had become the strongest and closest-knit professional group in the country, protected both by its trade unions and by its permanent occupation of positions of power.

As for Sir William, his brilliant career ended in tragedy. In 1972 when Edward Heath as prime minister began navigating his difficult U-turn towards state intervention and an incomes policy, he brought in Sir William to be his chief adviser, effectively by-passing the cabinet. Armstrong soon began to show worrying signs of strain, including bouts of religious mania, culminating in a nervous breakdown. His colleagues and his deputy, Ian Bancroft, were discreetly loyal and Armstrong soon retired to become chairman of the Midland Bank, whose directors were unaware of his breakdown. ('I never really believed in all the journalists' talk of an Establishment,' one Treasury man recalled to me, 'until I discovered that cover-up.') Armstrong's rapid move to the private sector at the (then) huge salary of £34,000 a year raised angry questions about the impartiality of civil servants. When I talked to him the next year he was reflecting sadly about the difficulties of changing the bureaucracy and about the public resentment against him ('Why do they pick on me? Why don't they talk about the other salaries?') When he died in 1980 there was little public reference to his strains, but his case-history had become regarded by the civil service as an object-lesson in the dangers of excessive political exposure—like the case of Sir Horace Wilson forty years earlier, who had been used by his prime minister Neville Chamberlain to advise on almost everything including the dealings with Hitler. The moral seemed clear: civil servants should keep their heads below the parapet.

SIR IAN AND SIR ROBERT

Armstrong had been succeeded in 1974 by the former head of the Treasury, Sir Douglas Allen (later Lord Croham), who lacked his predecessor's reforming ambition. He retreated from close political involvement, rarely talked with his prime minister Harold Wilson and shunned personal publicity. The Civil Service Department, the centrepiece of Fulton, soon lost its independence from the Treasury from which it had sprung. 'It never really worked,' one permanent secretary assured me in 1978. 'Armstrong's authority came from the Treasury, and later from Heath. Now it's got no real power, and I'm glad not to be running it.' When Mrs Thatcher came to power in 1979 she soon made clear that she wanted to abolish it: its main purpose of achieving a more dynamic and specialised service had long ago faded.

When Allen retired in 1977 there were two obvious contenders to be Head of the Civil Service. The more interesting was Sir Frank Cooper, the shrewd permanent secretary at the Ministry of Defence (see chapter 17), who was full of iconoclastic ideas: so it came as no surprise when the other was chosen in accordance with Brook's law.[4] Sir Ian Bancroft's career had been a model of orthodox administration: the son of a Middlesborough schoolmaster, he went from Coatham school to Balliol, as an English scholar. In Whitehall he rose as private secretary to a succession of ministers, becoming expert in pay and personnel. He was a courteous and civilised

---

[4] Brook's law—formulated by the late Lord Normanbrook, the former head of the civil service—states that 'There are two reasons for making an appointment. Either there was nobody else; or there *was* somebody else'.

administrator, much respected by his colleagues. He accepted in theory the need for more openness and less mystification and welcomed the new select committees as an educational forum. But he had seen the dangers of the Armstrong syndrome, he disliked personal exposure, and his instinct was to withdraw behind Fortress Whitehall—all the more after the arrival of a combative new prime minister.

By the late seventies the civil servants were retreating back into their traditional posture of long-suffering and misunderstood scapegoats. As Lord Bridges, the wartime head of the service, had described them thirty years earlier: 'We shall continue to be grouped with mothers-in-law and Wigan pier as one of the recognised objects of ridicule.' It was the special mark of the mandarin (as Richard Wilding, the secretary of the Fulton Committee, said in March 1970) 'that he should feel that to be misunderstood by the ignorant is inevitable, and that to be traduced is our peculiar badge of honour'. But the civil servants were now much more deeply unpopular than in Bridges' day: they were more visibly powerful, and also more prosperous and more secure than many other elites. They had gained a decisive victory under Ted Heath when their pensions, with those of other public servants, were linked to the cost-of-living index and thus proof against inflation. (They had first asked for them to be linked to the national growth-rate, which was then running higher; but Heath refused and offered them index-linked instead—which turned out to be far more valuable.)

In the following inflationary years, as their pensions steadily grew, the civil servants enjoyed a privilege which few private companies could match. It was an expensive political blunder, which following governments—particularly Mrs Thatcher's—tried in vain to undo. The civil servants were well organised, and retained their privilege—but at the price of mounting unpopularity. Small businessmen who had been bankrupted by the recession, or executives made redundant, could now watch retired civil servants who had never risked a penny increasing their pension year after year. When civil servants went on strike for more pay in 1981, disrupting airports, government computers and even dole payments, Mrs Thatcher could win political points by standing firm against them, while their image of dedicated public service was even more battered.

Yet the senior civil servants still felt unfairly traduced and unrecognised, even more so under Thatcher's stern rule: 'We don't feel privileged,' one of them told me in 1981. 'We've been hit both in the pocket and in the teeth.' Thatcher kept Bancroft on a short leash and when BBC radio produced a lively series about Whitehall called *No, Minister* she only reluctantly allowed civil servants to take part.

When Sir Ian appeared before a select committee in July 1981 he complained sadly about his thankless profession: 'There's a feeling among many people in the civil service that they are pretty peripheral to the needs of the country and that we as civil servants are a pretty unnecessary piece of baggage . . . an ounce of appreciation is worth a pound of money.'

Certainly Mrs Thatcher had succeeded in demoralising the mandarins as never before. 'What worries me,' as one of them said 'is that when young civil servants have converse with their friends in other professions, they don't reveal what their job is. It's not because they dread the old jokes, like Wigan pier. These attacks have a real edge.' But their sense of grievance attracted little sympathy among other professions in an increasingly insecure world, who saw them as still more privileged. Had the bureaucrats now passed beyond the control of any politicians? Had the growth of the public sector reinforced still further an elite which was insulated from risk-taking and enterprise?

By 1981 the political strains at the top of Whitehall were much more apparent. Mrs Thatcher did not conceal her impatience with the gentle and unassertive Sir Ian Bancroft: she had her own ideas about reforming Whitehall, and she still wanted to abolish the Civil Service Department. She put much greater faith in the occupant of the other top job in Whitehall, the Secretary of the Cabinet, Sir Robert Armstrong—no relation of Sir William—whose masterful style made him indispensable. Sir Robert was a much more confident and sophisticated mandarin: unlike most civil servants he had come up through the royal route via Eton and Christ Church, Oxford (where his father was the much-admired organist). As an undergraduate he seemed insulated from the world's troubles, with a cherubic and innocent look, and he was fortified by his own love of music—the traditional hobby of Treasury men. In the Treasury he rose effortlessly, becoming the ideal private secretary—first to Maudling, then to Butler, then to Jenkins, and then to Heath as prime minister. Armstrong's succinct minutes, written in an elegant Italianate hand, became legendary; and his patient and tactful style could reassure his successive masters.

Armstrong was cautious and naturally conservative, but he had some commitments, notably to Europe: he was invaluable to Heath in negotiating Britain's entry, and Jean Monnet was grateful to him as 'a most exceptional private adviser'.[5] After Heath's departure he stayed on to work for Wilson until he moved to the Home Office, which he ran for two years without showing any great interest in its reform. He was the obvious man to take over as Secretary of the

[5] Monnet: *op cit,* p. 304.

Cabinet in 1979 when Sir John Hunt retired; and before long he had—in spite of his friendship for Heath—become the trusted confidant of Margaret Thatcher. As head of the Cabinet Office—separated by a green baize door from Ten Downing Street—he had his own influence over policy-making and the secret services, and his contacts with cabinet ministers gave him some independence. But the prime minister could not do without him: he was the Jeeves of Downing Street. He knew everyone and could pour oil on the most troubled waters, while his musical life—he was now secretary to Covent Garden and a close friend of its chairman Sir Claus Moser—gave him an extra detachment.

As Mrs Thatcher became more irritated with Sir Ian—still more after the civil servants had struck—so she became more dependent on Sir Robert, and determined to deal with Whitehall directly. There was no sign of intrigue between the two rival mandarins; but Sir Robert, the suave Old Etonian, was much more adaptable and unflappable than Sir Ian, the grammar-school scholar. The prime minister suspected many of the senior mandarins to be too corrupted by the 'wetness' of previous administrations to carry out her policies enthusiastically, and her special adviser, Sir Derek Rayner (see below), warned her that the Civil Service Department was getting in the way of strict financial controls. By late 1981, after she had sacked Lord Soames (the minister in charge of the civil service) she was ready to move; and in November she announced her body-blow. The Civil Service Department would be abolished, Sir Ian Bancroft would be retired a year early, and the department's functions would be shared between the Treasury and the Cabinet Office. Sir Robert Armstrong would become responsible, on top of everything else, for all senior appointments in the public service.

The last major relic of the Fulton reforms had now disappeared. As Secretary of the Cabinet and Head of the Home Civil Service Sir Robert now had the same kind of concentrated influence which Sir Norman Brook had under Macmillan twenty years earlier, but with extra accretions in the Cabinet Office, including the secret services. After all the effort and promises the Whitehall system had ended up where it started, but more centralised than ever.

WHITEHALL WARS

The separate departments in Whitehall in the meantime were each demonstrating their own effective resistance to reforms. Newcomers to Whitehall are often surprised to find civil servants in different departments viewing each other with such suspicion that they hardly seem to belong to the same nation. The Treasury talks about 'those MAFF people' with disdain; Transport and Environment are constantly at loggerheads; the Foreign Office is treated like a rather hostile foreign power. Their separateness is not new: before the reforms of 1870 ministers each appointed their own private staff with no common recruitment policy. But as they expanded and multiplied the departments grew further apart, and the need for co-ordination became greater. The process of 'interdepartmental consultation' became a complex diplomacy of its own, providing unlimited scope for rival representatives to 'do battle' across the committee tables on behalf of their departments, whose populations were the size of big towns. These were the nine biggest departments with their staff in January 1981:

Defence	232,770
Health and Social Security	98,292
Inland Revenue	76,240
Employment	52,122
Environment	45,374
Home Office	35,482
Customs	26,945
Agriculture, Fisheries and Food	13,218
Transport	13,129

Each has developed its own pervasive character, regardless of any minister who in theory might control it. The Ministry of Defence which is by far the biggest (see chapter 17) is too busy with its own internal warfare between military and civilians to look much further down Whitehall. The Ministry of Agriculture, Fisheries and Food (MAFF) has its own all-absorbing love-hate relationship with the National Farmers' Union (NFU) over in Knightsbridge. The Department of Health and Social Security, the chief instrument of the welfare state, has its own web of offices throughout the country, intricately interlocked with local government. The Departments of Trade and Industry, behind their forbidding buildings in Westminster, make their own alliances with corporation executives. Each department represents not only its minister's policy, but the interests of its clients, whether farmers, industrialists or local councils.

Where, in this web of conflicting interests, is there any national purpose? The cross-purposes between departments are still more evident in capitals abroad, where each of them may have its own representatives in the embassy—a Labour Attaché, a Commercial Attaché, a Military Attaché—each of whom may pursue a different policy. In Pretoria the trade representative has encouraged British exports while the diplomats are supposed to be discouraging them. Brussels offers the greatest scope of all for confusion, where rival departments from ten nations can wage their own intricate battles, trying to put together a Community policy.

The most distinctive and the most disliked of the departments is the Home Office, which has resisted would-be reforming Home Secretaries from R. A. Butler to Roy Jenkins to William Whitelaw. Its vast range of responsibilities include the police and prisoners, liquor licensing, censorship and obscenity, taxis and immigrants, and the only consistent theme is regulation. It is the Home Office which most directly affects the freedom of the individual, and successive scandals have revealed its continuing insensitivity to human rights; as when for instance women immigrants were found in 1979 to be subjected to 'virginity tests' to discover whether they had produced a child. And in protecting individuals from computerised information the Home Office lags far behind most other European countries, and no reformer has succeeded in changing its defensive and secretive habits.

Like many Whitehall failings the wars between departments can easily be blamed on their ministers. 'They don their departmental livery rather too readily,' as one permanent secretary explained, and their diaries confirm that impression. In cabinet a minister is preoccupied with defending his department's budget on which his prestige depends, and his permanent secretary will judge him accordingly. The Treasury now tries to insist that a department will gain prestige by cutting down costs; but the total budget remains the yardstick of the minister's success.

It is only prime ministers who see over the high walls, and successive premiers have tried to break them down. Macmillan, Wilson and Heath each did their bit to create 'monster ministries' in the prevailing fashion for bigness, to try to limit the rivalries; and in 1970 Ted Heath created two huge new departments—Environment, and Trade and Industry. They would resolve conflicts (a White Paper confidently explained) 'within the line of management rather than by interdepartmental compromise', and they would be 'more answerable to parliament and the community at large'.

It was not long before they showed opposite tendencies: they were less accountable to parliament, under a single cabinet minister who could conceal their differences, while the conflicts continued inside them. 'I reckon it took about five years really to get the benefits of the merger,' said one permanent secretary. 'By that time they were ready to be de-merged.' By the mid-seventies the fashion was already changing from bigness to smallness, and the giants looked much less attractive. Environment was split up again, Trade and Industry re-arranged. Transport re-emerged as a separate ministry and the old Ministry of Power reappeared as the Department of

Energy, like Jonah from inside the whale. It was back again to the early sixties.

While much-publicised reforms were ending in fiasco, more discreet methods were slowly chipping away at the Whitehall granite. When Ted Heath was preparing for power in 1968 he asked the heads of thirty corporations to dinner and invited them to propose senior executives who could move into government. When he came to power two years later Heath brought some businessmen in, not with great success: some had been recommended as a means of getting rid of them, others lacked the analytical skill to adjust. But one man had a lasting effect, and his story provides some interesting lessons.

Derek Rayner had been put forward by Marks and Spencer, the legendary shopkeepers (see chapter 23) who had always rigorously analysed the costs and standards of their thousands of suppliers. He was a rather boyish-looking bachelor in his late forties, imbued with his firm's systematic management methods. Arriving in Whitehall he soon took a patient and humorous view of the natives, like an anthropologist visiting a foreign tribe; he found he could wheedle civil servants on to his side, and he only occasionally turned to temper. He began in the Ministry of Defence, reporting on how to cut down extravagant weapons procurement, and he was then asked—with the blessing of the civil servants—to stay on to implement his report. When the Labour government returned he went back to Marks and Spencer but Mrs Thatcher brought him back to Whitehall in 1979 as Sir Derek, her special agent for reducing waste and inefficiency, with her full personal support. If Rayner could not tackle the civil service, she thought, no one could. But he kept on his job at Marks and Spencer in Baker Street, half time.

Rayner was very sceptical of formal reforms such as Fulton's, and he regarded the Civil Service Department as an obstacle. What he wanted was to make Whitehall more interested in management and costs, and he soon observed that the mandarins who were running the nation's biggest organisation were far more interested in writing minutes on policy questions—which was how they got promoted— than in the workaday problems of management. It was part of the old amateur principle, reinforced by a classical education, that policy problems should be regarded, like analysing Greek verse, as being abstracted from mere administration. Rayner believed that efficiency could and should be measured. He insisted on getting outside the charmed half-mile of Whitehall which held the keys to promotion, to look at the 'great battalions' of civil servants in the provinces.

He concentrated on getting the jobs better done; he reckoned that three billion out of the eight billion a year spent by the civil service consisted of essential services, from paying benefits to keeping light-houses, which could not be cut, but which could be done more efficiently. He always asked the familiar business questions—'What have you saved, simplified, reformed?'—and he soon realised that many provincial offices were so bogged down in new tasks that they had no time to think about easing their burdens. He knew he must work inside the system, gaining the support of the permanent sec-retaries and motivating the younger civil servants; and he soon intro-duced a system of scrutinies, to be completed in sixty working days, which used teams of young civil servants to investigate cost savings inside each department, from pension payments to tax forms.

Rayner's trump card was the prime minister's personal support, which he used to give prestige to his teams. In two years 400 young civil servants took part in his scrutinies, whom Mrs Thatcher recog-nised with special parties in Downing Street. Rayner became more confident and outspoken, and by July 1981, when he gave evidence to MPs, he was insisting that promising young civil servants should be promoted more rapidly, with a 'model succession policy' to provide proper qualifications at the top. 'There must be rewards for positive actions and change in Whitehall,' he told me. 'The path to promotion must go beyond Whitehall, to people who show that they can do things better. There should be far more able young civil servants running local offices in the provinces.'

It remains to be seen how far Rayner's techniques and incentives will survive his departure (he is now vice-chairman of Marks and Spencer, and expected to become chairman). But there is little doubt that one resolute innovator has achieved more reform in Whitehall than all the much-proclaimed plans of Fulton and William Arm-strong. Several morals might perhaps be drawn: that effective reforms can only be made from inside the bureaucracies; that they must be supported by a prime minister; and that they are more likely to be achieved by someone who prefers (in Monnet's phrase) to do something, rather than be someone.

Rayner's achievements, though remarkable, were only a drop in the Whitehall ocean. In April 1982 the select committee of MPs chaired by Edward du Cann produced a report on civil service efficiency which sounded very familiar. 'There is no clear orienta-tion,' it said, 'towards the achievement of effectiveness and efficiency at the higher levels or in government generally . . . We suspect that the amount of money spent has been far more important to the Treasury than how effectively it has been spent.' The senior ranks in

Whitehall, said the MPs, should be opened up to specialists including accountants and economists; the internal auditors were much more interested in checking the regularity of payments than in getting value for money. But the committee blamed the politicians at least as much as the civil servants: 'Ministers should realise that ability to manage their departments is as important to the country as their performance on the floor of either House or in committee.'[6] The basic reason for the inefficiency in Whitehall was much as it had been two decades earlier: neither ministers nor civil servants had the will to cut down the superstructure on which their own prestige rested.

PERMANENT SECRETARIES

The chief nursery of the senior civil service remains Oxbridge as was the case a century ago. The top public schools have long ago ceased to be dominant and the nine 'Clarendon Schools' which in 1950 provided a third of the permanent secretaries, in 1981 provided only one in eight. But Oxford and Cambridge still provide the high road to selection and promotion. The more prestigious the department—so exquisite is Whitehall's class-consciousness—the more dominant is Oxbridge, which in 1977 provided 86 per cent of the senior officials (deputy secretary and above) in the Foreign Office; 77 per cent in the Treasury, 62 per cent in the Department of Employment, and 60 per cent in Energy.[7]

The advantages of Oxbridge emerge more strongly at each stage of advancement. Over the last twenty years other universities have protested about discrimination, and their proportion of senior recruits has slowly risen; but in the competition for administrative trainees in 1980 the Oxbridge candidates were still far more successful, with an 18 per cent success rate compared to only 3 per cent among graduates from other universities and polytechnics.[8] The 'fast movers' who are quickly promoted to under-secretary are more likely to come from Oxford. 'The only educational factor associated with career success,' said a study by the Civil Service Department in 1977, 'is attendance at Oxford.' At the very top of the tree (see table on page 178) all but one of the eighteen permanent secretaries in the biggest departments went to Oxford, Cambridge or Edinburgh. The Secretary of the Cabinet and one of the three Treasury knights both went to Eton and Christ Church, Oxford.

An ambitious administrative trainee, recruited from university,

[6] 3rd Report from the Treasury and Civil Service Committee, Session 1981–82.
[7] See Kellner and Crowther-Hunt: *op cit*, p. 193.
[8] Civil Service Commission Annual Report, 1980.

climbs up the well-defined rungs of the ladder with mock-humble titles which seem designed to confuse the outsider:

> Administrative Trainee
> Higher Executive Officer
> Principal
> Assistant Secretary
> Under-Secretary
> Deputy Secretary
> Permanent Secretary

It is this steady procession of graduates, crossing and re-crossing each other's paths in their self-enclosed London bureaucracy, which still determines the corporate character of Whitehall. Since the Fulton Report some of the 'executive officers' from the humbler ranks have reached the magic ladder as administrative trainees, but many fewer than Fulton had hoped. 'A decade after Fulton two worlds remain within the Administrative Group: the world of policy-makers, whose promotion is rapid and who work mainly in London; and the world of the clerical and executive staffs, whose promotion is usually slow, and whose managerial work is scattered round Britain.' [9] This divide, fortified by class differences, exacerbates the distinction between policy and management which so concerns Sir Derek Rayner.

Like most bureaucracies the senior civil service is a pyramid, but with a kink in the middle, at the stage of assistant secretary, where competition gets suddenly tougher and failure is clearly defined. Those who are not promoted do not leave the service, like army officers, but remain within it. Those who want promotion pay their own price in terms of strain and conformity. 'It's tragic to watch,' one ex-minister lamented. 'The young principals are some of the cleverest and most open-minded people you could imagine; then you see them worrying about promotion, not wanting to blot their copybooks, looking over their shoulders, knowing that if they're thought to be controversial, they won't be promoted. They become part of the system.'

In the classic route to the top the promising civil servant first shows his real skills as a private secretary to a minister. In the intimacy and camaraderie of the private office he can see at close quarters how power is really exercised, sharing the confidence of politicians and observing all the ironies and shortcomings that lie between policies and their execution. And here, very often, he stiffens his ambition to climb to the top rung of permanent secretary. The seven hundred civil servants with the rank of under-secretary or

[9] Kellner and Crowther-Hunt: *op cit*, p. 140.

above—the 'open structure' since the Fulton reforms—inhabit the
area with real political influence. And a permanent secretary is at the
heart of the Whitehall nexus, closely in touch with his colleagues in
other departments. Theoretically he is the servant of his minister;
but his promotion and prestige depend heavily on the Head of the
Civil Service, and the minister may find it difficult to get rid of him.
He is much more closely in touch with other permanent secretaries
than the minister is with other ministers. The characters of
permanent secretaries have become the subject of growing curiosity,
all the more since so many people outside Whitehall now depend on
their favours, decisions or patronage. 'Mandarin is the right name
for them,' remarked one businessman who moves widely in
Whitehall. 'They've got the most impassive faces. But behind them
they're tremendously emotional—they remind me of lady dons.
They're always sulking or taking offence.' But the mandarin style
and the sceptical features, the assumption of objectivity based on
deep familiarity with all the facts, can still easily demoralise most
outsiders.

The balance of status between a minister and a permanent secretary has noticeably shifted. 'There's much less caste difference,' R.
A. Butler told me in 1961. 'In the old days it used to be thought that
the minister was chosen by God, and the permanent secretary was
just an official.' But now the caste difference seems almost the other
way round, as the permanent secretaries accumulate perks, index-
linked pensions and a lucrative job on retirement, while the minister
might find himself without a job or even a seat the next year.

These were the senior permanent secretaries in charge of the
biggest departments, including the top four civil servants in the
Treasury, in mid-1981, with their educational backgrounds (twenty
years ago, two of the permanent secretaries were women: today none
are):

NAME	DEPARTMENT	SCHOOL	UNIVERSITY
Sir Robert Armstrong	Cabinet Office	Eton	Christ Church, Oxford
Sir Ian Bancroft	Civil Service Department	Coatham, Redcar	Balliol, Oxford
Sir Douglas Wass	Treasury	Nottingham High	St John's, Cambridge
Sir Anthony Rawlinson	Treasury	Eton	Christ Church, Oxford
Sir Kenneth Couzens	Treasury	Portsmouth GS	Gonville and Caius Cambridge
W. S. Ryrie	Treasury	Mount Hermon, Darjeeling, Heriots	Edinburgh

NAME	DEPARTMENT	SCHOOL	UNIVERSITY
Sir Frank Cooper	Defence	Manchester GS	Pembroke, Oxford
Sir Kenneth Stowe	Health & Social Security	Dagenham GS	Exeter, Oxford
Sir Lawrence Airey	Inland Revenue	RGS Newcastle	Peterhouse, Cambridge
Sir James Hamilton	Education & Science	Penicuik	Edinburgh
Sir Kenneth Barnes	Employment	Accrington GS	Balliol, Oxford
Sir Donald Maitland	Energy	George Watson's College	Edinburgh
Sir Kenneth Clucas	Trade	Kingswood	Emmanuel, Cambridge
Sir Peter Carey	Industry	Portsmouth GS	Oriel, Oxford
Sir Brian Cubbon	Home Office	Bury GS	Trinity, Cambridge
Sir Douglas Lovelock	Customs & Excise	The Bec	—
Sir Brian Hayes	Agriculture, Fisheries & Food	Norwich	Corpus Christi, Cambridge
Sir Peter Baldwin	Transport	City of London	Corpus Christi, Oxford

The relationship between a minister and his permanent secretary has always been fascinating as a meeting of opposites: the extrovert and the introvert, the talker and the thinker, the individual politician committed to election promises, coming up against harsh realities: 'Facts that seem to live in the office' (as Bagehot described them) 'so teasing and unceasing they are.' Every top job, it has been said, needs two people: one who *looks* right, and another who *is* right, who works behind the scenes. Politicians have enjoyed romanticising it: 'The relations between a minister and his secretary,' Disraeli wrote in *Endymion*: 'are, or at least should be, among the finest that can subsist between two individuals. Except the married state, there is none in which so great a confidence is involved, in which more forbearance ought to be exercised, or more sympathy ought to exist.'

But it was never quite like that, and the roles have often become confused, as they were when Richard Crossman, as Minister of Housing in 1964, encountered the formidable Dame Evelyn Sharp (the relationship which inspired the television series *Yes, Minister*). Crossman, who was almost totally ignorant about housing, felt like 'someone in a padded cell' and then 'like somebody floating on the most comfortable support'; and constantly suspected 'the Dame' of crushing all new ideas. The Dame, adept at drafting minutes and organising Whitehall support, could never achieve a sensible relationship with her minister. 'He was damned if he was going to rely on advice from us,' she recalled. 'He wanted to be a bull in a china shop . . . It was only later on that I came to realise that underneath he was actually a diffident man. Perhaps that was why he shouted so loud. I think he wanted to be loved. But I never saw anyone go about being loved in the way he did.' [10] It was the opposite of Disraeli's ideal.

The senior civil servants know how to flatter a minister, swamp him with papers, isolate him and engage the apparatus of inter-departmental consultation to frustrate him. The minister's private office is designed to make him feel important, smoothing his professional and private life, ensuring that he will always have a car and chauffeur, a draft for his next speech, answers to questions, and appointments stretching months ahead. Many ministers prefer the accoutrements of power to the exercise of it, and civil servants are as expert as courtiers in the trappings. Yet a minister who can be deflected by flattery can only blame himself.

The permanent secretaries have become a convenient scapegoat for the politicians' failure to make radical reforms—particularly the Labour left, who see them as the high priests of consensus: 'This central theme of consensus or Whitehall policies which have been pursued by all parties for the last twenty years or so' (complained Tony Benn) 'have been accompanied by a steady decline in Britain's fortunes which has now accelerated into a near catastrophic decline of our industrial base.' But the civil servants argue that the swings between opposite policies have been the real causes of disaster; and that only consistent long-term policies can achieve industrial recovery. Even to build a motorway will take twelve to fourteen years between conception and completion, while governments and economic policies come and go. To plan a nuclear power station, or to electrify a railway will take two decades. 'The adversary system isn't efficient,' one permanent secretary insisted, 'and it's not very creditable. And it's got much worse since party manifestos have been written in indelible ink.' 'It is precisely those areas which have long lead-times, such as industrial investment and scientific research' (said Shirley Williams in reply to Benn's complaint) 'that have suffered most from U-turns and chopped and changed policies.' [11]

[10] See Crossman's account in *The Diaries of a Cabinet Minister*, vol I, and Dame Evelyn's reply in the *Sunday Times*.

[11] 'The Decision-Makers': lecture by Shirley Williams to the Royal Institute of Public Administration, February 11, 1980.

THE NEW ESTABLISHMENT?

It is when they leave Whitehall that senior civil servants show the full extent of their influence, moving into the supposedly autonomous public bodies—whether the British Council, the Arts Council, the Ombudsman's office, the Mersey Docks or the Nature Conservancy Council. Whitehall keeps its own book of the 'Great and the Good' full of names of outsiders who might be suitable for public appointments, for which any citizen can now recommend himself. But somehow the greatest and the best usually turn out to be the civil servants themselves. However diverse the activities of public bodies, from bird-watching to teaching foreign languages to investigating complaints against civil servants, they tend to end up with house-trained mandarins who know how government works, how to lobby for money and avoid making waves.

But their most spectacular migration has been into private industry, which has gathered speed over two decades. In the early sixties there was only a trickle, when Sir Leslie Rowan left the Treasury to take over Vickers; Sir Edward Playfair left Defence for International Computers; Sir Richard Powell left Trade for Albright and Wilson. But the trickle soon turned into a stream and after the Head of the Civil Service himself, Sir William Armstrong, became chairman of the Midland Bank the floodgates were open.

Most senior permanent secretaries now expect a clutch of new jobs after they retire at sixty. Lord Roll from the Treasury is now chairman of Warburg's bank and director of *The Times* and the Bank of England, among others. Lord Hunt, the former secretary of the cabinet, is now London chairman of the Banque Nationale de Paris and director of IBM, Unilever and the Pru. Lord Greenhill from the Foreign Office, Sir Leo Pliatzky from the Treasury and Sir Antony Part from Industry compete with arrays of directorships. Many younger civil servants, liberated by new pension arrangements, were lured away in mid-career: Sir Alex Jarrett became managing director of Reed International, Alan Lord took over Dunlop, Stanley Wright and Brian Hudson joined respectively Lazards and the Nordic Bank. Big companies and banks began to feel uneasy without an ex-civil servant on their board.

The life-cycle of an ambitious civil servant now looks very different. By his mid-fifties he will be searching anxiously for directorships with which to round off—or to crown—his career. 'You know I'll be sixty in two years,' one permanent secretary complained to me, 'and I haven't yet been offered a job' (he soon joined a nationalised corporation which he had recently been controlling, which raised at least two eyebrows). Retirement has a special terror for a civil servant accustomed to a heavy workload and a crowded diary, and a triumphant over-sixty could now boast: 'Never been busier in my life.'

This scramble for jobs, on top of index-linked pensions, did not endear the civil servants to others. Many jobs were obviously linked to previous activity: Sir Antony Part became a director of Lucas Aerospace only three months after leaving the Department of Industry; Sir Frederick Kearns left the Ministry of Agriculture, after a blazing row with his minister, to join the National Farmers' Union which depended on the ministry's favours; Angus Beckett, who had been controlling oil companies in the North Sea, became consultant to Texan oil companies. MPs complained that all the gamekeepers were turning into poachers, that the civil service was now in pawn to international capitalism. This English corruption, Lord Balogh suggested, was more effective than any crude passing of money; for a civil servant might now spend half his career pandering to industrialists, in the hope of a good job after retirement. But that was not how it seemed to them. 'It's our job to get close to industrialists,' one of them explained. 'If they ask us to join them, that's a sign of our success.' Had not Fulton himself called for more interchange between government and the private sector, as had happened during the Second World War?

The mandarins in business did not show spectacular commercial results. 'Whenever a civil servant becomes a chairman I sell my shares in the company,' said one banker. 'They never understand risks and hunches which is what business is about.' 'Look where it's got the companies,' said one current permanent secretary, listing the ailing corporations run by his former colleagues. 'It's only the civil servants who get out when they're young—like Weinstock—who do much good.' But many companies wanted their mandarins not for dynamic management but to bring them closer to the corridors of power ('old Tom can open a few doors'). The civil servants on the boards were the symbols of a private industry which was increasingly dependent on government favours.

There was similar movement in other Western countries, whether through the 'revolving door' between American government and industry, or through the *pantouflage* (changing slippers) of French civil servants into industry. But these foreign revolving doors moved people both in and out, bringing many businessmen into government—a rare phenomenon in Britain. And the dominance of the French *mandarinat* was based on the long history of state involvement in industry; it was an elite more thoroughly trained in economics or engineering and more fully responsible for its projects, with little interference from cabinets or parliament. The forceful planners among the French *inspecteurs des finances* made their counterparts in Whitehall look timid and amateurish.

The British mandarins were partly filling the vacuum left by the departure of the older 'Establishment'—that coterie of aristocrats, old soldiers or Tory politicians who were sprinkled through the boards in the fifties and sixties. As the old guard retired and died off, the company directors looked towards the men of Whitehall, with their aura of discreet power and omniscience; and the weaker industry became, the more reassuring they looked. Permanent secretaries who had long shrunk from publicity now cultivated the style of a new Establishment, appearing at bankers' banquets or oilmen's receptions as the representatives of their nation, the inner circle who really understood how it worked.

Do they measure up to it? In their semi-retirement they are financially secure and liberated from the political constraints about which they so often complained. They are in a position to take risks, to make bold statements and explain the real mistakes and problems of the country after a lifetime's experience. A few ex-civil servants—like Pliatzky or Croham—have sometimes spoken out. But the character-formation of most civil servants goes deep: they are trained to minimise risks, to avoid provocation and to achieve compromises. So it is not surprising that, when they are given their freedom, they have little to say.

11

The Treasury: Can the Centre Hold?

They give you the figures.

Lord Derby to Disraeli (when he 'demurred' at
becoming Chancellor of the Exchequer), 1852

Experience shows that there is a natural tendency for plans to go wrong.
Sir Leo Pliatzky, 1982

ALL the Whitehall departments depend on the single building at the
corner of Whitehall and Parliament Square which controls the
purse-strings. The Treasury has always been the hub of Whitehall,
and around its circular centre, capped with a dome of stained glass,
all the rest must revolve. The Treasury officials who move through
its shabby high-ceilinged corridors have been the scapegoats of each
economic crisis, the butt of each opposition, sitting it out with their
collegiate loyalty and quiet superiority. But the Treasury's shortcomings always raise the questions: must Britain really have such
centralised control? And can any political masters impose their will
on this intricate machine?

Many rival institutions have tried to diminish its power. In 1964
Harold Wilson set up the Department of Economic Affairs (DEA),
with George Brown as its master, to supervise the economy and the
national plan: but its life was short and unfulfilled, and the Treasury
took back its functions in 1969. The management side of the Treasury was hived off into the Civil Service Department in 1968 (see last
chapter), but it never achieved an independent power: its influence
waned and after fourteen years it was finally killed off by Mrs
Thatcher in 1981, with some of its tasks going back to the Treasury,
some to the Cabinet Office. The Think Tank or CPRS was set up by
Edward Heath inside the Cabinet Office to give the Prime Minister
more information independent of the Treasury, but its influence,
too, has declined. The Cabinet Office under Sir Robert Armstrong
still has some weapons against the Treasury; and since Britain

joined the European Community many Whitehall decisions have to be vetted by a Euro-secretariat. But the Treasury's monopoly of money is roughly back to the position of twenty years ago, while each new economic crisis emphasises its central control.

The fun of the Treasury, one of its ministers said, lies in being the spider in the middle of the web. It is a small spider watching large and numerous flies. Other Whitehall departments tend to see the Treasury everywhere: 'as the Arabs regard the Israelis'. But Treasury men feel like a small isolated state encircled by powerful adversaries. They love the language of war and games when they talk about Whitehall: surrounded, beleaguered, beseiged; they 'lay down the rules of the game and then blow the whistle'.

The Treasury is constantly providing money for the government through taxation, borrowing, or selling assets. But its wider influence lies in taking the 'Treasury view'. It prepares its elaborate forecasts, feeding economic quantities into 'the Treasury model', adding more and more equations to its vital statistics. And it sets the financial framework for the nation with the two great events of the Treasury's year: the public expenditure statement in the autumn, and the budget in the spring. In the summer the departments say what they will need; the Treasury tries to beat them down, and then presents the estimates for the cabinet to fight over. Then the statement is published, and for the next six months the Treasury works out how to pay for it. The Treasury looks after taxation and expenditure under one roof, and its officials are constantly aware of their colleagues' worries, so that an under-secretary on the revenue side by walking down the corridor can get a run-down of what the nationalised industries are spending.

The Treasury always has to see Britain's economy as a whole. At the top of the tree the permanent secretary and the highest officials meet in the Policy Co-ordinating Committee, to pull together the threads, and to forge—at least in theory—a gleaming Treasury View. Sometimes they cannot agree; in 1979 two Second Permanent Secretaries resigned after arguments in the PCC. But the PCC is usually the instrument for silencing dissident voices, and normally the Treasury presents a united front. There is always a Treasury ethos: Saying No.

PUBLIC SPENDING

The most appalling task of the Treasury men has been to comprehend and control public spending, which has provided successive pitfalls and traps. They always have to base their calculations of future spending on some picture of how the whole economy is behaving; but the forecasting side is always under attack. ('I want to do for forecasters,' Denis Healey once said, 'what the Boston Strangler did for door-to-door salesmen.') The Treasury forecasters worry that their predictions may be self-fulfilling as soon as they are published; if a government publicly admits that it thinks wages will rise by 12 per cent, they probably will. So the Treasury has to use forecasts whose assumptions were made in bad faith, because they dreaded the public reaction to their real assumptions.

The Treasury tried to tighten its control through its new cash limits, which Denis Healey introduced when he had to make his heavy cuts in 1976: each department had to account for any extra spending above its allocation, which must come from a limited fund, not from the bottomless pit of general revenue. But the cash limits proved to be one of the worst bones of contention between the Labour government and the TUC. 'They simply refused to accept that cash limits were sensible,' said Joel Barnett, 'either in socialist terms, in planning the best use of resources, or in seeking to fit expenditure to the priorities originally agreed.'

In the end the Treasury has no statutory power over spending departments, and much less real control than for instance in France: the Chancellor cannot bully departments like a French finance minister, because the cabinet can always subvert his neat calculations. Treasury officials try to work out agreements with the departments, but they remain under the control of cabinet. With no defined powers, the Treasury officials have to use all their guile, in a succession of Whitehall games: the skill lies in appearing to know as much about the department as its finance officer. They do not have the resources to tell a department how to run itself, and they only blow the whistle when it steps over the line.

At the head of the team controlling expenditure is the Chief Secretary to the Treasury, the unloved minister who plays the role of Oddjob (as Denis Healey told Joel Barnett) to the Chancellor's Dr No. He knows that the reputation of each spending minister depends on what he can get out of the Treasury, and that politicians who in theory are most opposed to public expenditure turn into big spenders in expensive departments (even Mrs Thatcher, when she was Minister for Education in 1971, boasted that she had achieved 'the biggest ever development programme for further education and polytechnics'). The Chief Secretary has to dissuade each spending minister, and what he cuts will depend partly on his government's priorities, but also on each man's political clout, and on doing a deal: 'You can have your twenty million if you support me in cutting X's and Y's budgets.' But in a major dispute he must have the support of the prime minister and the Chancellor; and that Trinity is hardly ever over-ridden.

Most politicians who have been through the allocation of public expenditure have been shocked by the arbitrary decisions. 'It is a vast book-keeping exercise,' says Bill Rodgers, the former cabinet minister, 'marked by horse-trading and ad hocery of alarming proportions . . . The real need is to seek to determine priorities for social policy long before the Public Expenditure Review begins.'[1] Joel Barnett, who was Chief Secretary for five years till 1979, has described the kind of pressures and lobbying which lay behind the decisions on spending, not least from the TUC.[2] In the final bargaining considerations of how the money is spent and what benefits it will produce have long ago been lost sight of: it is a contest between departments, personalities and pressures, where the size of the sums are the only yardsticks of victory or defeat. And the figures themselves are constantly suspect, as they acquire their political content. 'I thought I had done a fair amount of juggling with figures as an accountant,' wrote Barnett, 'but when it came to the sort of sophisticated "managing" and "fudging" I learnt as Chief Secretary, I realised I had been a babe in arms by comparison.'[3]

The complexities of taxation, too, are always liable to produce the opposite effects from what politicians intended, as simple rhetoric is translated into complex reality. When two left-wing Labour MPs, Jeff Rooker and Audrey Wise, put through an amendment to the Finance Bill in 1977 to raise the thresholds for paying income tax in line with inflation, they intended to help the poor and to reduce inequality. But the Rooker–Wise amendment, which indexed all tax-brackets, turned out to help the rich much more than the poor, so that in two years under Labour the gap actually widened, with the richest 10 per cent of the population earning 4.64 times as much as the poorest 10 per cent in 1978. And it was not until 1982 that the Tory Chancellor, by ignoring the Socialists' amendment, slightly narrowed the gap.[4]

Twenty years of trying to control public spending embraced many epics and disasters. In 1961 Sir Edwin Plowden (later Lord Plowden) introduced an elaborate new system for planning five years ahead, which assessed future spending not on a cash basis, but in 'volume terms' compensating for rising costs, which came to be called 'funny money'. But by 1975, as inflation gathered pace, public spending was visibly out of control; and the Expenditure Committee

[1] Rodgers: *op cit*, p. 128.
[2] Barnett: *op cit*, p. 62 ff.
[3] *Ibid*, pp. 21–2.
[4] See the *Economist*, February 20, 1982.

of the House of Commons, advised by the influential economist Wynne Godley, revealed that the Treasury had spent five billion pounds more (allowing for price changes) than they had planned three years earlier. By the following year the Treasury was submerged in a new crisis with spending still escalating and the pound sinking rapidly, so that by November 1975 Denis Healey had to apply to the International Monetary Fund for a loan of $3.9 billion. The harsh discipline of the IMF dictated new cuts in Labour's public spending which created a major cabinet crisis. But the Treasury's predictions, it turned out, were once again wrong: this time the spending was about £2¼ billion *less* than expected.[5] After all the anguish and soul-searching, as Denis Healey wryly reflected, they need not have borrowed from the IMF in the first place. By 1981 the Treasury had turned away from 'funny money', twenty years after Plowden had introduced it, back to controlling spending on the old-fashioned cash basis.

The Treasury talk about all the different claims on the nation—a gas pipeline here, a hospital there—conveys all the excitement of being at the centre of the web, knowing what others cannot know. But many politicians passing through the Treasury have felt the absurdity of it—trying to control half the nation's spending through numbers which have become so abstracted and unreliable. The more fallible the Treasury model, the more haphazard the cabinet's bargains, the more worrying they look. For a country like France, accustomed to decisive direction and a weak cabinet, the massive central distribution of funds might be viable. But the British cabinet ensures that decisions are never so rational; and as Britain becomes still more centralised—despite all the politicians' promises—the concentration of power in this central financial citadel looks still more worrying.

CHANCELLORS AND POLICIES

'Whichever party is in office,' said Harold Wilson in opposition, 'the Treasury is in power.' How far can any group of politicians, with only a few years in office, impose their will on this intricate machine? The frontiers of economic policy-making are always inscrutable. No individuals can decide policy, for the economic and political winds are constantly blowing them off course—as every government learns to its cost when it is faced with carrying out its manifesto promises. Economic policy is made in varying degrees by the prime minister, the Chancellor, the Cabinet Economic Committee, Treasury officials, economic advisers, wives, journalists, academics and (if

[5] See Leo Pliatzky: *Getting and Spending*, Blackwell, London, 1982, p. 159.

Labour is in power) the TUC. But the Chancellor of the Exchequer must still take the chief responsibility; and it is he who personifies the political will of his government.

The relationships of Chancellors, both with their prime ministers and the Treasury, have always fluctuated. Roy Jenkins, the Chancellor from 1967 to 1970, was largely left alone by Harold Wilson to face the sterling crisis of the late sixties; with the moral and financial support of the IMF he cut spending and pushed the government into a balance of payments surplus by £½ billion. Anthony Barber, who was Chancellor from 1970 to 1974, was much influenced by Ted Heath; the Treasury viewed his initial deflationary policy with suspicion, and when he made his U-turn they joined all too eagerly in the boom. Denis Healey came into the Treasury in 1974 committed to free collective bargaining while his top officials, rattled by inflation, were politely suggesting some incomes policy: and it was his officials as well as the IMF who persuaded Healey to press the cabinet to deflate in 1976. Healey was frequently sceptical of Treasury views, but he always listened to them, and they remember wistfully his pugnacious delight in arguments. His bullying tactics, usually backed up by Callaghan, forced through spending cuts which actually undershot the estimates.

When Mrs Thatcher chose Sir Geoffrey Howe as the Chancellor in 1979 she left no doubt that she saw herself (like Ted Heath) as the real boss of the Treasury. Howe was the quintessential barrister in politics, a scholar of Winchester with the kind of analytical, unimaginative mind for which the school was so famous. As a young Tory reformer he had a streak of idealism and became chairman of the radical Bow Group; but as he rose up he seemed prepared to defend any brief. His quiet speeches with their falling cadences were never very stirring, and he was easily bossed about by Mrs Thatcher ('Come on, Geoffrey') who saw economic and monetary controls as the key to her discipline. Privately he retained some radical views: he was worried about the segregation of public schools and wanted to work more closely with the unions. But installed at the Treasury with two convinced Thatcherites, Nigel Lawson and John Biffen, Howe could not afford to have serious doubts about her monetary policy, whatever the misgivings of Treasury officials and other cabinet ministers. He could be an obstinate arguer, but not with his prime minister.

The Conservatives were determined to navigate through the economic storms by the star of monetarism—a purer and brighter star than Healey ever followed. It was a remarkable change, as Sir Leo Pliatzky observed: 'In what was traditionally a party of practical men rather than theorists, which not many years earlier had in Sir

Alec Douglas-Home a prime minister reputed to do his arithmetic by the use of matchsticks, policy was now dictated by an abstruse doctrine on the money supply.'[6] The theory of monetarism had risen to prominence in Britain in the early seventies, when inflation was hitting new peaks. Keynesianism—which was primarily concerned with employment—had no answers, and the ratio of public expenditure to the Gross Domestic Product had risen from 50 per cent to 60 per cent in the three years to 1975, which prompted Roy Jenkins to warn that it endangered the 'plural society'.[7] The control of the economy through the money supply attracted the Tories as a mechanism which could alleviate inflation and other economic ailments through the invisible hand of the market; the government only needed to keep down the patient's temperature by maintaining a low and steady growth of monetary expansion. On this basis the Chancellor and prime minister worked out their 'medium-term financial strategy' and stuck to the theory despite growing scepticism from cabinet ministers. The strategy spectacularly failed to reach its targets, as public expenditure grew and monetary growth was still well above the planned 6–10 per cent.

Mrs Thatcher tried to blame both the Bank of England and the Treasury for trying to deflect her government's purpose. Certainly this pure monetarism was alien to the top Treasury officials, most of whom had been brought up in a Keynesian nursery, and believed in some kind of incomes policy—including the permanent head of the Treasury, Sir Douglas Wass, who had occupied his post since 1974. Wass was originally a scientific researcher for the navy, until he climbed up the Whitehall staircase, crossing and re-crossing his contemporary Sir Ian Bancroft (as Bancroft put it) like characters in Anthony Powell's novel-sequence *A Dance to the Music of Time*.[8] Reaching the top of the Treasury, Wass effectively dominated other officials, which encouraged the exodus of senior Treasury men in 1977. He worked relatively easily with Denis Healey, but he made clear in a lecture in 1978 that he would find difficulty in working with a staunchly monetarist government. When the Tories were elected there was much speculation about how Wass would get on.

But the Tory ministers had an effective technique against the Treasury men; they pretended they did not exist. For the first time in memory the politicians virtually ignored the views of the permanent secretary and the Policy Co-ordinating Committee. The Chancellor was surrounded by a team of five junior ministers, including the

---

[6] Pliatzky: *op cit*, p. 178.
[7] The Labour government soon reduced the percentage to 40 per cent by 1977–78 by the simple device of changing the definition of public expenditure. See Barnett, p. 80.
[8] Kellner and Crowther-Hunt: *op cit*, p. 116.

formidable Nigel Lawson, who was well-equipped to argue with officials about the complexities of City finance. They all met frequently together, often without Sir Douglas or any other official; they had little dialogue with officials, as earlier governments had, on broad questions of policy; they just left them to work out details, and to 'mind the store', while they took the major decisions without their knowledge or approval. Over the last twenty years no political team had thus imposed its policies against the advice of Treasury officials, or even of other Conservatives. The Select Committee on the Treasury, under the ambitious Edward du Cann (see chapter 2) began grilling Treasury officials and ministers in their upstairs room at Westminster, and produced uncomplimentary reports: they irritated officials and embarrassed Sir Geoffrey, but they did not visibly weaken the Treasury, and they drew ministers and officials closer together in a bond of solidarity against their persecution.

The Treasury ministers were also more sceptical of the Whitehall economists who had proliferated over the last twenty years. Since the very influential Chief Economic Adviser Robert Hall (now Lord Roberthall) left the Treasury in 1961 the post had become less important as other departments acquired their own teams of economists, and their individual influence had waxed and waned with political fashions; after the oil crisis of 1973, which no economist had predicted, their forecasts were even more suspect. But in 1980 Geoffrey Howe brought in a new Chief Economic Adviser, Terry Burns, a tousle-haired professor of only thirty-six who was already established as a bright young international monetarist at the London Business School, which had introduced computer forecasting into Britain, and shown the Treasury how to do it. Back in 1976, when the Labour government was reeling from inflation and the sterling crisis, the LBS had come up with an original package of monetarist proposals which fitted the kind of conditions that Washington and the IMF were demanding for a loan to bail Britain out; and Denis Healey turned to the LBS to give theoretical backing to the policies he was already pursuing. The influence of the LBS and of Burns now increased further under the Tories, and Terry Burns became probably the most influential policy-maker among the civil servants, and a crucial supporter of the government's medium-term financial strategy.

Mrs Thatcher herself was ambivalent about the Treasury. On one level she wanted to increase its power over other departments, and thought it had been too permissive about their spending. On another level she saw it as part of that wasteful public sector which was dragging down the economy. Many Treasury officials felt victimised by the Tory vilification of Whitehall: as one of them put it, 'We know that someone out there hates us.' When civil servants went on strike in 1981 most Treasury men remained loyal to the government, but many were aggrieved that they were being kept out of policy-making, and treated as innately untrustworthy public servants with suspect economic theories. The Thatcher government had imposed its will on the Treasury more effectively than any administration since the Second World War. But the centralised power of the Treasury building, equipped with the measuring-rods of monetarism, was now greater than ever.

NEDDY AND PLANNING

The Conservative members at the Treasury team were preoccupied with their economic strategy and controlling the money supply; and at first they were very little concerned with industrial strategy—believing it should be left to the laws of the market. Planning and government intervention, which had ebbed and flowed over two decades, was in full retreat.

The first surge of planning had begun under the Conservatives, when Harold Macmillan in 1961 had set up the National Economic Development Council (NEDC), known as Neddy. It was partly copied from the French *Commissariat au Plan*, which was then fashionable throughout Europe; but the British version had far fewer teeth, and was much more subject to the vagaries of politicians and democracy. Neddy was only designed to set general directions for the country's industrial future, with a tripartite membership from government, industry and trade unions, chaired by the Chancellor of the Exchequer. The Labour government in 1964 took planning much further, when George Brown at the new Department of Economic Affairs proclaimed his national plan; but the plan was hardly produced before the economic crisis of 1966 undermined it. Neddy still survived as the framework for 'voluntary planning', between the three sides; but when Ted Heath arrived in 1970 he largely ignored it until he made his U-turn in 1972, when he turned to Neddy as a convenient instrument for his own kind of intervention. The next Labour governments willingly used Neddy as a means of planning in concert with trade union leaders, but once again the economic storms wrecked most of the plans.

When Mrs Thatcher came to power she deliberately demoted Neddy, believing it was too influenced by cosy agreements between workers and management, an instrument of Labour's corporate state. Today Neddy is much less high-powered: 'It's full of mediocre people in employers' organisations,' as one of its members complained. 'It has no real institutional context for industry.' Yet it remains the only real meeting place between the three sides of the industrial triangle, and its Secretary-General, Geoffrey Chandler, a talkative enthusiast who was a loyal public relations man for Shell, has been determined to keep communications open. These were its members in late 1981:

Sir Geoffrey Howe	Chancellor of the Exchequer
Norman Tebbit	Secretary for Employment
John Biffen	Secretary for Industry and Trade
Nigel Lawson	Secretary for Energy
Sir John Greenborough	Newharthill Limited
Sir Alexander Jarratt	Reed International
Sir Jeremy Morse	Lloyds Bank
Sir Raymond Pennock	British Insulated Callender's Cables
Harold Whittall	Amalgamated Power Engineering
David Basnett	GMWU
Frank Chapple	EETPU
Geoffrey Drain	NALGO
Terence Duffy	AUEW
Moss Evans	TGWU
Len Murray	Trades Union Congress
Sir Richard O'Brien	Manpower Services Commission
Gordon Richardson	Bank of England
Sir Denis Rooke	British Gas Corporation
Michael Shanks	National Consumer Council
Geoffrey Chandler	Director-General

Neddy's first twenty years were hardly glorious, coinciding with Britain's declining industrial performance. But its difficulties always lay outside its conference, among the swerves of alternate government policies and the compromises of ministers. Politics were short, but planning was long; and any major scheme would outlive a single government. The revenues from North Sea oil, which might have boosted industrial investment, called for bolder government intervention; but Britain, like earlier spendthrift countries, was on the way towards using up her oil reserves with little to show for it.

The difficulties of planning and Treasury control always came back to the fundamental problem: how to mobilise an ancient and democratic nation into a sense of national direction and purpose. The French or Japanese systems which were so often invoked as models for Britain both rested on quite different democratic traditions; they had more co-ordinated banks and industrial groups, weaker unions and more unified national ambitions: their governments could be more decisive in abandoning old industries and channelling investment and credit towards new ones. The British were much more hampered by local and trade union pressures, and by all the proud old autonomous bodies. The bold plans and expectations inside the cabinet or the Treasury could all too easily become confused or frustrated when they reached the committees, the wrangles between rival interests, and the morass of local government.

12

Local Government and Regions: Decentralisation Defeated

The strength of free peoples lies in the municipality. Municipal institutions are to liberty what primary schools are to learning; they put it within reach of the people . . .

Alexis de Tocqueville

THE spiders' web of Whitehall was looking much less sensitive after all the switches of policy, the runaway spending, missing billions and breakdowns of control. The demands of the Treasury, and the powers of giant departments and nationalised boards, were drawing more power towards the centre; but local communities and regions each had different priorities and concerns—whether about their environment, their housing or their education—about which Whitehall could know little. Did the taxing and spending of distant communities have to be so closely controlled by Treasury systems which were so visibly fallible and incomprehensible?

Was the cumbersome machinery of the centralised nation-state, which had first grown up in an age of nationalism and wars, really suitable for regions in peacetime, with their own cultural identities and trading interests across frontiers? The international factors, including the European Community and multinational corporations, were already putting national capitals in a different perspective: the European nations looked too small for their own defence, technology or corporations; yet their centralised bureaucracies looked too big and too aloof to their scattered communities. Was a new pattern emerging, of a 'Europe of Regions', with old entities such as Provence, Bavaria or Wales reasserting themselves against the old nations?

DEVOLUTION

The most extreme challenge to London came from the original components of the United Kingdom which for a time threatened the unity of the nation; and the strange ebbs and flows of devolution revealed all the strains, but also the difficulties of assessing real popular feeling. The Westminster politicians were shocked that the idea of devolution ever got off the ground, for they had never taken regional frictions, except in Ireland, very seriously. But by the mid-sixties the resentments of Scotland and Wales were showing electoral successes in Westminster, while the violence in Northern Ireland was soon threatening to infect the mainland.

London governments had made small concessions to the regions' demands through the Scottish and Welsh Offices, with their own cabinet ministers and their own elegant buildings opposite each other in Whitehall, which were not answerable to any representative body, and were never politically animated. But the creeping centralisation of Whitehall and the welfare state aroused more resentment against distant decisions, and the entry into the European Community introduced a still more distant and incomprehensible centre of power.

Wales, which was first annexed in 1282, still had a prince and its own language—in spite of Henry VIII who banned its official use —and a survey in primary schools in 1978 showed that 63 per cent of pupils in Gwent could speak Welsh fluently. Welsh nationalism centred more on the revival of its culture than on political organisations: north and west Wales are the stronghold of the Welsh language, the Non-Conformist Church and the Liberal party; while in south Wales the immigration of Englishmen to work in the mines and steel works provided a solid working-class Labour element. Non-conformism found a strong voice in Westminster and even managed, through the Liberal party, to disestablish the Church of England; but since then its most evident political manifestations have been the sporadic Welsh referenda to decide whether pubs should open on Sundays (which Sabbatarians have increasingly lost). But Plaid Cymru, which had been set up as a cultural organisation in 1925, became a serious political force during the sixties, and by 1966 the candidate for Carmarthen, Gwynfor Evans, had won its first seat at Westminster.

The Scots were always less integrated than the Welsh. Although James I brought Scotland with him when he ascended the English throne in 1603, the two political systems were not joined until the Act of Union in 1707; and even then the Scottish educational and legal systems and the Church of Scotland were left carefully alone.

Scottish law, which was more firmly based on Roman law, helped to maintain the country's individuality, for any bills going through Westminster had to be specially adapted. The Labour party could not afford to offend Scotland which, being more working-class than England, was more solidly Labour. But while the economic fortunes of Wales were sinking with those of the mines and the steel works, the discovery of oil off the coast of Scotland in 1970 gave an impetus to northern economic life and self-confidence: Scotland, it seemed, need no longer be a poor relation of the prosperous south. Oil was the chief fuel for the Scottish Nationalist party, which won its first by-election with Winifred Ewing's spectacular victory in Hamilton in 1967, although she lost her seat three years later. By October 1974 the Scottish Nationalists were winning 30 per cent of Scottish votes, and returned eleven MPs.

The victories of Plaid Cymru and the SNP at last woke up Westminster to the discontent in the regions. To stall for time, in 1968 the Labour government set up a Royal Commission on the Constitution, first under Lord Crowther, then under a Scottish judge, Lord Kilbrandon, 'to consider . . . whether any changes are desirable . . . in present constitutional and economic relationships' between the parts of the United Kingdom. It took four years to report that it could not make up its mind. The majority of its members recommended some sort of regional 'devolution'—the word was becoming a very flexible catch-phrase—on the grounds that over-centralisation was deadening the political life of the regions. But they could not decide which parts should be devolved, how much, or in what ways: legislative, executive or administrative. They presented various options which were not much discussed and which were almost wholly ignored by the government. Like some other commissions it was not meant to achieve change, but to avert it.

The Conservative government had a chance to set up some sort of regional assemblies when it reorganised local government in 1972: instead it responded to the idea of devolution with apathy concealed by hypocrisy. But in 1974 an electoral phenomenon compelled the Labour government to swing reluctantly into action. In the February general election Labour was returned without an overall majority, while Plaid Cymru won two seats and the SNP won seven; and in the October election the SNP won four more and Plaid Cymru one more. Labour's tenuous hold now depended on the two nationalist parties: devolution was the price of their support, while their victories made it clear that they wanted something done. The union of political expediency and popular feeling eventually produced a sad child, the Scotland and Wales Bill, which had a stormy passage through the Commons, for the SNP made it stronger than the Labour government intended; and which was eventually defeated by a cross-vote.

When the SNP withdrew their co-operation, the shaky Labour government reintroduced the bill in two parts and in 1978 the Scotland Bill and the Wales Bill became law. But Labour had been forced by their dissenters to agree to a crucial concession which proved to be fatal: that the measures would only come into force if a minimum of 40 per cent of the population in each region agreed to the proposals in a referendum. The bills provided no broad constitutional revision as suggested by Kilbrandon. They offered almost nothing to Wales—a representative assembly without legislative powers, like a glorified borough council. They offered more to Scotland—an assembly which could legislate for health, education, local government, law and order. But neither assembly would have the power to raise money, which would be allocated by Westminster every four years.

What might these assemblies have achieved? They might have caused a new constitutional crisis as their representatives came up against their actual limitations; as Labour hotbeds they might have created endless headaches for Conservative governments; or they might have become political backwaters, just visible enough to grouse about, not powerful enough to be interesting. As it happened, they were consigned, like so much else, to the dustbin of the seventies. The Welsh proved conclusively that they were not interested: with a low turn-out only 12 per cent of the electorate voted yes. The Scottish turn-out was higher, and the yesses beat the noes by 33 per cent to 31 per cent (a percentage higher than had voted many governments into power): none the less they had missed 40 per cent by a wide margin. The two bills died a quiet death, unmourned in Westminster. And soon afterwards, in the general election of 1979, the SNP lost all but two of their members of parliament.

The word devolution, which had agitated and confused so many people over the last decade, suddenly disappeared again from the political vocabulary; and another British adventure returned to square one. The Tory government for the time being had no need of Scottish or Welsh votes, and only Northern Ireland remained as a huge question-mark over the unity of the kingdom.

LOCAL GOVERNMENT

But the broader resentment against the centre was still seething, not only in Scotland and Wales but in England itself. As the Conservatives began to cut down spending in the eighties a new crisis was brewing up between Whitehall and the local councils—which uneasily shared responsibility for so many day-to-day services, including schools, houses, buses and roads. Successive governments in their election manifestos had promised greater decentralisation, but had then increased their central powers. Like parents with teenage children they insisted that local councils should take more responsibility, until they tried to exercise it, when the government insisted: 'not like *that*'. Yet so long as the local governments were not given real responsibility, they were unlikely to behave responsibly.

Local councillors had long been regarded as second-class politicians, arousing indifference or contempt. Many Englishmen who can name the mayor of New York (who is directly elected) have never heard the name of their own local mayor, whom his fellow-councillors elect every year. The British mayors, with their associations with local trade and shops, are rarely seen in the same company as members of parliament, and the members of the Greater London Council, across the river at County Hall, feel thoroughly cut off from Westminster. Many senior French deputies in Paris, such as Mendès France from Louviers, or Gaston Deferre from Marseilles, have continued to be mayors of their home towns. But British MPs, though several of them have served in local government (such as Clement Attlee who was mayor of Stepney) usually break their ties with town halls when they arrive at Westminster.

Yet local government has longer roots than the national government: and the county courts in the Middle Ages, made up of freemen of the shire, had far-reaching powers. It was not until the Poor Law Act of 1834 and the Public Health Act of 1848 that the counties began to feel the impact of London, which increased with later social reforms. In the early twentieth century British local councils controlled huge and dynamic areas of spending, including not only houses, roads and police but water, gas, electricity and sometimes local trains and docks. Some mayors of the bigger cities, such as Joseph Chamberlain in Birmingham, were ambitious entrepreneurs, more like contemporary American mayors, who left a deep mark on their cities. But centralisation, government grants and nationalisation steadily diminished the scope and status of councillors. Westminster politicians preferred discussing distant colonies to the drains or schools on their doorstep, and public school boys preferred ruling the empire to the more humdrum government of their own natives.

Local councils are still responsible for a quarter of all public spending, but their powers to actually govern are strictly limited, caught up in a confused relationship with central government. No actual constitution describes their powers, which have developed in a typically British muddle. Unlike French local councils they have no powers independent of parliament—they can only carry out policies which have already been decided at a national level. If local councillors step outside their area they can be taken to court—and can be made to pay personally for unauthorised spending.

Over the years Westminster and Whitehall have increased their hold and their scrutiny, partly because they have contributed more of the local authorities' income, but also because both the main parties really *wanted* to control them more closely, to achieve their political goals. Labour was more concerned with social justice, as when they battled against local councils to introduce comprehensive schools. Conservatives were more concerned with cutting down waste and bureaucracy.

The relationship was obviously unsatisfactory and a succession of committees, commissions, and White Papers proposed different reorganisations. When the Labour party came into power in 1964 it showed little interest in local government, which had occupied only half a page in Anthony Crosland's *Future of Socialism*. Wilson and Crossman appointed a royal commission headed by that universal optimist of the sixties, Sir John Maud (later Lord Redcliffe-Maud), but they gave little thought to Maud's report in 1969. It was left to the Conservatives to push through the new Local Government Act of 1972, only partly based on Maud's report, which reorganised the whole of England and Wales except London (which had already been reorganised in 1963). It redrew the lines of 124 county and borough authorities and over a thousand district councils, and substituted fifty-three county councils with larger areas.

Many local traditionalists were appalled when ancient names such as Rutland and Cumberland were abolished, while new ones such as Cumbria, Avon and Cleveland appeared on the map; and many travellers have still not caught up with the fact that Lothian, for instance, includes Edinburgh. Six of the new councils were 'metropolitan', representing big cities and conurbations with dense populations. The chart on the facing page shows the six, together with London and the two biggest 'regions' in Scotland, followed by the tiers of other councils.

In keeping with the fashion politicians on both sides assumed that bigger units would be more efficient, and few predicted that they would create lumbering new bureaucracies with overlapping tiers which became still more remote from the ratepayers. Between 1961 and 1974 jobs in local government went up by 54 per cent, while the new bureaucrats were safeguarded by their expanding union, NALGO.

Most Westminster politicians remained happily ignorant of local government, and confused about the relationship. Many ministers of education, of housing, or of social services were surprised to discover

Greater London	6.9 million
Greater Manchester	2.6 million
West Midlands (Birmingham)	2.7 million
West Yorkshire (Wakefield)	2.0 million
Merseyside (Liverpool)	1.5 million
South Yorkshire (Barnsley)	1.3 million
Tyne & Wear (Newcastle)	1.2 million
Strathclyde (Glasgow)	2.4 million
Lothian (Edinburgh)	750,000

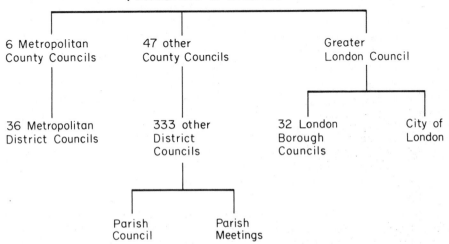

(ENGLAND & WALES)

themselves devoting much of their time arguing with local authorities who spent most of the money. When Richard Crossman, having already been in parliament for nineteen years, became Minister of Housing in 1964, he was astonished to discover that 'the ministry does no house-building at all. The people who build are either the local authorities or private-enterprise builders .. It's a ministry very remote from anything Harold suggested when we talked about organising a housing drive.' [1] Central government was allocating still bigger grants to local councils which were paid for by the taxpayer, topping up the councils' revenues from ratepayers, thus increasing the uncertainty about who held the real responsibility. So long as the economy was expanding, no one minded too much: but once Whitehall had to retrench, the relations with town halls moved towards a showdown.

[1] Crossman: *op cit*, vol 1, p. 43.

WHITEHALL V TOWN HALL

The bureaucracies of the enlarged counties and London boroughs were even harder to control than Whitehall departments. Far fewer voters participated in the local, as opposed to general, elections round the country, and many councils had huge class-based majorities—such as the Tories in Kensington and Chelsea, or Labour in Tower Hamlets—which were unlikely to be deposed. Many London councils commemorated their greater size with palatial town halls, to the fury of ratepayers. Kensington put up a vast fortress designed by Sir Basil Spence, with a sumptuous council chamber for their monthly meetings. Southwark, one of the poorest boroughs, planned a civic complex to cost £70 million. Camden, enriched by its high commercial rates from Holborn and Covent Garden, became the most notorious of all the big spenders.

By the mid-seventies the local spending spree was exasperating central governments trying to fight inflation. Anthony Crosland, the Labour Minister for the Environment, cut back the support for rates and announced, 'the party's over'. But councillors did not agree and they could borrow independently to keep up their spending. By 1974, they were causing so many problems that the Labour government appointed another committee under Frank Layfield, a barrister who was an expert on local planning, to report on local finances.

The Treasury was now paying for no less than 65.5 per cent of local councillors' spending and wanted to monitor it to prevent them disrupting its careful economic strategy. But the local authorities complained to Layfield that the more they depended on central government, the more unreliable their finances became, since the Treasury could suddenly cut back their grants to suit its strategy, forcing them to impose huge rate increases.

When Layfield reported in 1976 he complained that this muddled relationship violated the old principle of 'no taxation without representation'; he recommended that local councils should retain their autonomy, and be given the power to tax as well as to spend. He proposed that the central government should contribute only 40 per cent, leaving the other 25 per cent to be raised by a local income tax. The Treasury, which wanted to impose its own priorities on local councillors, was opposed to the idea, and the Labour government was predictably unenthusiastic. In 1977 it produced a White Paper which argued that a more clearly defined system would be less flexible and advocated more central controls, to ensure that local authorities reflected national priorities, managed their finances efficiently, safeguarded minorities, and maintained local democracy.

The centralising thrust was soon to be sharpened by the Conservatives. In opposition they had depicted the town hall bureaucracies as the villains of inflation, and when Mrs Thatcher came to power she appointed the ambitious tycoon-politician Michael Heseltine to the Department of the Environment, who was soon set on a collision course with spendthrift councils. He warned them that they must cut back their budgets; he reduced the central government's grants; and by 1980 he was insisting on penalising local authorities who overstepped their limits. The battle between Whitehall and the town halls became much more political, for many big-spending councils were run by highly-organised left-wing groups committed to more public ownership, who depicted Heseltine as a straightforward capitalist enemy. The borough of Lambeth in London, led by the Marxist Ted Knight, became the prototype of these radical spenders; and in 1981 their example was followed by the Greater London Council, when the left took control.

As the giant of local government, the Greater London Council magnified all its problems. The ninety-two councillors control much of the machinery of the capital, including the schools in the Inner London Education Authority (ILEA), and the network of buses and trains in London Transport. The ponderous palace of County Hall on the Thames, with its maze of courtyards and corridors, contains a bureaucracy of over 8,000 people, spending over a billion pounds a year, with a complexity more Byzantine than any of the Whitehall departments across the river. The councillors talk of the Palace of Westminster as if it were as distant as the Kremlin.

The leadership of London had become famous in the thirties under the Labour politician Herbert Morrison, who first created London Transport, and later became the prophet of nationalised industries; he was London's nearest equivalent to an American mayor. But his successors were much less visible, submerged in the intricate politicking, and it was not until the eighties that the leadership became equally famous.

With the Labour victory in 1981 London suddenly acquired a flashy new leader, Ken Livingstone, aged only thirty-five, who soon saw himself as a national figure. He is an engaging personality, a compulsive talker with a touch of showbusiness (his mother was a chorus girl). He started work as a hospital technician, but was propelled into politics in 1968—the climacteric year of the left. In his home suburb of Norwood he was politically educated by Gerry Healy, the Trotskyist leader, and by Ted Knight of Lambeth. Once installed in County Hall, Livingstone was part of a close and militant group including two of Tony Benn's advisers, Tony Banks and Frances Morrell ('Big Lil'): they were committed to rapid reforms, including slashing transport fares which would be recouped from higher rates.

There were in fact strong arguments for increasing transport subsidies, as on the Continent, to attract more passengers: private enterprise alone could never solve the worsening traffic problems; and other English councils, including West Midlands and Merseyside, had already introduced cheap fares. But Livingstone and Heseltine were now set for a fight, billed as the champions of public ownership and private enterprise; the government soon withdrew the Whitehall block grant to London Transport, in reprisal. Bromley Council brought a case against the GLC, complaining that it had exceeded its powers, and the battle shifted to the judges: finally the Court of Appeal, led by Lord Denning, ruled that Livingstone's council had acted illegally, and the judgment was confirmed by the Law Lords. The fares went up again, the extra rates were withdrawn and the left blamed the judges for frustrating democracy, with the slogan 'Who voted for Denning?' It was a classic case of the dangers confronting judges in political areas. I asked Denning whether he wasn't now siding against the underdog: 'No, it was Bromley which was the underdog, against the abuse of the GLC's power.'

The bitter arguments over transport worsened still further the relationship between County Hall and Westminster: 'The government use central powers so pragmatically that we don't know where we are,' the former deputy-leader Illtyd Harrington complained to me. 'The central government lack so much faith in individuals,' said the GLC's director-general, Sir James Swaffield, 'that they allocate huge funds for control and regulation.' In the meantime Heseltine, urged on by his prime minister, proclaimed a new discipline which set ceilings on rates and compelled councils to hold local referenda if they exceeded them. Tory as well as Labour councillors were outraged. 'The government seems poised,' complained two professors of government, George Jones and John Stewart, who had been on the Layfield Committee, 'to take a gigantic leap towards direct central control over local authorities, destroying the basis of local self-government.' Heseltine was compelled to withdraw his plan for referenda, but bided his time.

TOUCHSTONE OF DEMOCRACY?

Traditionally the left was keener on centralisation than the right, whether in Britain or on the Continent. Bold national reforms called for greater powers at the centre, while Conservatives could preach decentralisation as part of capitalist freedom of choice and non-interference. But the Tories in their crusade against inflation were now emerging as the most ruthless centralisers, while many left-wing councils—like the many communist councils in France or Italy—were trying to build their ideal society from below. The Social Democrats, together with the Liberals, were committing themselves to policies of decentralisation. Social Democrat candidates during 1981 gained unexpected victories at local by-elections, riding on a wave of new interest in participation; while the party committed itself to introducing local income tax with more local accountability as Layfield had proposed. But the local elections in May 1982 at the height of the 'Falklands Fever' showed how widely local politics were still influenced by the national mood, and gave unexpected successes to the Conservatives.

The confrontations with town halls at least served to dramatise the basic political problem; how to control local government without destroying its independence. Local councils were the only British bodies beside parliament which had the legitimacy of democratic elections; as such, they could provide a much-needed counterweight to the growing powers of the Treasury. But they are too unrepresentative and too dependent on grants from Whitehall to defeat the 'creeping centralisation'; they can only become more independent if they raise more finance locally, and become more accountable by attracting more voters in local elections.

Decentralisation is much easier said than done. Many politicians who espouse it turn out to centralise still further, in the name of reform and good management; and few government ministers willingly diminish their own powers. The strains between Whitehall and town halls were part of a growing tension all over Europe as the centralising pressures mounted, as European local authorities made clear at a conference at the Council of Europe in 1981. 'The degree of autonomy of local authorities,' said the *rapporteur*, M. Harmegnies, 'is the touchstone of a true democracy. When public affairs are entrusted to bodies directly elected and controlled by local citizens, this leads to a more careful weighing of costs and benefits than when the citizens' own money is scarcely perceived as being directly involved.'[2] But countries such as Germany or Italy still have much stronger regional counterweights in their Länder or provinces, while France and Spain are both seeking to reverse their historic centralising trends. The British, are now in danger of becoming the most tightly centralised nation in Europe, controlled not only by Whitehall and the Treasury but by other London headquarters including (as later chapters will suggest) more centralised banks, companies, television stations and newspapers.

[2] Report on 'The Principles of Local Self-Government', Conference of Local and Regional Authorities of Europe, Strasbourg, September 21, 1981.

13

Police: The Sharp End of Government

It is difficult to reconcile an effective system of police with that perfect freedom of action and examption from interference which are the great privileges and blessings of society in this country.

Robert Peel, 1822

Each nation's police force is a mirror of its inhabitants' values. If we today ignore the police and their problems, we cannot complain if we are getting the police we did not want.

Ben Whitaker, 1979[1]

THE problems of democratic control—whether through town halls, through Whitehall, through parliament or through the law courts—converge on the police. They are, as Sir Robert Mark, their ex-Commissioner put it, 'the anvil on which society beats out the problems of political and social failure'. To most British people 'The Law' does not mean the courts or the judges, but a policeman. The separation of the police from the judiciary and juries, who may reject their evidence, is critical to democracy. But most citizens are uncertain about it, and the question of how to control the police has loomed larger in the last decade.

Britain is still one of the few countries where all police are in theory servants of the public, subject to common law and with no special arm—like the CRS in France or the Carabinieri in Italy—under direct government control. Without any such 'third force' both police and government know that they cannot fall back on any reserve force except, in extremity, the army. But the British police are also, as Lord Gardiner, the former Lord Chancellor, described them, 'the most powerful and least accountable of any in Western Europe. Nowhere else do they have the power to prosecute without any independent evaluation: and in other countries forces are accountable through a minister.'[2]

[1] Ben Whitaker: *The Police in Society*, Eyre Methuen, London, 1979, p. 318.
[2] *Ibid*, p. 283.

The police are the most vulnerable part of that elaborate confidence trick which is government. Ministers, judges or civil servants require the passive obedience of the population; but the police have to enforce it: and they have to conceal the smallness of their force—only 120,000 people in 1982, one in 500 of the population—by a process of bluff. As people become more questioning and less respectful of authority, the bluff has become harder to maintain, and the conduct of the police has been more exposed to debate. In the last decade they have moved much closer to the centre of the political stage.

The police are in the midst of society, yet regarded as being right outside it, and this ambivalence was clear in their beginnings. In the seventeenth century the very idea of the police was regarded as foreign, particularly French, and particularly undesirable, and it was not until Robert Peel set up his 'new police' as a separate force in 1829 that policemen began to replace the old part-time constables.

The core of Peel's force was the Metropolitan Police in London, 'The Met', who were firmly separated from the rest of the country, and who remain quite unlike the provincial forces. They have a quarter of all British policemen—25,000 out of 120,000 with their own famous headquarters at New Scotland Yard, near Victoria. They have always come directly under the Home Secretary, who appoints the Commissioner, Deputy Commissioner and four Assistant Commissioners, who give up their police status to become known as plain Mister or Sir. The Commissioner himself is in a position of rare personal power, difficult to control, or to sack, and subject to inspection by no one.

For five years from 1972 the Met was dominated by a very unusual Commissioner, Sir Robert Mark, who became a symbol of the policeman exposed to politics—more like the Continental 'Chief of Police'. He was a questioning intellectual who enjoyed publicity; he had been a wartime major and a fellow of Nuffield College and he had lectured round the world; but he was first and foremost a dedicated policeman. He was seen as a liberal but he was basically a very intelligent authoritarian. He made his name by cleaning up corrupt detectives at Scotland Yard—though some colleagues thought he was not thorough enough, including Frank Williamson, the former Chief Constable of Cumbria, who was the chief scourge of corruption and who eventually resigned in frustration. Mark complained that the courts were too lenient, that juries should be able to convict on a majority vote, and that some lawyers were corrupt in defending criminals. He insisted above all that Scotland Yard should maintain its autonomy, and that the police should themselves look after complaints. Like lawyers and academics he readily associated freedom with the inviolability of his own profession. 'The operational freedom of the police from political or bureaucratic interference', he wrote, 'is essential to their acceptability and to the preservation of democracy. The police must not even seem, in dealing with industrial disputes or political demonstrations, to reflect the wishes of the government of the day.'[3]

It was on the handling of complaints that Mark came into collision with the Home Secretary, Roy Jenkins, who had first appointed him. After mounting evidence about police misconduct and violence, Jenkins was insisting by 1976 that complaints must be investigated by an independent body enjoying the confidence of the public. Mark was indignant, insisting that this would undermine police discipline and make investigation *less* effective; when Jenkins' bill went through he decided to resign rather than administer an act which he found repugnant. 'Now that discipline is to be administered by political nominees he (the Commissioner) inevitably becomes an administrator rather than a leader.'[4] But when the Police Complaints Board, under Lord Plowden, produced its first report in 1978 it showed little sign of undermining the Commissioner: at the same time there were growing demands for more thorough independent investigations of complaints.

Mark's successor, Sir David McNee, appointed by the next Home Secretary, Merlyn Rees, was much less politically sophisticated. Faced with worsening problems of racial conflicts, picket lines and National Front marches, he called for greater powers to search and detain, to limit demonstrations and to refuse bail. But he was not an expert administrator, and moved from Scotland to Scotland Yard with no past experience of its elaborate machinery. It was not altogether surprising when he announced his early retirement in 1982. His successor, Sir Kenneth Newman, had been tipped for the job five years earlier and was regarded as one of the toughest and most efficient administrators. He had begun his career in the post-war Palestine Police and in 1976 had taken charge of the Royal Ulster Constabulary, which he reorganised and modernised with scientific equipment and mobile patrol groups when it took over security from the army. He put his men on a war footing, and they were accused of using brutal methods for interrogating detainees; but he also developed 'responsive policing' which tried to get closer to communities. The problems of London were now not completely unlike the problems of Ulster.

[3] Robert Mark: *In the Office of Constable*, Collins, London, 1978, p. 202.
[4] *Ibid*, p. 212.

CHIEF CONSTABLES

The provincial police forces in the meantime, under their separate chief constables, were also coming under political fire. When Peel had set up the Met in 1829 he had left the provincial forces to look after themselves, but later governments gradually tried to co-ordinate them; and by 1856, in return for paying half their costs, the government was allowed to inspect each constabulary. The inspections were often perfunctory and it was not until 1919 that the Home Secretary was able to regulate pay, clothing and conditions. Now, under the Police Act of 1964, seven inspectors visit every police force in the course of a year, under the Chief Inspector, Sir James Crane, who was formerly Commander of the Fraud Squad at New Scotland Yard. The Inspector's influence over local forces is essentially through persuasion and argument; but his office has to approve all grants and short lists of chief constables, which helps his persuasion.

The forty-seven chief constables in England and Wales still have a formidable power; they are theoretically responsible to the local 'police authority', made up of councillors and magistrates, but in practice their personalities have great independence and local gran-deur: an intelligent and ambitious policeman can move relatively easily up the social scale ending up in the heart of 'county' society alongside the lord lieutenant and the high sheriff. The 'Chief' is a grand figure in the county, with a big subsidised house, a fast car and driver; many councillors may be in awe of him, and his views about immigrants, drunken driving, or pot can affect the policing of the whole county.

As crime has increased, criminals have become more organised and communications have quickened, more critics have demanded a national police force. The Willink Commission of 1962 decided that chief constables should retain their powers; but the objections return with each scandal about local police forces—such as the prolonged failure to track down the Yorkshire Ripper. The police have already been discreetly more co-ordinated: the Met are responsible for such national organisations as the Special Branch, the Fraud Squad, and connections with Interpol. But Commissioners are not always con-vinced of the advantages of centralisation: 'Whilst nationalisation or regionalisation may confer administrative benefits,' said Mark in 1968, 'neither would have any effect at all on the incidence of crime or the proportion of crime cleared up.'[5] And the Met with its own stubborn autonomy and refusal to be inspected by others, is not a reassuring advertisement for centralisation. As John Alderson, the

[5] Robert Mark: 'The Police, the Public and the Law', talk at the Inns of Court School of Law, October 9, 1968.

former Chief Constable of Devon and Cornwall, who worked at the Met, put it to me in 1981: 'The Met is the biggest, the least accountable, the most influential. If we can get it right, it will affect all of us. But the centre isn't holding together as well as some of the provincial forces.'

Police centralisation involved much larger democratic issues, including the protection of individual rights against data banks and computers. The British have always instinctively resisted central codification, and they celebrated the end of the Second World War by abolishing identity cards: Britain is one of the few European countries whose citizens have no number and need not carry any identification—which many police deplore. Centralised computers can enable the police to put together information about individuals much more efficiently but also more secretively, which calls for much closer scrutiny by parliament or its representatives.

'Police are conservative almost by nature,' said John Alderson, 'but they get more so when they're under fire, compounded by political influence.' During the seventies the Police Federation (the trade union of most policemen except the top ranks) became more visibly Tory. They retained a right-wing Conservative MP, Eldon Griffiths, to succeed James Callaghan as their representative in parliament, while the Superintendents' Association retained another Tory MP, Bernard Braine. The chairman of the Federation, James Jardine, publicly called for the death penalty and wrote to all candidates in the 1979 election calling for stricter sentences, while the Tories soon gave preferential treatment to police pay. The Conservative Home Secretary, William Whitelaw, warned the police superintendents, at their annual conference at Torquay, that they must not 'become the preserve of any one political party'; but the outbreak of riots in the summer of 1981 provoked the police to more political outbursts. 'I don't give a damn for the bleeding hearts,' said Jardine, 'the so-called liberals and Marxist agitators.'

Each chief constable had his own attitude to policing and crime, and now aired it much more publicly. The chiefs in the shires could afford to be more relaxed than those in the six metropolitan areas (see last chapter), faced with crumbling inner cities and rootless minorities, whose problems were spotlighted by the riots. The most notorious crime region was Merseyside, which already by 1977 was described as having the worst teenage-unemployment problem in Europe and the worst law-and-order problem in Britain. The authoritarian Chief Constable, Kenneth Oxford, at the time warned that, unless conditions improved, the city centre might need an 'army of occupation' by 1980.[6] Oxford insisted on tough measures

[6] James McClure: *Spike Island*, Macmillan, London, 1980, p. 13.

against Liverpool crime, and in the face of growing complaints of police brutality—particularly over Jimmy Kelly who died in detention—he resisted any outside investigation. The local police committee were already worried by Oxford's intransigence, and the riots in Toxteth, in the decaying centre of Liverpool, revealed all the toughness of the Merseyside police. The committee strongly criticised Oxford's methods and pointedly delayed authorising extra riot equipment while Oxford did not conceal his contempt for the councillors.

When the rioting spread from Toxteth to Moss Side in Lancashire, the spotlight turned on the Chief Constable of Greater Manchester, James Anderton, who had even firmer ideas about crime, and was obsessed by the dangers of Marxist conspiracies. A Methodist lay preacher, he was firmly anti-racist, zealously cleaned up pornography, and spoke much about community contact; but he had little patience with his local council. When citizens complained about police brutality against rioters the council supported a local committee of inquiry, but Anderton refused to give evidence to 'any Tom, Dick or Harry', and submitted his own report to the police committee. Anderton soon extended his attack to police committees in general, and in March 1982 he accused them of fighting 'a secretive and acrimonious battle' for power, and proposed that they should be abolished and replaced by non-political boards—an outburst which Roy Hattersley, the Labour shadow Home Secretary, described as 'inflammatory nonsense'.

The authoritarian responses of chief constables provoked the most liberal of them, John Alderson of Devon and Cornwall—not to be confused with James Anderton—to publish his own views on police behaviour, just when the Met were defending their own conduct to Lord Scarman, who was enquiring into the riots in Brixton. Alderson had already expounded his own ideas in his book, *Policing Freedom*, where he complained that the force had become too professionalised and divorced from the community: 'The police,' he explained, 'must be seen to be on the side of the little man.'[7] Now in his submission to Lord Scarman, he criticised the police relations with their communities and their tactics with rioters, and proposed that the Met should henceforth be supervised by a London committee including local councillors.

Alderson's advice infuriated other chief constables who mocked him as a soft liberal accustomed to policing tourists and sheep; but the resulting debate raised new doubts about the supervision of the police. However rigorous the Home Secretary and the Chief Inspector, only local citizens could really know about their community's

[7] John Alderson: *Policing Freedom*, Macdonald and Evans, London, 1979.

needs and their chief constable's behaviour: but most local committees were too feeble to control him, and could easily be accused of
being unrepresentative and politically motivated. The British compromise between local and central control had left, as in other
spheres, a large unaccountable gap in the middle; only a stronger
and more responsible system of local government and elections
could provide more effective control of the police, without still
further centralisation.

When Lord Scarman, the tireless trouble-shooter among the Law
Lords, eventually produced his report on the Brixton riots in
November 1981, he showed his customary political tact. He com-
mended the police strategy and tactics: 'they stood between our
society and a total collapse of law and order'. But he believed that a
major cause of the riots was the young blacks' hostility and loss of
confidence in the police; and he blamed the 'hard' policing methods,
the lack of consultation, the distrust of complaints procedures and
the racist attitudes of some policemen. 'The weight of criticism and
complaint against the police is so considerable that it alone must give
great cause for concern.' The Scarman Report reopened the controversy about the relations between the police and the law. 'I rather
regret,' Lord Denning told me, 'that Scarman suggested that the
police didn't do a good job.' 'I do not share Lord Scarman's conclu-
sions,' said Sir Robert Mark, 'about the adequacy of the law or the
effectiveness of the justice system.' But the report gave powerful
evidence that the police were inadequately supervised and that
without changes there would be more dangerous confrontations in
the future.

14

Scientists and Engineers: Frustrating the Future

The innovator has for enemies all those who have done well under the old conditions.

Machiavelli, quoted by
Sir Monty Finniston, 1979

It is the fate of the policymaker to live in a paper world and to risk being deceived into thinking that it is the real one.

Sir Alan Cottrell, 1981

Of all the intransigent forces confronting Whitehall and the Treasury, the most uncontrollable have been the scientists who can spend so much with so little to show for it. Governments which pay for more than half their country's research have repeatedly tried to pin down the scientists to national objectives; the scientists have resented every infringement on their freedom; while the communications between the two sides have remained rudimentary. Cross-purposes between scientists and administrators are common to all countries, but in Britain they are exaggerated by differences of class, schooling and pay which have made many scientists feel themselves outsiders, and by the gulf between the devotees of the past and the future. It is the fear of the future which most obviously distinguishes British attitudes from those of the western United States or Japan; and it is scientists who most easily conjure up that fear.

The last twenty years have seen a succession of tragi-comic encounters between British politicians and scientists, as governments have tried to bring scientists within their field of comprehension. When Macmillan appointed Lord Hailsham, who knew nothing about science, to be Minister of Science in 1959, Hailsham was confident that he was 'exactly suited to the job'; when I visited him in his office in the old Richmond Terrace, going up in a rickety lift, he was talking about the need for a new kind of builder's hod. He was 'disgusted' by the talk about two cultures, and maintained that his classical education was the best equipment possible for understanding nuclear physics.[1] When Harold Wilson appointed Richard Crossman, another classical scholar, as shadow Minister of Science, Crossman was equally confident. After quickly mugging up science papers he told Wilson: 'We've got through this science barrier.'[2] And a few days later Wilson made his famous speech about the white-hot technological revolution. In his first government Wilson created a new Ministry of Technology under Frank Cousins, the trade unionist, and brought scientists including Lord Snow and Lord Bowden into the government. The government spent vast sums on such projects as the 'world's most sophisticated aeroplane', the TSR2, the RB211 aircraft engine which was expected to capture American markets, and the development of nuclear fusion. But the spending had no visible effect on Britain's economic competitiveness, while the environmentalists were mobilising themselves against the social costs of new technology.

Sir Alan Cottrell, the former Chief Scientific Adviser (later vice-chancellor of Cambridge) described the changing government attitudes to scientists in terms of four periods, like periods of art. The Primitive Period began with the appointment of the first Master of the King's Ordinance in 1414 and progressed through innovations such as the Royal Observatory in 1675, the first publicly-funded scientific institution. The First World War, which made all governments realise the importance of science, ushered in the Classical Period. Venerable committees were set up to supervise research, including the Medical Research Council (MRC) in 1920 and the Agricultural Research Council (ARC) in 1931; government establishments such as the National Physical Laboratory (NPL) and the Royal Aircraft Establishment (RAE) became large research centres; the Department of Scientific and Industrial Research (DSIR) tried to apply science to industry. The scientists would retain their autonomy from commercial pressures in keeping with the 'Haldane Principle', enunciated by Lord Haldane in 1918, which said that the relevant minister should be 'immune from any suspicion of being biased by administrative considerations . . .'.

The Second World War brought in the Romantic Period, when nations saw scientists as possessing the keys to their future:

The experiences of the second war established a new era of faith in science and technology. Together they formed in people's minds a magic wand for solving national problems and achieving great missions. Science told you what you could be doing and technology

---

[1] Hailsham: *op cit*, p. 183.
[2] *The Backbench Diaries of Richard Crossman*, p. 1020.

told you how to do it. Together they provided irresistible power, the power of new ideas embodied in material strength.[3]

Ministers and civil servants both wanted to leave scientists with the greatest freedom, and to allow them to be judged by their peers. 'In this way, bread was cast upon the scientific waters in vast amounts and the pure scientists enjoyed a golden age that lasted for some twenty years.' The research councils expanded and were augmented by two new ones, the Natural Environmental Research Council (NERC) and the Social Science Research Council (SSRC). This Romantic Period witnessed spectacular world developments, including radio astronomy, molecular biology and solid state physics, while technology produced space satellites, transistor radios, computers and rockets. In Britain Wilson's white-hot technological revolution promised a close new relationship, and many scientists looked towards a brave new world of rational co-operation. 'Is there any way,' asked C. P. Snow (later Lord Snow) in his Godkin lectures in Harvard in 1960, 'in this great underground domain of science and government, in which we can arrange to make choices a little more rationally?' 'At the time I was impressed,' commented Sir Fred Dainton, 'but twenty years on I realise it was a ridiculous question.'

But by the late sixties the more sceptical Modern Period was already dawning. The Labour government was beginning to worry that its vast scientific spending was not cost-effective, and at the Ministry of Defence Denis Healey was insisting on supervising his thousands of scientists more carefully. Successive military and civil projects were abandoned—from Black Arrow and the TSR2 to the Channel Tunnel and tracked Hovercraft. By 1971 Shirley Williams was announcing that for scientists, as for local councillors, 'the party was over'; and she complained that 'there are far too few meeting places between the scientists, the social scientists and the politicians who make the decisions'.[4] But economists and civil servants were now beginning a long counter-attack against the scientists.

The disillusion was international: in 1971 the OECD described in its report on *Science, Growth and Society* how all Western governments had changed their minds about the benefits of science. The disenchantment in Britain was greater, however, for there was a wider gap between civil servants and scientists, who had a greater aversion to more practical research; and the lack of achievements was more striking. As Cottrell put it in 1981:

[3] Sir Alan Cottrell: *What is Science Policy?* Royal Institution; the Maxwell/Pergamon Discourse, 1981.
[4] *The Times*, February 27, 1971.

The total effect of all the government's policies over this post-war period, has, I am forced to conclude, been to achieve the *very opposite* of what it intended. *Pure science*—the less commercial the better—has prospered under these policies, but industrial *applied science* has been discouraged . . . . Thus we have the extraordinary result that, after thirty years of government science policy in which the primary aim has undoubtedly been to apply the results of scientific research more purposefully to our national production effort—to use Sir Harold Wilson's words—the practical effect of governmental policies has been to make pure science strong and industrial science weak.[5]

Britain was still stuck with her century-old problem. Her scientists continued to win Nobel prizes; her old centres of excellence such as Cambridge and Imperial College, together with a few new centres such as Manchester, Liverpool and Leeds, could compete in pure research with the great institutions of Europe and America; her academic scientists, including the old families such as the Hodgkins and the Huxleys, maintained their originality and dedication with a striking continuity. But the problem of how to connect up science and technology with industry, which had concerned British technocrats a hundred years earlier, was still unsolved, and the gap of prestige between the pure research laboratory and the factory floor was wider than ever.

A SCIENTIFIC ESTABLISHMENT?

As they faced the criticism and cuts from Whitehall and the Treasury, the scientists were very conscious that they lacked the cohesion and close communication of 'the Whitehall village'; and scientific research was now much more fragmented and specialised. They could look back with some nostalgia on the seventeenth century, when the Royal Society founded by King Charles II attracted all kinds of scientists and amateurs: Newton, Halley, Dryden and Pepys could gather to chat about telescopes, gravity or comets and at least pretend to understand them. But since the nineteenth century the Renaissance ideal of the 'universal man' had steadily faded; after 1901 the Royal Society excluded the 'human' sciences like economics or philosophy, and their proceedings became less intelligible not only to laymen but to scientists in other fields. The Royal Society (like the Royal Academy for painters) became absorbed in its own mumbo-jumbo and self-admiration.

Before 1939 the top British scientists were still relatively close-knit. In the words of Alexander King, the first Secretary of the Advisory Council for Scientific Policy:

[5] Cottrell: *op cit*.

Up to the Second World War, the size of the British science system was small enough for internal adjustments and policy direction to be in the hands of a few, outstanding personalities belonging to the same coterie. Coherence and mutual understanding were probably achieved rather effectively, if utterly informally, through frequent, easy, but often unplanned contacts between the leading figures of the Royal Society, the research council secretaries, and senior civil servants, all of whom were habitués of the Athenaeum Club.[6]

But in the post-war years, in the midst of the vast expansion and specialisation, the scientists felt themselves much more isolated, and it was not difficult for politicians to play off one against the other. Lord Hailsham, during his brief reign as Minister of Science, was struck by how little one scientist might understand another: 'There is a real sense,' he wrote, 'in which there is no such thing as science but only sciences.'[7]

The scientists have tried to assert their common interest against the politicians and civil servants; and in the sixties the Royal Society made great efforts, particularly under the presidency of Lord Blackett, to become more relevant and adventurous. They now award medals for contributions 'leading directly to national prosperity', and they have increased their annual quota of fellows to include applied scientists, technical directors and such worldly men as Sir Arnold Hall and Lord Kearton. But the fellows are very aware that their own interests diverge, and that government has usurped much of their influence: in 1981 the Society submitted a report to parliament complaining about the down-grading of scientific advisers in Whitehall, and the government's resistance to first-class scientific advice.

A similar quandary faced the 'scientists' parliament', the British Association for the Advancement of Science. It was founded in 1831 to rescue science from its low status, and it was mocked by Dickens as the 'Mudfog Association for the Advancement of Everything'; nevertheless it became the setting for Victorian scientific debates, including the historic argument between Huxley and Bishop Wilberforce in 1860 about Darwin's *Origin of the Species*. A century later, however, the 'British Ass' had become a peripheral body, providing readable papers by popular professors at its summer meetings. In 1970 its stately proceedings at Durham were interrupted by radical young scientists demanding that it must face up to the political repercussions of science, and it has since tried to widen its appeal. It has a flourishing youth movement, and it has

[6] Philip J. Gummett: *Scientists in Whitehall*, Manchester University Press, Manchester, 1980, pp. 224–5.
[7] Hailsham: *op cit*, p. 183.

formed useful study groups, including an inquiry into engineers' training which led to the Finniston Report (see below). But while it is less conservative, it is more fragmented, and by the time of its 150th anniversary members were still uncertain of their proper role: were they a scientists' parliament or a shareholders' meeting?[8]

The scientific establishment, such as it is, remains largely cut off from the rest of the British power-structure. While lawyers and economists—those earlier prophets of government—were tamed and brought into the heart of Whitehall, scientists were more resistant to becoming 'house trained'. They have achieved much more recognition: nearly half the university vice-chancellors are now scientists or engineers, and many of the younger senior civil servants now have scientific degrees. But the top scientists are more aloof from the political world than those in France or America. They are nearly all from grammar schools, many from Redbrick universities. They talk with a refreshing originality and lack of pomp, with boyish enthusiasm and very little snobbery, often retaining a cheeky attitude to Whitehall or to Head Office; I have found their conversation a relief after the more guarded responses of bureaucrats and business executives. But the ideal of the politically sophisticated scientist who can bridge the gap between his speciality and the public—a prospect which the prime minister herself seemed to offer—seems as distant as ever.

While most practical scientists come from Redbrick, the aristocracy of science who pursue pure research still come from the university which has been their centre for the past century. Of the documented Fellows of the Royal Society elected since 1971 (excluding those educated abroad), 33 per cent came from Cambridge, 11 per cent from Oxford, 21 per cent from London, and 35 per cent from all other universities.[9] The Cavendish Laboratory in Cambridge, where Lord Rutherford presided over the team which split the atom, has produced about eighty Nobel prizewinners, including four during the seventies; and the dominance and intense competitiveness of the Cavendish shows every sign of continuing. Cambridge continues to perpetuate its own kind, attracting ambitious scientists as Oxford attracts politicians, and nearly all the Cavendish researchers have Cambridge degrees: for scientific excellence there is no substitute for the hot-house. But while new research at the Cavendish may lead to important industrial opportunities, in micro-electronics or chemical catalysts, it attracts more interest from American than from British industrialists.[10]

[8] See chapter by David Morley in *The Parliament of Science* (edited by Macleod and Collins): London Science Reviews, 1982, pp. 237 ff.

[9] Survey by Dr Herbert Eisener, *New Scientist*, December 1981.

CHIEF SCIENTISTS

The uncertain status of British scientists has been reflected and magnified by the fluctuating role of the top advisers in government. Throughout the sixties Whitehall science was dominated by the tireless zoologist, Sir Solly (now Lord) Zuckerman who was Chief Adviser first to the Ministry of Defence and then to the whole government. He was a sparkling and witty talker who could make science seem comprehensible and exciting to prime ministers, but he revelled in his political power and infuriated both civil servants and other scientists with his easy access to the top, as a 'court scientist' like Lord Cherwell in Churchill's time. When he finally left government in 1971, to run the London Zoo and become Professor-at-Large, his rivals did not conceal their relief.

His successor as Chief Scientific Adviser, Sir Alan Cottrell, was much less flamboyant, a professor of metallurgy from Birmingham with bushy eyebrows and untidy hair; and he worked partly alongside the head of the new Think Tank, Lord Rothschild, an outspoken individualist who had run Shell's research. The two men managed to cut back several scientific white elephants, and tried and failed to stop Concorde; in 1972 they predicted a huge increase in the oil price, though hardly anyone believed them. But the magic reputation of scientists was already fading as the civil servants counter-attacked. When Cottrell retired in 1974 the position of Chief Scientific Adviser was abolished and his role was only partly taken over by scientists in the Think Tank, who had access to power only through the Cabinet Office.

The down-grading was partly paralleled in the United States, where the post of president's adviser was likewise abolished in 1973: in both countries (as the politicians explained) each department now had its own scientific adviser.[11] But British scientists faced a more serious setback in the face of a stronger civil service. 'There's no really intelligent scientific focus in the Cabinet Office, which is what is most needed,' Lord Flowers, the Rector of Imperial College, told me. 'Ministers must be confronted at first hand by experts who can say when the administration has been wrong.' Or as another scientific authority complained: 'The heads of the research stations are now far less powerful than after the war: they're like branch managers responsible to Whitehall. The civil servants can always get between them and the ministers.' In 1981 the House of Lords Select Committee on Science reported strong evidence that 'the power and influence of chief scientists have declined over the last five years';

[10] See the *Economist*, February 27, 1982.
[11] See Gummett: *op cit*, p. 50.

and when the prime minister appointed a new Chief Scientific Adviser Robin Nicholson, a professor of metallurgy and businessman, his appointment was hardly noticed.

The alphabet of committees which had multiplied in the fifties and sixties now provided the battleground between civil servants and scientists. The Treasury men tried to translate the scientists' vague speculations about the future into detailed projections of public expenditure, while the scientists despised their lack of imagination: 'civil servants *hate* the future'. Faced with growing complaints about the cost of research, Lord Rothschild at the Think Tank produced a controversial report in 1971, which proposed a much more practical system, based on the experience of big industrial organisations such as his old firm, Shell. The government should henceforth deal with applied research and development as a customer deals with a contractor: 'The customer says what he wants; the contractor does it (if he can); and the customer pays.' Each department would be a customer, dealing with its relevant research council, the contractor; and the departments would control a quarter of each research council's funds. It was a reversal of the proud academic autonomy of the councils enshrined in the old 'Haldane Principle'. The scientific establishment wrote long protests to *The Times*, made speeches in the House of Lords and gave evidence to the select committee; but they still had no real unity and some of them, including Cottrell, supported Rothschild. By the end of 1972 the government had carried out most of Rothschild's proposals. Each department now has its own chief scientist while the old 'scientists' cabinet', the Council for Scientific Policy, has been replaced by the committee of scientists called the Advisory Board for the Research Councils (ABRC).

The new system has obvious advantages to more sceptical politicians. The chief scientists within each department can bring a closer understanding of critical advances: for example the microchip which threatens to revolutionise industrial production, or the development of biotechnology which promises to use genetic engineering to harness organisms to man's needs. There are some hopeful signs of more serious collaboration between scientists and industry. The Advisory Council for Applied Research and Development (ACARD) was boosted after 1980 under the brief chairmanship of the late Alfred Spinks, the pharmacologist and former research director of ICI, who used ACARD to try to educate the government about innovations in industry. Even the venerable Science Research Council has decided to come closer to industry: under Sir Geoffrey Allen, Professor of Chemical Technology at Imperial College, it changed its name to the Science and

Engineering Research Council (SERC), and is now chaired by the young Professor of Mathematics at Oxford, John Kingman.

But the relationships between councils and departments remained tangled; and when Sir Alec Merrison, the nuclear physicist, became chairman of the Advisory Board in 1979 he complained that the changes had set up an 'unnecessarily elaborate machinery'. 'Science is still too much tied up with committees,' as Sir Frederick Dainton, the Chancellor of Sheffield and elder statesman of science put it. 'The government pours money into science and then worries that the money isn't flowing out at the other end; but it's industry which fails to pick up the ball when it's put at their feet. The interface between government and scientists has to be met from both ends. Governments must allow scientists the freedom, but scientists must use their freedom responsibly.'

Why had Britain so uniquely failed over twenty years to harness science and technology to her needs? All industrial countries had suffered some disillusion; but most of them had more to show for it. Sir Alan Cottrell insisted to me that governments blamed scientists for what was really their own inability to give proper direction; and that British scientists had fallen uncomfortably between two stools. Or as he put it to the House of Lords select committee in 1981:

> There is what you might call the German-American model which is really a sort of benign laissez-faire in which you do not interfere much with industry, but you create broad conditions under which industry by its own efforts can prosper. Then there is the French-Japanese system which is a *dirigiste* system. I think we have constantly tended towards the French-Japanese system, without ever understanding it. The first thing is to understand that you need a completely different kind of administrative civil service.

ENGINEERS

The failure of reform is more glaring in the profession of engineers, who provide the critical links between inventions and their application. The half a million people who call themselves engineers range from factory technicians to professors at Imperial College; but the highly-qualified professional engineers play the decisive roles, and they are very conscious of having lost out. They can look back at a glorious history of heroes such as Brunel, Telford or Stephenson, but their status has declined since the nineteenth century, as Britain retreated from industrial innovation. The best consulting engineers still enjoy high reputations and lucrative contracts abroad for building bridges, dams or industrial plants: but at home they are all too easily outmanoeuvred by accountants and civil servants more skilled in communication and political intrigue. Even engineers who are venerated and honoured, such as Sir Dennis Pearson, the former head of Rolls Royce, can find themselves suddenly toppled from their pedestals by bankers and politicians.

The engineers and their institutes must themselves take much of the blame; for they have resisted reforms which were in their own interests. Over twenty years successive critics have complained about their fragmentation into rival institutions which look at each other with jealousy and suspicion. These are the biggest, with their dates of foundation and secretaries in 1981:

Institution of Civil Engineers	1818	Robert Campbell
Institution of Mechanical Engineers	1847	Alexander McKay
Institution of Marine Engineers	1889	J. Stuart Robinson
Institution of Production Engineers	1921	Raymond Miskin
Institution of Chemical Engineers	1922	Trevor Evans

The oldest, the 'Civils' (bridges, roads, dams) always took a high-handed line with newcomers, and it was their refusal to admit George Stephenson which led to the foundation of the 'Mechanicals' (trains, cars, aeroplanes). The two early institutes built their palazzos, like gentlemen's clubs, next door to each other behind Parliament Square—convenient for lobbying Victorian MPs—where they still glare at each other. By 1919 the engineers already had more than a hundred societies; but the different branches are now much more interdependent, and a dam can involve Civils, Mechanicals and Electricals, working closely together.

The fragmentation not only limited their scope, but prevented any common system of qualifications and common outlook. 'If engineers are to gain their old position of policy makers and financial controllers,' warned Sir George McNaughton, the president of the Civils twenty years ago, 'they must be able to express views on wider fields than the purely technical.' Two years later Geoffrey Feilden, a Mechanical who specialised in gas turbines, published his *Report on Engineering Design* which blamed the institutions—particularly the Mechanicals—for their narrow attitudes and lack of interest in design, which was all too obvious to consumers grappling with British cars, central heating or lawn mowers. The institutes half-heartedly tried to co-ordinate, and twelve of them formed a joint council to speak with one voice. But it had no real independence and could not even produce its own register of qualifications.

The shortcomings of engineers looked more worrying as Britain faced growing competition from European cars or Japanese electronics which showed much more sophisticated design. In 1977 the

Labour government, pressed by Arthur Palmer who was both a Labour MP and an electrical engineer, appointed a committee chaired by the former head of British Steel, the outspoken Scottish metallurgist Sir Monty Finniston. He was distressed by his profession's subservience, 'falling into a subordinate role like well-schooled butlers' (as he put it in his report). 'In Germany or America engineers were regarded as right at the top, next door to doctors,' he told me, 'but here we found that engineers were rated below male models.' He asked his staff to look at all the previous reports—going back to 1852 when Sir Lyon Playfair first described the superiority of German engineers—and realised that none of them had been followed by effective action.

When he produced his report in 1979 Finniston was determined that this one would be acted on: 'Unless urgent action is taken to advance the engineering dimension on national economic life,' he warned, 'industrial decline is inevitable, with unprecedented and undesirable social consequences.' He listed eighty recommendations for improving the engineers' training, status and industrial influence; but he insisted that they all depended on a single proposal to introduce a new Engineering Authority, to be set up by the government as the chief engine for change. It could enforce its will on the stubborn old institutes, to supervise education, qualifications and licensing; and it could bring together employers, government officials and universities to enlarge what Finniston called 'the engineering dimension'.

The treatment of the Finniston Report soon became another political fiasco. The Conservatives were now in power, with Sir Keith Joseph at the Department of Trade and Industry, who first seemed to welcome the idea of a new Authority. But he took fright at intervening against the spirit of the new Tory philosophy—just when his own disastrous restructuring of the Health Service was being dismantled—and could not bring himself to impose a new body. He delayed endlessly, while the institutes were once again digging in. The Civils, the oldest and most stick-in-the-mud, regarded themselves as unique and unchangeable. The Electricals, the richest and biggest, first supported the new Authority but then went against it. The president of the Council of Engineering Institutions, Dr Percy Alloway, insisted that 'we want much more time to consider our position before we give up any of our powers'.

Joseph and his permanent secretary, Sir Peter Carey, decided to compromise and proposed a much weaker chartered body where the institutes would be fully represented, but without proper teeth. By August 1981 they had appointed a chairman, Sir Kenneth Corfield from ITT, but three months later he still had not decided on staffing or membership. 'What I wanted was an engine for change,' Finniston told me. 'Instead we have got a shunter moving along disjointed lines.'

Without changing their professional structure, the engineers, as Finniston had warned them, could do little about their education and status. Their Victorian institutions had proved more resistant to pressure for change than medieval schools or universities. They were still the Cinderellas amongst the industrial professions, cut off from others by their outdated institutes and narrow horizons, still an easy prey to tycoons and accountants. It was not altogether surprising that they were bewildered and inarticulate when they faced the political outcry about nuclear power.

THE NUCLEAR DILEMMA

> If a problem is too difficult to solve, one cannot claim that it is solved by pointing at all the efforts made to solve it.
>
> *Hannes Alfven (quoted by*
> *Lord Flowers, 1976)*

By the late seventies most of the grandiose national projects of scientists and engineers were fading into disillusion: the TSR2, the Channel Tunnel, even Concorde were ending in tears. But one scientific controversy was more critical and enigmatic than any: the question of nuclear power.

After the world energy crisis of 1973 the possibility of large-scale nuclear energy was more tantalising than ever, and far more politically exposed. The furious subsequent debates were not only about the dangers of the 'Faustian bargain', by which governments could buy energy at the cost of their people's safety. They were also about the centralisation of power. Each expansion of energy through history—from wood fires, to coal, to national gas and electricity, to oil from distant countries, and now to vast long-term nuclear programmes—had made local communities more dependent on a distant bureaucracy, taking decisions in inscrutable ways. The protests against nuclear power in the seventies were linked to other movements including the environmentalists and the proponents of 'small is beautiful'. 'The real driving force behind the anti-nuclear movement,' Sir Alan Cottrell suggests, 'is socio-political. It is the manifestation of a more general aversion to modern Western society, to massive industrialisation, high technology, central bureaucracy and security forces, and to free enterprise and economic growth.'[12]

[12] Alan Cottrell: *How Safe is Nuclear Energy?* Heinemann, London, 1981, p. 110.

The two meanings of power, political and physical, were becoming mixed up. The continuing debate about nuclear power and its warlike connections brought back all the old suspicions about the relationship between scientists and government. The critical nuclear choice was still darkened and confused by the British obsession with secrecy, and only if voters could begin to trust and understand the nuclear programme would they consent to this new leap into the future.

The British experience of civil nuclear power had been particularly tantalising, littered with false hopes. The Atomic Energy Authority (AEA) had been created with great expectations in 1954 and two years later completed the world's first commercial plant for generating atomic energy at Calder Hall. Scientists twenty years ago still sounded confident that Britain could lead the world in producing safe, peaceful nuclear energy. The atomic research station at Harwell was full of dedicated boffins watching ghostly machines, while politicians were rashly promising magical breakthroughs such as ZETA, which would turn the sea into energy.

In the following years vast rectangles and spheres rose up along the coastline, accompanied by high hopes from scientists and growing suspicions from environmentalists. But the dreams of cheap, safe energy were dissolving as the real costs and difficulties emerged. Rival British consortia were competing unprofitably, while the scientists could never decide which system was the most promising—gas-cooled or water-cooled—and their advanced gas-cooled reactors suffered delays and escalating costs: by 1973 British reactors were actually generating less electricity than in 1968. The American companies were now investing billions, and the giant Westinghouse Corporation was designing advanced pressurised water reactors which were cheaper to build than British designs.

The secretiveness of the British Atomic Energy Authority gave full scope for the fears of anti-nuclear protesters, and the scientists were now looking much more capitalist. The AEA was now interlocked with British Nuclear Fuels Ltd, based near Warrington, which sold fuel to the world market. Its chairman since 1971, Sir John Hill, began to sound more like a salesman than a scientist. Most new contracts for nuclear reactors were now held by the giant General Electric Corporation, run by Sir Arnold Weinstock, who relentlessly questioned the scientists, cutting them down to size with his mastery of statistics. 'If he comes out from behind his desk,' complained Walter Marshall (see below), 'that's an adventure.'

The global stakes were doubled and redoubled after 1973, when the rising oil price made every nation long to move rapidly into a nuclear age. Britain, though she was built on coal and surrounded by oil, still had high nuclear ambitions and in 1975 the debate opened up when Tony Benn, becoming increasingly populist, arrived at the Department of Energy. His chief scientist, Walter Marshall, was a big booming Yorkshireman who had been at the AEA from its beginning, with intervals in America, and was now also its deputy-chairman. He tirelessly defended the pressurised water reactor (PWR), which had been developed by Westinghouse and adopted by General Electric. But Benn was inclined to favour the advanced gas-cooled reactor (AGR) and he was instinctively suspicious of the Weinstock–Westinghouse lobby. 'In my political life,' he wrote afterwards, 'I have never known such a well-organised scientific, industrial and technical lobby as the nuclear power lobby.'[13] His parliamentary secretary, Brian Sedgemore, was still more sceptical about Marshall: 'He expressed himself with a certainty on the awesome issues of atomic and nuclear power that I found unnerving.'[14]

Benn and Marshall were soon locked in a noisy deadlock: Benn complained that Marshall could not open his mouth without referring to the pressurised water reactor; Marshall complained that Benn would never commit himself to anything. Benn maintained that the nuclear decision was far too critical to be taken without involving the public, and when the ageing plant at Windscale began to reveal 'worrying events', he demanded that each 'event' was reported to him personally and made sure they were publicised. But he still could not decide about future reactors, and eventually Callaghan as prime minister insisted on getting his own advice from the Think Tank in the Cabinet Office—which turned out to reflect strongly the views of Marshall and the PWR lobby. Benn indignantly rejected the advice, which he and Sedgemore saw as part of the civil servants' conspiracy, and soon afterwards eased Marshall out of his job (four years later he became chairman of the Atomic Energy Authority). But Marshall's successor, Sir Hermann Bondi from the Ministry of Defence, though quieter and more relaxed, turned out also to support the PWR. Benn continued to support the AGR against the unscrupulous opposition (as he saw it) of the arch-capitalist Weinstock: and finally in January 1978 Benn announced that instead of a massive programme of PWRs he had authorised the building of AGRs. 'The triumph is complete,' Sedgemore recorded in his diary. 'A great victory for Tony against great odds.' The triumph was short-lived: two years later the Conservatives, back in power, authorised a modified programme for building PWRs subject to new safeguards. But the public ignorance and suspicion remained profound: 'From first to last,' as Sedgemore com-

---

[13] Benn: *op cit*, p. 81.
[14] Brian Sedgemore: *The Secret Constitution*, Hodder and Stoughton, London, 1980, p. 107.

plained, 'parliament had taken no part in the decision-taking process.'[15]

In the meantime in 1976 the secrecy of the scientific establishment
had been shattered from within. The august nuclear physicist Sir
Brian (later Lord) Flowers had been asked by parliament to report
on the nuclear danger to the environment. Flowers had been an
atomic expert ever since the joint wartime Anglo-Canadian project,
and as a member of the Atomic Energy Authority he was now inside
many confidential debates. But he was concerned about his colleagues' complacency, and worried about the dangers of secrecy: 'I
worked under secrecy-wrappers for years,' he told me, 'and there's
nothing like secrecy for stopping you thinking about things.' He
thought that the commercial nuclear industry 'plays down the fact
that it's safe to supply to other countries, so as not to damage the
British industry'. When Flowers and his colleagues produced their
report in 1976 they warned that the dangers of building power
stations had not been properly disclosed, and that the problems of
disposing of nuclear fuel were still unresolved. They were afraid that
'there may be a gradual step-by-step progression to overriding
dependence on nuclear power through tacit acceptance of its
inevitability'; they warned against the dangers of moving into the
'plutonium economy'; and they insisted that Britain should lessen
her future dependence.

The Flowers Report provided new fuel for the anti-nuclear movement, and infuriated many scientists. 'Some of them saw me as a
traitor,' he said later, 'because I spoke from within their ranks.'
'Flowers did a disservice to the nuclear industry,' Walter Marshall
complained to me. 'If he had fundamental worries he should have
tried to get his way on the AEA.' 'It was a bad and silly report,' said
Sir John Hill, the head of British Nuclear Fuels. 'We should have
refuted it more strongly.' But Flowers had compelled the chief
scientists to try at last to explain themselves. 'We didn't realise early
enough,' admitted Marshall, 'that we had to meet this gap with the
public, to be understandable and authoritative.' 'The gulf between
us and the public is extraordinary,' said Hill. 'They're concerned
about dangers which don't worry us at all, while we're concerned
about dangers which don't worry them.' Hill now produced
speeches and articles answering the environmentalists, admitting
some past mistakes, and promising better public relations. But the
public were not easily reassured after the long record of secrecy.

In March 1979 the nuclear lobby faced a new blow, when the
reactor at Three-Mile Island in Pennsylvania developed a serious
fault; the pumps feeding water to the boilers cut out, causing what

[15] *Ibid*, pp. 122, 124.

Cottrell called 'the most alarming accident in the history of civil and nuclear power'. The population suffered no physical damage, but the subsequent Kemeny Report showed how easily human error could disrupt all the technical precautions. The lack of candour at Three-Mile Island was as disturbing as the fault itself, and the secretiveness of government was reinforced by the secrecy of big business.

Under this cloud of public suspicion the Conservatives inherited the nuclear problem in 1979, with David Howell at the Department of Energy. 'It's impossible to get a disinterested view,' one politician in the department complained to me. 'The nuclear lobby, the coal lobby, the oil lobby, the electrical lobby—they're all being truthful in their own way, but none sees the whole truth. Perhaps Tony Benn was right after all: perhaps only the people can decide.' The commercialisation of nuclear research caused much less disinterested enquiry than the original questioning spirit of the AEA. 'Whoever could work at Dounreay,' said Flowers, 'and believe that nuclear power had no future?' The Tories were back with indecision. Mrs Thatcher, who had been a scientist, had once said that she did not need a minister for science because she could decide; and some scientists hoped for a new decisiveness at the top. But in two years the prime minister gave no evidence of having taken any scientific decision.

The government agreed to a public enquiry on the next power station, to bring all the fears and arguments out into the open and the protesters were now focusing on the little hamlet of Sizewell on the Suffolk coast, where the government wanted to build a new PWR reactor, not too unlike that in Three-Mile Island. Sizewell presented a typical conflict of local interests: it already had one much-criticised ageing reactor, on a cliff looming over the Minsmere bird sanctuary, just north of the unspoilt eighteenth-century town of Aldeburgh; but it was also next door to the Victorian industrial town of Leiston, which had once built the first steam-harvesters but was now full of unemployed looking for work.

How could a sensible decision be reached about the nuclear future? The scientists had very different viewpoints. From Cambridge Sir Alan Cottrell complained that the general public 'has been let down by nearly everyone concerned'—including the nuclear authorities who had alienated many people by their secretiveness and 'daddy-knows-best' attitudes, and the media who played up every sensation.[16] More radical scientists complained that conservatives like Cottrell were reducing the nuclear debate to a cold-war

[16] Cottrell: *op cit*, pp. 3ff.

issue, implying that attacks on nuclear power were strengthening the Soviet hand. Lord Flowers insisted on a middle way between the simplifications of populists and the media, and the closed world of experts and businessmen. 'You can't allow decisions to be taken by two men. You can't solve the problem by narrow agreement, any more than by populism,' he says. 'You can only make progress with some kind of informed consensus.'

No country has solved the problem, and each country's debate about nuclear power reflects its own political character. In France the government, which was accustomed to bold planning decisions (and which controlled television coverage), could more easily take a gamble, suppressing public debate until the first power stations were built. The United States had a more extensive and informed debate than anywhere, but also more powerful commercial pressures. But the British have been the most indecisive. The scientists can convincingly blame the politicians: 'Life is so complex nowadays,' as Marshall put it, 'that politicians avoid any decisions which are emotional or controversial.' But the politicians complain in their select committee that the scientists' evidence has been thoroughly unconvincing, as they insist on the superiority of one different system after another; and the scientists are reluctant to recognise that they depend on some kind of democratic process.

The nuclear dilemma turns out to be an extension of Britain's political dilemma: the failure to give democratic direction. The essential plans for the future depend on both politicians and experts taking decisions boldly but carefully, acting on all the information available and knowing that the results will be felt for decades to come. But the cross-purposes between scientists and Whitehall, and between scientists and the public, have made bold decisions increasingly difficult. 'It doesn't matter how well you build nuclear power stations,' as Sir John Hill put it to me, 'if the public won't let you build them.'

15

Diplomats: Salesmen and Spies

If foreign ministries did not already exist, they surely would not have
to be invented.

Zbigniew Brzezinski, 1970

In the control of society's foreign affairs democratic governments do
appear decidedly inferior to others.

De Tocqueville: Democracy in America

THE most persistent of all Whitehall wars has been the conflict
between Treasury men and diplomats, who are heirs to opposite
traditions: the clerks and the knights. Home civil servants not surprisingly resent the hauteur and extravagance of diplomats, the most
self-contained of Britain's elites, who so often seem to represent the
Foreign Office rather than Britain. As Edmund Wilson said of
Harold Nicolson in the twenties, 'In spite of his travels he has only
resided in one country—the British Foreign Office, approaching
foreigners from a special caste.' The diplomats have been the most
evident symbols of a country with a great imperial past, reluctant to
come to terms with a commercial and workaday future.

Every democratic country treats its diplomats with suspicion, as
operators in a rarified international network who are cut off from the
emotions of ordinary people, and too readily come to terms with
foreigners; while the diplomats, as Tocqueville suggests, are apt to
regard democratic debate as an unwelcome intrusion into a subtle
and secretive art. But the British diplomats have long incurred
special suspicion and envy. They have established their own loyalties and networks, even more effectively than the home civil servants,
so that ex-ambassadors can slip into jobs as company directors,
heads of institutes or colleges. Unlike permanent secretaries they
write confident memoirs, with titles like *The Ruling Few* and *The Inner
Circle*, revealing the follies of politicians; and they perpetuate the
image of an Establishment which alone understands the real prob-

lems of the world. The rest of Whitehall is not altogether sorry when the diplomats are periodically made fools of.

The attempts to reform the diplomats provide a familiar saga of frustration. The most ambitious attempt was begun in the worst phase of the Second World War, when Eden and Bevin tried to widen the narrow circle of diplomats and to bring in specialists and even women. They managed to integrate the separate branches of diplomacy including consuls, and to widen recruitment, but the Foreign Office still kept much of its exclusive arrogance. In 1962 another committee under Lord Plowden complained about the diplomats' amateurism and lack of specialisation, but still without much effect. Six years later the Treasury, appalled by the extravagance of the diplomats, insisted on *another* committee, headed by a mining entrepreneur, Sir Val Duncan. He and two colleagues produced a forthright report pointing out that Britain was now 'a major power of the second order', and was like a man who has to give up his Rolls Royce in favour of a smaller car. They made some devastating criticisms: much embassy accounting was 'in or near the quill pen era', many attachés were dispensable, and many jobs could be done much more cheaply by flying diplomats out from London. In reply the Foreign Office mounted a powerful lobby in Westminster and frustrated most of the committee's intentions.

The most drastic criticism of all came in 1977 from the cabinet Think Tank—a team of young economists, including two women, under Sir Kenneth Berrill. They travelled extensively and were shocked by the waste and extravagance in the embassies: the houses were too big and there were too many cars. The diplomats were out of touch with events at home and spent far too much time on 'cocktail party circuits' and 'insubstantial entertaining'. The service was overmanned with highly-paid people, including twelve men of permanent secretary rank. 'It is misleading and dangerous,' the report summed up, 'to think that the United Kingdom can maintain its position in the world by keeping up appearances.' They recommended more cuts, more specialisation in exports, and more interchange between the foreign service and the home civil service.

Many younger diplomats had themselves complained about the overmanning and wastefulness of their service (at least until they reached the age when they themselves might become redundant). But a public attack, as in so many attempted reforms, made them close ranks; and the Think Tank had made a tactical blunder in extending its criticism to the British Council and the BBC Foreign

Services (which employed many journalists whose support the diplomats could count on). Senior ambassadors led by Sir Nicholas Henderson in Paris spent much time trying to demolish the report, spreading stories about the Think Tank 'butterflies'. Retired diplomats made speeches in the House of Lords and wrote letters to *The Times* pointing out the essential role of grand representation. Popular papers even printed photographs of 'dippy' wives demonstrating about their hard lives. In the uproar the critics suffered more than the diplomats. It was not until two years later, under the Thatcher government, that the foreign service began to face serious cuts; and even then it could deflect part of the damage away from its own embassies, towards the BBC. The diplomats who were employed to represent their country were certainly adept in representing their own interests.

DIPLOMATS AND EUROPE

Whitehall's dislike of the diplomats was based not only on their extravagant style, but on the suspicion that on important issues they were usually wrong, because they were cocooned from Britain's economic realities, and never thought clearly about her future role in the world. And critics could point with some justification to the record on Europe.

When the European Community was being created in the mid-fifties, and eagerly inviting Britain to join, the British diplomats, like most politicians, were still basking in past Atlantic glories. They were mostly bored by economics and trade, and when Europe began to revive and unite they scarcely noticed it. When the movement was launched in Messina in 1955 the British ambassadors in Europe advised against taking it seriously and the ambassador in Paris, Sir Gladwyn Jebb, was not then (as he has explained)[1] a convinced European; as a result only one British observer from the Board of Trade, Russell Bretherton, watched the birth of the Common Market in Messina. The Foreign Office was far more interested in the United States, and American influence extended further into Whitehall in 1956 when Sir Roger Makins, former ambassador to Washington, became joint head of the Treasury. Even after the Treaty of Rome had been signed in 1957 and the Common Market was visibly working, the Foreign Office regarded it largely as a trade question to be left to the Treasury, and the treaty was not even properly translated into English. And it was the Treasury which first began to take Europe more seriously when Sir Frank Lee, a newly-convinced European, became its head in 1960.

[1] Lord Gladwyn: *Memoirs*, Weidenfeld and Nicolson, London, 1972, p. 288.

After Macmillan had tried and failed to join the Common Market in 1962, the diplomats were at last converted to the idea of Europe. But they were not very subtle Europeans. They were soon locked into a feud with de Gaulle, believing they could isolate France by wooing the other five members; but de Gaulle had the veto, and the French were still the key. The Paris embassy went into a sulk, cultivating what George Brown called an 'arid frigidity',[2] and even stopping Princess Margaret from going to a party in Paris. Only when a political ambassador, Christopher Soames, was appointed in Paris was there some movement; but when Soames had a secret talk with de Gaulle, the Foreign Office quickly leaked it to the other five to make sure that relations would not get further. It was an incident (as Douglas Hurd, now Minister of State in the Foreign Office, put it) which only made sense 'if one remembers this ancient bitterness between the two great diplomatic services of Europe.'[3] It was Ted Heath as prime minister, not the diplomats, who broke the deadlock by negotiating directly with Pompidou in 1971, and who eventually got Britain into Europe in spite of the diplomats. Not until the mid-seventies did the Foreign Office fully come to terms with Europe—encouraged by a new generation of diplomats with more European than American wives, who had a more realistic view of Britain's economy.

But Whitehall soon suspected that the Foreign Office was becoming *too* preoccupied with Europe, engrossed in the intricate negotiations about common policies, initiatives and declarations, and forgetting about the rest of the world. The Commonwealth's own department had been absorbed to create what was officially called the Foreign and Commonwealth Office; but India, Africa and the Caribbean now appeared very secondary to the European capitals, and their High Commissioners had to look for support to the Commonwealth Secretariat in Marlborough House, or even to Buckingham Palace.

The diplomats' obsession with Europe—interspersed with occasional forays into the Middle East—made them more unpopular with many politicians: and when the Labour party came out against the Common Market after 1979 any appearance of a bipartisan foreign policy was broken making the diplomats more vulnerable to attack. Mrs Thatcher herself was very suspicious of her diplomats' Eurospeak and their insistence on a European consensus, which she saw as deflecting the national purpose.

---

[2] George Brown: *In My Way*, Gollancz, London, 1971.
[3] Douglas Hurd: *An End to Promises*, Collins, London, 1979, p. 58.

EMBASSIES AND EXCELLENCIES

Successive reforms have gradually changed the characteristics of diplomats, and recruits are nowadays less distinguishable from home civil servants; none the less the Foreign Office still has a higher proportion of public school men and graduates with first class degrees, and the uprooted career of a British diplomat sets him apart with that combination of grandeur and insecurity which can often generate pomposity. The first years can be exciting, when young diplomats can participate in decisions and share the secret telegrams of the great, and the collegiate atmosphere has its advantages over the lumbering bureaucracy of American diplomats; but the comradeship can also reinforce the resistance to change and specialisation. (Diplomats are still criticised for being amateurish, even in languages, and in 1980 a committee of MPs complained that only half of the staff in the Paris embassy spoke tolerable French: 'They get by,' mocked the MP for Hertford, Bowen Wells, 'by speaking English very loudly.')

It is in their thirties that many diplomats become frustrated, as they continue their nomadic career, nagged by their wives about their recurring exiles in rented houses, and finding the roads to the top overcrowded. Some of the ablest leave in their thirties; some are given early retirement in their early fifties; and even ambassadors may be eased out before the retiring age of sixty. While the diplomats have resisted being integrated with the workaday home civil service, their way of life has miseries as well as splendours, and by their late forties many of them reveal that well-known *déformation professionnelle*—the incuriosity and reluctance to listen, the 'male menopause', the nostalgia for a vanished life-style at home.

The path to the peaks of diplomacy can be very dispiriting. The British foreign service, unlike the French, resents young high-fliers, and perpetuates 'Buggins' turn', promoting ambassadors according to seniority rather than appropriateness, sending a man to Paris who hardly speaks French, a man to Jerusalem who cannot stand the Israelis, a man to the magnificent embassy in Rome who is bored with entertaining Italians. 'The odd thing about the Office,' as one ex-ambassador complained, 'is that they don't really know who is a good diplomat and who isn't.' Once he becomes an ambassador, a diplomat still enjoys a special splendour: His Excellency represents the Queen and is a miniature monarch in his own embassy. But the greater his dignity, the more exasperating his loss of influence, when his political masters at home can easily by-pass him with jet planes, telephones and telex.

Ambassadors nowadays like to dispel the atmosphere of rarified

old-style diplomacy and present themselves as hard-hitting salesmen—particularly arms salesmen. They rattle off details of contracts
and companies, and welcome visiting businessmen to lunch, who
twenty years ago would have been left to the commercial attaché.
(But are they entertaining for the future of their country or for
themselves, an unkind sceptic might wonder, when a retired ambassador reappears later as a company director?) Sometimes the
diplomats' enthusiasm for trade has gone *too* far. The British
embassy in Tehran before 1979 looked more like a trade fair, full of
brochures, posters and travelling salesmen: and the diplomats were
so eager to encourage exports to the Shah's regime that they took
little notice of the reports from the bazaars and the mosques that the
Shah would soon be toppled. The Foreign Office later commissioned
their own secret report on why they had been taken by surprise by
the Iranian revolution: it showed that the traditional Islamic expertise of the diplomats and the 'Friends' in the secret service—which
had been so useful in helping to reinstate the Shah in 1953—had been
neglected in the commercial excitement and preoccupation with
communism.

The traditional top postings are to the two grandest embassies,
Paris and Washington, which each cast spells over their inhabitants.
The Paris embassy is one of the most magnificent private residences,
bought from Napoleon's sister, with a theatrical staircase, a ball-
room and a huge garden going down to the Champs Elysées; but
since Lord Soames left in 1972 no ambassador has had a grand
enough style to live up to it. The present occupant is a career
diplomat confusingly called Major John Fretwell, whose first name
is Major but who prefers to be called John. He went from Chester-
field Grammar School to Lausanne University and Cambridge,
married a French wife and served in Moscow, Pekin and most
recently as minister (no. 2) in Washington, where he was tipped for
high promotion. But it is too soon to know his form in Paris; and the
actual requirements of the ambassador are never quite clear in an
age when politicians, civil servants and Eurocrats are constantly
shuttling across the Channel.

The Washington embassy has long been the despair of reformers
and critics, with its staff of 600 providing a miniature Whitehall,
mostly insulated from contact with Americans; and its bureaucracy
is so cumbersome that senior diplomats in London prefer to fly to
Washington themselves to get through to their American counterparts. Past ambassadors have alternated between career diplomats
and politicians, but after David Owen appointed his prime minister's son-in-law, Peter Jay, his successor Lord Carrington preferred
to appoint professionals after retiring age. He first chose Sir Nicholas

Henderson, the debonair former ambassador in Paris who had recently espoused the Tory cause, whose tall shape and long drooping hair hovered over visiting ministers. He was tipped to be succeeded by Sir Anthony Parsons, an Arabist who was ambassador to Iran during the fall of the Shah, but who survived to become representative at the United Nations. He is an unconventional and unpompous man with many American friendships; and he showed his skills as a patient and courteous negotiator over the Falklands.

The more influential top diplomats, who are less obviously grand than the ambassadors, are the cluster of knights in the great Foreign Office palazzo in Whitehall who are engaged in perpetual policy-making alongside their political masters. They still belong to a very rarified world. Twenty years ago Sir Harold Nicolson, in a lecture on 'The Old Diplomacy and the New', explained that 'today it is as difficult for an aristocrat to enter the foreign service as it would be for a camel, loaded with the bales of Eton and Balliol to pass through the eye of a needle'. Today the Foreign Secretary and Head of the Service are both Etonians, and the deputy-head is a Balliol man.

Sir Antony Acland, the permanent under-secretary—the misleadingly humble title for the top diplomat—rose up through the most traditional route, from a landed family to Eton to Christ Church, to the school of Arabic, to being private secretary to the Foreign Secretary and eventually ambassador in Madrid. He is urbane, courteous and has no known political views. His deputy, Julian Bullard, is a more original and academic diplomat, who holds the post of Political Director, in charge of co-ordinating policy with other Europeans. He comes from the heart of the Balliolocracy: his grandfather was the great Master of Balliol, A. L. Smith; his father, Sir Reader Bullard, also from Balliol, became ambassador in Tehran; and Julian, like his brother, went from Balliol to the foreign service. He remains an intellectual more than an apparatchik, with a questioning long-term view of the world.

FOREIGN SECRETARY

When Lord Carrington became Foreign Secretary in 1979, moving into the ornate Victorian room, he was soon seen as the 'diplomat's diplomat', a welcome relief after the abrasive style of his predecessor, David Owen, who enjoyed deflating his ambassadors and officials. Carrington immediately went round the old building shaking hands with nearly everyone, spreading his charm and breezy style. He was already the model of the modernised Tory aristocrat, having held office under Macmillan, Home, Heath and

Thatcher, fitting in with all of them. With his comic face, drooping chin and huge spectacles he could disarm the most wary critic, always apparently delighted to see any acquaintance, desolated to see them go. His throwaway humour, with a touch of P. G. Wodehouse, was a useful smokescreen and he liked to use frivolity as a weapon—though it could exasperate Americans—dismissing what he disliked as boring. He had a short attention span—particularly about economics—but he was quick at assessing people and sizing up arguments. He could impress Africans and Asians as well as Labour MPs, but behind his jollity he was basically pessimistic, inclined to assume, like Lord Melbourne, that all change was for the worst, and easily depressed by the Third World.

Carrington had a special political significance as a link between Thatcher's lower-middle-class Tories and the dwindling aristocratic tradition. His ancestor Thomas Smith set up a bank in Nottingham which became a financial power in the eighteenth century—its entrance is still visible next to the Royal Exchange—before it was absorbed into what is now the National Westminster Bank. His descendant Robert Smith, who lived in Whitehall, was banker to the prime minister William Pitt, and one day he asked him for the privilege of driving through the Horse Guards. 'No, I can't give you that,' said Pitt, 'but I will make you an Irish peer' (a cheap way to reward political service). So Mr Smith became Lord Carrington.[4]

The present Lord Carrington went through Eton and Sandhurst and the wartime Grenadier Guards without going to university. As a young peer he could slip effortlessly into politics: eventually Macmillan made him First Lord of the Admiralty and Heath made him Minister of Defence. When Mrs Thatcher was elected leader Carrington deployed all his charm to reconcile Heath to her, but in vain. Thatcher was wary of his political past, his giggly style and his charming way with foreigners, but she found him indispensable; and he knew, unlike most of his colleagues, how to treat her as a woman. He was sometimes talked of as the next Tory prime minister, but he had one fatal disqualification: he was still in the House of Lords. He could have renounced his title in 1963 as did Home and Hailsham, but it would have looked too silly (he once told me) for all three to become commoners: and he thought he did not want to be premier anyway. His presence in the Lords eased the task of being Foreign Secretary, and he could leave the rough questioning in the Commons to his number two, first Ian Gilmour, then Humphrey Atkins. But it added to the occupational hazard of diplomats, who can easily lose touch with the politics of the market-place.

As Foreign Secretary Lord Carrington had great strengths. He

[4] G. W. E. Russell: *Collections and Recollections*, Smith, Elder, London, 1904, p.217.

had easy access to the Reagan administration, tried to moderate some of their cruder anti-communist attitudes and persuaded them to press for an independent Namibia. He was assiduous in trying to establish a common European foreign policy, particularly regarding the Palestinians. And he achieved a public triumph in successfully negotiating for an independent Zimbabwe. Several other factors contributed to that success. Mrs Thatcher herself, after Carrington had first persuaded her to switch her line, kept pressing for an overall settlement when Carrington was not hopeful; the unconventional young diplomats tirelessly kept the talks going; the Commonwealth Secretariat kept the lines open to Robert Mugabe, whom Carrington never expected to win power; Lord Soames gained Mugabe's confidence during the transition. But Carrington had skillfully presided over one of the most remarkable of many ex-imperial turnabouts, which had transmuted the 'Marxist terrorists' into a responsible independent state, anti-Soviet and pro-British.

Despite this Carrington remained largely preoccupied with Europe: 'I see my European opposite numbers,' he explained, 'rather more often than I see some of my colleagues in the cabinet.' And he was easily bored by less pressing issues—including the North-South debate, most of the Commonwealth and . . . the Falkland Islands. Many politicians and diplomats were bored by the problem of 1,800 islanders in the South Atlantic, who stubbornly resisted any settlement between Britain and Argentina, who had been sporadically negotiating for the last twenty years. The British and Argentinian diplomats were often not far apart: 'Some of my more *insouciant* British colleagues,' one British former negotiator told me, 'may have given the Argentinians the impression that we'd be quite glad to get rid of the islands.' When the Argentinians once again became more threatening in March 1982 and then took over the island of South Georgia the Foreign Office, with all their intelligence networks and thirty diplomats in Buenos Aires, still appeared conciliatory and even approved the sale of spare parts for their weapons. Even some hours after Argentinian troops had actually landed on the Falklands, Carrington still appeared to think that they were not very serious.

Then the next day parliament was recalled and the politicians burst out with all their newly-found passion; the diplomats were denounced as appeasers, and the fleet was mobilised. Carrington made a mild speech in the House of Lords but was then invited by Whitelaw to listen to the stormy debate in the Commons. He was appalled by the rush of demagogy and agonised by his own misjudgment; and after a weekend of anguish he insisted on resigning—not in protest against the government's policy but in acknowledgment of his own mistake. It was the first real resignation on a point of honour since Carrington's boss at the Ministry of Agriculture, Sir Thomas Dugdale, had resigned over the Crichel Down scandal in 1954.

In the frenzied new political atmosphere, Mrs Thatcher had to reassure all wings of her party, and she turned to a man who had been increasingly critical of her economic policies, Francis Pym. He had hoped to become Foreign Secretary three years earlier, but had been made Minister of Defence, until he was moved after his resistance to Thatcher's cuts. Pym had even longer Tory roots than Carrington, from an old land-owning family going back to the great parliamentarian, John Pym, who opposed King Charles I in the year 1629. He was a duller man than Carrington, without his panache: he has a nervous habit of pulling down the bottom of his suit-jacket. He has no obvious views on anything, but has natural political skills and an instinctive feel for the House of Commons, where he was a much-admired chief whip. He is difficult to dislike, with a relaxed and genial style; and he has one great advantage—a voice, a deep, strong voice which carries conviction. Moving into Carrington's job, he was soon able to reassure his party as the naval armada set sail for the South Atlantic, without saying very much but promising in full voice that 'Britain does not appease dictators'. And his position in his party was now almost impregnable, for the prime minister could not afford to disregard him.

The humiliation of Carrington and the Foreign Office had a flick in the tail. The critical days after the Falklands' invasion rapidly tested Britain's friendships. The Commonwealth Secretariat, which the Foreign Office had long disdained, was swiftly able to rally most African, Asian and Caribbean countries in Britain's defence, thus confuting charges of neo-colonialism. The Washington administration which Mrs Thatcher had so loyally supported through their most unpopular policies, insisted for three weeks on remaining 'even-handed' between Britain and Argentina, while the Europeans whom she had despised as compromisers unanimously denounced the Argentinian invasion and imposed their own sanctions. But the Europeans were soon back in disfavour, when they overrode a British veto on higher farm prices, and their support for the British policy on the Falklands waned as it became more warlike. And the Falklands crisis still exposed the diplomats to the recurring complaints: why could they never think ahead, to foresee Britain's future role in the world?

SECRET SERVICES

He that has a secret should not only hide it but hide that he has it to hide.

Thomas Carlyle

Under the spreading chestnut tree, I sold you and you sold me.

George Orwell, 1984

In the shadowy regions between diplomacy and defence, the British secret organisations have long generated a fascination out of proportion to their numbers. Secrecy is one of the British obsessions, like class, which seems to express a deeper psychological need, as if it were a substitute for the mystery of a religion. Power in Britain originated in secrecy, as in America it thrived on publicity. Many of the attitudes of Whitehall administrators, cultivating their own mystery, go back to their origins as 'the secret garden of the Crown'; there is a special magic for others as well as James Bond in being 'On Her Majesty's Secret Service'. But civil servants can easily use secrecy as a means of protecting themselves from accountability and questioning rather than as a genuine defence against external dangers: 'Of course secrecy is the easiest way to protect ourselves,' as one permanent secretary explained. While most public documents are released after thirty years, many historical secrets are still safeguarded. 'There are some secret documents about the Napoleonic Wars which the Foreign Office still won't release,' a distinguished historian complained to me. 'They explain that their contents might offend the French.'

While the American security services, the FBI and the CIA, exhibit themselves with proud buildings and signposts, the British still prefer to pretend that their secret services simply do not exist, which makes MI5 and MI6 much more exciting to thriller writers and paranoiacs. Their directors' names are kept secret with the help of 'D-notices' sent to newspaper editors; spies and spymasters, even when knighted, are described in *Who's Who* as part of the foreign service, while diplomats refer to them as 'the Friends'. Their anonymity helps them to move in the conventional world without recognition or awe; but their names are well known to any interested foreign power. MI5 and MI6, though often confused, have quite separate functions and characters. MI5, which is concerned with Britain's own security and catching foreign spies, has basically cautious officials, not recruited until they are over twenty-five, and many of them professional men. MI6, otherwise known as the Secret Intelligence Service (SIS), operates its own espionage and intelligence abroad, and recruits more buccaneering and tricky people, with a good deal of aggression or acquisitiveness. 'The most idealistic people,' said one ex-MI6 official, 'turn out to be the most venal in the end.'

In the seventies the British public became still more fascinated with the mystery of the secret services, encouraged by a vast output of spy-thrillers and by revelations which appeared to corroborate the fiction. The novels of John le Carré, exploring the psychological subtleties of deception and treachery, seemed to compete with the true-life epics of defecting British diplomats; while the character of George Smiley, le Carré's fictional head of MI6, seemed to merge with the actual former director, Sir Maurice Oldfield, who was called back to Northern Ireland before he died in 1981. Oldfield himself was appropriately enigmatic; a podgy round-headed bachelor with thick glasses and a slow charm which attracted women. The son of a Derbyshire farmer, he became a medieval historian at Manchester University, but kept his country roots. In the buccaneering sub-aristocratic world of British espionage he was the 'sceptical spider' who could get under other people's skin and understand their hidden springs.

The subtler spy novels about conflicts of loyalties and seedy treason, together with the revelations about actual traitors, were especially enthralling in a period of retreat from world power and certainty. 'The British are obsessed with treachery and deception,' one espionage expert explained, 'as the Germans are with terrorism, and the Israelis with commandos.' But the secret service was itself in some decline, only partly concealed by its relationships with American intelligence. The limitations of both were painfully revealed in 1979 in Iran, where twenty-six years earlier they had planned the coup which reinstated the Shah on the throne; and the failure to foresee the importance of the Ayatollahs was a bitter humilation to the older professionals, including Oldfield. Like the armed forces, the secret service has retreated from its previous world role; and Northern Ireland now provides the chief challenge to its skills.

Yet the frenzy of interest in spies and spymasters was itself a kind of decoy: the public, as in other fields, was becoming fascinated with them just when their importance was fading. Electronic systems of bugging and interception, which could pick up messages round the world without dealing with dubious intermediaries, were becoming much more valued. The British have developed their own elaborate systems, under their own secret department SIGINT, or Signals Intelligence; but they are also closely linked through NATO with their American counterparts, including the National Security Agency (NSA), more secretive and expensive than the CIA. To record conversations inside cars in Moscow or in committee rooms in Tripoli seemed to open up a huge new area of both espionage and diplomacy. The politicians in the Ministry of Defence in Whitehall value their links with Washington intelligence not just because of the actual information, but because of the thrilling sense of sharing the world's eavesdropping.

British governments are even more secretive about the existence of SIGINT than about their older intelligence agencies, and they disclose nothing officially about its base, known as Government Communications Headquarters (GCHQ), in two big office blocks in Cheltenham. Some past secrets of British wartime interception and code-breaking have been revealed since the publication of the book, *The Ultra Secret*, by Group Captain Winterbotham in 1974, and some of the wartime history of MI5 and MI6 is now emerging semi-officially, in books written under the pseudonym of Nigel West, with co-operation from former agents.[5] But these help to provide a diversion from contemporary electronic secrets; and the global expansion of monitoring systems since the Second World War has remained under wraps. The British system is linked to the Americans, and also with Canada, Australia and New Zealand, to provide a world network, including ex-imperial outposts such as Malta, Ascension Island and Mauritius; the Foreign Office dreads that revelations might cause diplomatic convulsions, cutting them off from American and other intelligence.

Yet the British obsession with secrecy can often work against itself, attracting attention by its obvious anxiety; this was very evident in 1977, in the extraordinary story of Colonel B. It began when the magazine *Time Out* published an article by two journalists, Mark Hosenball and Duncan Campbell, which referred to British electronic installations and links with the NSA. The British intelligence chiefs were alarmed: Hosenball, who was American, was hastily deported, while Campbell, a young English journalist who had specialised in electronic information, was a marked man. Soon afterwards Campbell and another journalist interviewed a former intelligence corporal about the workings of SIGINT—which revealed very little—and all three were arrested and charged under the Official Secrets Act. At the preliminary hearings the prosecution produced an intelligence officer who gave evidence under the name of Colonel B, whose real name was censored by a 'D-notice' to newspapers. But the mystery merely attracted the curiosity of radical journalists, who quickly revealed him in their union magazine *The Journalist* as Colonel Hugh Johnstone, and were then charged

[5] See Nigel West: *MI5: British Security Service Operations 1909–1945*, Bodley Head, London, 1981 (to be followed by a volume on MI6).

with contempt of court. When the journalists held their annual union meeting at the seaside the police followed them, to prevent the name being repeated; but Johnstone's name was already written in the sand, and delegates shouted it at the conference. Then four Labour MPs repeated the name in parliament, using their privilege; the Director of Public Prosecutions warned editors not to publish it, but even *The Times* mentioned Colonel Johnstone, explaining that it had been its duty to report parliament faithfully for the last two hundred years. Colonel Hugh Johnstone was now the most famous officer in the British army.

The trial of Duncan Campbell and the two others followed the next year, and the Attorney-General now used all his legal weaponry, charging them under the harshest section of the Official Secrets Act, directed against 'spies and saboteurs'. But the defence counsel, Lord Hutchinson, was able to show that every piece of information in the original article in *Time Out* was available in already-published sources, including the journal of the Royal Signals Association, *Wire*, which was among Campbell's favourite reading-matter. The judge clearly disapproved of the more extreme charges, and eventually insisted that they should be dropped; in the end he gave the two journalists a conditional discharge, and the corporal a suspended sentence. The whole case had been counter-productive: far from scaring journalists away, it had focused national interest on official secrets, and Campbell now continued to uncover facts about electronic intelligence, phone-tapping and secret installations in the left-wing *New Statesman*. The blundering military tactics were despised by more sophisticated civilian intelligence experts: 'Military intelligence,' Sir Maurice Oldfield was heard to remark, 'has the same kind of relationship to real intelligence as military music has to real music.'

The intelligence services remained outside the supervision of parliament, or even the cabinet; and it was always possible for them to use secrecy to protect themselves rather than the nation. Members of parliament found it impossible to investigate and reassure themselves about the frontiers of intelligence, even though they were concerned that the secret network could be used not only against enemies abroad, but against enemies at home. While Congress in Washington has devised its own system of scrutiny, British MPs achieved nothing when they questioned the prime minister, who is responsible for the intelligence services. As Harold Wilson put it in *The Governance of Britain*: 'The prime minister is occasionally questioned on matters arising out of his responsibilities. His answers may be regarded as uniformly uninformative.' [6]

[6] Harold Wilson: *The Governance of Britain*, Michael Joseph, London, 1976, pp. 167–8.

A long-standing rivalry separates Signals Intelligence on one side and MI6, or 'Human Resource Reporting', on the other. Old-fashioned espionage has been partly discredited by the record of defections and doubtful loyalties; but electronic espionage, with its massive output of 'raw' intelligence, presents its own problems of assessment and interpretation, which depends in the end on highly intelligent men at the top. During the Second World War the head of MI6, Sir Stewart Menzies, insisted on maintaining control over the crical de-coding headquarters at Bletchley, with its team of dons supervised by Alexander Denniston, which was the original of the later network of SIGINT. But the two systems are now very separate, each providing very different material to the diplomats in charge of each country or region in the Foreign Office. It is in the Cabinet Office, next door to the prime minister's own secretariat in Downing Street, that the secret services have been centred, more thoroughly since the reign of Sir Burke Trend, the durable Secretary of the Cabinet under Harold Wilson. And it is in the Cabinet Office that the different intelligence networks come together, under the Joint Intelligence Committee which is made up not of ministers but of civil servants and intelligence officers, who are responsible to the prime minister, through the Cabinet Secretary.

It is the Joint Intelligence Committee and its secretariat which decides on the 'tasking'—directing the intelligence towards particular areas and concerns—and which assesses the information that comes back, whether from MI6, from SIGINT or from America and other NATO sources. The JIC is the real battleground between the intelligence systems and the chairmanship is one of the most crucial, and most secretive, jobs in Whitehall. For some years the post was occupied by a man from GCHQ, Sir Leonard Hooper (who was involved in the case against Duncan Campbell) and who caused some resentment among MI6 people. Now the position is held by a former diplomat, Sir Antony Duff, who has past links with intelligence. He is an admiral's son who began his career as a regular naval officer and married a naval captain's daughter; but he moved into the Foreign Service after the war, and rose rapidly. When Lord Carrington needed the best possible team to negotiate the Rhodesia settlement he chose Duff to lead it, which he did with great skill, and Duff became Deputy Governor of Rhodesia under Lord Soames, during its transition into Zimbabwe. When Duff was due for retirement in 1980 he was asked to take over the Joint Intelligence Committee in the Cabinet Office, and thus entered the heart of the secrecy world, working alongside the Secretary of the Cabinet, Sir Robert Armstrong, but directly responsible to the prime minister. It was an indication of Duff's central importance that he was, unlike Armstrong, appointed as a Privy Councillor when he took the new job—an honour usually restricted to former cabinet ministers, senior judges and some peers. The secret services still retained their historic links with the Crown.

It is Duff and his committee who have to weigh and assess the significance of all the conflicting messages about international crises—whether about Iran, or about Poland or about the Falkland Islands, which provided their most recent test. British intelligence was well-placed to assess the true intentions of Argentinian governments, with the help of the big embassy and of Signals Intelligence, which could use the signals station on Ascension Island to pick up Argentinian messages. The Labour MP Ted Rowlands, who was a minister in the Foreign Office up to 1979, involved in negotiations over the Falklands, explained that the British had been able to listen in to Argentinian conversations and read their telegrams. Lord Carrington was well aware that the Argentinian fleet was moving towards the Falklands on a naval exercise in late March 1982, and the occupation of South Georgia already gave warning of the new tension.

Given the flow of signals, human resource reporting and political assessments, how could the Foreign Office be so unprepared when the Falklands were in fact invaded? However comprehensive the intelligence system, it still depended on very human assessments and human mistakes; and the past blunders, whether over Iran or over Vietnam, have shown the fundamental difficulty of all political intelligence: that it is very difficult to tell politicians what they do not want to know.

16

Armed Forces: the Victory for Secrecy

The British forces have nothing but generals, admirals and bands.
General George S. Brown
(former Chairman of the US Joint Chiefs of Staff)

Army, Navy,
Medicine, Law,
Church, Nobility,
Nothing at all.

Cherry-stone Rhyme

THE place of the armed forces in the national psyche has always been uncertain. Britain has liked to regard herself as one of the least military of nations, able to put away the symbols of war as soon as peace is declared. The links between politicians and the services are slender: since the Duke of Wellington no military man has become prime minister; Major Healey, Colonel Heath and Brigadier Powell soon abandoned their titles when they left the wartime forces. But military values still play an unseen part in the country's thinking, like an old pistol kept in a cupboard. The sense of military hierarchy and the ancient class division between officers and NCOs can still be perceived through the ranks of industrial corporations: the army's sense of order and structure appears more attractive to many people as civilian society becomes more confused and indisciplined. In moments of national humiliation or bewilderment, the British can still summon up almost instantly the memories of the Second World War, which her former enemies had no difficulty in forgetting.

The three services have been the most obvious symbols of Britain's declining world role, whittled down with each economic crisis, and subjected to drastic and often contradictory reassessments. While the Foreign Office could never decide about Britain's future world role, the services suffered most from that indecision. In 1957, when there were still 720,000 men under arms, Duncan Sandys as Minister of Defence concluded his ruthless Defence

Review which concentrated on small mobile forces and the nuclear deterrent and abolished conscription. In 1964 Denis Healey cut down the nuclear force and cancelled Britain's fighter-bomber, the TSR2, and in 1967 he began withdrawing British forces from East of Suez. By 1975 the Labour government had reduced the defence budget to 4½ per cent of the GNP, cutting back overseas bases still further. By early 1981 the total forces were 330,000—less than half the number a quarter-century earlier.

The generals, admirals and air marshals had seen more rapid changes in their role and technology than almost any elite, as the territory they were defending had dwindled from a quarter of the world's population to the frontiers of Western Europe—including Ulster, the threatened corner of the United Kingdom itself. Yet they had kept their morale and prestige more intact than most other professions: while politicians or bureaucrats were constantly under attack the generals were largely outside the political firing-line.

The services were so effectively cut off from most people's lives that they were largely forgotten. Since national service was abolished they have had less contact with ordinary civilians, to the relief of many regular officers. ('Conscription may have been good for the country,' said General Sir Richard Hull in 1962, 'but it damn near killed the army.') The army and navy are still among the most tribal institutions, with their own families, regions and retiring-grounds; dedicated and loyal and proud, but often politically naive, easily out-argued by politicians or civil servants. 'For the first time the boards don't have admirals and generals who fought in the Second World War,' said a senior civil servant in Defence. 'The military experience is much narrower and more specialised—moving between Britain, Ulster and Germany—and other civil servants find it harder to deal with them.'

MINISTRY OF DEFENCE

The segregation of the forces is aptly expressed by the Ministry of Defence, in its desolate stone fortress between Whitehall and the river, the most impenetrable of all the Whitehall bureaucracies. The overmanning, the perks and the fleets of military cars have long been the despair of the Treasury and civil service reformers; even Derek Rayner, though he managed to rationalise procurement, was baffled by the labyrinthine structure of the ministry. Since Harold Macmillan twenty years ago abolished the political heads of the three services, including the ancient post of First Lord of the Admiralty, the minister has had much greater power, responsible for the whole population of the services as well as the civilians; but the vast apparatus has become still more cut off from public inspection.

Since then successive politicians have tried to integrate the three services into a more unified structure, but of all the many mergers of the sixties and seventies this has been the most resistant. A succession of committees—in 1962, 1965 and 1966—recommended reorganisation to avoid the overlaps between the services; and a committee in 1969 proposed to abolish the separate ministers for the navy, army and air force. But the subsequent Tory and Labour Ministers of Defence, including Lord Carrington and Roy Mason, never grappled with the internecine battles, and it was left to Mrs Thatcher finally to abolish the separate service ministers in 1981, replacing them with junior ministers whose tasks involved all three services.

The services still retain much of their traditional triplication, always trying to reproduce three hierarchies, three messes, three hospitals, three chaplains. At the ministry they keep their lumbering machinery for consulting all down the line of each service, before trying to reach a common policy. At the top, 'the sanctification of the Chiefs of Staff ritual', as Lord Carver (the former Chief of the General Staff) calls it, makes life much harder for the minister, with the service chiefs bargaining with each other; while the top man, the Chief of Defence Staff, has to be appointed from each service in turn, the most immutable example of 'Buggins' turn next', a procedure which is not interrupted even if one of the service chiefs dies. The CDS is always supposed to leave his old service loyalty behind him, but he will always reflect the bias of a lifetime. So strong are the services that ministers still cannot appoint the best man for the job, or interfere with the promotion and patronage within each service; and no reform of the ministry can be really effective until it goes further down the ladder.

Integrating the three British services has been desparately slow; and integrating the British forces and equipment with NATO is still harder. Gradually Britain has been compelled, by rising costs and the logic of alliance, to collaborate more closely with the Continent. The decisive figures in European defence policy are not the Chiefs of Staff but the NATO commanders with outlandish names such as Saceur, Comanaucent, Chinchan or Cincent, defending frontiers where the concept of purely British interests has become meaningless. But Britain has not yet settled down to a role entirely within NATO; and there are still a few outposts of empire which provide counter-attractions.

At the top of this intricate structure sits the Minister of Defence, with a task which needs years of experience; but ministers have come and gone with legendary speed, and only Denis Healey stayed for more than four years. Healey loved out-arguing the admirals and generals but he never really grappled, according to his civil servants, with the internal jungle. 'Reorganising the ministry,' he said later, 'was like having an appendix operation while you're moving a grand piano.' Each minister is caught between needing the services' loyalty and needing to cut down their extravagant hierarchies. 'You must remember,' Lord Carver warned Roy Mason when he was minister, 'that we're not only the managers of the military: we're their trade union leaders.' Conservative ministers since 1979 have been even more caught between their posture of robust support for the military and the economic pressure from the top to cut costs. When Francis Pym failed to wield the axe ruthlessly he was reshuffled in favour of the banker John Nott, who saw the bottom line and obeyed his prime minister.

The minister presides over three top officials—the Chief of Defence staff, the permanent secretary and the Chief Scientific Adviser—whose divergent viewpoints give wide scope for disagreement: the top civil servant is always trying to rationalise the ministry, while the chief scientist threatens to undermine them both with prospects of new technologies and costs. ('If we could only lock up all the scientists for five or six years,' the former minister, Harold Watkinson, said twenty years ago, 'we might have a consistent defence policy.') The present Chief Scientific Adviser, Sir Ronald Mason, a professor of chemistry at the University of Sussex and an expert on radiation biology, is less far-reaching in his influence than was Solly Zuckerman in his day: he has been at the ministry for five years, but like other scientific advisers his scope has narrowed and he has to contend with chief scientists in all the three services. The Chief of Defence Staff, Admiral Sir Terence Lewin, is one of the most broadminded, and least hawkish, men to have held the position; but like his predecessors he is caught up with the problems of having to represent all three services in 'the Chiefs of Staff ritual'. It is the permanent under-secretary, Sir Frank Cooper, who is the real master of the building, where he has spent most of his career: after Oxford he became a wartime RAF pilot and then moved into the air ministry as a civil servant, and thence into the Ministry of Defence where he has remained, with intervals in the Civil Service Department and the Northern Ireland Office, until he reached the top job in 1976. Sir Frank is a shrewd mandarin with a political feel, whom many colleagues wanted to head the whole civil service; but he is one of the few people who are thought to understand the real workings of the Defence ministry and it is he who holds all its complex and secretive strands together.

The invulnerability of the Ministry of Defence is reinforced by the traditional cult of secrecy, which provides an obstacle, not only against democratic control, but often against sound political judgment. The self-enclosed circle at the top of the Ministry of Defence and the Foreign Office has its own engrossing, but very incomplete, view of the world: 'I can't tell you how much it means,' said one newly-arrived politician in the Ministry of Defence, 'to be in the middle of all those intelligence reports.' A long-standing minister, such as Healey or Carrington, can be sucked into the assumptions of the military mind; and David Owen has described how, as Minister for the Navy, he became suddenly aware of the breakdown of a highly sensitive intelligence mission which he had authorised:

> A fairly detached, almost routine, outlook was replaced by an acute awareness of how close to the knife edge so much of our military activity has become. The insidious process of military indoctrination, a heady mixture of pomp and secrecy to which most politicians are susceptible, tends to blunt one's normal sensitivity. One can easily become a part of the very military machine that one is supposed to control.[1]

Some politicians on the left see a darker danger behind the secret world of defence. 'What has happenened since the Glorious Revolution of 1688,' says Tony Benn, 'is that technology has shifted the balance of power more sharply towards the military in every country, and we must not allow it to displace democratic accountability. The parallel between the old standing army and the modern security services is that in the old days armies were rarely used for foreign wars, but were primarily instruments of domestic repression.'[2]

The ministry conceals many worrying secrets; but some of the most sinister are to be found in the great showroom in the dark heart of the building, which displays the British weaponry offered for sale to foreign governments. Submachine guns, hand-held missiles and mortars with 'maximum lethality' are laid out on gravel; a high-explosive shell is shown with armour-plating alongside, pierced with a six-inch hole; a diorama shows a village encircled by British-made tanks, controlled by a British-made radio system; and one corner shows weapons for internal security, developed since the Ulster troubles, including rubber bullets and a remote-controlled gun on wheels. It is to this showroom that the chief government salesman,

[1] David Owen: *The Politics of Defence*, Jonathan Cape, London, 1972, p. 14.
[2] Tony Benn, *op cit*, p. 176.

Sir Ronald Ellis, takes visiting Arab potentates or Latin American admirals, to persuade them to buy British equipment—with far fewer restrictions in recent years. The deals made with foreign governments in the Third World are among the most carefully-guarded secrets in the ministry, immune from parliamentary questioning: 'There's nothing to be gained from publicising sales,' as one defence official told me. 'We don't want to give ammunition to our critics.'[3] But they sell plenty of ammunition to foreign countries—including potential enemies.

The most secretive regions of all in the ministry are concerned with the maintenance of an independent nuclear deterrent, which has dominated every defence budget over the last three decades. Britain's A-bombs and H-bombs have remained in obscurity ever since the huge cost of first developing them was concealed in the defence estimates, and few members of parliament concern themselves with the complexities of nuclear defence. 'Compared to the United States,' said David Owen, 'the poverty of public debate on defence matters . . . is a disgrace.' The secrecy was maintained by Jim Callaghan as prime minister, when he decided to 'harden' the missiles on Polaris submarines with the Chevaline programme, which cost about a billion pounds and was concealed from most of the cabinet: 'It suggests,' as the anti-nuclear campaigner Edward Thompson commented, 'that the level of official mendacity is today very high indeed.' It was not until January 1980, when the House of Commons held one of its rare debates on defence, that the Tories officially revealed this expensive nuclear programme—when it was almost completed.

Thatcher and Nott took a bigger secret decision when they decided to replace the Polaris system with Trident, at a cost estimated at £5 billion over fifteen years, affecting the whole balance of conventional forces. Most cabinet ministers were kept in the dark, and the decision was only debated after it had been made. Many military experts as well as left-wing disarmers had already come out against Trident: 'I can't imagine any responsible British prime minister,' said Lord Carver, 'ordering a nuclear strike against the Soviet Union if the US had already refused to do so.' But the Trident remained the fixed commitment among all the cuts.

THE ARMY

The army took the most obvious buffeting in the post-war decades, defending indefensible positions in successive colonial enclaves, cutting down regiments, retreating from the Far East and

[3] Anthony Sampson: *The Arms Bazaar*, Hodder and Stoughton, London, 1977, p. 297.

Africa into Europe, and now moving between West Germany and Ulster, where it risks its soldiers' lives in one of the most thankless operations in British history. The British Army of the Rhine (BAOR) which contains about 55,000 soldiers, a third of the army, is now the modern equivalent of the old British army in India. It is almost equally separated from the natives, but under much more comfortable conditions, with family barracks, winter sports, frequent journeys home and (for officers) subsidised education for children at public schools. During the long retreat from the empire there have been periodic scares that the army might refuse to accept Britain's dwindling role; and in the early seventies there were short-lived rumours about a coup, featuring the former Commander-in-Chief in Northern Europe, General Sir Walter Walker. But the army's discontent was never serious. Army officers, though most are Tory, remain politically aloof. Army pay has steadily risen until it is now higher than that of civilians with similar qualifications (the table below shows their salaries in 1981, with their equivalents in other services). Fighting in Ulster and the Falklands has boosted rather than discouraged recruiting, while increasing the army's prestige with the British public. The troops have been much more adaptable to change than most factory-workers: 'I think,' said one Sandhurst observer, 'it's because the shop-floor leadership is much better.' The army is still very tribal: among the ten serving full generals in 1981 four were sons of army officers (and one a canon's son). But officers and troops have both moved closer to a civilian life-style, many of them living in houses and flats away from the barracks; and army wives and children have exerted their own pressure to keep officers away from the mess.

SALARY 1981	ARMY	ROYAL NAVY	ROYAL AIR FORCE
£35,845	Field-Marshal	Admiral of the Fleet	Marshal of the RAF
£33,170	General	Admiral	Air Chief Marshal
£26,215	Lt-General	Vice-Admiral	Air Marshal
£21,935	Major-General	Rear-Admiral	Air Vice-Marshal
£20,900	Brigadier	Captain (Senior)	Air Commodore
£17,480–19,319	Colonel	Captain	Group Captain
£15,012–16,589	Lt-Colonel	Commander	Wing Commander
£11,304–13,494	Major	Lt-Commander	Squadron Leader
£8,979–10,424	Captain	Lieutenant	Flight-Lieutenant
£7,789	Lieutenant	Sub-Lieutenant	Flying Officer
£5,950	Second Lieutenant	Acting Sub-Lieutenant	Pilot Officer

THE GUARDS

You can always tell a Guards officer, but you can't tell him much.
Old Saying

The most apparently unchanging soldiers are still the Guards, the seven regiments of the Household Division who guard the Queen and march outside Buckingham Palace in black bearskins. The three oldest foot regiments — the Grenadier, Coldstream and Scots Guards — all date back to the Civil War, when they helped to restore King Charles II to the throne; and the senior cavalry regiment, the Life Guards, were appointed by the same king in 1674 'to attend the King's person on foot wheresoever he walk, from his rising to his going to bed'.

The 400 Guards officers are rooted in a social structure that pre-dates popular democracy and industrialisation. They have slightly broadened their intake since the Second World War: they now take a few recruits from state schools; a private income, though advisable, is not now essential; and officers can live modestly in London — even south of the river — without being ridiculed. But the Guards remain closely linked to the public school tradition, and particularly to Eton which ever since 1860 has had a full time army officer, usually from the Guards, to run its cadet corps. Military families will put down their son for the Brigade at birth and the headquarters write to parents when they see the announcement of a baby boy in *The Times*. The way of life of Guards officers remains interlocked with horsey occasions, debutante dances and state rituals; and many heirs to big estates still remain Guards officers until they inherit. Their status is supported by barracks in London's Royal Parks, which in theory help them to protect their Queen, and which involve them in the world of the monarchy. Their class-consciousness has exasperated many radicals, and there are still no black or brown Guardsmen (though their public relations officers insists there is no colour bar).[4] Their arrogance and ceremonial obsessions seem largely irrelevant to the rest of contemporary Britain.

But in times of military crisis, as in the Falklands, they re-emerge in the forefront. They have been able to connect their traditions with contemporary technology and their chief instrument, behind all their horses and pageantry, is the Chieftain tank; and all the Household regiments except the Irish Guards have served in Ulster. The Guards' values can attract surprising people, including the Archbishop of Canterbury who won the Military Cross in the Scots

[4] John de St Jorre: *The Guards*, Aurum Press, London, 1981, p. 198.

Guards. 'I do not share most of the political and social views of my Guards friends,' he explained, 'but I shall always be grateful for the way in which integrity, idealism and sticking to the things you believed in were genuinely respected behind all the banter and the privilege.'[5]

SAS

But the Guards are now rivalled by the more ruthless crack troops of Special Air Service (SAS), the regiment of highly-trained soldiers who have become more important with the spread of terrorism. Like the Guards, they pride themselves on excellence and discipline, particularly self-discipline; but they insist that they have no class distinctions. In the words of their buccaneering founder, Colonel David Stirling, himself a Scottish aristocrat, 'In the SAS we share with the Brigade of Guards a deep respect for quality but we have an entirely different outlook. We believe, as did the ancient Greeks who originated the word "aristocracy", that every man with the right attitude and talents, regardless of birth and riches, has a capacity of reaching that status in his own lifetime in its true sense . . . All ranks in the SAS are of "one company" in which a sense of class is both alien and ludicrous.'[6]

As warriors in peacetime the SAS are cut off from the rest of society, living in their own world of potential violence with their own values and rules and their motto: 'Who Dares Wins'. They tend to see all security in terms of force: some have left to become mercenaries, and David Stirling himself once talked about establishing an army to protect Britain against trade unions and revolutionaries. When Ian Smith illegally declared independence for Rhodesia in 1966, Harold Wilson's government could not be sure that SAS troops would fight against the white Rhodesians; and the Rhodesians' own SAS soldiers were soon brutally effective in tracking down and interrogating black guerrillas. Any government using the SAS has to be sure that it can contain them. 'Like the guerrilla army, the modern SAS uses force sparingly,' says their historian Tony Geraghty, 'as a precise cutting edge for political policy.'

The evolution of the SAS followed Britain's most exposed interests—beginning in North Africa in wartime, continuing into colonial wars in the Third World, and more recently involved with antiterrorism in Europe and Northern Ireland. As early as 1969 some SAS soldiers were operating in Ulster, but it was not until 1976 that

[5] *Ibid*, p. 234.
[6] Tony Geraghty: *Who Dares Wins*, Fontana, London, 1980, p. 4. I am indebted to this book in this section.

Harold Wilson formally announced their presence. The spread of terrorists through Europe increased the demand for counter-terrorists, particularly after the Munich massacre of 1972; and the SAS developed their own techniques of counter-revolutionary warfare (CRW) which came into the open when two of them helped German anti-terrorists to rescue hostages from a hi-jacked airliner in Mogadishu. Soon afterwards Callaghan as prime minister authorised the SAS to extend their role in Britain itself, using more sophisticated training and equipment at their headquarters in Hereford. But their presence and techniques were kept very secret, and it was not until the siege of the Iranian Embassy in 1980 that they publicly revealed themselves—dangling from ropes, creeping in through windows, stunning the terrorists with 'flash-bangs' and rescuing the hostages in eleven minutes.

The rescue turned them into public heroes and boosted Britain's national pride, but it opened up the awkward questions of legal and political responsibility. The Home Secretary, William Whitelaw, was authorised by the prime minister to use the SAS, under the charge of the Ministry of Defence; but the unleashing of soldiers with wartime techniques strained the assumption of legality in a country in peacetime. The SAS soldiers were trained to shoot terrorists even if they were apparently surrendering, and they did so. When they appeared in court at the trial of the terrorists they were disguised and nameless.

Like other anti-terrorist groups the SAS may well become more important as new weapons call for expert training, whether against terrorists at home, or against enemies in adventures abroad. The SAS has its equivalent in the Royal Marines, called the Special Boat Service (SBS) which claims to be able to do everything that the SAS does, 'but with flippers on', and both services played a key role in the Falklands. These clandestine warrior elites, with their peacetime 'licence to kill' may eventually present Western democracies with problems of control, like the problem of the French *paras* who emerged in the fifties as a political force in metropolitan France. But these secretive black-clad figures, like mythological avengers, have become apparently indispensable to contemporary warfare and counter-terrorism.

AIR FORCE

The Royal Air Force, unlike the army, was born into uncertainty and rapid change, and from its beginnings in the First World War its existence had been bitterly resented by the army and the navy. Air force officers were accustomed to be looked down on by the other services: they were more democratic, more mobile and individualist, encouraging a democracy of the air which had its own wartime impact on Britain's social system on the ground. The officers were often better educated than those in other services, but less concerned with the old 'officer-like qualities' and more with self-discipline and technical mastery: 'We don't believe in bull — planes have their own discipline'. In peacetime the pilots have become increasingly expensive to train and commercially more valuable, and many move on to become highly-paid pilots in British Airways. At the top, the air marshals become accustomed to seeing their squadrons transformed every few years, as piston-engined planes gave way to jets, which gave way to the first supersonic planes. The intricate new planes of the eighties, led by the Anglo-German Tornado, make up what the RAF regards as their most comprehensive programme of re-equipment.

By its nature the air force was prepared to be flexible and to undertake tasks which the other services could not; but it was even more confused by Britain's changing view of its world role. In the sixties the RAF was in the midst of successive colonial conflicts, operating in Kuwait, Brunei, Borneo, South Arabia or Aden, and had to be ready to fly the army across the world; but by the seventies, when Britain had retreated from East of Suez, it became much more preoccupied with defending Europe and Britain itself. The RAF now has only three commands: Strike Command, which was merged from the old Bomber and Fighter Commands, providing the 'front-line teeth' within Britain, and which is now almost completely integrated within NATO, with the British commander Cincukair serving under Saceur. The second Command, RAF Germany, is the most closely integrated into NATO, constantly training with the European air forces as part of the Second Allied Tactical Air Force (ATAF). The third, the Supporting Command, based in Cambridgeshire, was merged with the old Training Command in 1977, and provides the back-up and training for the other two.

The current Chief of the Air Staff, Sir Michael Beetham, has a career which spans all the great changes over the past forty years: the son of an army major, he trained as a pilot in wartime and flew in Bomber Command; he served in East Africa in the fifties, in Britain and in Aden in the sixties, and in Europe in the Seventies, ending up as commander of the RAF in Germany, and the Second Allied Tactical Air Force. With its many joint operations with the rest of NATO, the RAF has become the most accustomed to the internationalisation of defence; but it is still faced with the basic uncertainty which had always made planning so difficult; would Britain still need its own independent strike force outside Europe?

THE NAVY

The Royal Navy was always the service most jealous of its traditions, mounting heavy political artillery, while the stubbornness of admirals was legendary; it was the top-heavy navy which originated the famous law of Professor Parkinson: 'work expands so as to fill the time available for its completion'. The private empires of the Commanders-in-Chief at Devonport (Guzz), Portsmouth (Pompey) and Chatham (Chats) defied intervention: their dockyards covered several parliamentary constituencies, and they could influence the politicians. The confidence of the admirals was reinforced by their separate naval tradition and by their intermarried families. When Admiral Sir Edward Ashmore became First Sea Lord in 1970 the hereditary principle scored a new triumph: he was the son of a vice-admiral; he had married Elizabeth Sturdee, whose father and grandfather were admirals; and his brother was also a vice-admiral, who had married Patricia Buller, whose father and grandfather were admirals. (Since retiring Sir Edward has followed another naval tradition, by becoming a director of an arms company, Racal.) The navy remains very close-knit, and of the five serving full admirals today, two are sons of naval officers, while the present Chief of Defence Staff, Sir Terence Lewin, is the son and brother of a naval officer.

The admirals have needed all their fire-power; for their arguments in favour of maintaining a large surface navy within NATO in a nuclear age looked increasingly doubtful. The most valuable vessels were the hunter-killer (SSN) submarines, costing £160 million each in 1980, which could if necessary be armed with cruise missiles carrying nuclear warheads. But the admirals insisted on also maintaining a large surface fleet, including a giant new aircraft carrier, the *Ark Royal*. But this, the other services complained, assumed that a Soviet attack on Europe would be followed by a protracted war—which few experts could visualise.

By 1981, when the Treasury was insisting on cutting defence costs, the new Minister of Defence, John Nott, demanded that the navy take most of the cuts while the admirals doggedly defended their fleet, encouraged by their Navy Minister, Keith Speed, himself a reserve naval officer. Speed publicly protested that to run down the navy would 'ignore this country's history, its geography, its economic trading base and the security facts of life as members of NATO'. Nott promptly asked Speed to resign, and when he refused Mrs Thatcher sacked him. Nott went ahead with his cuts: he arranged at last to shut down the vast Chatham dockyard, and planned to scrap ten warships: one aircraft carrier, HMS *Invincible*, was sold to the Australians for delivery in 1983; another, HMS *Hermes*, was to be withdrawn, together with the assault ship HMS *Fearless*. The cuts were not quite as savage as the right wing portrayed them: smaller warships would take the place of the big ones, creating a slightly bigger navy. But the vision of a big surface fleet with a world role seemed finally defeated. The admirals were on the run.

THE FALKLANDS CRISIS

We go to gain a little patch of ground
That hath in it no profit but the name.
Shakespeare (Hamlet)

No one, not even Keith Speed, had foreseen the kind of crisis that would appear to vindicate the admirals; when the Argentinians captured the Falkland Islands in 1982 the action did not fit into any naval thinking. The *Fearless*, as it happened, had been reprieved from the scrapyard, but the *Hermes* was covered in scaffolding. When John Nott faced the House of Commons on the day after the invasion he infuriated both sides by making cheap political points, provoking calls for his resignation, rather than Carrington's. But over the weekend Nott quickly changed his style and the Ministry of Defence could well blame the Foreign Office. The three Chiefs of Staff quickly achieved an importance they had not had since Suez twenty-five years ago—with an admiral, Sir Terence Lewin, as their Chief.

With the government determined to show its strength, the navy was mobilised with a speed which astonished almost everyone, not least the diplomats: it was as if the Ministry of Defence had declared war on the Foreign Office. The *Hermes*, the *Invincible* and the *Fearless*, which were all on their way out the year before, now led the armada to sail eight thousand miles to the Falklands, to retrieve the position which the diplomats had lost. The fleet sailed out of Portsmouth, watched by cheering crowds and weeping fiancées, as if they were part of an old war movie; and as it steamed slowly across the Atlantic the big surface fleet seemed to have suddenly emerged from the admirals' fantasy-life to become Britain's critical weapon. Its commander, Rear-Admiral Sandy Woodward, a former submarine commander who had become Director of Naval Plans, became the most famous admiral for forty years, as he gave bold if contradictory interviews about the forthcoming battle.

The other two services faced their own challenges. The army was strained to its limits to provide paratroops on top of its commitments in Germany and Ulster, but a paratroop force was embarked on the rapidly-requisitioned cruise liner, the *Canberra*. The RAF quickly converted old Vulcan bombers—which were also soon due to be scrapped—to carry conventional rather than nuclear bombs. The SAS and the SBS were prepared for secret landings on the islands. The great expedition provided the kind of test of tri-service collaboration, on sea, land and air, which planners might have dreamed of: the British had the advantage of knowing more about the islands than the enemy, and they knew a great deal about warships which they themselves had sold to the Argentinians. The navy remained the centre of attention, as the service on which the other two totally depended; and the extravagant aircraft carriers which had so often been threatened and mocked were now facing their greatest test. Would the ministry have to revise all its thinking about the navy of the future?

But the armada, for all its splendour, remained a kind of illusion. However effectively it might re-take the Falklands, it could not possibly defend them permanently. The logic which had led the Foreign Office to seek an agreement and to yield sovereignty to Argentina remained overwhelming, for Britain could not undertake to defend 1,800 islanders 8,000 miles away. Unlike the gunboat diplomacy of the last century this expedition was not part of a master plan: its eventual object was not to occupy the islands but to give them away. In the context of naval history it was a freak case—an anomaly left over from the empire, a throwback to an earlier age which gave no strategic lessons for the future.

Yet the Falklands armada had released a surge of aggressive patriotic emotion which took most politicians and commentators by surprise. Television and tabloids conjured up a militant mood in language echoing the Second World War, with outraged revelations about the Argies' atrocities which had attracted no interest a month earlier. The Ministry of Defence revealed all its capacity for secrecy and news-management, with its brisk and impersonal bulletins. The prime minister, always much influenced by the Churchillian era, fitted naturally into the role of a new Boadicea, encouraging our boys to the fight and vowing to liberate the Falklanders from 'the iron heel of the invader'. The great expedition acquired its own popular momentum: retired admirals and air marshals explained the strategy on television while defence experts pondered over maps, diagrams and clips of old propaganda film. The armada provided a far more vivid and comprehensible epic, with goodies and baddies, than the intricacies of nuclear strategy, or dry statistics about trade figures or money supply.

The Falklands expedition seemed to be giving the British the sense of national purpose for which they had been searching since the Second World War. In the first flush of patriotism all the political leaders except Tony Benn approved the armada, the recapture of South Georgia and the bombing of the Falklands: and the Tories soon showed their greatest popularity since their election. The unity and decisiveness, which politicians and civil servants had so lacked as they tried to plan Britain's industrial and economic future, was now suddenly mobilised behind a military expedition which made no real economic sense. Britain's older elites of admirals and generals summoned up their traditional following, as if industry and economics were merely distractions in the nation's real character-development. The echoes from the Second World War were almost deafening—while the contrast with Britain's ex-enemies was extreme. Germany and Japan had managed to transfer their military enthusiasm and discipline into their industrial competition, putting their national purpose behind exports, management and industrial research, deploying salesmen and chairmen as seriously as if they were parachutists or generals. Britain seemed unable to escape from her military tradition, and could not take her industry as seriously as her infantry.

Was the upsurge of the warrior spirit a sign that Britain had never really come to terms with its role since the Second World War, as a medium-sized power which had to pay its own way through commerce and industry? Was the country still stuck in the old wartime spirit, kept alive with memoirs and movies, so that it needed only a catchword to release the long-pent-up aggression from the national subconscious? Or was the war in the Falklands an expression of national resolve and unity, which lay at the heart of Britain's self-respect: a reminder that real patriotism still depends on courage, firmness and the military virtues, and not just the ability to make money?

PART

THREE

Finance

17

The City: the Permissive Old Lady

My Word is My Bond
Stock Exchange motto

THE City has always been cut off from the rest of London. Walking eastward past St Paul's any visitor can notice the change in atmosphere across this invisible moat. The pace is more hurried, the clothes more formal and the shops bleaker, as the office blocks rise higher above the canyons. Clerks and typists stream out of the stations in the morning like an invading army, and then leave it deserted at night, with only the new Barbican Centre as a hive of night-time activity. Narrow bars, fruit-stalls or basement restaurants are squeezed into odd corners and backyards between the stone palaces. But in the last two decades the contrast between the City and the rest of Britain has become more extreme. Bankers and dealers have become more international while industrialists and others have been bogged down in the country's economic constraints, and politicians have pursued their own national policies. The square mile of the City has become like an offshore island in the heart of the nation.

The separation is deep in Britain's history. The City's most famous institutions, including the Bank of England, Lloyds insurance market and the senior merchant banks, began long before the industrial revolution, when they depended on foreign trade and the ships that came up the Thames. While the self-made factory owners in the north were changing the face of Victorian Britain, most City bankers remained aloof from industry and made new fortunes from buying and selling commodities, gold or minerals from the empire and beyond. In the austere years after the Second World War, when the Labour government went through its social revolution and economic crises, City families were reclaiming their tribal territory with bowler hats and umbrellas; and Labour had to grant tax concessions to Lloyds and others to keep them in the country. In the late fifties London bankers were still surrounded by strict exchange controls, but they found huge new profits by dealing with Eurodollars, creating the world's most sophisticated money market.

No stretch of land in the world has had such a continuous commercial experience. The square mile still displays nearly every stage of its history since the Normans built the Tower of London on its eastern edge. Other old financial centres such as Venice or Florence have survived as tourist attractions, but the City is still the biggest financial centre in Europe, with glass skyscrapers next to medieval churches and computerised offices next to Roman walls.

It was always a collection of markets. Round the Norman church of St Bartholomew the street names such as Cloth Fair and Hosier Lane reveal their medieval origins, and behind high office blocks little trading villages still buy and sell their own specialities. At the Metal Exchange dealers bid for copper, tin, lead or zinc, while the little street of Great St Thomas Apostle deals in furs and skins. But most City companies long ago turned away from dealing in materials to dealing in money. Stockbrokers or bankers still like to belong to the old 'livery companies', such as the Fishmongers', Goldsmiths' or Armourers,' whose magnificent halls proclaim their old trades. But they have never wrought gold or gutted a fish, and their forbears long ago found more profit in buying and selling shares, insurance or money. The concentration of the City of London, its tribal closeness and its comparative freedom from constraints and lawyers, gave it a speed and expertise which had attracted 450 foreign banks by 1982; office space costs more per square foot than anywhere except Hong Kong. Over the last decade, while British industry has become still less competitive and more defensive, the City has held its own despite the troubles of sterling and the growing power of foreign banks.

The inhabitants of this extraordinary island—like those of other banking islands such as Hong Kong, Singapore or Manhattan—view the world very differently from those on the mainland. They can see across the whole globe, but they see it only through money; they clearly perceive Britain's economic problems, but they see the British people through balance sheets. They are constantly dealing with bits of British industry, restructuring companies, joining their boards, merging them or rationalising them. But they still remain aloof from the real industrial problems; and their business (as Jim Slater described it) is making money, not things.

BANK OF ENGLAND

In the centre of the square mile, opposite the Royal Exchange and the Mansion House, stands the fortress of the Bank of England, the centre-piece of the City's confidence and stability. The Bank's sense of ritual has diminished slightly in twenty years: a detachment of Guards no longer marches in bearskins through the City every evening at rush hour, to protect the Bank from rioters; and the whole building is now being modernised at the cost of £10 million. But attendants in pink morning coats still guide the visitors across the polished mosaic floors, through the high arches to the inner parlours where the senior officials hold court. The style of the Bank suggests a financial monarchy, with its own courtiers and king, such as was set up in 1694.

Most of the work of the Bank is very humdrum. On the ground floor the practical men conduct the everyday market operations—selling bonds, dealing with reserves, the exchange rate, interest rates—working under the Chief Cashier whose name appears on every bank-note. Upstairs are the brains of the Bank, the intelligence units and economists—who have multiplied since the Radcliffe Report in 1959 complained that the Bank did not know enough about the economy—who now constitute a kind of university of money. Though the present Governor has tried to integrate the two sides they are still rather disconnected. But all the Bank's employees are conscious of being grander than their equivalents in Whitehall: they get not only index-linked pensions but cheap loans for mortgages, superior lunches and higher salaries, and about thirty-five of them earn more than the permanent secretary of the Treasury.

The monarchic style is still supported by the 'Court' of eighteen directors who meet every Thursday in the palatial Court Room. The kind of membership has changed very little in the four decades since the Bank was nationalised. There are five executive directors, a token trade unionist, five industrialists and four merchant bankers. The Bank has wondered whether to include other financial groups, such as the clearing banks, the building societies or the pension funds which all long ago outgrew the merchant banks in their wealth: but if they chose one, they explain, they would offend others. The Court has very little to say in running the Bank: as Cecil King complained after he had resigned in disgust in 1969: 'The directors have been surrounded with an entirely bogus aura of knowledge and power.' But the aura still remains. Overleaf are the eighteen directors, for what they are worth, in 1982.

The Bank's relationship with the government is constantly

DIRECTORS OF THE BANK OF ENGLAND, 1982

NAME	JOBS	SCHOOL AND UNIVERSITY
Sir Gordon Richardson	Governor	Nottingham High School; Cambridge
Kit McMahon	Deputy Governor	Melbourne Grammar School; Oxford
George Blunden	Bank of England	City of London School; Oxford
Sir Adrian Cadbury	Cadbury Schweppes	Eton; Cambridge
Sir Robert Clark	Hill Samuel Bank	Highgate; Cambridge
John Clay	Hambros Bank	Eton; Oxford
Leopold de Rothschild	Rothschild's Bank	Harrow; Cambridge
Geoffrey Drain	General Secretary NALGO	Preston Grammar School; London
John Standish Fforde	Bank of England	Rossall; Oxford
Sir Jasper Hollom	Chairman, Panel on Takeovers	King's School, Brunton
Sir Hector Laing	United Biscuits	Loretto; Cambridge
Anthony Loehnis	Bank of England	Eton; Oxford
Lord Nelson of Stafford	General Electric	Oundle; Cambridge
John Brangwyn Page	Bank of England	Highgate; Cambridge
Sir Alastair Pilkington	Pilkington	Sherborne; Cambridge
David Scholey	Warburg's Bank	Wellington; Oxford
Sir David Steel	British Petroleum	Rugby; Oxford
Lord Weir	Chairman, Weir Group	Eton; Cambridge

shifting, and it has never been consistently subservient since it was nationalised, when Sir Stafford Cripps said 'the Bank is my creature'. The Governor writes his own stern speeches, and the Bank puts out its own views and assessments in its Quarterly (though it shows drafts to the Treasury). It always advises the government about how to implement policies, and in times of economic crisis, or when the exchange rate is worrying, its influence usually increases. 'From your own experience and mine,' Harold Wilson said to the Governor when he was taking evidence for his committee on the City, 'there have been occasions when the Bank has had to read the riot act to the government of the day.'

The Bank of England has wider scope and more influence than most central banks. It lacks the statutory independence of the German Bundesbank or the Fed in Washington which can both set their own interest rates. But it is more independent than the Fed in managing reserves; it manages government debts, which no other central bank does; and it supervises the other banks, which only some others do. Moreover, the City for which it is responsible is the most international of all financial centres, which gives more scope for disasters. The Bank must worry constantly about shaky foreign banks and the effects of the explosion of Eurodollars which has transformed the City over twenty years; and this international responsibility has removed it further from Whitehall. Foreign clients, particularly OPEC governments, have deposited billions of Eurodollars in the London branches of American banks, assuming they were free from American controls. But what is the real nationality, if any, of this money?

The Iranian crisis gave the Bank a sudden glimpse of the dangers on this grey frontier between international politics and finance. When the American hostages were captured in Tehran, President Carter retaliated by freezing all Iranian deposits, including those in American banks in London. The Bank of England was horrified by this threat to the City's independence; the European banks resented the American high-handedness; and a mass of lawsuits followed, to challenge the legality of the freeze. When the Americans began negotiating the release of the hostages in exchange for unfreezing the assets, the Bank of England was chosen as the intermediary; both sides trusted the Bank and few other central banks could handle a vast increase in their foreign currency overnight. After a week of discreet negotiations in London, the back view of the Deputy Governor, Kit McMahon, could be seen on television disappearing into an aeroplane bound for Algiers. It was a tense time for the Bank, for the hostages might have been blown up after McMahon handed over the guarantees, but the operation went smoothly, and the Bank gained international prestige as the honest broker. But the Bank was partly disappointed with the outcome; for when the Iranian assets were unfrozen, the law suits were dropped and the central question remained unresolved: are these billions of Eurodollars under any nation's control?

Fifteen months later the Bank was on the other side of the argument; when Argentina invaded the Falklands, the British government insisted on freezing Argentinian assets in London, worth $1.4 million, and on cutting back any new loans. The Bank of England handled the crisis, as it said, 'more adroitly' than Washington two years before, fearful of offending foreign banks which were hit by the freeze and withdrawal of loans, and worried that Argentina might have to default on her existing large loans from British banks led by Lloyds. But the sudden restrictions as a consequence of a British dispute nevertheless worried many foreign bankers: was the City such a safe offshore island after all?

THE GOVERNOR

In spite of democratic encroachments the Governor remains the prince of the City, with a special splendour to magnify his views. He presides in grander surroundings than the prime minister, let alone the Head of the Treasury—which is poignant because the latter, Sir Douglas Wass, was at the same grammar school in Nottingham as Sir Gordon Richardson, the Governor. Richardson is certainly the more stylish—with a fine profile which, as one American banker enviously said, might have been ordered by central casting. As a young man he had no banking connections: after Oxford and a war in staff college he became a very successful barrister and then moved into the City, becoming a director of Schroder's Bank to which he gave a new reputation and authority. He was seen as a natural choice to succeed Sir Leslie O'Brien as Governor in 1973. He is both gregarious and totally discreet, willing to talk about anything except the Bank. He has perfected the bankers' omniscient style—'if you knew what I know'—as if he were playing twenty questions, with the final answer always withheld.

Richardson soon found himself facing the City's biggest financial crisis in forty years, which revealed all the hazards and responsibilities that lay behind the Bank's grandeur. The day-to-day tasks of regulating the market and implementing government policies were not exacting; but a crisis brought out all the tensions behind the Bank's relationship with the rest of the City, as the authority which had to prevent the system collapsing. Like an anxious parent, it had to watch to pull the child back from the cliff, and in late 1973 the brink was very close, and very steep.

The Bank itself was partly to blame. In the permissive first years of the Heath government it had allowed too many 'fringe banks' to grow up, borrowing money short-term and putting it into booming property development. When the government began to squeeze credit the interest rates rose, property prices fell, and investors were in trouble. Gerald Caplan's London and County Securities was the first to reach the cliff-edge, threatening to shatter confidence in others. The Governor quickly gathered together the company's chief bankers, National Westminster, and its major shareholders, who formed a consortium which undertook to hold up London and County. Then the shares in Cedar Holdings were suspended and Richardson, who had seen it coming, negotiated hectically with their bankers, Barclays, and their major shareholders, including the Electricity and Unilever pension funds, to drag it back from the brink. By now the market was panicking, and more fringe banks were tottering towards collapse.

Just before Christmas 1973 the Bank launched its 'lifeboat' of emergency funds. Jasper Hollom, the Deputy Governor, met with the big banks two or three times a week to decide how to distribute the funds, to which the banks had to contribute, until by the end the Lifeboat had used up about £1.2 billion. The Bank used all its moral pressure to make other institutions aware of their danger, and to induce the co-operation of reluctant pension funds, and they eventually mobilised vast private funds, in spite of the risks, into public channels. During 1974 the British crisis was compounded by collapses abroad—of the Herstatt Bank in Germany, the Sindona empire in Italy, and the Franklin Bank in New York. By November 1974 the National Westminster was rumoured to be nearing the edge, and it had to take the extraordinary step of publicly announcing that it was *not* in difficulties. By now the shoring up of shaky structures was straining all the clearing banks: the Bank of England itself put £85 million into the fund, and had to shoulder more responsibility until it ended up owning two major groups, Slater Walker and Edward Bates, and even had to rescue the Burmah oil company by buying its shareholding in BP.

When the City eventually returned to some kind of normality in mid-1975 the Bank had learnt many lessons. Of the twenty-six fringe banks which it had been supporting, it allowed eight to collapse. Only a few individuals went down, such as William Stern, whose property empire collapsed with debts of about £100 million, though he continued to live in style. Some financiers went to court or were investigated, such as Jim Slater and Gerald Caplan; but the

Bank was accused of being too compassionate in many of its rescues, and five years after the lifeboat was launched, it had only got half its money back. The Bank of England had shown it could deal swiftly and efficiently with a crisis, but it had also shown itself much too permissive; and after the crisis had to strengthen its supervisory powers with a new Banking Act.

When Thatcher came to power in 1979 Richardson was thought to welcome the new regime. He was keener than the Treasury on restricting the money supply, and the Conservatives had implied that the Bank should be more independent. But there was soon high tension between the Bank and the Treasury: the government based its financial strategy on reducing the growth of the money supply, but during their first year it went on growing, at about double the target-rate. Many Conservatives felt that the Bank was either incompetent, or deliberately sabotaging their policy, and Mrs Thatcher thought that the Bank had let her down. She was impatient with Richardson as he lectured her at length like a lawyer with a well-prepared brief; while Edward du Cann's committee, which was grilling the Treasury, showed more sympathy for Richardson and the Bank, which made the government still crosser. Relations reached their nadir in the autumn of 1980, when Richardson was rumoured to be retiring early, but they later improved; and after the Royal Wedding in 1981 the Bank gave a party where the Governor and the prime minister actually received foreign dignitaries together.

The Governor, in spite of the stronger banking laws, still rules the City very personally, like a tactful but dominating parent; not through commands, but through advice, requests and warnings. Most of Britain's major institutions are within a stone's throw, which gives him a great advantage over the Chairman of the Fed or the Comptroller of Currency in Washington who has to supervise 14,000 banks through his intricately computerised system. ('How I envy Gordon,' as one former Comptroller said to me. 'Only six banks, all within walking distance.') The Governor knows the chairmen intimately through his Old Boy Net, and they have to trust and confide in him. The Bank always tries to avoid too many rules, which encourages armies of lawyers to get round them, and prefers to 'invite' bankers to 'discuss their problems', and to make them responsible for following guidelines. Many American bankers are surprised and relieved by a process which is much quicker and cheaper than legal confrontation.

Behind its formal façade the Bank of England has one of the most informal of all systems in the world, and other central banks are beginning to prefer the firm hand and the gentleman's agreement to the iron claw of statutory control. But the Bank's personal approach, like any banker's, depends on knowing its clients and maintaining a mutual sense of trust. As the City becomes more cosmopolitan and the world's biggest banks become increasingly multinational, can the Governor maintain his gentlemanly control over the financial jungle? It was a question which came to a head in his relationships with the big British banks.

18

Bankers: The International Island

It is necessarily part of the business of a banker to profess a conventional respectability which is more than human. Life-long practices of this kind make them the most romantic and the least realistic of men.

Lord Keynes

WITHIN a short distance of the Bank of England stand the palaces of all the Big Four banks—Barclays, National Westminster, Midland and Lloyds—whose branches can be seen in every high street in the country, and which are the chief repositories of British savings and the chief sources of credit. The easy profits of these banks, their lack of competition and their rigid hierarchies, have amazed many foreigners and exasperated many British customers. They include some of the biggest and most profitable banks in the world; and in 1981 Barclays' profits were the biggest of all. While British industry was reeling under the full rigour of the world recession and monetarist discipline, the British banks were under no great competitive pressure, and could make their record profits out of their 'endowments'—the current accounts of customers to whom they pay no interest. Even the bankers' own paper, the *Financial Times*, was forced to protest in May 1980 that 'something is seriously wrong with Britain's retail banking system . . . It is class-based, diverse and sleepy. It is dominated by a handful of institutions known as the clearing banks whose profitability is the envy of commercial banks all over the world, yet its UK management is wholly in-bred and often less than sparkling. It is a system badly in need of a shake-up.'[1]

The banks long inhabited the twilight world between nationalisation and free competition, whose rules are obscure. They adopted the high-minded style of public servants, while their chairmen—the 'old spinsters' as Keynes called them—pronounced every year on the state of the nation as if they were part of the Treasury. They

[1] *Financial Times*, May 3, 1980.

allowed rival credit-mongers such as building societies and hire purchase companies, with more vulgar associations of commerce, to creep up behind them and take much new custom. During the sixties and seventies they gradually competed more openly, and after the Heath government relaxed credit control they earned huge new profits from the property boom. But they closed their doors at 3.30 p.m. and on Saturdays and never encouraged working-class customers, so that the British are still the 'great unbanked', with proportionately fewer bank accounts than other Europeans. Many people preferred to put their cash into building societies, which hugely increased their share of personal deposits, from 22 per cent in 1963 to 47 per cent in 1979, while the National Giro, run by the post office, provided a simple new way to pay bills. It was only in 1979 that the big banks began to compete seriously with the building societies by lending for house mortgages, which soon provided an important part of their profits. By 1982 some banks began opening on Saturdays again.

All the Big Four have shown the same kind of creeping centralisation, moving from strong provincial roots and links with local communities towards heavy concentration in London. During the merger-mania of the sixties they became much more concentrated. In 1967 there were still eleven clearing banks (for ordinary customers) in Britain, including the smaller ones such as the National Commercial in Scotland and Martins, a strong regional bank with old Liverpool connections. Then the Bank of England, with customary obscurity, 'made it plain' that it was not averse to further amalgamations, and there was an unseemly rush to merge. The aggressive Midland tried to marry Lloyds, which then rushed over to Barclays and tried to merge with it. The government then turned the proposal over to the Monopolies Commission, which eventually decided that three big banks would be too few; but they allowed the National Provincial to marry the Westminster, and Barclays to gobble up Martins: Liverpool no longer had its own strong credit base, which many people believed contributed to the further economic decline of Merseyside. The Big Four now dominated British credit, and even the three remaining Scottish banks, though they still printed their own bank-notes, were not quite what they seemed: the Clydesdale Bank was 35 per cent owned by Midland, and the most dynamic part of the Royal Bank of Scotland was its London affiliate, Williams and Glyn's. Overleaf are the six major clearing banks with their chairmen and deposits in 1981.

Each of the Big Four, it is true, still has a distinctive character. Barclays, which was first created in 1896 as a federation of Quaker family banks, keeps some of its regional structure and tradition; but

Bank	Gross deposits £million	Chairman	Education
1 Barclays	42,834	Timothy Bevan	Eton; Guards
2 National Westminster	39,709	Robin Leigh-Pemberton	Eton; Oxford; Guards
3 Midland	38,000	Sir David Barran	Winchester; Cambridge
4 Lloyds	25,309	Sir Jeremy Morse	Winchester; Oxford
5 Royal Bank of Scotland	6,698·8	Sir Michael Herries	Eton; Cambridge
6 Bank of Scotland	2,524·6	T. N. Risk(!) (Governor)	Kelvinside; Glasgow

it is also the most dominated by old banking families, who take turns to provide the chairman. 'It has always been relatively easy,' as the bank's official history puts it with engaging candour, 'for a scion of the old Quaker families to reach a high position in Barclays.'[2] For twelve years until 1962, the bank was dominated by Sir Anthony Tuke, 'the Iron Tuke', and after an interval he was succeeded by his less steely son, also Anthony Tuke. In 1982 it was the turn of Timothy Bevan, the director descendant of Silvanus Bevan who joined the original Barclays in 1767. Bevan presides over a board which still includes a Pease, a Tritton and a Goodenough; of the board of twenty, six are Etonians and four are Wykehamists. But the Quaker tradition has not deterred the bank from supporting apartheid policies in South Africa, from which it derives large profits.

The National Westminster (NatWest) also boasts its historical and regional connections: 'our roots are our branches'. It long ago absorbed Coutts bank, the bankers to the monarchy, and it includes a Money-Coutts on its board; but it has never quite recovered its reputation in the City since the crisis of 1974 when it had lent far too much to shaky property companies. It now has few links with its old provincial past; its chairman, Robin Leigh-Pemberton, an amiable landowner and barrister, travels conscientiously through his territory; but the NatWest board, complete with an earl, two viscounts, three barons, a baronet and nine Etonians, is a kind of monument to Britain's past, with few links with the industrial present.

The Midland originated outside London, as its name implies, and it was known as the small man's bank, with a rugged independence and adventurousness. More recently it has proclaimed itself in advertisements as 'The Listening Bank', but the friendly image was quickly offset by a succession of customer disasters, beginning when

[2] Julian Crossley and John Blandford: *The DCO Story*, Barclays International, London, 1975, p. 229.

a student went into a Midland branch and was promptly arrested for having an overdraft. The Midland is now firmly London-based, with a former head of Shell, Sir David Barran, as its chairman (soon to be succeeded by his Scottish near-namesake Sir Donald Barron). It has the most industrial board of any bank, including the current chairmen of Standard Telephones, GKN, Brooke Bond, Reed International and Swan Hunter, and several ex-chairmen—of ICI, Cadbury, Dunlop and Rowntree. But they have not much helped the commercial sense of the Midland, which is run autocratically by its general managers, and it has become the least profitable of the big banks, suffering from a succession of collapsed companies, including Stone Platt and Laker Airways (see below).

Lloyds, like Barclays, had Quaker origins, with much custom in Wales, although it now has hardly a Welshman in sight. Its chairman is the most mandarin of bankers, Sir Jeremy Morse (an international monetary expert) and its board includes a clutch of industrial chairmen, a former Lord-in-Waiting, Lord Lloyd, and the Queen's representative at Ascot, the Marquess of Abergavenny.

All four banks have maintained their class-distinctions like the army and the navy; or like cricketers divided between the 'gentlemen' on the boards and the 'players' in the offices who work their way up towards the peak of chief general manager. All of the banks have become increasingly centralised, reaching all their key decisions within the square mile. Manchester, Liverpool and Birmingham have all lost financial influence in this shift to the capital, and the main boards, with their fondness for old families and giant companies, reflect few of the many-sided activities which their deposits and loans represent. Can the diversity of Britain really be effectively represented by these four chairmen of the banks, two from Eton, two from Winchester?

Fortified by their rising profits the big banks have all ventured further abroad, whether by buying London merchant banks, by lending through their own subsidiaries, or by buying up foreign banks. All four have bought banks in the United States, culminating in Midland's purchase of the venerable old Crocker Bank in California, the thirteenth biggest in the United States, which rocked the old San Francisco establishment and exasperated other American bankers who were not allowed, by their own McFadden Law, to buy banks in other states. ('It becomes increasingly ridiculous,' complained Walter Wriston of Citibank, 'to say that Midland can buy Crocker, but Citibank can't: we both speak English.') American banks were also moving across the Atlantic, and Citibank is now the sixth biggest bank in Britain in terms of loans. But the big British profits lay in the clearing banks with their high-street branches.

Would a foreign bank ever be allowed to break into that cosy circle?

THE ROYAL BATTLE

It was the sudden contest to take over the somnolent old Royal Bank of Scotland which lit up the obscure outlines of British banking like a flare above the trenches—and which raised awkward questions not only about foreign buyers, but about centralised money. The Royal Bank, incorporated by a charter in 1727, was proudly based on its temple in Edinburgh, with branches all over Scotland, and it had already fought off a bid from Lloyds in London. But its chairman, Sir Michael Herries, worried about takeovers and longed for stronger international connections, and in 1981 he supported a merger with the Standard Chartered Bank—an ex-colonial bank based on London with large interests in white South Africa and in Hong Kong, headed by the former Chancellor of the Exchequer, Lord Barber. Herries and Barber both cooed over the marriage, which would create a 'fifth force' to compete with the Big Four; while the Governor of the Bank of England, Gordon Richardson, to many people's surprise blessed the union.

But the wedding preparations were soon shattered by the arrival of a more dashing and dynamic suitor from the Far East, the Hong Kong and Shanghai Bank: it was quite traumatic for the British to see *two* ex-colonials coming back to the old country full of money to claim this old property. The 'Honkers and Shankers' had a dominating position on its own island; it did much profitable business with mainland China and it had already extended round the world, buying the Marine Midland in New York, the British Bank in the Middle East and Antony Gibbs the London merchant banker. Its restless chairman, Michael Sandberg, was now determined to build a bigger European base, beginning with the Royal Bank of Scotland. The Governor was appalled: he insisted that the Hong Kong Bank was much less controllable than Standard Chartered and made clear that the bid was—using one of the most terrible words in his dictionary—'unwelcome'. To his horror Hong Kong took no notice of this signal and persisted with their bid—even darkly hinting that the Governor was favouring Standard Chartered because Barber had appointed him governor eight years earlier. It was an overt challenge to the Governor's tribal authority; but the Foreign Office and the Department of Trade, anxious not to disturb the Chinese connection, took the side of Hong Kong. The government, much embarrassed, referred the rival bids to the Monopolies Commission.

The commissioners under their deputy chairman, Jeremy

Hardie, an intellectual master-accountant, then heard evidence from all parties including the Governor, who made it clear that since the Hong Kong people had disobeyed him in the first place they could not be trusted. Hardie was more worried about the effects of a merger on the Scottish economy, and the commissioners went up to Edinburgh to inspect the scene. The Scots warned them of the consequences of a 'branch economy': how many local industries, from insurance to cars to electronics, had suffered from centralised managers, and how morale in Scotland was being weakened. 'Entrepreneurial spirit and business leadership depend critically on self-confidence,' the commissioners decided, 'and on balance we believe that such self-confidence has been weakened.' The Royal Bank, they found, was 'an important company in an exceptionally important and prosperous Scottish industry'. A merger, they boldly argued, 'may be seen as part of a process of economic centralisation which has been seriously damaging to Scotland and to some other regions in the United Kingdom'. 'There is a value,' they said plaintively, 'in preserving such independent local centres of business initiative and opinion as survive in the United Kingdom.'[3]

The commissioners were now unsympathetic to both the suitors. They were sceptical of their promises to keep their hands off Edinburgh, and though they were concerned about the concentration of the Big Four, they were doubtful about Barber's claim that a fifth force would produce 'a radical new departure in retail banking'. They were not convinced by the Governor that he would find it impossible to properly supervise the Hong Kong bank (though they 'should hesitate to treat lightly the Bank's concern'), but they agreed with him that there could be divergent interests between London and Hong Kong. So they came out against both bids. The government quickly endorsed their judgment, the Royal Bank remained on its own, the Scots rejoiced in their independence, and the Governor was deeply relieved that his authority had been upheld. Self-regulation and voluntary agreement, he explained, were essential to underpin the British financial system: 'The customary authority of the Bank, exercised steadily and in rational discussion—not by mysterious oracular contortions on my part—is vital to this underpinning. That is why I have done my best to uphold it.'

But the affair still raised questions beyond the immediate controversy. Could and should these British banks keep their cosy circle, protected from foreigners by the Governor, while they spread themselves abroad? Was Scotland really being saved from further

[3] Command 8472, January 1982.

centralisation? (For soon after the bids were defeated, the Royal Bank brought in a new chief executive—from London.) And what about all the other regions—including the wastelands of the north-east and north-west—which had already seen their finance drained towards London—with effects that (as the commissioners had warned) were 'seriously damaging'? What benefits had they seen from the mergers which the Bank of England had so calmly approved thirteen years earlier?

MERCHANT BANKS

The merchant bankers, in contrast to the clerkdoms of the clearing banks, have shown a more aggressive spirit of profit-making and individualism, like cavalry compared to the infantry. Most of the merchant banks (as the table overleaf shows) are at least a century old, and they deliberately cultivate a mahogany gravity; but those with the gravest expressions may be taking the most daring risks. The merchant banks reveal the profit motive at its keenest, pervading every activity. Many civil servants and politicians who move into their offices find themselves acquiring new incentives as they trade not in words but in money and rush round the world with a single-minded ambition which they did not know they possessed. The banks can offer clever and presentable young men more money and more exciting prospects than industry or Whitehall, with a cosmopolitan life-style very different from the rest of the country. The moat seems wider than ever.

The bankers provide continuing replays of two familiar City epics. In one, the outsiders of one generation become the insiders of the next; in the other, old money gets its revenge on new money. Twenty years ago when I first visited their parlours the old merchant bankers provided a kind of caricature of stuffy aristocrats, as if they were part of a left-wing farce. The most famous bank, Rothschilds, provided lunches among their old trophies and bric-à-brac; Rothschilds was run by Rothschilds, Barings by Barings, Hambros by Hambros. Lazards and Morgan Grenfells were the two chief Gentile banks, which closed ranks to keep out outsiders. Lazards, which had begun as a Jewish bank in New Orleans, had become thoroughly British, owned by Lord Cowdray and run by Lord Kindersley, Lord Brand and his brother, Lord Hampden. Morgan Grenfell, though first established by the American J. P. Morgan, was headed by two British landowners, Lord Bicester and Lord Harcourt.

The old bankers' attitudes were essentially defensive: 'They're like the British empire,' Jack Hambro explained to me. 'There's nothing more to gain and quite a lot to lose.' The banking families, many of them inter-related, clung closely together: and all their clannishness, with a hint of their anti-semitism, emerged when they tried to defend themselves against Siegmund Warburg, a far more able newcomer from Hamburg who dared to set up his own bank in 1946. When he was engaged in selling British Aluminium to American bidders, the old banks, led by Morgans and Lazards, closed their ranks to try to stop him, accusing him of being unpatriotic while trying unsuccessfully to make their own American deal.

The old banks gradually woke up. They soon realised that they could, like Warburg, make big profits from mergers, takeovers and property deals as British companies realised their hidden assets; and as the City boomed, clever young men without banking connections came in with spectacular success, setting up investment companies, fringe banks and bucket-shops. Many old bankers in their excitement with profits forgot much of their caution and discretion, and the most phenomenal newcomer, Jim Slater, was so dazzlingly successful that three of the senior merchant banks—Lazards, Warburgs, and Hill Samuel—nearly merged with him. Spiralling property values and stock-market prices conspired to encourage the bubble, and forty years after the Great Crash most City people had no memories of how money-mania could overcome the most sober establishments.

The more cosmopolitan banks with foreign experts and dealers, such as Warburgs, Montagus, Rothschilds or Kleinworts, had also discovered a huge new source of profits in the market for Eurodollars which began in the late fifties and multiplied through the sixties. This burgeoning international trade, encouraged by American trade restrictions, helped to re-establish London as a world financial centre: British bankers themselves controlled relatively small funds, and sterling was one of the most fragile currencies, but they knew how to make money out of other people's money. The speed, concentration and permissiveness of the City of London attracted the biggest banks from all over the world and Lombard Street, where Italian bankers had first set themselves up five hundred years earlier, now displayed an array of banks from five continents. London's geographical position was an added attraction: an exchange dealer could talk to Tokyo in the morning, to New York at lunch-time and to California in the afternoon. But the continuity and stability of the City was its greatest asset: as Walter Wriston (the chairman of Citibank in New York) put it to me: 'The Eurodollar market exists in London because people believe that the British government is not about to close it down. That's the basic reason, and that took you a thousand years of history.'[4]

The British boom which had made the fortunes of so many out-siders soon collapsed in the crash of 1974. The wonder-men of the sixties—such as Jim Slater, Pat Matthews, or Christopher Selmes—found their empires toppling, and were either rescued or drowned. The old bankers liked to forget that they had ever admired Slater, and remembered that old money and families were much safer. When Lord Cowdray asked Lord Poole, who ran Lazards, how he had managed to avoid lending to the crashed financiers, Poole replied: 'Quite simple: I only lent money to people who had been at Eton.' The old epic had come round again, full circle: the players after all were not gentlemen.

The merchant banks had come through, but they were not the same. The Eurodollar business had survived the crash and while industry was collapsing the moneylenders could still prosper. The old banks had brought in new blood, with more aggressive money-making instincts. They arrived earlier at work and had shorter lunches: Barings even stopped serving wine. The more dynamic banks had to be involved with the rest of the world, and their cosmopolitanism contrasted sharply with the parochialism of indus-trialists and most politicians.

The club of merchant bankers, the 'accepting houses' who were underwritten by the Bank of England, had experienced some con-vulsions. Montagus had been bought up by the Midland Bank; Brandts, which had been run entirely by the Brandt family, was taken over by Grindlays, owned by Citibank. Arbuthnot Latham, after revealing some shady dealings, was bought by a subsidiary of the American Dow Chemical Company; Singer and Friedlander was bought by the Tory entrepreneur, Keith Wickenden, who had made a fortune by building up European Ferries; Antony Gibbs, founded by the family who made their fortune from guano, was bought by the dreaded Hong Kong Bank and after much protest from its chairman, Sir Philip de Zulueta, was excluded from the accepting houses.

None the less, most of the old banks have survived with modifica-tions, most of them dominated by a few individuals. Rothschilds went through bitter battles for control between the two cousins, Evelyn and Jacob Rothschild, until Jacob, the more aggressive and ambitious, left the bank to run his own investment trust. Barings is still run by a committee of Barings—John, Nicholas and Peter. Morgan Grenfell is now divorced from Morgans in New York, and has built up its own international business, first under Sir John Stevens, now under his successor William Mackworth-Young. Siegmund Warburg ostensibly retired ten years ago, delegating

[4] Anthony Sampson: *The Money Lenders*, Hodder and Stoughton, London, 1981, p. 113.

his bank to Lord Roll and David Scholey, but he can make his influence felt from Switzerland. Hill Samuel, the merger of two old banks in 1970 is run by Sir Robert Clark, yet still bears the marks of the man who first merged them, Lord Keith. The most individualist banker has been Lord Kissin, the Hungarian entrepreneur and commodity trader who bought up the once-Irish bank Guinness Mahon. In 1980 he appeared to retire, leaving the bank to be run by the ex-Labour cabinet minister, Edmund Dell; but when the profits collapsed Dell soon found himself barely in command and the board, after much intrigue, replaced him with Alastair Morton, an ex-South African who seemed able to keep Kissin at bay.

The more aggressive bankers show all the acquisitiveness of individuals unrestrained by bureaucracies, crossing over frontiers and continents so easily that it is often hard to know where they really belong. With the growth of Eurodollars the City has rediscovered some of its nineteenth-century cosmopolitanism and a little of its daring. But the bankers have much less connection with British life on the other side of the moat—with the endless, slow problems of industry, technology, labour and unions. Viewed from the boardrooms of the old banks, Britain's industrial effort looks a phenomenon which has come and gone, while banks go on for ever.

ACCEPTING HOUSES

Founded	Bank	Assets 1981 £ million	Chairman	Education
1763	Baring Brothers	489	John Baring	Eton; Oxford
1804	Rothschild's	603	Evelyn de Rothschild	Harrow; Cambridge
1804	Schroder Wagg	1,845	Lord Airlie	Eton; Guards
1810	Brown Shipley	252	Lord Farnham	Eton; Harvard
1830	Kleinwort, Benson	2,713	Robert Henderson	Eton; Cambridge
1831	Hill Samuel	1,443	Sir Robert Clark	Highgate; Cambridge
1833	Arbuthnot Latham	206	Andrew Arbuthnot	Eton; Guards
1836	Guinness Mahon	332	Graham Hill	Winchester; Oxford
1838	Morgan Grenfell	1,578	Lord Catto	Eton; Cambridge
1839	Hambros	1,389	Jocelyn Hambro	Eton; Cambridge
1853	Samuel Montagu (Midland)	1,580	Malcolm Wilcox	Wallasey GS
1870	Lazard Brothers	735	Ian Fraser	Ampleforth; Oxford
1880	Charterhouse Japhet	485	Malcolm Wells	Eton
1907	Singer & Friedlander	283	Keith Wickenden	East Grinstead GS
1919	Rea Brothers	109	Walter Salomon	Hamburg
1932	Robert Fleming	194	W. R. Merton	
1946	S. G. Warburg	981	Lord Roll / D. G. Scholey	Abroad; Birmingham / Wellington; Oxford

BANKS AND INDUSTRY

Were the bankers to blame for not investing in British industry? It is an old argument, going back to the bleak years of the thirties, or to the post-war years when the Japanese and Germans were putting all their capital into their industry, which was leaping ahead of the British. The British banks preferred to provide credit for ordinary customers who could repay their loans quickly; and when they lent to industry they preferred established companies, however dubious their future, such as British Leyland and Rolls Royce. Their conservative outlook and their elderly boards encouraged their preference for the past, and their distaste for the adventurous small companies of the future. The most effective alternative source of credit, the building societies, attracted funds into houses which thus increased the disadvantage of industry. The Wilson Committee on the City in 1980 expressed some doubts about the banks' relationships with industry, and the argument soon became more acrimonious as banks made record profits from lending while small companies were being bankrupted or were stillborn.

A forceful case against the banks was made in 1980 by Lord Lever, the former cabinet minister, and George Edwards, a post office economist. 'Many of Britain's economic ills,' they said, 'can be traced in whole or part to the historic distortion in our credit system . . . the financial arrangements which enable us to buy and confidently maintain our houses are not available for our factories.' The British failure to channel savings into investment, they complained, had fuelled inflation and set back prosperity: Japanese, French or German companies all borrowed more from their banks on longer terms, while British industrialists had to find most of their money for expansion from their own profits. Lever and Edwards wanted the government to press banks to provide more long-term funds for investment, and to put a ceiling on other bank loans. 'Unless we do act to revive investment, our decline is assured at a more rapid rate than in the last decade.'[5]

Lever's attack provoked hurt responses from the bankers. Leigh-Pemberton of NatWest blamed the lack of industrial enterprise: 'No bank can lend money,' he explained, 'unless a customer asks for it first.' Christopher Johnson, the economic adviser to Lloyds Bank, insisted in suitable bankspeak that 'any direction of lending would be an unwarranted intrusion by the state in the allocation of financial resources according to commercial criteria', while his chairman, Sir Jeremy Morse, replied in loftier style: 'Banks have often been unpopular in hard times because, like doctors, lawyers and under-

[5] *Sunday Times*, November 1980.

takers, they are seen to do relatively well while others are doing badly . . . If and when industrial activity picks up, the banks have long-standing guidance from the Bank of England to make room for industry's needs.'

But several business customers agreed with Lever: 'Some bankers lack any knowledge and insight as regards business,' wrote Per Lindstrand from Oswestry; 'They simply have no idea of the requirements of the market,' wrote Bryan Rawlins from Kent. And four former members of the Wilson Committee wrote to support Lever, complaining that the British system failed 'to encourage projects with long-term pay-off periods'.

The Bank of England maintained a pained silence, as if the argument were too vulgar to join; and it was not until sixteen months later that the banks produced their measured response to Lever's attack, and to similar criticisms produced by a parliamentary committee headed by the Conservative MP Michael Grylls, the chairman of the Small Business Bureau. The Banking Information Bureau produced a report by two economists which criticised Lever's statistics and insisted that the pattern of lending was now not very different from that of France and Germany; only Japan, they reckoned, had channelled much more of its national income into investment, and even Japan was now moving more towards the European pattern; while British banks were now lending longer-term, to fill the vacuum left by the disappearance of corporate bonds.[6]

It was true that the Bank of England had pressed the banks to develop a more helpful and enduring relationship with industrial companies since the crash of 1974. The Bank still shrinks from intervening with investment by pension funds and insurance companies (see next chapter), but it has tried to provide new mechanisms to channel funds into industry, including 'Equity Capital for Industry', which it set up in 1976 jointly with the clearing banks—although its first results were disappointing. Since the recession in the eighties the Bank has felt compelled to provide more lifeboats to try to save sinking companies: it invites company directors, bankers and pension fund managers to sit round the table, pressing them with all its mysterious moral authority, to try to stave off a bankruptcy.

But to suggest that bankers should be 'guided', as in Japan, to lend money in some directions, and not others, remains a heresy to British banks who still prefer to survey the past rather than the future. The social divide between bankers and most industrialists makes them

[6] Dimitri Vittas and Roger Brown: *Bank Lending and Industrial Investment*, Banking Information Service, March 1982.

all the more hesitant, and the opaque language of bankers' documents reveals their instinctive reluctance to welcome new customers. When they *do* take an interest in a fashionable new business, they are apt to switch suddenly, all together, from extreme caution to uncritical enthusiasm; for bankers move naturally in herds, and behind their grave expressions they can be (as Keynes warned us) 'the most romantic and the least realistic of men'.

The bankers showed all this repressed romanticism when, led by the Midland, they began lending large sums to the exuberant airline operator, Sir Freddie Laker. He was such a persuasive salesman and popular hero, blessed by both political parties, that when he rashly bought more big planes in the midst of the world recession in 1980 the bankers could not resist him: while he borrowed from American banks to buy five DC10s he also borrowed from a syndicate of banks, led by the Midland, to buy three European Airbus planes. By 1981 his borrowings amounted to seven times the value of his equity, while he faced growing troubles as other airlines tried to undercut his fares across the Atlantic; but he could still borrow more from the Clydesdale Bank, the Midland's Scottish subsidiary. It was only when Laker's position became desperate in October that the Midland and the Bank of England were worried enough to ask a merchant banker, Ian McIntosh from Samuel Montagu (now owned by the Midland), to try to reschedule the vast debts; but the German and Austrian banks in the syndicate now took the gloomiest view and wanted to sell off the planes while they could. The Bank of England tried to organise help from the aircraft manufacturers: the Airbus company was adamant but McDonnell Douglas who made the DC10s agreed to put up another £5 million, provided that Laker's earnings did not decline. During that winter Laker's planes were only 40 per cent full and travel agents were scared away by growing rumours of crisis. While Laker was proclaiming in February that he was out of his troubles and 'flying high' the banks knew he needed another £10 million to survive for two months, and were closing in. The Midland directors spent a whole day with Sir Freddie analysing the dismal projections and refusing to lend any more. The next day the posters proclaimed the national calamity: LAKER GOES BUST.

Could the banks have prevented it? Many City experts were surprised, not so much by the overreaching ambitions of Sir Freddie, as by the rashness of the Midland which had so readily lent so much to a company with such small capital and now stood to lose at least £10 million. 'It is hard to escape the conclusion,' said the *Financial Times* the next day, 'that if the bankers had taken a more hard-nosed approach, yesterday's sad story might have been averted.' The bankers could claim that they had done everything they could to prevent a bankruptcy; but they had shown that fatal generosity which can bedevil the relationships between insiders and outsiders: they had given a man enough rope to hang himself.

19

Pensions and Insurance: the Reluctant Owners

The growth of pension funds during and since the middle 1970s has created the biggest revolution in the British financial scene in this century. Surprisingly it was almost totally unperceived by political or even financial commentators until very recently.

Harold Wilson, 1979[1]

WHILE bankers were arguing about their responsibility for industry, and while politicians were pressing to nationalise or de-nationalise, the actual ownership of industry was being transformed behind their backs through a mechanism which few of them foresaw. The rise of insurance companies and pension funds—the 'institutions' as they are obscurely called—with their vast sums waiting to be invested, has introduced a bewildering new force into the midst of late industrial society. They seem to belong half to capitalism, and half to socialism, and their responsibility has only been seriously debated in the last few years.

INSURANCE COMPANIES

The pension business began quite separately from the City of London, when groups of working men in the mid-nineteenth century first organised savings groups to give them security, which grew into insurance companies aloof from the traditional financial strongholds. The biggest and most famous, the Prudential, originated in 1848: its agents began collecting weekly savings through the Potteries and the weaving districts of Cheshire and Lancashire from artisans and workers who were dedicated to self-help and determined to avoid state aid. By the 1880s the Pru had collected more than seven million policies, and held three-quarters of the new life-insurance business which had developed from small savings. Its

[1] Harold Wilson: *Final Term, The Labour Government, 1974–1976*, Weidenfeld and Nicolson, London, 1979, p. 146.

continuity is commemorated by the pink castle, the most spectacular of all Victorian monuments, which stands in Holborn appropriately just outside the square mile. Its Gothic corridors, ecclesiastical boardroom and fairyland roofs, now lovingly renovated, mark the triumph of working-class security; but no Victorian director could have predicted the subsequent development of this giant piggy-bank.

The Prudential first became famous for the 'men from the Pru' who collected money from house to house, offering both life insurance and pension schemes. But as its great central fund accumulated, waiting to be paid out after the retirement or death of millions of savers, the Pru acquired a more awesome significance for City men and industrialists. For it invested its millions not only in government stock, but in industrial shares—on a scale which by the 1950s was already making the Pru the biggest single shareholder in many giant companies, while the new money pouring in from their small savers was eclipsing all other sources of finance. These were the ten biggest 'life companies' in Britain in 1981 with their annual income from premiums and their chairmen:

LIFE INSURANCE COMPANIES

Company	Chairman and education	Life funds £ million
1 Prudential	Lord Carr (Westminster; Cambridge)	6,222
2 Legal and General	Professor Robert Ball (St Marylebone; Oxford)	3,993
3 Standard Life	Alexander Hodge (Fettes; Edinburgh)	2,925
4 Commercial Union	Sir Francis Sandilands (Eton; Cambridge)	2,229
5 Norwich Union	Michael Falcon (Stowe; Heriot-Watt)	2,105
6 Guardian Royal Exchange	John Collins (King Edwards; Birmingham)	1,648
7 Scottish Widows' Fund	Edmund Clutterbuck (Winchester; Oxford)	1,574
8 Eagle Star Holdings	Sir Dennis Mountain (Eton; Guards)	1,363
9 Pearl Assurance	Frederick Garner (Sutton County)	1,324
10 Sun Life	Philip Walker (Epworth, Rhyl)	1,238
11 Royal Insurance	Daniel Meinertzhagen (Eton; Oxford)	1,153
12 Hambro Life	John Clay (Eton; Oxford)	1,073

The chairman of the companies include a smattering of the hereditary City establishment, including four Old Etonians: Daniel Meinertzhagen maintains his family's links with Lazards Bank; John Clay of Hambros is the son of the former Conservative economic adviser to the Bank of England; Sir Francis Sandilands worked his way up Commercial Union and is now the elder statesman of insurance, a veteran of government committees; and Sir Denis Mountain followed his father Sir Brian as the chairman of the family business, Eagle Star. The boards have become slightly less influenced by bankers and old families as the companies have become more confident of their own importance, and in 1981 the insurance world experienced a fearful shock when the German giant Allianz made a bid for Eagle Star, buying 28 per cent of its shares before Mountain fought back, leaving the company with an uncertain future ownership.

The men in these companies who are most important to industry are not the chairmen or directors but the investment managers, who are quite outside the old City traditions. By training they are nearly all actuaries—that tiny and rarified profession of mathematicians who are expert in calculating probabilities, but have little experience of industry or politics. They are mostly quiet men from grammar schools, cut off from the louder and more confident world of bankers or stockbrokers, and rightly preoccupied with their fiduciary role—they love that word—as trustees for their policyholders. But they could not avoid being involved in boardroom battles when directors petitioned them as shareholders for support. By the fifties the Pru—which sometimes had twice as much money as any other shareholders—was worried to find itself being asked to decide who should control a company.

The Pru's power first dramatically broke on the public in 1956, when their investment manager Leslie Brown helped to dislodge Sir Bernard Docker, the flamboyant toff who was chairman of the British Small Arms Company. Since then the company has intervened more frequently, usually secretly, and in 1970 it made history by leading a shareholders' revolt against the unprofitable old arms company, Vickers, forcing the board to appoint its own nominee, Peter Matthews, as managing director. The current joint investment managers, Ronald Artus and Brian Medhurst, have become more actively involved with industry than their predecessors, and they have had to reflect carefully about the Pru's role, particularly since the ordeals of 1974 and the world recession. 'We have to recognise that the world doesn't owe the Pru a living,' as one of them said. 'The recession has done more than the Pru to shake up British industry.'

Ronald Artus, the senior investment manager, is a fast-talking economist who moves appropriately between two worlds: he is proud of his working-class roots (he displays his grandfather's membership certificate of the dockers' union in his office); and he married into the Touche family, linked to the stockbrokers Touche, Ross and the NatWest Bank. He deplores the arrogance of fund managers who try to make social rather than commercial choices, but he believes the Pru must face up to new responsibilities. 'The residual role of the proprietor,' he explained to me, 'isn't being exercised by anyone: but I hope the institutions can for the first time counterbalance the power of self-perpetuating managers. In the early joint-stock companies proprietors and managers were virtually the same, but with the advent of mass shareholders there was no conceivable challenge to the boards, except the market forces. Now the big institutions are beginning to exercise some control in extreme cases. But you mustn't exaggerate our catalytic role: it's really peripheral to the development of industry.'

PENSION FUNDS

The insurance companies with their huge funds and conservative boards are still politically exposed, a favourite target for the left. But they have been partially eclipsed by the newer and more nebulous power of the pension funds. The large industrial companies employ their own investment managers to handle the growing portfolios for pensioners, which by the sixties were beginning to rival those of the Pru. They were supposedly trustees for their employees' savings, but they were so little regulated that the funds could easily be used to bolster the company. That might suit the workers: in a few cases the pension fund of a small company is now its single biggest shareholder, which protects it from being taken over, and gives workers an extra interest in its profits. But an investment manager who is protected from disclosure can use his pension fund to shore up the wobbly company without even telling the workers, which can threaten their security. When, for instance, the food company J. Lyons was in perilous straits in 1976, it sold some of its property to its own pension fund, most of whose trustees were also its managers—including the chairman.[2]

The largest of all the pension funds are those of the nationalised industries, which have the most workers; and the eight largest nationalised funds in 1981, with their assets and chief managers, are shown overleaf. The managers of these funds work in an extra political dimension, for they are directly responsible to trustees including trade unionists, who thus find themselves responsible for huge chunks of private industrial investment. It was an odd sequel to the original nationalisation three decades earlier. 'The nationalisation of coal in 1946 cost the government £393 million,' said Harold Wilson when he was investigating the City in 1978. 'I guess the coal industry pension funds today are probably involved in buying other

[2] See the *Economist*, November 4, 1978.

NATIONALISED INDUSTRY PENSION FUNDS, 1981

	Assets (million)	Members (thousand)	Chief Managers
Post Office	3,800	400,000	Ralph Quartano
National Coal Board	2,665	303,000	Hugh Jenkins
British Railways	2,000	215,000	John Morgan
Electricity Council	1,825	136,000	Bob Gibson
British Steel	1,400	118,000	Paul Oldham
Gas Council	1,033	93,000	Alan Phillipson
British Airways	1,032	46,000	G. Burwood
Water Council	500	58,000	J. C. Richards

people's industries at the rate of £393 million every eighteen months. That is an extension of nationalisation in a creeping way, not necessarily in the way that parliament intended.'[3]

These huge funds came into existence haphazardly. Nationalised pensions could have been arranged, like civil servants' pensions, through 'pay-as-you-go'; the present generation of workers could pay for the pensions of those who have retired (provided the industry continues to exist). But they were in fact paid for by 'funding': the workers contributed during their working life and were repaid after they retired. Funding thus accumulated a pile of money which could exceed the assets of the parent corporation.

Because these funds grew up unexpectedly, governments did not establish any mechanism like company acts to make them accountable: they only needed to produce accounts for their members. The biggest funds remain very private organisations which are largely ignored by the rest of the financial establishment: none was represented on the Wilson Committee, or on the Court of the Bank of England. A few pension fund managers want to be recognised, but most seem to enjoy their anonymity. One fund manager saw himself as a gnome, with his profile under the table; it was a ridiculous idea, he thought, that the public had a right to know about what he did with the money. But their anonymity, without any overt power base, encourages the legend of a secret cabal of faceless men manipulating their financial power, or conspiring to stage 'investment strikes'. Certainly the managers of the biggest funds know each other, lunch each other and meet at the National Association of Pension Funds (NAPF) which looms large in many City debates. Sometimes they join forces to achieve changes in a company of which several hold shares. But they are also in competition with each other, which limits their collusion, and there has been no real evidence of serious conspiracy.

[3] Speech to the London branch of the British Institute of Management, September 8, 1978.

The fund managers are improbable representatives of the new owners of Britain—even more improbable than the actuaries who run the insurance companies. Many are 'beardless boys' as Harold Wilson calls them, working in small offices in modest surroundings; they come from different trainings, but many have worked up through the pension business. Few of them come from the public school or Oxbridge background of bankers and stockbrokers, and there are some faint rumblings of class warfare. The old guard treat them with wary politeness, as they might treat upstart millionaires who have suddenly become lords of the manor.

Merchant bankers and stockbrokers still have plenty of scope for managing pension funds, and even some of the biggest funds leave part of their money with the bankers: Hill Samuel manages about £2 billion worth of pension funds, including half the British Rail Fund which they jointly manage with Warburgs. Many City people still regard pension fund managers as wet behind the ears, and some have been able to take them for a ride. The smaller funds tend to go automatically to a bank or a stockbroker, who may feel little competitive pressure, but the big funds can compare their own team's performance with a merchant bank's and leave the bank if it cannot compete.

POSTMEN, MINERS, RAILWAYMEN

Much the biggest British fund comes from the Post Office, the biggest employers in Europe, with about 400,000 members in 1981; and the pensions for this army of postmen and telephone operators have flowed into a lake of money which now fills up with over £1 million a day. Posfund, as it now calls itself, is run by a committee of nine who sit every three weeks, including four trade unionists, four nominees of the Post Office board and the fund's chairman who is responsible for the broad pattern of investment.

The previous chairman, Alfred Singer, who resigned in 1979, was an outspoken accountant who had spent much of his life in industry, including Tesco. 'With my background I'm in favour of stirring up companies,' he told me in 1978, 'but if we dig into questions of industrial performance, we have no credibility.' He was succeeded by a more orthodox chairman, Sir Daniel Pettit, a former schoolmaster, sportsman and Unilever manager. But most of the responsibility for the fund lies with the chief executive, who for the last eight years has been Ralph Quartano, a former chemical engineer and journalist who joined the Post Office and found himself running the pension fund rather by accident. He is genial and humorous, but very conscious of his fund's responsibility and power; and he has shown his weight in a succession of boardroom battles.

What is the real responsibility of a big fund? Posfund has taken pride in investing in inner cities, and in local authorities' property schemes, but it does not take risks with 'social' investments. The union leaders want to diversify the fund among countries as well as industries, and 10 per cent is now invested outside Britain—including the great arcades along the Rue de Rivoli in Paris. Trade unionists are frequently in a tricky position as trustees of pension funds: they want to get the best returns for their members, while this may conflict blatantly with their union's own political views. When the shares in the British National Oil Corporation were put up for sale in 1981 pension funds saw them as a good buy, although many unions were committed to a policy of renationalisation without compensation—which would make the shares valueless. Workers want their savings, as Tony Benn lucidly explains, 'not only as income when they retire; but to sustain and create jobs while they are at work, and so to guarantee that they will retire in a buoyant economy';[4] yet the equation is not as simple as it sounds. The union trustees, as one fund manager put it, are 'particularly good at wearing two hats'; they argue that their unions' policy is a risk they must take into account in buying the shares. They are not enthusiastic about investing in labour-intensive industries which could boost employment, or about confining investments to Britain: 'They're more capitalist than you or me: it's hard to restrain them from investing everything abroad,' one fund manager said. Even if trustees officially stick to their political views, the fund managers often ignore them.

The same kind of conflict is evident in the Coal Board pension fund, where the miners' leaders sit on the board. The fund manager, Hugh Jenkins, is a chartered surveyor who came up through property (which accounts for 30 per cent of the fund's investment); he now has a staff of twenty dealing with marketable securities, and his fund owns over 5 per cent of many big companies. He sees the heads of the largest informally about once a year, trying to maintain a dialogue and to avoid public clashes; but he is particularly keen on investing in small companies, which require more attention, and he is certain that pension funds will have to pay more time to finding good managers for industry. The pension funds, he insists, are often more positive and more robust than insurance companies: 'the real problem is *accepting* our power.'

The British Rail fund, the third biggest, is run by a more conventional City man, John Morgan, who spent eight years in Warburgs

[4] Benn: *op cit*, p. 150.

bank and moved from Rothschilds to British Rail in 1978; but he is proud of his working-class roots as a member of the Rugeley Progressive Working Men's club in Staffordshire. He runs the fund from an elegant neo-Gothic office in the old Great Eastern Hotel in the City, looking after about £2 billion. He seems puzzled, even upset, that a journalist should want to visit him, and insists 'we're just technicians'. The British Rail fund, however, gained much publicity by its controversial venture into art collecting: while the postmen were buying up parts of Paris, the British Rail fund built up a rich hoard of paintings and sculptures in partnership with Sotheby's. Its annual purchases made up only 5 per cent of its total investment, but it could still buy more than the British Museum and the Tate Gallery combined. It was criticised for collecting too rashly, and for being too closely linked to Sotheby's which had its own interests at heart; and by 1979 it had stopped collecting. But it was less rash, it turned out, than investing in a venerable British company such as Leyland.

Do the fund managers exert their power as a block? They insist that they each have their own ideas and perspective, but they compete less obviously than insurance companies, and they are all interested in long-term and secure investments. Most of them are very conscious of being outside the old City establishment of interlocking directorships. The four groups of major investors in the City—the insurance companies, the pension funds, the unit trusts and the investment trusts—each have their own 'protection committee' to look after their common interests. They all come together every two months in the Institutional Shareholders' Committee, a body first proposed by the Bank of England, to safeguard shareholders' rights as a kind of long-stop to the other committees, but which also provides a sounding-board for members' attitudes. And the pension funds, which have become much more aware that they control most of the money, have increasingly made the running. 'What happens,' (Harold Wilson asked) 'when the boys grow up?'

THE OWNERS' DILEMMA

In the early seventies the insurance companies and pension funds faced shocks which showed all the perils of their ownership of industry. The bankrupting of Rolls Royce in 1971 and the collapse of British Leyland in 1975 left most of their big investors with devalued shares; and the crash of 1974 sent all British shares—particularly property shares—reeling. As investors began to recover, they had to think more carefully about their relationship with industry. They could not easily 'vote with their feet', like American funds, by selling their shares in big companies whose management they distrusted; for heavy selling could induce panic in the relatively small British stock-market. They were therefore pressed to intervene more boldly with the managers of industry.

The left wing of the Labour party in the meantime was clamouring to nationalise the insurance companies; and at the party conference in 1976 the new prime minister Jim Callaghan deftly deflected the left by promising to appoint a commission to investigate the whole City, to be headed by his predecessor. Harold Wilson and his colleagues on the commission were soon touring the insurance boardrooms and bankers' parlours, making sporadic statements to keep the issue alive; it shortly became clear that Wilson did not favour nationalisation, but he was fascinated by the power of the pension funds. 'They could be more powerful than the cabinet,' he said to me, 'and they leak a lot less.' He saw that the fund managers were in a dilemma: 'If they interfere in industry they're exerting a power which was given to them for quite other reasons; and if they don't interfere they're accused of having power without responsibility. They can't win.'

The meetings of the Wilson Committee, on top of the fiascos of 1974, helped to stimulate a good deal of self-questioning in the City, which was trying to pre-empt outside criticism. 'Institutions can no longer ignore the wider responsibilities that come from being part of a whole sector,' said Peter Moodie of the Prudential in October 1978, speaking to the Institute of Actuaries. 'They cannot afford to be labelled as "absentee shareholders" or regarded as totally passive. With more than 50 per cent of all equity in institutional funds, the sector as a whole cannot dispose of problems by selling its shares . . . the willingness of institutional investors to take a more positive role, which has been growing over the last two decades, must continue to grow.'

When the Wilson Committee published their report in 1980, they did not express any serious concern about pension funds; but Wilson himself, with four others, signed a note of dissent supporting a proposal first put forward by the TUC: that the funds should put 10 per cent of their money into a fund which would take a longer view than commercial investors of potentially productive investments; the government would guarantee them a rate of return at least equal to gilt-edged stock, if necessary making up the difference. But the pension managers predictably resented the prospect of placing part of their billions in the hands of a separate institution outside their control; they argued that they were responsible to their members, not to the British economy, and that any government subsidy for long-term investment would be more efficient without this kind of smokescreen.

The proposal was dropped, but it reflected a recurring criticism: that pension funds take too short a view of returns from industry, and are too wary of devoting venture capital to longer-term schemes. They are in a difficult position: by law they are responsible for their members' money to trustees who review their accounts yearly so that they cannot ignore short-term rewards. They can tell cautionary tales such as that of the Electricity Supply Industry fund, which had to be reorganised in 1980 after it had got into deep water, particularly that of the Brighton Marina Company. Many fund managers, like the bank chairmen, argue that industry never really asks for more money. Hugh Jenkins of the Coal Board set up a special fund for investment capital: 'We tramped round many companies over a period of eighteen months offering this facility,' he told the Wilson Committee, 'and in only three cases did we get any positive response.'

However some fund managers now feel more responsible for encouraging specific companies and industries—whether because of criticism like Wilson's, or because of the vogue for small companies, or because they believe that the pension funds must contribute to economic growth in their own self-interest. The funds of the Coal Board and British Steel have helped to start up alternative industries in coal and steel areas. Posfund is proud of having invested in small companies in East Anglia—including one which has cornered the market in African violets and is now diversifying into geraniums. But these investments are still relatively tiny and the funds employ very few people to spend a great deal of money. 'Thirty million pounds is about the right size of an investment,' as one of the Posfund staff explained. 'Thirty thousand pounds is rather more of a problem.'

As the millions pour into the pension funds and insurance companies, at the rate of over £40 million a day, they have to look further afield to try to invest the money safely. They have bought farming land, art collections and commodities to try to hedge themselves against inflation, and they are having to change their traditional attitudes to industry. They have been stealthily exerting more leverage: as in the showbiz spectacular of Associated Communications (see chapter 28) or the less publicised and more important case of International Computers (ICL) in 1981, where three big institutions, including Posfund, intervened with encouragement from the government to put in a new chairman, Christopher Laidlaw. The Pru is now looking more carefully at new companies, partly because, they explain, 'it's much harder to change old companies than new ones', partly because they need to look further into the future. They now have their own venture capital fund called Prutech, which had invested about £20 million by early 1982, including £1 million invested in the Scottish company, M and D Technology, based on a new kind of medical 'scanner' invented at Aberdeen University.

But most of the institutions have also been sending more of their money abroad in pursuit of greater profits, and by 1981 they were investing £2.3 billion of new money in overseas shares. This foreign investment seems sensible enough in their members' interests, as Britain's own prospects look dimmer, and the trade unionists, as we have noted, remain very ambivalent. Yet the flow of funds could eventually damage Britain's industrial prospects still further: 'At what point,' asks one recent critic of the institutions, 'does this apparent pessimism about British economic prospects become self-fulfilling?'[5]

The financial power of the pension funds has grown up in parallel with the political power of the trade unions—both consequences of organised workers, through their savings and their labour. The leaders in both areas were reluctant to face up to their responsibilities, preferring to remain passive and protective and keeping outside the older structures—the cabinet on the one hand, the banks on the other. The old clearing banks in the City, with their detailed knowledge of industrial accounts, might seem more equipped to intervene and revive industrial companies. But the new pension funds, with their smaller staffs and shorter experience, wield the real money-power.

The private corporate state (as the *Economist* calls them) of pension managers is constantly influencing the structures of British society—whether by financing property development, by propping up industrial directors, or by moving their funds into new regions or cities. They have grown up discreetly on the backstage of the financial community, beyond the ken of politicians and parliament. Some economists see them as representing a form of socialisation of industry, but if it is socialism it remains remarkably unaccountable. It is an odd twist to the story of capitalism that the critical choices, behind the pomp and gravity of old bankers and brokers, should be taken by unobtrusive accountants in small rooms who are helping to change the face of the nation without even realising it.

PENSIONABLE PEOPLE

No future pensioner can feel altogether reassured by the past performance of the great companies on which his savings depend.

[5] John Plender: *That's the Way the Money Goes*, André Deutsch, London, 1982.

He is encouraged to use them by the tax system which gives relief to people investing in the funds, but they cannot offer greater security than an individual who invests his own money in a house, and they have too often, like the bankers, put their money into ageing giant companies which have sunk or collapsed. They have been too passive either to invigorate industry or to safeguard their savings, as they followed some of their most disastrous investments—whether Leyland, Burmah, or Rolls Royce—over the edge of the cliff.

The pensions industry has grown in thirty years from a mouse into a mammoth, but can it avoid the fate of a mammoth, in a much harsher climate? In the past most companies promised fixed pre-arranged pensions until inflation made them a mockery, and they now relate most occupational pensions to a person's final salary. But their investments may be so eroded by inflation that they may not be able to fulfil their promises, and may have to cut the real value of the pensions. As the Chancellor, Sir Geoffrey Howe, warned the pension funds in May 1981: 'Our society is locked into providing benefits without having made the economic adjustments necessary to sustain them.'[6]

The promise of pensions is part of the dilemma facing every old industrial country, particularly in a time of recession: how can a nation facing all the risks and uncertainties of world competition promise indefinite security to its ageing population? Why should retired civil servants as well as company executives expect to receive two-thirds of their final salary for the rest of their lives, keeping pace with inflation—a promise which dates back to more prosperous times—to be paid for by younger people struggling to maintain a lower standard of living? A society of pensionable people becomes conditioned to living without risk and enjoying the fruits of their savings, encouraged by every insurance advertisement; but the realities of competitive industry, on which their pensions depend, are much harsher and less certain. The insurance castles and palaces of the City, with all their reassuring promises—the Rock of Gibraltar, the umbrella, the country home with roses round the door—all depend for their fulfilment on a very changeable industrial society, to provide the exports which alone can enable Britain to pay her way.

[6] Speech to National Association of Pension Funds, May 8, 1981.

FOUR

Industry

20

Farmers: the Pre-industrial Revival

Land ownership in this country can bring with it inestimable and unjustifiable power and influence for a tiny minority of our citizens—a minority whose interests are frequently in direct conflict with the good of the community.

Labour Policy Document, 1982

BRITAIN's oldest industry remains the most prestigious and politically influential, though it employs less than 3 per cent of her people. Land ownership, the original basis of political representation, still has close links with the Tory party, and the present cabinet includes four farmers and landowners (Whitelaw, Pym, Prior and Heseltine). The Labour party has its own weakness for farmers, many of whom reckon they have done better under Labour governments than under Tories. ('What a subtly corrupting thing it is to marry into a farm,' Richard Crossman told his diary, in 1959, after he had married a farmer's daughter. 'Slowly you start to believe you have something to do with it!') The more uncertain the future of other industries, the more reassuring is the business which is rooted in the land itself. But the finite quantity of land—60 million acres for 56 million people, or one acre per person—sets an obvious limit on how many people can enjoy owning it; as Mark Twain said: 'Nobody's making it any more'.

As in other pre-industrial activities—in banking, insurance, theatre or gardening—Britain excels in agriculture while she falls back in manufacture: the entrepreneurial energy and innovation which has been so lacking in new industries is very visible in the countryside, where dynamic farmers rip up hedges, plough up national parks, lay concrete yards and build silos in beauty-spots with inexhaustible enterprise, and the country air is loud with the rural sounds of chain-saws, tractors and helicopters. Well-educated graduates who would never be seen inside a factory or office-block can acquire sudden incentives and business acumen when facing the land.

It has long been an important paradox that the most urbanised country in Europe should be the most fascinated by the countryside. Many historians have blamed country estates and rural romanticism for the decline of British industry in the late nineteenth century: the very fact that the British countryside emptied so rapidly (as Martin Wiener points out)[1] enabled the new urban rich to move into big estates, imposing their own romantic views on rural life, while the growing suburban population insisted on living in little houses with gardens rather than in apartment blocks like most Continentals. But this long love-affair with the countryside has taken a new twist with the farming boom of the post-war decades, culminating in Britain's membership of the European Community; and behind the apparently timeless and immutable rural values there are very deliberate economic and political forces, which are often concealed but must be understood.

For over a century after the Corn Laws of 1846 British agriculture was the least protected in the world, and consumers benefited from cheap food imported from wherever it could be found. Canada, Australia, South Africa and New Zealand were all low-cost exporters and even when imperial preference was introduced, prices were not substantially increased. The British farmers were almost unsubsidised and hit by regular depressions as low prices abroad made domestic production uneconomic. In the 1880s and 1890s and then again in the 1930s, land reached rock-bottom prices and farming became a very risky way to make a living. But the Second World War helped to change attitudes to farmers as Britain faced the U-boats with an unprepared agricultural industry, and after the war governments introduced a range of economic measures to stimulate home production and limit foreign competition. The Agriculture Act of 1947 (followed by other acts in 1957, 1964 and 1967) set up a system of government support based on an annual review of farm incomes, costs and profitability.

The National Farmers' Union sat on one side of the table arguing their poverty; the civil servants from the Ministry of Agriculture sat on the other pointing to the farmers' wealth; the Treasury pursued its ritual dance and complained that the farmers' lobby had a tame ministry; the cabinet eventually adjudicated each year between a Minister of Agriculture eager to do well by his farmers and a Chancellor determined to stop the feather-bedding. The result was a set of guaranteed prices for the farmer, regardless of how much he produced, maintained by a government subsidy, which topped up the prices that the farmer got in the market. These 'deficiency payments'

[1] Martin Wiener: *English Culture and the Decline of the Industrial Spirit, 1850–1980*, Cambridge University Press, 1981.

had two great advantages. The consumer got the food as cheaply as the free market would allow and it was all consumed, not stockpiled or destroyed. It served the country effectively until 1973, and Britain remained one of the largest importers of foodstuffs, at very low prices, in the world.

But the whole system of agriculture was profoundly changed when Britain joined the EEC in 1973, and British farmers found themselves sharing the privileged and protected position which Continental farmers had long assumed to be their right. The Ministry of Agriculture was turned from a sleepy backwater into a department which virtually ran its own foreign policy, and agriculture was a major factor in European politics as the battles raged over the costs and benefits of the Common Agricultural Policy (CAP).

The CAP is based on quite different principles from the British deficiency payments, deriving from centuries of European protectionism and agricultural dominance. Under the CAP the farmer gets his return from a market which is managed in order to bring prices up to guaranteed levels. This is done by erecting high tariff barriers against food from outside the Community (from 'third countries'—a revealing phrase) and by buying up the surpluses, which then build up the famous butter mountains and wine lakes: butter, wine and skimmed milk powder have all now been in surplus for years. 'Community preference' means that European food always gets favourable treatment whatever its costs or quality, and the consumer must pay the full manipulated market price. Economists have endlessly argued whether the old deficiency payments would have cost less (they probably would in a country such as Britain with relatively few farmers). What is certain is that the European system encourages excess production with its high prices, and subsidises the overseas consumer by exporting the surpluses below cost; while the deficiency system subsidised the home consumer and gave him cheap food.

The high cost of the CAP became one of the chief complaints of British anti-Marketeers. It is not intrinsically inefficient, but it has many absurdities and extravagances, and it has certainly kept prices too high—because the agriculture ministers of the ten countries, who take the critical decisions, depend for their backing on their farmers' lobbies. Each of them will explain to their own Treasury at home that it was the fault of the others. The result is over-expensive food, too many special subsidies to placate member countries, and too much surplus.

The unfairness of the CAP, and the power of European farmers which lay behind it, defied successive attempts at reform. John

Silkin, the Labour Minister of Agriculture until 1979, was the only minister who tried to take on the Continental lobby—inspired more by domestic political ambition than by any passion for reform—but he too was bought off with special arrangements such as subsidising butter for the British consumer. It was not until 1980 that European ministers admitted that the policy was going seriously wrong: in return for Britain's huge contribution to the budget they committed themselves to reform the CAP, which was now making up over 70 per cent of the Community's budget.

Britain's underlying problem was always that she had to pay more than her share of the running costs of the club she joined in 1973. The Community's income comes partly from the high tariffs on imported food, and since Britain imports more than the others she contributes more; while since she does not produce surpluses and get subsidies from exports, she gets less money in return. When Britain signed the Treaty of Accession she expected to get compensating benefits from social and regional policies, but they never developed in the bad times of the seventies: by 1979, when the transitional period had ended and the full huge payments became due, the government had to do something. The Europeans temporarily agreed to put ceilings on Britain's contributions but the arguments still rage over a long-term solution, and the showdown in May 1982, when the British veto against higher farm prices was overruled, showed that the French still see the CAP as their price for European unity.

THE FARMERS' LOBBY

British farmers, in the meantime, adapted quite easily to their new political environment. The National Farmers' Union has swiftly become Euro-minded: its past president, Sir Henry Plumb, became chairman of COPA, the pressure group of European farmers, and then leader of the Conservative group of European MPs. The current officials of the NFU know the Brussels and Strasbourg run only too well, and they have recruited civil servants from the ministry, including the former second permanent secretary, Sir Frederick Kearns, to help to influence Whitehall and the European institutions. British farmers themselves have become expert in the arcane specialisms of monetary compensatory amounts, sluice-gate prices and sheepmeat clawback. And agricultural production increased steadily during the 1970s, so that Britain now produces 70 per cent of her own food.

The relative success of British farmers has caused fundamental political arguments. If agriculture is the most efficient industry, the farmers suggest, the government should devote still more funds to agricultural subsidies, to back proven winners rather than lame ducks. But since farmers already get extensive free advice, tax concessions and grants for capital investment, plus a guaranteed end-price, the sceptics argue that it is hardly surprising that they do well; the lesson is surely that other industries should get the same treatment. The argument could embarrass both main political parties. The Tories do not want to create an example for intervening in industry, while the socialists wish it was not the rich landed interest which reaped most of the benefits of subsidy and planning.

The profits from farming are having some effect on the social structure of the countryside. Big landowners are still powerful in many counties such as Northumberland or Wiltshire, but they are less dominant: more important are the industrialised farmers, such as Bernard Matthews who did to the turkey what others did to the chicken in the 1960s. Professional managers have entered the farming scene, spending their careers running efficient units for absentee owners, including the pension funds and the new rich, who want to buy the status that only land seems to confer. Tenant farmers are becoming rarer since they got greater security in the seventies, for the new legislation made owners much more reluctant (like house-owners with their tenants) to rent their land.

The backbone of British farming is now provided by the owner-occupier, and the average farmer is a relatively well-off small businessman who is rich in terms of land-value and lives well off the firm, though he may have less ready cash than his Rover and smart farmhouse might suggest. Compared to other country-dwellers the farmer is now prosperous, thanks to the protection and subsidies which came first from the nation, then from Europe. But British governments have shown far less interest in protecting the consumer and supervising the companies which process and market the food, apart from some nods in the direction of food standards and labelling. The Department of Prices in its five years made no impact on agricultural policy, and the idea of a national nutrition policy has found no favour with politicians.

But if farmers have gained financially, they have lost much of their public popularity. The image of romantic rural life has suffered heavily from battery chickens and zero-grazing, from the wrecking of landscapes, the burning of stubble, the spraying of pesticides which kill off wildlife, and above all from the discrepancy between the good life in much of the countryside and the poverty of the inner cities (which Continentals still tend to see the other way round). The division between town and country has become in many ways more extreme in Britain than on the Continent, where the rapid flight from the land in the sixties and seventies was accompanied by an industrial boom in the cities, and the French and Germans deliberately tried to keep people in rural areas, with the help of craft and light industries. The British farms were rapidly shedding their workers, replacing them with machines, and creating a new agricultural revolution while urban industry was much less efficient. 'The average farmer,' says Sir Richard Butler, the President of the National Farmers' Union (and son of 'Rab' Butler), 'farms 50 per cent more land with a third as many men as in the fifties.'

The British farmers were able to become much more productive, with virtually no union problems and no restrictive practices: at first most of the redundant farm workers could get better-paid jobs in the towns, while the country villages filled up with middle-class weekenders and retired couples living on pensions. But with mounting unemployment this distribution looks much less socially attractive: the farms get bigger and more highly mechanised with the help of their subsidies, providing still fewer jobs, while the inner cities provide a bleak and rootless background for mass unemployment. 'Other countries have perhaps been a little more farsighted than we have,' said Sir Henry Plumb.

The prosperity of farming might appear to provide some compensation for a de-industrialising country—a reversion to the Jane Austen kind of Britain of settled families and unchanging values which has survived all the convulsions of the industrial revolution. The disproportionate success of the British farmers' lobby—with the help of their tame ministry, the landowners in the cabinet, and the European farmers—testifies to the continuity of old British attitudes. But it is dangerous to be misled by the romantic associations of old farmhouses, duckponds and stables. For farms are rapidly being transformed into large units of agrobusiness; the divide between town and country has become more of a class division; and land is becoming once again an explosive political question. Land, particularly in scenic areas, becomes increasingly sought-after in an age of greater leisure; but the economic trends suggest that its ownership—whether by old aristocrats, new businessmen or pension funds—is becoming more concentrated. The attitudes of conservationists can easily spill over into an ancient conservatism favouring great estates, old families and the interests of game rather than urban people, with the Nature Conservancy in league with big landowners. The Labour party is once again calling for the nationalisation of the land, to cut back the landowners' influence: 'Only through the public ownership and control of the land,' said their draft policy statement in 1982, 'will we be able to eliminate that power and influence.' But the land is a classic case of the limitations of democracy; as more people own it, so its social value diminishes.[2] The subsidising of farms may help to make Britain more self-sufficient in producing her own food; but it will do little to mitigate the economic and social difficulties of a country whose future must depend on cities and manufacturing industry.

[2] See Fred Hirsch: *The Social Limits of Growth*, Routledge, London, 1977, pp. 32–6.

21

Companies: Bigness and Smallness

The interest of the dealers, however, in any particular branch of trade or manufactures, is always in some respects different from, and even opposite to, that of the public.

Adam Smith: The Wealth of Nations

IT was not just the land that was more concentrated. With extraordinary speed a succession of mergers transformed British industry in the sixties, more drastically than in other Western nations. The country so proud of regional diversity and local autonomy, the family hotel and corner shop, was now above all the home of giant corporations. The hundred largest British companies in 1958 made 32 per cent of the country's manufacturing output; by 1972 they provided 41 per cent. Most British industries were now more concentrated than in other European countries, and in some industries the five biggest companies produced over 90 per cent of all the goods. A third of the giant corporations of Western Europe (with turnovers exceeding £250 million), were now based in Britain.[1]

Any shopper could notice some of the consequences: the same kinds of bread, sugar, shoes or frozen foods extending throughout the country in the same chains of supermarkets. But the most ruthless concentration afflicted the most famous and diverse of all British institutions, the pub.

THE FATE OF THE PUB

There were no great grounds for nostalgia about the old brewing families, who had established and fortified their local monopolies over the centuries. The old eighteenth-century owners whose names covered the inn-signs—the Cobbolds, Trumans, Charringtons, Youngers or Whitbreads—got richer by buying up local pubs to

[1] *A Review of Monopolies and Mergers Policy,* Command 7198, HMSO, London, May 1978.

build up their 'vertical integration', from the vat to the bar-room, which is unique in Britain (and which would be illegal in America).[2]

Today only a quarter of the 66,000 British pubs are 'free houses' which can sell anyone's beer. Thus protected, the brewing families felt no serious competition, and the richer ones were elevated to the 'Beerage', retreating from active trade into country houses and rural pursuits. But the sleepy owners gave scope for individual landlords, and their beers and pubs were part of the local scenery. In 1950 there were still six hundred separate brewing companies enjoying different degrees of regional monopoly.

But in the late fifties the development of pasteurised or 'keg' beer enabled the same product to be sold across the nation, while the new TV commercials could advertise it more powerfully, and the screen kept people away from pubs. The standards of beer and service were falling, while the pubs were tempting assets for take-overs. A Canadian invader, Eddie Taylor, began buying up brewers in the north, and in 1958 the dreaded Charles Clore tried to buy one of the oldest and biggest companies, Watneys. The old brewers now panicked, and began recklessly forming their own mergers in self-defence. Watneys bought up a succession of other breweries to fortify itself—including Wilsons of Manchester, Ushers of Trowbridge, Phipps of Northampton and both Norwich breweries—only to fall like an old dray-horse into the hands of Clore's rival tycoon, Maxwell Joseph of Grand Metropolitan Hotels (see below).

Ind Coope of Romford, having merged with Taylor Walker, bought up Tetleys in Leeds and Ansells of Birmingham to create Allied Breweries—the biggest alcohol company in Europe which included a sixth of all Britain's pubs, Double Diamond beer, Harvey's wines, Cockburn's port and Whiteway's cider. All this came under the control of the Showering cider family, who had built up their new fortune by promoting their fizzy cocktail, Babycham, on TV. Mitchells and Butlers, based in the Midlands, took over Bass and Charrington, to form the biggest beer-producer of all. Whitbread first made alliances with a succession of famous brewers, including Flowers, Tennants, Strongs and Birchwoods, and then gobbled them up. Courage took over Simmonds of Reading, Georges of Bristol and Smiths of Tadcaster, only to be itself taken over by Imperial Tobacco. By the early seventies six companies (excluding the Irish stout company Guinness) dominated British beer, and provided 70 per cent of beer production. Overleaf are the Big Six today, with their numbers of pubs (which do not necessarily reflect their overall size).

[2] Price Commission: *Allied Breweries (UK) Ltd*, HMSO, London, 1978.

Bass Charrington	8,000
Allied–Lyons	7,500
Whitbread	7,000
Courage	5,300
Watney Mann & Truman	5,000
Scottish & Newcastle	1,400

These new giants, run by centralised accountants, relentlessly rationalised their pubs and breweries into uniformity. They shut down the local breweries and built new factories like chemical plants to mass-produce their national beer, and the new lagers which began to take over from keg and bottled beer. Whitbreads, with all its famous old brews, now had one big beer factory at Luton; Watneys painted all their pubs red, advertising the 'Red Revolution'; Bass Charrington put plastic toby jugs on their once-elegant façades; while TV commercials proclaimed the new uniform beers.

Gradually beer-drinkers realised the enormity of the change, and by the late sixties they began to revolt. In 1971 a group of young pub-crawlers founded CAMRA, the Campaign for Real Ale, to protect the fast-vanishing traditional draught beer against the inroads of pasteurised beer or 'Euro-fizz'. They sought out the few smaller breweries which still made proper beer and soon became one of the most effective of all consumers' lobbies, attracting 30,000 members and even buying their own pubs. Eventually they forced Watneys and others to reverse their whole strategy; the big companies brought back 'real ale' and began carefully to conceal their uniformity, re-painting their pubs in different colours, disguising their common ownership with their old local names, and creating brand-new traditional pubs with fancy lettering and decor to attract foreign tourists. Instead of mass drinkers joining the Red Revolution the TV commercials now showed Pickwickian landlords in eccentric country pubs.

The financial advantages of centralisation soon proved an illusion. The costs of transporting the beer from the new factories were soaring with the wages of lorry-drivers and the price of petrol. The big new plants were much more vulnerable to strikes, so that thousands of pubs could be at the mercy of six brew-house workers. Bewildered central managers could not control their intricate networks of pubs, and their lorry-loads of beer were sometimes found to be making long journeys quite unnecessarily. The big companies began painfully to rethink their national policies. Watneys sold off some of their least profitable pubs to individual owners—who could soon make money out of them as free houses selling other beers. Max Joseph eventually admitted that if he had realised the problems of managing Watneys he would never have bought it.

The giant companies turned out to be less profitable than the smaller ones. In 1977 the Labour government's Price Commission investigated the brewers' monopolies, spurred on by angry complaints about the price of beer, which made up 3 per cent of the average household's spending. The Commission found that the big companies not only charged more for their beer than the smaller ones, but that their profit margins were significantly smaller—a combination which, as they nicely put it, 'gives rise to fundamental questions about the trade and its organisation'. The big companies, with their control over pubs, their heavy concentration and their lack of foreign competition, revealed 'classic conditions for a monopoly which is likely to operate to the detriment of consumers'.[3]

Only about seventy smaller brewers survived the merger-mania, but the best of them produced better beer, better pubs and better profits. A few became nationally famous for their local brews—such as Adnams of Southwold, with its forty small Suffolk pubs; Wadsworths of Devizes; Youngs of Wandsworth; or Greene King of Bury (still controlled by the Greene family which produced the novelist, a former BBC director-general and the present chairman of Jonathan Cape). Enterprising managers could make good profits from small breweries without wrecking their characters. But for most pubs it was too late: the local roots had been pulled up, and could not be replanted.

HOTEL CHAINS

The fate of hotels was equally melancholy. They do not look very concentrated according to the statistics: a survey in 1974 showed that the twenty biggest groups owned only 15 per cent of the hotel bedrooms in Britain. But the choice of good hotels in London and other big cities has been steadily narrowing, while some towns offer virtually no choice of ownership. With their captive packages of foreign visitors, hotels become easily interlocked with other sections of the tourist industry including food, drink, entertainment and gambling; and while they are the most visible of industries they are controlled by secretive tycoons.

The biggest of the leisure groups, Grand Metropolitan Hotels, which includes the Watneys pub chain, was one of the most spectacular results of the merger-boom. It was founded by a young financier, Maxwell Joseph, who was an estate agent in north London until he began dealing in property, and realised that many British companies were sitting on undervalued assets. He was fascinated by

[3] Price Commission Report No. 31: *Beer Prices and Margins*, pp. 41–5.

reading Arnold Bennett's *Grand Babylon Hotel*, he explains, and soon bought his own small hotel: by 1961 he had twenty-three hotels, and had launched a public company, whose booming shares soon became a stock-market legend. He took over stately London hotels, including the Britannia, the Europa, St Ermin's and the Mayfair, and moved into other businesses including Express Dairies, Berni Inns, Nagle Bookmakers, Mecca dance-halls, Trumans and Watneys breweries and International Distillers, the alcohol combine which includes Gilbey's Gin, J & B Whisky, Piat wines and the elegant Château Landon in the Médoc. As the tourists swept into Britain Joseph could make profits from nearly everything they did, and by 1980 the conglomerate of Sir Max (as Joseph became) was the twelfth biggest company (by sales) in Britain.

Any traveller through Britain is likely to come across the long hand of Grand Met; the Schooner and Berni Inns purvey standardised food, with the same prices and decor, subjecting famous old inns to the same discipline. The conglomerate pays homage to its old traditions, including a coat of arms with symbols of its two old breweries, Watneys and Trumans; but they do not interfere with quick profits, and in 1977 Sir Max sold off Truman's heirloom, Gainsborough's portrait of their founder, Sir Benjamin Truman. Since the tourist boom ended in Britain Sir Max has turned to the United States, taking over the drink and tobacco company, Ligget and Meyers, and then buying—in a remarkable coup in 1981—the eighty-three Intercontinental Hotels from Pan American Airways, at the knock-down price of £270 million. But Britain remains the heart of his leisure empire.

In the late sixties Grand Met was Britain's biggest hotelier, but in 1970 it was overtaken by its rival, Trust House Forte, whose growth had been equally spectacular. It was built round the success of one man, Charles Forte, a restless Italian entrepreneur who was educated in Dumfries and combined brio with canniness. His family owned seaside ice-cream cafes and when he was twenty-five he bought his own milk-bar in Regent Street, becoming expert at costing cheap food. He opened more cafes round Leicester Square, and made quick profits from catering for the Festival of Britain in 1951. He then moved upmarket, buying up the old Café Royal restaurant and then his first hotel, the Waldorf, quickly followed by others. But mass feeding remained a major source of profits—in the airports, on aircraft or in motorway cafes.

In 1970 Forte merged with a dignified group of hotels with an almost opposite character: the Trust Houses had been founded by Quakers who insisted on their own austere standards (they would not make profits from alcohol, which added to the appeal of their bars), and their chairman, Lord Crowther, was the former editor of the *Economist*. The two groups married warily with a nicely-balanced board but Forte soon moved to sack Crowther's choice as chief executive. A public boardroom battle ensued, with each side accusing the other of exploiting the company, revealing much dirt about hoteliers' perks. Crowther accused Forte of personally costing the company a million pounds a year, including his private plane, suites, cars and entertainment; Forte revealed that Crowther had his own suite at the Grosvenor House and his own private staff of researchers. But Crowther was no match for Forte, who brought Lord Robens on to the board as a director who turned out to be committed to Forte: Crowther lost out, and died soon afterwards.

Forte could now extend his mass-catering methods through British country hotels, which quickly fell into the lap of Trust House Forte: their insides were gutted, their purchasing centralised, their meals ruled by 'portion control', and their prices jacked up to what the market would bear. In many towns THF soon provided the only major hotel. Forte built a chain of new Post Houses throughout the country, bought up Little Chef roadside cafes and spread his net far abroad, catching such august hotels as the George V and the Plaza Athénée in Paris and acquiring 460 hotels and motels from the Californian Travelodge company. But his real concentration was in London: he bought thirty-five hotels from the food company, Lyons, and also bought shops, travel agents and bars. A tourist in London can now easily spend all his time within the THF confines: he can walk down Park Lane from the Cumberland to the Grosvenor House, have lunch at the Serpentine Restaurant, buy clothes at Lillywhites and have a drink at one of the Henekey Inns. He can buy his air ticket at a Milbanke travel agency, eat a THF snack at the airport, buy liquor at a THF duty-free shop and find himself eating a THF meal on the plane.

Forte ran his empire in an imperial style: he owned 16 per cent of the shares, and fended off a raid from Allied Breweries. His son Rocco joined the board and his sister redesigned his 'flagship' hotel, the Grosvenor House. He had few union problems, partly because the annual turnover of staff was about 70 per cent. He brought Tory dignitaries on to his board, and chose Lord Thorneycroft as chairman who also became chairman of the Conservative party (to which THF gave £25,000 a year). He built up his own mini House of Lords on his board of trustees, including a Marquis (Exeter), an Earl (Westmoreland), a Viscount (Bridgeman), an Astor (Hugh), and an ex-Tory cabinet minister (Boyd-Carpenter). By New Year's Day 1982 Forte himself was a peer.

THF was now presented as the world's great hotelier, and advertisements emphasised the personal service and creative chefs in the friendly hotels. But gastronomes were less impressed; of the thirty-two British restaurants awarded a rosette in the 1982 *Michelin Guide*, none was owned by either THF or Grand Metropolitan.

Forte had only one major setback, when he tried to buy up the famous Savoy group of hotels. The battle between the two groups provided a new episode in the long-running British serial: the embattled Establishment besieged by a dynamic outsider. It looked like a caricature on both sides. The Savoy's style was disdainful and very conscious of its romantic tradition: their chairman, Sir Hugh Wontner, was a former Lord Mayor of London, an actor's son with a smooth manner who lived in Claridges and entertained guests in princely style. The vice-chairman, Dame Bridget D'Oyly-Carte, who lived in the Savoy, was the granddaughter of the impresario who helped to found the hotel. Wontner insisted that a proper hotel could never be part of a chain, and he confined his Savoy group to Claridges and the Connaught (with the best food in London), the Lancaster in Paris and the new Berkeley in London which he claimed was 'the last really de luxe hotel in Europe'. He fought off successive raiders, including Charles Clore and Max Joseph, while the board fortified themselves with voting shares; but in 1980 the group lost nearly £2 million and had to sell off part of the old Savoy building.

Forte, who had been waiting to pounce, saw his new chance to bid for the group in 1981, and the two elderly chairmen, both seventy-two, each wooed the shareholders and each carefully denigrated the other side. Forte insisted that his first aim was to improve the run-down hotels; Wontner scornfully referred to Forte's roadside snack bars. When Wontner was criticised for his extravagant perks and suite at Claridges, he explained that he had to sample the hotel services at first hand to maintain the standards. The old men's battle raged for two months: Forte had 14 per cent of the Savoy shares and the support of Kuwaitis who owned another 21 per cent; but the small shareholders loyally rallied round Wontner, and the directors and their families still controlled 35 per cent of the votes. Forte was denied the prize he most longed for. London's grandest hotels were still controlled, not by a global chain, but by an eccentric group of hereditary directors living in their own properties.

Forte's empire was not technically a monopoly: in 1978 the Price Commission reckoned (in an unpublished report) that THF owned only 4 per cent of hotel bedrooms in Britain. But in thirty towns the only hotel recognised by the AA was a THF hotel; thirty more had only two hotels, of which one was the THF. In London, which accounted for 38 per cent of all THF accommodation, THF hotels stretched across three sides of Hyde Park.

Was this concentration and uniformity inevitable? The rapid expansion of tourism in the sixties and seventies, with package tours, charter flights and computerised bookings, was bound to threaten the independent smaller hotels. The old family-owned country places which catered for a leisurely middle class were quickly undermined by mass tourists on one level and by expense-account businessmen on the other, while mass-catering on the new motorways was quickly contracted to big companies—as all over Europe, though with more appalling results. The new uniformity of hotels could be justified, as in America, as the price of extending opportunities in a democracy. 'Thirty years ago,' as one Labour ex-cabinet minister explained, 'a family like mine would never have stayed in a hotel. We can't be too worried if they all look rather alike.' But the concentration of hotels, as of pubs, did not necessarily produce lower costs and better service: it was their corporate clout and tax benefits which gave the giants their real advantage. And as the merger-mania subsided and smaller units came back into fashion, the great hotel-chains with their top-heavy management and impersonal controls began to look less attractive to both customers and shareholders.

MUDDLED MERGERS

The chains of pubs and hotels were only the most visible consequences of the wave of mergers and take-overs, which produced a new cluster of diversified companies or 'conglomerates'. There was a parallel trend in America in the late sixties, where the stock-market boom had likewise encouraged aggressive companies to extend themselves, claiming that merged companies through the processes of 'synergy' and 'economies of scale' were much more efficient. But the scope in Britain was still greater: companies were sleepier, anti-trust laws were weaker, and the field (as we will note) was dominated by only a handful of entrepreneurs.

Existing giant corporations, with far less enterprise, were also buying up other companies, in order to put their eggs in several baskets—or because they felt they had to buy *something*. The Rank cinema chain, which earned vast profits when they bought the British rights to Xerox, moved into hotels and leisure; the Beecham group, which had first begun with pills, extended itself into domestic products from Lucozade to Badedas. The Booker company, which was based on sugar, rum and African trading, moved into engineering, drink shops and health-foods and even bought shares in best-selling authors such as Ian Fleming and Agatha Christie. Vickers, the old armaments company and 'merchants of death', moved into Roneo, hospital equipment and light engineering.

Among the old dogs trying to learn new tricks were the two tobacco giants, British American and Imperial (Bats and Imps), the third and sixth biggest companies by sales in the country. Since 1902 they had carved up the tobacco world between them, until they had to break up their cartel when Britain joined the Common Market; and both companies, worried by the shortage of smokers, felt the need to buy into more promising lines. Bats bought up cosmetics (including Yardleys and Lenthéric), the Wiggins Teape paper group, the seven hundred shops of International Stores, and the Argos shops. They also moved into America, buying up Gimbel's department stores, the Saks Fifth Avenue group and later the Marshall Field shops based in Chicago. Imperial Tobacco embarked on a deliberate buying programme in 1960, beginning with Golden Wonder crisps, HP sauce and Smedley's tinned foods. By 1969 they had bought the second biggest frozen food company, Ross; two years later Plastic Coatings; and the next year the Courage brewing company, with its 6,000 pubs. Imps, like Bats, moved also into America, buying the Howard Johnson chain of motorway cafes at a very high price just before the recession. Imps had no real entrepreneurial drive: it had grown with its own lazy momentum like a snowball rolling downhill. And both Imps and Bats, after all their hectic diversification, were still making most of their profits from tobacco.

But to control these corporate rag-bags needed much more rigorous techniques than those needed for cigarette-making or shop-keeping. The men at the top could only comprehend their scores of different products through numbers, and the experts with their hunches or their 'feel for the product' were pushed aside by the army of accountants who entered their kingdom, with their impedimenta of computers, discounted cash-flows and dreaded bottom lines. They had to plan their investments into the far future, but their achievements were reckoned by their short-term results: and many bigger companies turned out to be more reluctant to take risks than smaller ones—for their control depended on rigid budgets, and their shareholders, including pension fund managers, were insisting on jam today, not tomorrow. Creative and risk-taking industries, such as entertainment, publishing and even some retailing, depended on the judgment of managers who could defend their own flair against pessimistic accountants; but the bigger the company, the harder was their struggle, which was often complicated (like other conflicts in Britain) by suppressed class-warfare from accountants who had climbed doggedly up the corporate back-stairs.

Every merger was first proclaimed as increasing efficiency and profitability; but many of them, like the brewers, gradually turned out to be less efficient and profitable. The new superstructure and head offices added to their overheads while many of their 'economies of scale' were never achieved. When two merged companies were making the same products, they frequently continued to duplicate them, merging their boards and headquarters but not their plants. The managers at the top, who always like to extend their own empire, were keen on the mergers, while the shareholders were apt to find themselves with declining dividends.

Some of the biggest take-overs proved to be disappointments: Bats faced mounting losses in their shops in Britain and America, of which they had little experience, and after a boardroom row they fired the director of the stores. As for Imps, they faced greater problems with their mixture of beer, chickens, frozen foods and HP sauce—made worse by the poor results from their Howard Johnson chain in America. Their gentlemanly chairman, Malcolm Anson, the former deputy-chairman's son who came up through cigarettes, followed a 'hands-off' policy towards the other businesses while their troubles mounted, until he was sacked with a golden handshake of £300,000—to be replaced by a more aggressive chairman who had also come up through cigarettes, who promised to follow a 'hands-on' policy. But the company's far-flung interests provided chronic headaches for the central board.

By the mid-seventies the merged companies, particularly when they were diversified, were often less profitable than those which remained intact. The Labour government's report on mergers policy in 1978 examined reports from several economists and concluded that 'the evidence suggests that in something like half of the merger cases studied, profitability was reduced—or at any rate was not increased.'[4] And as companies faced the testing years of the early eighties they showed more clearly the dangers of diversifying into industries they did not understand. 'The race has tended to go, not to the widely spread and the wealthy,' wrote Robert Heller in 1981, surveying the 'growth league' in *Management Today*, 'but to the swift—to the companies that exploit narrow opportunities to the broadest possible extent.' And looking at the 'profitability league' he gave the same message: 'The lesson that rings out loud and clear is that of the virtues of specialisation.'[5]

Sophisticated chairmen were now taking a more sceptical attitude towards all diversification and mergers. 'I don't believe in the idea

[4] Command 7198, May 1978. See also Gerald D. Newbould and George A. Luffman: *Successful Business Policies*, Gower Press, Farnborough, 1978.

[5] *Management Today*, June and October 1981.

that a manager is a manager is a manager,' Sir Peter Baxendell of Shell told me in 1982. 'I think diversification has to come from below, where the ideas and entrepreneurs are. Managers often don't realise themselves how much they fly by the seat of their pants. I remember when things went wrong with our subsidiary General Atomic: the feeling that you weren't on the seat of your pants was pretty damn awful.'

Why had so many company chairmen been so eager to merge and diversify into businesses about which they knew so little, with such slender evidence of the benefits? With hindsight, most businessmen I asked had little doubt: 'The mergers suited no one, except the people at the top,' as one of them said, 'but the directors always wanted bigger companies, because they meant higher status, bigger head-quarters—and higher salaries.' The expression 'empire-building' was very apposite, for these chairmen seemed to be translating old imperial attitudes into their new industrial structures. They were more interested in the size than the profits.

But the merger-mania had been only one manifestation of the prevailing passion for bigness which had shown itself in the monster ministries of Whitehall, the enlarged local councils and the gran-diose town halls—and perhaps most significantly in the architec-tural fashion for tower blocks, concrete complexes and housing estates which transformed Britain's cities. Whatever the economic shibboleths, these giant structures clearly had an underlying emo-tional appeal, as if they were promising rationality, security and permanence. But they also, it turned out, provided an escape from personal responsibility and identity, and few people had worked out how they should be run, or who should control them. 'Rather like the Peter Principle, in the absence of competition organisations tend to grow beyond the point where they are manageable.'[6] They soon achieved their own inertia, protected by their managers, inhabitants and trade unions; but they survived into the eighties as monuments to the evasions of the earlier generation. Each party attacked the other for its own mistakes of gigantism: the Tories attacked the nationalised industries and big unions while Labour attacked multi-nationals and banks. But both parties had played along with the movement which had left individuals and consumers the poorer.

SMALL BECOMES BEAUTIFUL

By the late seventies small companies—those that had sur-vived—were back in fashion, whether among managers, economists or politicians. As unemployment raced up politicians realised that

[6] Nicholas Falk: *Think Small*, Fabian Tract 453, London, 1978, p. 10.

most giant companies were not going to provide extra jobs: their new automated plants were designed to cut down jobs, not to create them, and they were constantly increasing their ratio of capital to labour. Many of the giants were firing thousands of workers in the lean years of the early eighties; but a few of those workers found they could set up their own business with their redundancy money, which provided the first major source of new capital for ordinary people since the post-war gratuities in the forties—which had themselves been the origin of several post-war entrepreneurs. Small companies were much more likely to create jobs, particularly in the service industries which depended on people, and American statistics were showing that most new jobs came from small companies. But Britain had relatively fewer small firms than most of her industrial competitors.[7]

There were plenty of incompetent small companies and family firms, run by the sons and grandsons of the founder who had lost interest in the trade, or lost sight of the real competition; and the merger-mania of the sixties revealed the somnolence of the smaller companies as much as the ruthlessness of the raiders. But a *new* small company nearly always has a dynamic boss, looking for innovations and opportunities, and in America many major inventions now originate with small companies or individual inventors, while computers and microprocessors are likely to increase the future scope for small manufacturers. Yet small businessmen in Britain have more difficulty than the giants in raising money from banks and the City, and the Wilson Committee in 1980 confirmed that 'compared to large firms, small firms are at a considerable disadvantage in financial markets'. Big companies can often get bigger discounts for materials, and exert more leverage with the shops; and many of them demand cash on-the-nail from their small customers, while delaying payment to their minor suppliers for three months.

Both the big political parties by the late seventies were promising more support for small companies, while a few big businessmen, particularly in the oil companies after 1973, were becoming worried that they would overwhelm their more modest colleagues, destroying some of their own customers. The former head of Shell, Sir Michael Pocock, tried actively to help small companies, and Shell in Britain now tries to give advice and encouragement to new firms, promising to pay its own bills promptly. Other giants such as ICI and Marks and Spencer have also helped to set up small businesses through 'enterprise agencies' in industrial areas.

There was one kind of very small business that was clearly thriv-

[7] See Graham Bannock: *The Smaller Business in Britain and Germany*, Wilton House, Farnborough, 1976.

ing, unrecorded by government statistics or tax-collectors: the individuals or groups working in the 'black economy'—the hidden, informal, underground or irregular economy, as it was called according to moral attitudes to it—who dealt only with cash. In 1968 Sir William Pile, the head of the Inland Revenue, suggested it was 'not implausible' that undeclared income might amount to $7\frac{1}{2}$ per cent of the Gross National Product; and an independent survey two years later concluded that 'it was difficult to believe in a figure less than 5 per cent'.[8] As unemployment increased there was growing evidence that much more money was being earned than the official wages and dole payments recorded. Chain stores such as Sainsbury and Marks and Spencer were surprised to note that their shops in regions of high unemployment were not selling noticeably fewer goods than others; and MPs for those areas were struck by signs of unusual activity and lack of leisure.

Moreover the individuals who paid no taxes clearly worked much harder and more zealously than ordinary company employees: one Treasury man who was studying fiscal policies and incentives was surprised (he told me) to discover that when he found a plumber to fix his own central heating for cash, all the traditional obstacles such as absenteeism, tea-breaks and overmanning suddenly disappeared. A whole underground network of self-employed entrepreneurs was clearly forming itself, with the common bond of not paying taxes and (an almost equal relief) never filling in forms, so that statistically they did not exist. It was as if, in the cracks between Britain's decaying bureaucracies, a new entrepreneurial energy was beginning to start up from scratch; and a similar phenomenon was observed in many other countries, including the Soviet Union. No government could officially come to terms with this flouting of the law, particularly since many of these underground workers collected the dole while earning large tax-free incomes. But as unemployment rose further the black economy was clearly mitigating the hardship, and it was impossible to stamp out.

These free-booting tax-dodgers, however, could never be a substitute for organised small industrial companies, which were so important for Britain's future. And the harsh winds of the early eighties, with climbing interest-rates and diminishing markets, blew much more fiercely through the small structures than through the giants' strongholds. Small companies could not afford to borrow more from the banks at high rates and some of the most enterprising ones, which had rapidly increased their exports, faced the extra hazards of a strong pound which benefited their foreign competitors. Thousands of small companies, despite all the politicians' goodwill,

[8] Michael O'Higgins: *Measuring the Hidden Economy*, Outer Circle Policy Unit, July 1981.

went into bankruptcy. Britain had become more than ever a country of large corporations.

GOVERNMENTS AND MONOPOLIES

The two major parties were ambivalent about the giant companies. The Conservatives proclaimed the magic of the market-place and the virtues of small businessmen, and attacked the corporate state of nationalised monopolies fortified by Labour governments and the unions. But the Tories depended on the giants such as Trust House Forte for their funds—or for directorships when they were out of office—and they were much less vocal about the semi-monopolies of private industry which formed their own kind of corporate state. The free-enterprise lobbies, led by the Institute of Economic Affairs, paid homage to their hero Adam Smith (they celebrated the bicentenary of the *Wealth of Nations* in 1976); but they rarely quoted Smith's warning that 'people of the same trade seldom meet together, even for merriment and diversion, but the conversation ends in a conspiracy against the public, or in some contrivance to raise prices.' (They were words, said Ronald Grierson, a champion of free enterprise, which might have been describing Neddy, the arch-embodiment of the corporate state.)[9]

The Labour party was also muddled and divided. 'The workers think monopolies are bad,' as one cabinet minister put it to me in 1978, 'but they think competition is worse: they associate it with cut-throat conditions and low wages.' Monopolies never had the same evil connotations as in America, where workers associated them with the exploitation and strike-breaking of Rockefeller or Carnegie—which led to more effective anti-trust laws. British trade unionists were more inclined to see giant companies as the safeguarders of their jobs, and easier to handle than small bosses whose workers were hard to organise, if they were unionised at all. Giant unions felt more at home with giant companies, each with their opposite numbers and rituals of negotiation. In these cosy arrangements, only the consumers and the shareholders were the losers.

Successive governments had set up a cumbersome machinery to supervise monopolies over four decades. The Labour government in 1948 first set up the Monopolies Commission, which has since been extended. It is headed by a lawyer—at present a cautious Channel Islander, Sir Godfray Le Quesne—assisted by economists, accountants and others, but its powers are feeble: it can only investigate when the government asks it to, its reports are not binding, and

[9] R. H. Grierson: 'The Mirage of the State's Entrepreneurial Role', lecture at the Royal Society of Arts, March 13, 1978.

behind its legalistic and impartial style it may be influenced by the political atmosphere. After the spate of mergers in the sixties there was more pressure to protect the consumer, and in 1973 the Conservatives set up an Office of Fair Trading to represent the consumer, to look into restrictive practices and to report potential monopolies to the Commission. The next year the Labour government went much further, establishing a special Department of Prices and Consumer Protection under a cabinet minister (first Shirley Williams, then Roy Hattersley). The department would ensure fair trading with the help of a Price Commission which could forbid an increase in prices, and with a National Consumer Council to protect shoppers.

The Price Commission was seen as a surrogate for the real market-place: 'We try to make prices what they would be,' as one Labour minister told me, 'if there *were* competition.' Their reports helped to expose restrictive agreements and incompetent mergers, but the Department repeatedly ran into political cross-winds, for the Labour cabinet was also pursuing its industrial strategy which usually favoured big companies and mergers. However damning the evidence of inefficiency, other Whitehall departments could easily be persuaded by big companies that their mergers were in the national interest in the battle against foreign competition, and trade unions still favoured mergers as a way to protect jobs. Even Tate and Lyle or Allied Breweries, which were sworn enemies of Labour, made their case for mergers. 'The nastier the company.' (one cabinet minister complained) 'the further we have to lean over backwards to be fair.' A classic confrontation loomed up in 1978, when the Imperial group wanted to add Eastwood chickens to their food empire, which would give them 32 per cent of the market in 'oven-ready poultry'. The Office of Fair Trading complained and Roy Hattersley wanted the Monopolies Commission to investigate; but the farm workers felt safer with the merger, and their union pressurised the compliant Minister of Agriculture, John Silkin. The workers won, and Imps got their chickens.

At the apex of the industrial pyramid, where trade unionists, industrialists and ministers meet together at Neddy, all sides have been inclined to favour mergers. In May 1968 the Prices Department put out a 'Green Paper' which after analysing the unprofitable past mergers put forward modest suggestions to restrict them in future: the government should examine the dangers of companies abusing their market power, and should look more sceptically at oligopolies as well as monopolies. But at Neddy's next meeting nearly all the members, including the trade unionists, were opposed to further restrictions: only the Secretary for Trade (Edmund Dell) and the head of the Consumer Council (Michael Shanks) sided with the

Secretary for Prices (Roy Hattersley). At the peak of the corporate state, giant companies made planning and negotiation simpler for everyone, with no tiresome complications about efficiency or consumer choice to get in the way.

When the Tories came back in 1979 they quickly changed the policy once again: they abolished the Department of Prices and concerned themselves (with the help of a new Competition Act) with monopoly power in the unions and nationalised industries, rather than in the private corporations. The policy towards monopolies came under heavier fire when a new wave of mergers went through at a time when the public was much less sure of the benefits of bigness: the Thorn electronic company bought EMI, Racal bought Decca, GEC bought Avery's weighing machines. The controversial Lonrho company was allowed to buy the Scottish and Universal Investment Trust 'Suits' and the *Observer*, though not Harrods (see next chapter). The government did not even ask the Commission to investigate before Rupert Murdoch bought *The Times* and (more serious) the *Sunday Times* (see chapter 27). The Commission, as we have seen, refused to allow the merger of the Royal Bank of Scotland (see chapter 18); but that was interpreted as protecting British banks against foreign competition. 'I don't think there's any doubt,' said the Commission's chairman Sir Godfray, 'that if a person has a monopoly he is in a position to do good to himself at the expense of the public.' But John Biffen as Secretary of Trade was a convinced non-interventionist: 'There's got to be a very good reason,' he told me, 'to stop anyone taking over anyone else.' As the mergers went on the City and the Press became more worried about the Commission: 'Is the machine out of control?' asked *The Times*. 'Britain's trustbusting lacks rhyme and reason,' complained the *Economist*.[10]

It is the control of monopolies and mergers which shows the most obvious need to escape from the political influence of the corporate powers, whether of industrial companies or of trade unions, who support the two old political parties. The need for entrepreneurial drive, as the next chapter will suggest, is greater than ever in a country which has been so long inclined to industrial lethargy; but that drive must always be counterbalanced by rigorous and independent constraints. For businessmen however enlightened are an order of men, as Adam Smith warned, 'whose interest is never exactly the same with that of the public, who generally have an interest to deceive and even to oppress the public, and who accordingly have upon many occasions, both deceived and oppressed it'.[11]

[10] *The Times*, June 9, 1981; the *Economist*, December 19, 1981.
[11] *Wealth of Nations*, Book 1, Chapter II.

22

Entrepreneurs: the Outsiders Come Inside

Avarice, the spur of industry.
David Hume, 1741

WHILE companies were becoming bigger, more diversified and more multinational they were not necessarily, as most people had expected, becoming more impersonal at the top. Twenty years ago the 'managerial revolution', which was first proclaimed by James Burnham in 1941, was still believed to be overtaking big corporations so that they would be controlled by committees of managers, anonymous accountants and computers working according to the economic laws of the market. But business leaders or entrepreneurs were soon making a spectacular come-back—not so much in starting new companies, as in buying up and transforming old ones.

Even some of the biggest corporations were dominated by a single powerful personality who (like the prime minister in the cabinet) can make nonsense of theories about committees of equals. Only slightly smaller companies, with populations of tens of thousands, found themselves suddenly changing hands to be controlled by a single ruthless financier (the word ruthless, which businessmen two decades ago regarded as libellous, is now used as a compliment). The entrepreneurs provided large new bogies for the left. 'Workers have no legal rights to be consulted when the firms for which they work are taken over,' said Tony Benn. 'They are sold off like cattle when a firm changes hands with no guarantee for the future.'[1]

SHARKS V. MULLETS

The success of the entrepreneurs cannot be explained only in economic or sociological terms, like so much else in Britain. They belong more to the world of anthropology, or even zoology, as if they

[1] Benn: *op cit*, p. 49.

belonged to a different species from a strange habitat. While ordinary workers and managers move in their well-worn sheep-tracks,
the entrepreneurs swing above them like chimpanzees, jumping
from tree to tree and only occasionally dropping to ground level; and
like chimpanzees they cavort mainly with each other, whether fighting, playing or mating, but always restlessly moving between trees.
Or as Sir James Goldsmith, the Anglo-French financier, explained
to me, they are like sharks, who can chase away the bigger fish and
thus benefit the small ones:

> When a friend of mine visited the Galapagos Islands he saw hun-
> dreds of thousands of anchovies being attacked by diving birds. The
> sea was a gory mess. The anchovies could not escape because they
> were also being attacked from below by large mullets which were rising
> from deeper seas and forcing the anchovies to the surface. Suddenly
> the mullets dispersed, the anchovies swam to deeper waters and the
> birds flew away. The reason soon became obvious. Sharks had been
> attracted to the scene and attacked the mullets who fled to safety. The
> sharks saved the anchovies.

All the real entrepreneurs, as opposed to pure money-jugglers or
stock-market speculators who remain in back rooms, have outsize
personalities; and they can motivate, cajole or intimidate others
through their physical presence, projecting face-to-face power. Most
of them are big muscular men, whom no one can miss when they
enter a room; and even the small ones such as Murdoch or Forte can
quickly generate electricity around them. When they negotiate
together they circle round each other like cats, preparing for their
battle of wills. 'Have you ever talked to Jimmy Goldsmith?' the City
financier Jim Slater asked me in his heyday, when he was fascinated
by will-power and 'positive mental attitudes'. 'You feel his personality so strongly that the air seems to be impregnated with it.
And when Jacob Rothschild rings up the whole line seems to be
crackling.'

The most ambitious entrepreneurs are irrepressible and infinitely
resilient, thriving on adversity which sets their adrenalin running:
'They have to feel they've got their backs to the wall to perform
properly,' as one of them explained. 'If they make a lot of money they
have to get rid of it, like gamblers, so that they're at risk again. I'm
told that Jimmy Goldsmith wakes up in the middle of the night
thinking he's bankrupt.'

The most recurring loser has been Robert Maxwell, the Czech-
born financier who has continued to move through British institutions over the last twenty years like a whirlwind, turning them
upside down without staying long inside them. 'You really *need* to go

to the meteorological office to find a description for him,' one of his colleagues advised me. After serving in the British army, and in the occupation forces in Germany, he made his first fortune by publishing German and other scientific papers after the war which became the nucleus of his company, Pergamon Press. He looked for some years like the tycoon of the future, a Labour MP as well as a publisher and international financier, with close links with Russia and Germany; and his massive frame and dominating manner had all the marks of the unstoppable entrepreneur. But in 1969 Maxwell faced a major disaster, when he tried to sell Pergamon to an equally ruthless American financier, Saul Steinberg, who after buying a block of shares challenged Maxwell's figures and pulled out of the deal. Maxwell was voted off the board and a subsequent enquiry by the Department of Trade stated that he could not be relied on 'to exercise proper stewardship of a publicly-quoted company'. Despite that, he soon recaptured Pergamon, making it a private company and pushing up its profits for a few years before it was hit by the recession. In the meantime he had tried and failed to buy a whole succession of companies, including the *News of the World*, the *Sun* and *The Times*—in each of which he was foiled by Rupert Murdoch (see chapter 27). By the late seventies Maxwell looked like a man of the past.

But then he saw a new chance to take over a crumbling company, the British Printing Corporation which he had first tried to buy twenty years earlier. BPC was an unhappy mixture of printing works and publishers including famous old printers such as Waterlows, Sun and Hazell Watson and Viney, which had suffered successive traumas over twenty years: it was a model of how not to merge. The company had been created by a brilliant but autocratic accountant, Wilfred Harvey, who made high profits during the publishing boom but squandered his own money on gambling; and in 1965 Harvey was ousted by the august Sir Geoffrey Crowther (of Trust Houses and the *Economist*), who put in an orthodox management team, followed by a succession of dignified directors who tried inadequately to clean up the mess. But BPC went from bad to worse, with its vast plants lying idle after the slump in magazine sales and with unions extracting exorbitant wages. By 1980 it was heading for bankruptcy, and at this point Maxwell swooped down, buying 30 per cent of its shares for less than £3 million, which he later increased to 77 per cent. The board of BPC, as Maxwell described them, 'looked as though they'd swallowed a dead rat'.[2] But it was just better than bankruptcy, and Maxwell moved in with all the force of his personality to try to rescue the doddering old giant. Whatever the outcome, it was an extraordinary sign of Maxwell's resilience, and

[2] *Management Today*, February 1982.

other entrepreneurs were not slow to draw their own morals. As Goldsmith put it:

> Who was the good man in the BPC? Was it Wilfred Harvey who built it? Was it Geoffrey Crowther who brought in the new management which destroyed it with all the best intentions? Or was it Robert Maxwell who goes back in there and saves it? You have to decide not who means well but what is the result rather than the purpose. It would look as though the sharks have helped the anchovy more than the mullet.[3]

Like princes the entrepreneurs cajole with charm and show disapproval with an eyebrow: they can arouse a sense of both dependence and adventure among their employees, as if they had always needed a dominant father-figure which no management committee could provide. But the entrepreneurs can never be real father-figures, for they are driven by their restless and rootless ambition. 'Some people are born with a bug inside them,' Harley Drayton the master-financier told me in 1960. 'If they are, they can do anything. If they're not they might as well settle down to be a clerk.' Or as Goldsmith said in 1981: 'Dynamism is usually the result of disequilibrium. My disequilibrium comes from the very simple reason that I'm a foreigner over here. I'm a Jew to Catholics, a Catholic to Jews, an Englishmen to the French and a Frenchman to the English. I've always been neither one nor the other—which is a very unsettling thing to be.'

THE BRITISH DISTASTE

Every entrepreneur is a kind of outsider, with a detachment which enables him to see and exploit opportunities. Many expatriates—like the Chinese in Malaya, the Syrians in West Africa or the Indians in Britain—play a dynamic part in their adopted country, while their countrymen at home seem lethargic. But the English have been especially resistant to new forms of trade and money-making, and it is symptomatic that the English have no word equivalent to the French *entrepreneur*. Britain has thus offered glittering prospects to aggressive outsiders: 'There must be something wrong with this country,' Lord Thomson of Fleet liked to say when he was making his huge fortune from television, newspapers and oil after retiring to Scotland, 'if it's so easy to make money out of it.' 'What's especially interesting is why the Canadians and Australians are so successful in Britain,' says Goldsmith, 'because they're really ethnically the same, with the same origins and ethics as the English. A Canadian or

[3] Interview with author, June 23, 1981.

Australian who comes to England is outside the class system, doesn't have to be classified, and therefore can get on with everybody; whereas in England even today the class system still has an influence, and is a container of energy. Everybody is desperate to be respectable in their own little group.'

What were the real roots of Britain's aversion to entrepreneurship and money-making, which was so notable in the post-war decades? Certainly the public-school system which emphasised the team spirit and old military virtues played a part (see chapter 7); though a few public schoolboys—such as Terence Conran and Alexander Plunket Greene (Bryanston), Algy Cluff and Nigel Broackes (Stowe), Clive Sinclair (Highgate) or Goldsmith (Eton)—broke through the taboos to make their own fortunes. ('All the people for whom success seemed unavoidable at school have disappeared,' as Broackes put it to me. 'I'm unusual as a middle-class entrepreneur, but I think I was influenced by my mother's poverty after my father died.') The universities, as Algy Cluff suggests, provided a greater disincentive to business enthusiasm, encouraging graduates to see every side of each question and to prefer theoretical to practical arguments.

But the British distaste for trade had deeper roots than these institutional structures: already by the mid-nineteenth century the first enthusiasm for industrial progress was leading to a relapse into disillusion, rural nostalgia and the search for an unspoilt old England. The early Dickens, excited by modern manufacture, gave way to the sceptical Dickens of *Hard Times* and *Our Mutual Friend*. The rugged enterprise of early northern engineers and mechanics gave way to the respectability and gentrification of the professions and institutes. The sons of industrialists were cleansed of trade and commercial ambition by the burgeoning public schools, and re-treated into country estates.[4]

Some historians have blamed the Victorian novelists for encouraging anti-business attitudes, and one contemporary London financier, Nicholas Stacey, has even suggested that the early women novelists were particularly responsible, spreading their contempt for vulgar Victorian tradesmen.[5] Certainly British writers showed a striking lack of interest in the office life and business activities that were growing up around them, or treated them with a moral disdain, as in Trollope's *The Way We Live Now*. But this was equally evident in the revulsion of American novelists, such as Edith Wharton and Henry James, who both deplored the brash new commercialism which was invading old New York.

[4] See Wiener: *op cit.*

[5] 'The Sociology of the Entrepreneur': lecture at McMaster University, Canada, October 18, 1980.

What was more significant in Britain was the continuity of an aristocratic or would-be aristocratic tradition which while being enriched by trade still kept it at arm's length, and returned to country roots in search of more lasting values: 'The world's first great industrial nation,' as Professor Wiener from Texas puts it, 'has never been comfortable with industrialism.'[6] In terms of political stability and continuity, there may have been merits in this counter-balancing force at a time of social upheaval; but at a time of nostalgia and industrial stagnation the contempt for business could easily encourage the stagnation.

Whatever the underlying social causes, for two decades after the Second World War British companies were sitting ducks for the predators—sitting on valuable assets, with weak managers and passive shareholders. The old family brewers, shop-owners or ship-owners strikingly demonstrated the British lack of interest in business. A handful of Jewish entrepreneurs—including Charles Clore, Isaac Wolfson, Max Joseph, Jack Cotton and Max Rayne—bought up their companies and properties cheaply and developed them to rapidly push up their profits and share-prices. Within ten years the pattern of ownership had already drastically changed.

By the late sixties the scope for making quick gains from take-overs was diminishing, as managers became more efficient and companies could no longer sit on wasting assets. An unexpected opportunity for entrepreneurs of a different kind came when oil was discovered in the North Sea, which was to make Britain into an oil-producer on the scale of Kuwait. It gave potential profits not only to the oil companies but to any company which could supply oil rigs, pipelines, labour and servicing in the 'off-shore supply industry'. But British companies and entrepreneurs were pathetically slow in responding to the demand for equipment and engineering, and to make money from the new industry along their own coastline. A few companies in Aberdeen, Peterhead or Great Yarmouth made good profits from provisions and servicing oil rigs; but the oil companies had to buy most of their equipment from foreign suppliers, and British Petroleum was embarrassed that it could not buy British. It was not until the late seventies that British companies, after much prodding by government, were providing two-thirds of the North Sea market, but by then the business was past its peak.[7]

The long boom of the sixties produced many new City millionaires who bought and sold companies, stripping or exploiting their assets; but their business, as Jim Slater assured me, was 'making money,

[6] Wiener: *op cit.*

[7] See Michael Jenkin: *British Industry and the North Sea: State Intervention in a Developing Industrial Sector*, Macmillan, London, 1981.

not things' and they did little or nothing to make British industry more competitive. Genuinely productive entrepreneurs involved in innovation and future technology were much rarer, and their progress much more tricky as they tried to make connections between speculative inventions and highly competitive world markets.

One of the few has been Clive Sinclair, the forty-one-year-old computer manufacturer who has combined spectacular innovations with a willingness to take new risks. He began at a public school, Highgate, but, like a good entrepreneur, left early and set up his own firm at twenty-two. He invented the first pocket calculator, Britain's first digital watch and a tiny cheap TV set, until he was over-extended, had to be bailed out by the National Enterprise Board and left his own company. But he bounced back at thirty-nine with a new company, Sinclair Research, and launched a successful new personal computer, followed by a cheaper version which now sells about 60,000 a month. He operates from modest offices in Cambridge with a staff of thirty, carefully delegating the production to others; with a projected research lab for computers in Winchester, close to the researchers at Southampton University, and with his boldest new project—for an electric city car—being developed jointly with Exeter University. But Sinclair's success story is a rarity compared to the proliferation of electronics companies in California or Massachusetts, and his innovations are in sharp contrast to most British entrepreneurs who buy and sell existing corporations.

Under Ted Heath, as well as under Wilson and Callaghan, the entrepreneurs were still very suspect: but by the late seventies the word was losing some of its opprobrium, as the British became more disillusioned with bureaucracy, and more concerned with competition. It was also much harder to make money out of industry: 'The net return on new industrial equipment,' said Broackes in 1982, 'is down to 3 per cent: twenty years ago it was 15 per cent, all over the West.' Managers, permanent secretaries and even ambassadors, as well as businessmen, began to fancy they had an entrepreneurial drive. But the idea of the nation being run by entrepreneurs, or even of a businessmen's cabinet, was inherently absurd. For no real entrepreneur could be concerned with people's long-term security; and no civil servant or politician should be allowed to practise the kind of risk-taking that could lead to bankruptcy. The aggressive and nomadic instincts of the entrepreneur would and should always be at odds with the protective territorial role of the state. Global tycoons looked forward to abolishing national frontiers, a concept that was not tolerable to any likely government, or electorate.

The more ambitious entrepreneurs were no longer operating in a purely national framework, and the global expansion of the sixties and seventies gave new opportunities to clever operators who could buy and sell between countries, marrying products to markets across the exchanges. They belonged to no single country or set of laws, and they could move far more quickly than their predecessors, with planes, phones and telex, leaving national governments plodding behind them. They thrived on the mystery and unpredictability of their journeys, which gave a sharper edge to their bargaining. The more bureaucratic corporations and governments became, the more the entrepreneurs could manoeuvre and zigzag between them.

THE 'REVOLUTIONARY CAPITALIST'

Among the global entrepreneurs Tiny Rowland became a kind of caricature of the species. His tall shape and long face, suave and soft-spoken, popped up without warning all over the world: in Zambia, in Kuwait, in Mexico or London. He belonged to no nation—born in India, half German half English, beginning his career in Southern Rhodesia. Traditional British bankers and businessmen dreaded and distrusted him, but he flourished on their rejection and he showed an irresistible charisma to his own followers, as he led them on to new adventures, keeping one step ahead of his rivals. Rowland liked to call himself a 'revolutionary capitalist', but he never discussed his management methods: like his American colleague Daniel Ludwig he never wanted to be tied down or recorded, and shrouded most of his operations in secrecy. 'His success rests on three things,' an aide explained. 'His unconventional background, his capacity for hard work, and his single-mindedness. He was brought up against a background of restless danger, so his mind never worked in conventional ways. He looks for opportunities and deals where other people least expect them, and he makes use of his relationships with his famous persistence.'

Rowland operated like an old-style imperial adventurer in Africa, but adjusting his methods to the post-imperial age; with his towering personality and mastery of figures he could do business with black countries which more orthodox companies had written off. 'It can be easier to make money out of chaos than out of order,' explained one of his rivals, 'provided you know what you want.' He began in white Southern Rhodesia, where he saw prospects in a sleepy company called London and Rhodesian Mining and Land, represented by an ambitious but trusting aristocrat, Angus Ogilvy—who later married the Queen's cousin. Ogilvy rashly brought Rowland in to revive Lonrho (as it was shortly called) and Rowland soon left the other directors panting behind him.

He rushed round the newly-independent black states, establishing close personal relationships with their leaders with his customary hospitality, acquiring concessions, trading rights, newspapers and even a railway in Malawi. ('Everyone said that I was mad because railways never make money,' he said afterwards, 'but it enabled me to obtain other interests.'[8]) He helped many black leaders through their political struggles, including Kenneth Kaunda, Joshua Nkomo, Jonas Savimbi and Julius Nyerere, and though Nkomo lost out and Nyerere took against him, others remembered his favours.

But his black interests did not interfere with very profitable business in South Africa, including platinum mines and printing works, and he began building another base in Britain, including a steel works (Hadfields), distillers (Whyte and Mackay), the Volkswagen agency and later a group of casinos. He handled Britain rather like Africa, finding local chieftains and making them dependent on him: he recruited a succession of old war-horses on to his board, to help pull his chariot—including Churchill's son-in-law Duncan Sandys, Sir George Bolton the adventurous banker, Lord Shawcross the veteran lawyer, and Edward du Cann, the financier MP and ex-chairman of the Tory party. But they all knew there was only one boss; they were all in awe of him, and he used them for his characteristic operations—sudden ambushes, secret penetrations, and deadly raids.

Rowland was a throwback to an earlier, more Victorian version of capitalism, and he never respected the formalities and niceties of the City of London; by 1971 his banker Sir Siegmund Warburg—who had backed many other outsiders—decided that he could no longer represent Lonrho. By 1973 Rowland's autocratic style had so appalled his staider directors that they staged a boardroom revolt led by Sir Basil Smallpeice, a mild-mannered former chairman of BOAC. 'The irresponsibility of Mr Rowland,' Smallpeice complained in a deposition, 'outweighed any benefit to be derived from his abilities and contacts.' The ensuing scandal revealed that Rowland, among many personal favours, had paid Duncan Sandys (now his chairman) $100,000 a year tax-free in the Cayman Islands.

Rowland put his faith in his shareholders at an extraordinary general meeting in May 1973, and with a huge majority they rallied to Rowland and voted to throw out Smallpeice and the rebels. Rowland's reckless methods, defying national taxation, were too much for the prime minister Ted Heath, who called them the 'unpleasant and unacceptable face of capitalism'; the phrase haunted Heath, as other tycoons threw it back at him. But the face

[8] Cronje and Ling: *Lonrho, Portrait of a Multinational*, Penguin, London, 1976, p. 30.

was acceptable to the shareholders, and Rowland trebled Lonrho's turnover and profits in the next three years.

Rowland soon faced a new enemy: the Department of Trade was investigating Lonrho, and its team of investigators spent eighteen months preparing evidence. The prospects looked bad to British investors and by August 1974, as the London stock-market slumped, the Lonrho shares bottomed at 47 pence. But Rowland was never dependent on London alone: already in February 1974—when the energy crisis had just quadrupled the wealth of the Arab oil-producers—he was publicly predicting that joint projects with Arabs and Africans would 'become the most important aspect of our business'.[9] A year later Kuwaiti investors had brought 22 per cent of Lonrho, as a means to invest more in the Third World, particularly Africa, and Lonrho's share price had bounced back with the general recovery to 150 pence. Rowland had cleverly become part of a critical new triangular relationship—between Arab capital, Western technology and Third World markets and products. The Department of Trade, which reported later in the year, criticised his business methods in devastating detail, but his friends could reply that only unorthodox methods could succeed in business with developing countries that were erratic, corrupt, and desperately in need of entrepreneurial skill.

Rowland still nursed ambitions within Britain, and he soon had his eye on the House of Fraser, the biggest chain of department stores whose crowning glory was Harrods. The stores had been inherited by Sir Hugh Fraser, a weak and confused man who was addicted to gambling; he needed stronger management for his holding company, Scottish and Universal Investment Trust and unwisely invited Rowland to join him. Sir Hugh (like Ogilvy before him) seemed to regard Rowland as a father-figure, but he was like a lamb sharing a cage with a lion. Rowland soon bought up enough shares in Suits to control it (including the Outram newspaper group headed by the *Glasgow Herald*) and put his sights on the Harrods group of which through Suits he already owned 10 per cent.

Rowland's siege of Harrods became another episode, like Forte's siege of the Savoy, in the recurring British saga of august British institutions threatened by dreaded intruders; but this was a more ferocious engagement. Sir Hugh was supported by Warburgs Bank, now Rowland's vowed enemies, who appointed their own man to his board: Professor Roland Smith, a tall, quiet professor of marketing who combined company directorships with lecturing at Manchester (it gave him, he assured me, a useful detachment). Fraser and Smith

[9] Cronje: *op cit*, p. 9.

tried to convince their uneasy shareholders that their team was thoroughly reliable, but Rowland knew they had a very weak link—Sir Hugh's continuing passion for gambling. Rowland soon revealed damaging evidence including bounced cheques to the rest of the board, and prepared to sell all his Harrods' shares, which now amounted to 30 per cent.

But then in a complete turnabout he secretly met with Sir Hugh in Scotland, dominating him once again and, to the horror of Warburgs and the other directors, Sir Hugh and Rowland emerged as old friends. The board hastily sacked Sir Hugh from the chairmanship and replaced him with Professor Smith. Rowland and Sir Hugh now plotted together to capture control of Harrods, making a new cash offer to shareholders.

At this confused stage the bid was referred to that old umpire the Monopolies Commission, which took nine months to deliver judgment. They had already allowed Rowland to acquire Suits and the *Observer* (see chapter 27), but Harrods was too much for them. They decided that Lonrho was 'seeking to acquire a very large company which may, if the merger takes place, lose a number of its most experienced executives'; and that a merger would be 'adverse to the public interest'. Professor Smith was elated, but still apprehensive: 'A very competent adversary,' he said about Rowland, 'but we win all the battles.' 'These are skirmishes,' retorted Rowland, in his most menacing mood. 'It is he who wins the war that matters. The professor knows we are there, and he will see us in his dreams. He will need two Mogadons instead of one each night.'

The Commission's verdict reflected all the British ambivalence towards unrestrained free enterprise. Rowland's restless drive had undoubtedly benefited his shareholders and brought new energy to his companies: he may already have helped to make Harrods more efficient (as he proudly pointed out) by forcing them to appoint a serious chairman. Yet Rowland was unmistakably a lone buccaneer who thrived on insecurity, disrupting any organisation and set of rules; or as the Commission put it, 'Lonrho's management lacks depth'. Now his jungle methods were invading not just newspapers and casinos, but a conservative landmark such as Harrods. It was one thing to unleash competitive capitalists, but quite another to be at their mercy.

The emergence of these global entrepreneurs was only one symptom of more fundamental changes in the British economy. Companies had to face far more intensive competition in world markets in the seventies, with structures which were too rigid, too bureaucratic and too overmanned. In this harsher climate stately old corporations, and even nationalised industries, were beginning to realise that they could no longer be run as if they were part of the public service, with committees of managers and boards of directors retired from Whitehall. The whole concept of the semi-permanent corporation was coming into question, and individualist business leaders were reasserting themselves everywhere.

23

Corporations: the Chairman and the Conscience

Did you ever expect a corporation to have a conscience, when it has no soul to be damned, and no body to be kicked?

Lord Thurlow (1781–1829)

THE social characters of British corporations had been undergoing significant changes. In the balmy days of the sixties, with mounting mergers and easy profits, they were becoming increasingly comfortable and paternal while their managers fortified themselves against the outside world. The combination of incomes policies and high taxation encouraged companies to offer more perks or fringe benefits instead of high salaries. 'Remuneration consultants' set themselves up to negotiate whole packages of tax-free benefits for new recruits, bargaining with cars, medical services, university scholarships for children, cheap holidays, country-house weekends, low mortgages, cheap loans and even tailors' bills. The senior executives of British Aluminium had their own yacht (ostensibly for 'testing paints'); ICI provided grants for university fees; BP gave generous loans; British Oxygen offered free furniture. Ford offered not only cars, but second cars, to their senior men.

It was the car which loomed largest as the chief British symbol of executive status, with Ferraris, Alfa Romeos or Mercedes superseding Marinas or Cortinas, while the Inland Revenue winked at the fiction that cars and chauffeurs were purely for business. By 1981 about two-thirds of the cars on the roads were owned by companies, who also paid for the petroi:[1] it was hardly surprising that however much the price of petrol went up, the queues of cars into the cities each morning refused to go down.

The managers inside their company wombs were pampered whether they liked it or not. The home loomed smaller as the office loomed larger, and the company took over more of the role of the

---

[1] *Financial Times*, February 20, 1982.

father, both of the manager and of his family. The British in the past mocked such paternalism as belonging to autocratic companies in less fortunate countries, such as Krupp, Sony or Fiat. But the British corporations, encouraged by the tax system, were now also becoming the universal guardians and providers of whatever the state did not already provide.

Corporate lunch-rooms became more elaborate as executives were paid with food and drink instead of extra money. The Labour government had clamped down on expense-account meals in restaurants in the mid-sixties, but that only set off a new round of culinary competition in company dining-rooms which were much more discreet and could charge only nominal sums. When the Labour government restricted all wage increases the companies stepped up 'fringe benefits' until the fringe was really the centre, and the lunches became more lavish, sometimes with butlers, wine-cellars and chefs outdoing public restaurants: any realistic *Michelin Guide* would now award most rosettes to the lunch-tables of corporations and merchant banks, like *Chez Courtauld*, *Au Shell*, or the *Brasserie BP*. American observers were amazed by this lunchtime contest: 'The British eat like crazy,' the former American ambassador Kingman Brewster told a reporter in 1977. 'You find they're really in competition with each other, trying to see who can serve the finest food.' No private individual could compete with these tax-free feasts: he would always be more lunched against than lunching. The apparatus of hospitality encouraged managers to spend most of their lives with other company men, while the headquarters became still more self-enclosed. Foreign travel, far from broadening their contacts, could narrow them further, as the company hospitality waited to meet them at the other end.

Was this corporate paternalism harking back to some earlier, pre-industrial pattern? Perhaps as tribal Africans maintain their chiefly hierarchies in modern cities, the old British patterns were re-emerging disguised as Shell or ICI. Some company lunch-rooms seem like Oxbridge high tables, while bars and clubs echo an army mess. Corporate hierarchies are often reminiscent of the elaborate gradations of the Victorian country house: the grand staircase becomes the express lift to the directors' suites; the servants' hall becomes the typing pool; the kitchen becomes the canteen. The nannies, the tweenies, the housekeepers, the governesses, the aunts and extended families, are all reincarnated in different kinds of secretary. At Christmas-time the office block takes on the domestic atmosphere of the great hall or the nursery wing, strewn with decorations and Christmas cards addressed to 'Dear Fifth Floor' or 'Dear Office'. At the office party the bosses flirt with the secretaries for a one-night fling, and return to decorum when the green baize door swings back in the New Year. Old social patterns constantly seem to reassert themselves in companies' obsessions with status—the directors' lavatories, the gradations of carpet, the prestige of the secretaries and secretaries' secretaries, the chauffeur, the boxes at the opera. The great country house, producing everything for its own needs, still seems to represent some ideal of self-contained security. The corporations could certainly give their employees a sense of community and security for which they were grateful, particularly when they were ill, or going through a domestic crisis. But a company could never be a real substitute for the family or local community; for to be profitable it had to be constantly changing, aggressive and flexible.

When the Conservatives came back in 1979, cutting the highest tax-rate from 83 to 60 per cent, many people expected companies to cut back on their perks—all the more as they were facing fiercer competition in a world recession, while the Tory philosophy stressed individualism and self-help. The Confederation of British Industries conceded that perks should be reduced, and Sir Geoffrey Howe condemned them as 'wasteful and inefficient'. But many businessmen now regarded perks as their right, often more precious than the equivalent salary increase, and the car manufacturers complained that any cuts would create more unemployment. There were some reductions in the hardest-hit corporations and Shell (I was told) stopped paying for their executives' suits. But when in August 1981 the Charterhouse Group published their annual survey, it showed little sign of diminishing perks: the average director of a larger company had a company car costing about £15,000 with free petrol, medical insurance, free meals and newspapers, help with telephones and free financial advice; 16 per cent had a second company car, and some companies even gave jobs and cars to the. directors' wives.[2]

Yet the harsh new climate of global competition was now testing more seriously many of the corporations' assumptions, not only about their paternalism, but about their permanence. Their benevolent image looked ironic when they were firing workers and senior executives—often with golden or silver handshakes, but with small prospects of alternative jobs. The old picture of the solid and centralised corporation like a Whitehall department was now very misleading: many big groups had cut back their headquarters staff and de-centralised their scattered divisions so thoroughly that they began to look more like quite different companies. The corporations turned out to be not at all like country houses, colleges or regiments;

[2] *The Times*, August 17, 1981.

and it was the state which was left to look after their cast-offs and rejects.

MANAGERS AND WORKERS

What had happened to the old 'industrial triangle', between industrialists, the government and trade unions? The three sides were looking much more disjointed in the eighties, when they tried to connect at the meetings of Neddy and elsewhere. The businessmen's chief representative body, the Confederation of British Industries, had been formed from a merger of three employers' bodies in 1965—at the height of merger-mania—and had come to see itself as part of the fabric of the corporate state. Some right-wing Conservatives complained from the start about the dangers of becoming thus institutionalised: 'Remember Caligula,' warned Enoch Powell, 'who wished the Roman people had only one neck, so that he could cut it off?'

But the CBI came to echo much of the style of the TUC, as if it were itself a trade union. It issues statements and economic policies from its new headquarters at Centre Point within a stone's throw of the TUC in Bloomsbury; and it assembles at the seaside each year, two months after the TUC conference, to deliver speeches about the role of business. But its purpose became even less clear than that of the TUC, and it fell into the habit of self-pitying complaints about the unions' behaviour ('You must stop wishing the trade unions would go away,' said Clifford Rose of British Rail in 1978). And the directors were much less confident than the general secretaries about whom they represented.

After the return of the Conservatives in 1979 the CBI faced greater political confusion, when many industrialists were suffering from high interest rates and a high pound which the Thatcher government did nothing to mitigate; and at their 1980 conference their new director-general, Sir Terence Beckett from Ford, created a furore by challenging the Conservative government to 'a bare-knuckle fight'—which was only partly offset by a conciliatory visit to Number Ten two days later. Some pro-Thatcher chairmen promptly withdrew their membership and looked towards more loyal business outfits—such as Aims, the Free Enterprise Organisation run by the resourceful propagandist Michael Ivens; or the Institute of Directors, the palatial businessmen's club opposite the Athenaeum presided over by Walter Goldsmith, a passionate admirer of Mrs Thatcher. Many Tory businessmen complained that the CBI was now talking the same kind of language as the TUC, and was no more than a relic of the bad old days of corporatism.

The old ding-dong between the CBI and the TUC in the mean-time did not hold out hopeful prospects for a new pattern of industrial management; for they both appeared to relish the familiar battles between labour and capital, left and right. Some politicians on both sides—particularly those with experience abroad—were insist-ing that Britain could only resolve her industrial troubles by introduc-ing a more democratic system, involving workers in management decisions and sharing the responsibility for a company.

Industrial democracy came more into vogue in the early seventies. Only a few trade unionists supported it seriously, but they included Jack Jones, then general secretary of the Transport and General Workers' Union, and the assistant general secretary of the TUC, David Lea, who both battled from the late sixties to have it included in the Labour party manifesto. When the Labour party was wooing the trade unions under the social contract they made a vague com-mitment, and set up a committee in 1975 under Lord Bullock, to try to take it further. But the TUC insisted on maintaining its influence, and their three members on the committee (Jack Jones, David Lea and Clive Jenkins, the left-wing secretary of ASTMS) were ranged against three industrialists (Sir Barrie Heath of GKN, Sir Jack Callard the ex-chairman of ICI, and Norman Biggs, chairman of Williams and Glyn's Bank).

When Bullock published his report in 1977 it recommended that companies' boards should have an equal number of workers' and shareholders' representatives, with all the worker-directors chosen by the unions. Industrialists, led by Sir John Methven, who was then director of the CBI, refused to accept the unions' 'single channel', and about half the cabinet agreed, including Edmund Dell the Trade Secretary. But Albert Booth the Employment Minister argued that the unions were bound to be the only source of worker-directors, whatever the law. The CBI favoured limited and voluntary reforms to provide more consultation, while many trade unionists were very unsure that industrial democracy would be in their own interests. If there were workers on the boards, co-operating with managers and shareholders, what would happen to the whole adversary system of industrial relations, on which so many jobs and incentives depended on both sides?

The Labour government set up a cabinet committee including Shirley Williams and Tony Benn to try to reach a compromise, but when they published a White Paper in 1978, which accepted the TUC's 'single channel' the CBI thought it too extreme while the TUC thought it too watered-down. The spate of interest in indus-trial democracy was soon eclipsed by the growing unpopularity of the unions and the defeat of the Labour government, and the Conservatives showed little interest in reviving the question. But some politicians, particularly Liberals and Social Democrats, still insist that worker participation will become essential, particularly in companies undergoing rapid innovations and technological change which must have their workers' co-operation. 'Industrial democracy could usher in much better relations in industry,' says Shirley Williams, 'greater co-operation in improving the productivity of all factors of production, and a better understanding of the need for voluntary incomes and prices policies to combat inflation.'[3]

Britain remains years behind many other Western European countries in worker participation. West Germany, Holland, Belgium and Scandinavia have both participation laws and better industrial relations—though they are never quite clear which is cause and which is effect. Many critics told Bullock that Britain had to have reasonable industrial relations before workers and managers could co-operate. Britain still has only a few companies with profit-sharing schemes (such as the John Lewis Partnership whose employees have owned the company since the twenties) and a few companies with workers on the board, including two nationalised industries, the Post Office and British Steel. But the prospect of a nationwide system for industrial democracy has been lost in the general acrimony between unions and employers, between left and right, as both sides retreat into their familiar class assumptions.

LEANER AND FITTER?

The chief executives were more in command than ever; and during the dark early eighties many of them went through experiences they will not soon forget, as they had to abandon their predecessors' plans for expansion, close down new plants, or lay off tens of thousands of workers. These upheavals undoubtedly made companies, in Thatcher's phrase, 'leaner and fitter', increasing their productivity and profitability. A few chairmen were dismayed that the government was not grappling with the problem of vast unemployment which was the inevitable consequence of the new ruthlessness. But many businessmen were openly grateful to the government for compelling them to slim down and put their corporations in order. In November 1981 a clutch of corporate chairmen reaffirmed their Conservative loyalty, including Ronald Halstead of Beechams, Sir Arnold Hall of Hawker Siddeley, Sir James Hanson of Hanson Trust, Lord Inchcape of Inchcape and Malcolm McAlpine of McAlpine. 'The government's resolute stand since 1979,' they wrote to *The Times*, 'alas against the background of the worst world

[3] Williams: *op cit*, p. 140.

recession since the war, has compelled even the most lagging managements and workers to confront the long-neglected reality that we all have to earn our own living in a tough competitive world.'

But why (I asked several chairmen) did they need the combination of Thatcher and the recession to induce them to become more competitive and profitable—in a capitalist system in which shareholders as well as executives are assumed to be pressing for maximum profits? The answer, most of them agreed, lay in a fundamental change in the social and political climate. In the seventies most executives, even under worsening conditions, were not prepared to be so ruthless; they often felt themselves circumscribed not only by the fear of the unions but by their own social conscience, while there was no very powerful pressure from shareholders or chairmen. The recession, the new Tory philosophy and the sheer need for survival, had transformed the atmosphere, and as one company cut down its workforce so others found it easier to follow. The unions turned out to be weaker, the backlash from unemployment seemed less worrying, and reaction inside the company was less hostile than many managers had expected. And the harsh old laws of the market-place were beginning to assert themselves, as the fear of unemployment made workers work harder.

The chief executives nevertheless faced a more testing ordeal than had their predecessors, with a responsibility they could not readily abdicate. The relationships between chief executives and their corporations was becoming much more visible and direct, as the winds blew away the trappings, the false gods and accumulated delusions, as some of the following case-histories will suggest. In taking their disagreeable decisions they became more conscious of the gulf between the insecurity of their industries and the more protected world of the City, academia or the professions. It was a gulf, they could reflect, which was part of Britain's predicament; for all those other secure and comfortable superstructures ultimately depended on Britain's industrial exports. In the conditions of the early eighties none of the biggest British corporations looked the same as ten years before, and in most of them the role of chief executives and chairmen—as the following case histories suggest—was becoming more critical, and exposed. Opposite are the thirty biggest British companies by turnover, as compiled by *The Times, 1,000, 1981–1982*.

ICI AND HARVEY-JONES

Imperial Chemical Industries had been the most thoroughly British of the giants ever since it first brought together five companies in 1926, to counter the German chemical combine I.G.

COMPANY	MAIN ACTIVITY	CHAIRMAN or CHIEF EXECUTIVE	TURNOVER Total £000	EMPLOYEES
1 British Petroleum	Oil	Peter Walters	25,347,000	118,200
2 Shell Transport and Trading	Oil	Sir Peter Baxendell	15,846,000	—
3 BAT Industries	Tobacco	Sir Peter Macadam	7,497,000	177,000
4 Imperial Chemical Industries	Chemicals	John Harvey-Jones	5,715,000	143,200
5 Unilever	Food, detergents	Kenneth Durham	4,345,800	79,148
6 Imperial Group	Tobacco, etc	Geoffrey Kent	3,929,081	127,300
7 Shell UK	Oil	John Raisman	3,263,100	20,150
8 Esso Petroleum	Oil	Archibald Forster	3,219,400	8,614
9 General Electric	Electrical engineering	Lord Weinstock	3,005,800	188,000
10 Ford Motor	Motor cars	S.E.G. Toy	2,924,000	76,000
11 Rio Tinto Zinc	Mining	Sir Anthony Tuke	2,795,800	65,799
12 Grand Metropolitan	Hotels, breweries	Sir Maxwell Joseph	2,582,600	106,565
13 Czarnikow	Commodity brokers	Richard Liddiard	2,567,451	717
14 S & W Berisford	Merchant commodity trading	E. S. Margulies	2,452,539	4,607
15 Allied Suppliers	Food, drink, tobacco	James Gulliver	2,310,290	63,300
16 Rothmans	Tobacco	Sir David Nicolson	2,271,198	24,700
17 Allied – Lyons	Brewers, vintners, hotels	Sir Derrick Holden-Brown	2,267,700	83,971
18 P and O	Shipowners	Earl of Inchcape	2,240,269	14,599
19 George Weston Holdings	(Associated British Foods)	Garry Weston	2,157,375	72,601
20 Guest, Keen and Nettlefolds	Steel and engineering	Trevor Holdsworth	1,922,700	101,605
21 Texaco	Oil	Thomas Cottrell	1,883,000	4,373
22 Dalgety	Merchants	David Donne	1,876,000	28,567
23 Marks and Spencer	Shops	Lord Sieff	1,872,900	44,646
24 Gallaher	Tobacco, opticians	Stuart Cameron	1,835,781	27,536
25 Bowater	Paper	Lord Erroll	1,760,000	34,500
26 Lonrho	Mining	'Tiny' Rowland	1,744,990	140,000
27 Courtaulds	Textiles	Christopher Hogg	1,709,900	88,000
28 Thomas Tilling	Industrial Holdings	Sir Robert Taylor	1,696,600	45,700
29 Thorn EMI	Electronics	Sir Richard Cave	1,620,900	125,458
30 Great Universal Stores	Shops, mail order	Lord Wolfson	1,580,554	34,649

Farben. It thus grew up in a world of cartels and agreements with other companies. Its financier-chairman Lord McGowan wanted to sell chemicals through the empire (it still has huge off-shoots in Canada, South Africa and Australia); and its palace on Millbank, with its high nickel doors representing man's scientific progress, was a monument to its pre-war ambitions and its benign paternalism. But it was never as secure as it looked. McGowan's assumptions about the imperial market were hopelessly over-optimistic, and the great new chemical works at Billingham-on-Tees (where I was an ICI baby) was equipped to produce far more fertilisers than the empire could buy. And McGowan himself, it was later revealed, was a financial gambler who nearly went personally bankrupt and had little serious understanding of the industry he autocratically control-led.[4]

In the post-war years ICI had a remarkable team of chemists to compete with Duponts in America and the three big German com-panies (which had been split up from I.G. Farben) but it rested too easily on its laurels, and lacked the spirit of salesmanship and adventure. Its leadership veered uneasily from the benign scientific rule of Lord Fleck to the meaner ambitions of the accountant Sir Paul Chambers who overreached himself when he tried to buy Courtaulds in 1962. ICI became more seriously competitive and coherent; but its overmanning was legendary. (When a man from British Rail was boasting to an ICI man that his company was bigger, the ICI man replied: 'Aha, but we've got more *passengers*.')

The oil crisis of 1973 gave ICI its first serious shock, by putting up the price of an essential commodity and inducing a chemical reces-sion, after which its new chairman Sir Maurice Hodgson, a scientific master-planner, began seriously cutting down its great bureaucracy. When the new recession arrived, accompanied by Thatcher, he had to cut back from 90,000 workers in 1979 to 73,000 in 1981, though like other tycoons he admired Thatcher for forcing industry to get leaner. But ICI was still less agile than its three German rivals—each now bigger than ICI—and it was becoming less British, and more European and American, in its global contest.

Then in 1981 the board appointed a new chairman, John Harvey-Jones, who was neither a scientist nor an accountant: with his long straggly hair and untidy moustache he looks more like a musician. He began as a successful naval officer specialising in Russian intelligence, and his style still has a touch of the humorous spook who can get other people to reveal themselves, with a sugges-tion of melancholy behind his jolly extroversion. He left the navy

---

[4] For a candid and scholarly account of McGowan's operations see W. J. Reader: *Imperial Chemical Industries, A History*, vol 2, Oxford University Press, 1975.

when his daughter contracted polio and took a modest job as a works study officer in ICI, from which he rapidly climbed. What he brought to the company was a detached analytical mind, and a rare capacity to get others to work for him, with a disarming straightforwardness and willingness to listen. He dislikes the old paternalism of ICI, its military hierarchy and tiers of management; he even talks of trying to get rid of its palace on Millbank. He is worried by the corruptions of power, and determined to retain his individual viewpoint, at the risk of indiscretion: he is an open supporter of the Social Democrats and an outspoken critic of Mrs Thatcher. He faces the thankless task of cutting down the company still further, but he has the reputation of not evading responsibility.

COURTAULDS AND HOGG

Courtaulds, the old textile giant, suffered still more in the recession. There was nothing new about a textile crisis: since the beginning of the century British cotton, followed by fibres, had faced growing world competition and the old Lancashire mills were closed down in scores. But Courtaulds had survived too complacently, and it was not until ICI nearly took it over in 1962 that they showed more fight, much influenced by their deputy chairman Frank Kearton. Two years later Kearton became chairman, determined to make Courtaulds 'the Hong Kong of Europe', building up-to-date new plants to compete in world markets. But after Kearton left in 1975 the harsh winds from abroad blew with their full force. The new chairman, Sir Arthur Knight, began to de-centralise and rationalise his factories, while the competition became more relentless. Then in 1979 the board boldly chose a forty-three-year-old new chairman, Christopher Hogg, a lean and rigorous master-manager who still bicycles to the headquarters in St James's Square. Hogg had already been a banker, a Harvard business student and a graduate of the Industrial Reorganisation Corporation (see next chapter) where he was much impressed by Arnold Weinstock (who had taken over General Electric at the same young age). He was determined to apply Weinstockean principles (see below) ignoring shibboleths of company tradition, setting targets and cash limits for the divisions and then leaving them alone.

The Courtaulds crisis soon worsened, as the soaring pound made exports far less competitive, and the Thatcher government would not intervene; the brand-new plants that Kearton had planned could not compete and Courtaulds was fighting for its corporate life. In one agonising decision Hogg stopped making nylon altogether and in under two years he cut the work force by 35 per cent, to 65,000 people. He took advantage of the flexibility of textiles, whose units were smaller and more manageable than car or steel plants, and he weathered the storm: as the pound sank again Courtaulds became more competitive after two terrible years. But Hogg was very conscious that he had looked over the precipice.

GENERAL ELECTRIC AND WEINSTOCK

The most enduring of the chairmen is Arnold Weinstock, now Lord Weinstock, who for the last nineteen years has run General Electric while cabinets, permanent secretaries and even trade unionists have come and gone. His success was quite bitter for the left, for it had been Tony Benn who had encouraged him to take over first Associated Electrical Industries and then English Electric, to create a single British giant; but Weinstock's preoccupation with profits soon made him a bogy man as he closed down whole plants and eliminated tens of thousands of jobs, so that by 1980 Labour's national executive were complaining that GEC 'plays a particularly malign role in UK electronics', and demanded its nationalisation.

Already in the sixties Weinstock was the archetypal new capitalist, determined not to be misled by 'false gods': he abolished the extravagant palaces of his old rivals, sold off their furniture and wine and cut back their perks, while he ran his own empire from small headquarters behind Park Lane. He gave his scattered divisions apparent autonomy, while scrutinising budgets and costs with the eagle eye of a statistician. He saw himself driven by a lonely purpose: his Polish-Jewish parents died when he was young and he always felt a sense of special duty, he told me, as a survivor of the Jewish massacres. 'When things are going right I feel there must be something wrong, and when things are wrong I feel I've got to put them right.' He probably influenced Britain more than any other single businessman: not just by restructuring its chaotic electrical industry, but by providing a model for financial discipline and decentralisation which others followed.

Yet the consequences of Weinstock's methods were not very encouraging for the country. His rigorous controls took little account of the need for imaginative risks, and he was deeply sceptical of ventures into the unknown. His critics complained that he ruled through fear not love, and that he suppressed the engineering genius on which his industry ultimately depended. Much of General Electric's profits came from contracts with nationalised industries such as British Rail, which were often critical of the company, while Weinstock's lobby was not slow to influence governments. More worrying was GEC's 'cash mountain' of reserves which amounted to over £600 million by 1981, earning high interest in the midst of the recession, but revealing a depressing lack of faith in industrial investment. While the government was urgently trying to encourage high technology, its biggest manufacturing corporation was looking more like a bank.

FAMILY FIRMS

Was it by chance that two of the big companies which most effectively survived the recession were family firms run by the third or fourth generation? Both the famous chains of stores, Marks and Spencer and Sainsbury, combine careful training and benign paternalism (or maternalism?) with strict financial discipline and quality control. Marks and Spencer, which had grown out of a market-stall in Leeds, had been run since the turn of the century by interlocking Marks, Sieffs and Sachers who kept control with their voting shares while excluding their less commercial members from the board. They were single-minded in their pursuit of innovation and profits, steadily trading up from the first penny bazaars into sophisticated stores selling suits, luxury foods and fashion which made them a by-word first in Britain, then in Europe. The Sieffs and Sachers, though passionate about Israel, did not suffer the distaste for trade that overcame old English families; they were never ashamed to discuss underwear or price-tags at fashionable dinner parties. They developed a severely analytical approach to management which not only extended their range and profits, but had its own impact on Whitehall after the campaigns of Sir Derek Rayner (see chapter 10)—who is now their vice-chairman and may become the first non-family chairman.

The Sainsbury grocery chain showed even more resilience when it added 58 per cent to its profits in 1980, in the height of the recession. Since John Sainsbury first set up a dairy in Drury Lane in 1869 the business has stayed in the family, and for the last thirteen years its chairman has been Sir John Sainsbury, the great-grandson of the founder, and son of the previous chairman, Lord Sainsbury. Other board members include Sir John's cousin David Sainsbury (the finance director who is also prominent in the Social Democratic Party) and his brother Timothy (who is a non-executive director and Tory MP).

The Sainsburys maintain wide interests in the arts: Sir John married a ballerina and is a director of Covent Garden, while his uncle Sir Robert was chairman of the Tate Gallery and endowed the Sainsbury Art Centre outside Norwich. But the directors remain dedicated to groceries, strengthening their central hold through computers, laying down prices, displays and rules of hygiene: 'We never allow ourselves to forget the virtues of the small business,' Sir John claims, 'that cares about every individual customer and every individual employee.' While other supermarkets such as International and Tesco have faltered, Sainsburys continued to increase both profits and jobs during the slump.

'When a family firm goes wrong,' said one Sainsbury, 'it goes very wrong: but when it comes right it has great advantages. I think people still prefer a company which has a strong sense of identity.' The same thought comes from Prince Charles—from that other old family firm—who in his tours of industry was specially impressed by the identity of M and S and Sainsbury. Among all the anonymous giants which lost their sense of direction and purpose in the midst of mergers and management committees, the best family companies retained their drive and identity.

BRITISH OXYGEN AND GIORDANO

Perhaps the most surprising transformation was that of staid old British Oxygen, which had long sat back on its semi-monopoly, with its own privileged style (Lord Reith of the BBC had been its vice-chairman), and its reputation for extravagant perks. During the seventies it became more widespread and adventurous under its accountant chairman Sir Leslie Smith, and in 1978 it took over the American company Airco, which was run by a masterful forty-three-year-old, Richard Giordano, whom Smith chose to be chief executive of the whole international group—now called the BOC Group. Giordano is the model of the classless global manager: both his parents were Italian immigrants, and he worked his way up to Harvard and then to law school and became a master of cool management style, looking as relaxed as if he were floating on air. In the Hammersmith headquarters he was quietly surprised by the lack of control over subsidiaries round the world, by the demoralised state of the managers, the power of the unions and the widespread overmanning: 'People seemed to think,' he told me, 'that their main mission was job-creation.'

He administered the usual medicine, imposing stricter central controls, firing strings of managers and workers, communicating directly with them and not through their unions. He was baffled by the British class system but ignored it, not looking to Oxbridge for his new managers. He cut back the privileges—'If you're seen to be enjoying privileges, there's something wrong'—closed the company bar and rented off much of the headquarters building. He sold some of the company's more eccentric acquisitions, including a pizza-

maker and a trout farm, and concentrated on the main business—industrial gases, welding and carbon graphite products. He
shuttled across the Atlantic and looked at the British scene with
detachment: he is concerned about the widening gulf between the
employed and the unemployed, but insists that companies must not
confuse their values.

His results were sensational in the midst of the recession: in 1981
BOC profits were up by 50 per cent. His own salary, which included
bonus payments, was still more sensational: it went up from
£200,000 to £477,000—the highest in any British public company
and more than twice that of other top chairmen. The shareholders
showed little signs of worry while Giordano forged ahead with
expansion, but the unions were appalled for 80 per cent of BOC's
profits now came from outside Britain. In 1982 Giordano decided
without consulting them to build a big new plant in South Carolina;
Roger Lyons of ASTMS complained, 'Mr Giordano is trying to turn
BOC into an American company.' It was a cruel twist, though not
altogether surprising, that one of the few expanding companies in
the recession was run by an American making most of its profits
outside Britain.

Behind all the stories of leaner and fitter companies lay the same
basic transformation of attitudes at the top: chairmen and chief
executives could no longer feel responsible for the continuing security and welfare of their workers. From the mood of the sixties, when
many of them were 'hoarding' workers with an excess of zeal, they
had swung to attitudes which were often more ruthless than those of
other Europeans, while they could not, like the Japanese corporations which were more genuinely paternal, guarantee jobs in other
parts of their groups. The heads of British companies (I found) had
very varying attitudes to the gathering army of unemployed to which
they had contributed. Some saw the real blame as lying with the
unions; some, such as Giordano, were worried by the widening rift
between the employed and the unemployed; some, such as Baxendell of Shell (see chapter 26), were more deeply worried about the
long-term political consequences; some, such as Harvey-Jones, felt
impelled to become politically involved, to press for more humane
government policies. But everywhere—and not just in private industry—the assumption of a company's deeper social responsibility had
been blown away by the storms, and the ex-workers became like
ghosts outside the system.

24

State Capitalists:
Governments and Industry

If the men are wrong, nothing will be right.
*Sir Ronald Edwards (to the Select
Committee on Nationalised Industries), 1968*

WHAT was to be done with private companies which were tottering
towards collapse? How far should governments intervene to rescue
or restructure British industries which could not compete in the
world markets? The swings of policy towards industry had provided
some of the most glaring examples of British discontinuity as each
government tried to run its own version of a mixed economy which
combined free enterprise with national ownership and planning,
while each stopped short of giving decisive direction. But however
strong their ideological prejudices, like other Western governments
they could not in the end evade the problems of declining industries.

In the first Labour phase Harold Wilson had set up the Ministry
of Technology in 1964, first under Frank Cousins and then under
Tony Benn, to help introduce the white-hot technological revolution
into British industry; but the ministry was extravagant and confused, and Benn became over-excited with the game of tycoons. To
achieve more practical results, the Labour government in 1966 set
up the Industrial Reorganisation Corporation (IRC) to 'promote
industrial efficiency and profitability', funded directly from the
Treasury to by-pass political interference. Its chairman was
Labour's favourite industrialist, Sir Frank Kearton from Courtaulds, and its first director, Ronald Grierson, was a smooth
cosmopolitan banker who was very reluctant to intervene: 'It has
always seemed to me,' he wrote later, 'that the creative genius of the
British people in commerce and industry flourishes in almost exactly
inverse proportion to the amount of central tutelage applied to it.'[1]

[1] 'The Mirage of the State's Entrepreneurial Role', lecture to the Royal Institution, March
13, 1979.

But his successor Sir Charles Villiers was a more adventurous banker with a confident military panache. He and Kearton assembled a bright nursery from the City and industry and pushed through a succession of mergers to strengthen companies against fiercer foreign competition. They helped the young Arnold Weinstock to merge three electrical companies into one. They pushed through—heavily prodded by Benn—the ill-considered merger between Leyland and the British Motor Corporation. They prevented the Swedes from buying the ball-bearing company, Ransome and Marles, by quickly merging it with other British companies.

In retrospect the IRC must take some of the blame for the merger-mania of the sixties: as two of its executives John Gardiner and Geoffrey Wilkinson, reflected afterwards, 'the aim was laudable, but the thought that this objective could be achieved through mergers was laughable.' In the heady atmosphere of the time the IRC was too confident, like many bankers, that it could put industry right without tackling the human problems in the factories. But it helped to inject some realism into British companies which often welcomed its advice, and many of the IRC nursery went into industry later, to achieve very practical results: including Christopher Hogg, now chairman of Courtaulds; John Gardiner, now chief executive of Laird; Christopher Zealley, ex-chairman of the Consumers' Association; and Alastair Morton, now chief executive of the Guinness Peat bank.

When Heath came to power he rapidly disbanded the IRC, to the relief of merchant bankers who resented its competition. But he soon had to begin intervening more deeply in private industry; though he allowed Rolls Royce to go bankrupt he had to shore up its aerospace business in the national interest. When Labour came back in 1974, with Benn as Minister for Industry, they were rapidly faced with private companies collapsing in the wake of the oil crisis and the crash, culminating in the collapse of British Leyland which had to be rescued by the state (see below).

To control and oversee these lame ducks Harold Wilson set up a National Enterprise Board, which was the brainchild of the left-wing economist, Stuart Holland; and the NEB, with four trade unionists on its board of eleven, was at first seen as a child of the left. But its first chairman, Don Ryder from Reed Paper—Labour's new favourite tycoon—was determined to be strictly commercial; and his discipline was reinforced by his successor, Sir Leslie Murphy, a banker from Schroders. Murphy, a footballer's son who had once been Clement Attlee's secretary, regarded the NEB as 'a bridge between state ownership and private entrepreneurial activity'. He saw its development (as he described it to me) as being locked into the historical problems of late capitalism. The big private investors could no longer provide risk capital, the pension funds and insurance companies would not intervene in badly-managed companies, and someone had to exercise the power of ownership when there were disasters. In the integrated financial systems, like those of Germany or Japan, the all-powerful banks could drastically reform or revive companies; but in the looser market systems, like those of America or Britain, the state might have to provide the means to turn companies round.

The NEB struggled hard to control its most expensive charges, Leyland and Rolls Royce, and it turned round the Ferranti electronics company so effectively that—to the fury of the left—it made good profits for the Ferranti family. The NEB was not now loved either by the left, who saw it helping capitalists, or by the right, who saw it competing with the City and encouraging 'creeping nationalisation'. But it was the first convincing alternative to the outright nationalisation of collapsing industry.

Then in 1979 under the Conservatives the policy again switched 180 degrees. Thatcher and Joseph quickly cut down the NEB, removed Rolls Royce from its control and insisted, like Heath nine years before, that private industry must stand on its own feet. But the old pressures for intervention soon reasserted themselves. By 1981 the government could not ignore Britain's technological backwardness; and the free market clearly would not provide the capital or incentive for advanced technology. While the free-enterprise rhetoric continued, Kenneth Baker, a flexible Heathite minister, went to the Department of Industry with the special task of stimulating information technology. 'It is quite unrealistic,' he soon explained, 'to expect such new industries to grow in the market place without government prompting and assistance.'[2] And when Britain's chief computer company, ICL, fell into difficulties (see chapter 19) he had to intervene with help of the pension funds to put in Christopher Laidlaw as the new chairman.

The Tories reshuffled once again the alphabet of bodies operating between government and industry, and merged the remains of the NEB with the inactive National Research Development Corporation (NRDC) which had been set up thirty years ago by Harold Wilson and little heard of since. The merged body, called the British Technology Group (BTG) is now run by a young ex-civil servant, Brian Willott, who wants, like so many before him, to connect up university research and industry; and the chairman is Sir Frederick Wood, who had built up Croda, his father's chemical company on Humberside, before successfully running the National Bus Com-

[2] *Management Today*, October 1981.

pany from 1972. 'We hope to create an organisation which will work with the private sector,' Sir Frederick announced, 'in supporting the innovative, inventive, and the enterprising individual and company.' But there was some weary scepticism as to whether the merger could mobilise the sleepy NRDC or the demoralised NEB to this much-proclaimed task.

This chopping and changing over two decades have reflected all Britain's uncertainties about state capitalism. It was becoming clear, even to non-interventionist Conservatives, that private capital left to its own would not provide the huge investments required for the more advanced and risky technologies: Weinstock's General Electric preferred to keep its money-hoard locked up safely as cash. But could any government body within a democratic framework provide that prompt decisiveness which was essential if British industry were to respond to the intense foreign competition?

Successive British institutions, from Neddy to the IRC to the NEB to the new BTG, had tried in different ways to harness government and industry together, with an eye to Japanese or French models; but none of them had proven their success and all of them had suffered from the lurches between opposite political philosophies. They had all come up against 'problems of communication'—or total cross-purposes—between government, industrialists and trade unionists, problems whose roots went back more than twenty years. Behind the cross-purposes lay the basic fact that the British in their post-imperial phase were still confused and divided; they still could not mobilise the sense of national purpose or unity, which had been so evident in wartime, to the more contemporary challenge of industrial survival. Politicians and their voters found it easy to turn away from the ugly problems of industrial decline; and their reluctance to face up to the facts was most evident in their attitude to the car industry.

LEYLAND AND LITTLE MICHAEL

Through all the switches of policy the tragic story of British Leyland provided a succession of object-lessons—whether for managers, bankers, pension funds or governments—on how not to cope with an ailing company. It was a long illness. When the British Motor Corporation had been first created from the mass-produced car companies Austin and Morris the two were never properly integrated: the two big plants at Cowley and Longbridge still made the same cars, sometimes carrying identical parts in opposite directions. Their managers had grown up in the shadow of two autocratic tycoons, and they were slow to catch up with the techniques of costing and marketing, while London bankers were baffled or bored by the inarticulate Midlands engineers who had come up through the techs. By the mid-sixties BMC, in spite of the success of the elegant Mini, was beginning to lose ground seriously to foreign competition. Its chairman Sir George Harriman was a home-grown optimist who looked forward to joining the Common Market (at Longbridge he drew diagrams on an envelope to show me how his cars would invade the Continent). But already BMC was facing inroads at home, from Volkswagens, Fiats or Renaults.

By 1968 the Labour government was enthralled with mergers, and Tony Benn persuaded Donald Stokes, the legendary salesman-chairman of the Leyland bus company, to merge with BMC. ('If I'd known what a mess BMC was in,' Stokes told me a few weeks later, 'I'd never have agreed.') The Press proclaimed Stokes as the hero of exports, but the merger, like others, had happened only at the top: the factories were still unco-ordinated, each with its own complex pay agreements, while the industrial anarchy at BMC soon infected the more successful specialist cars such as Rover and Jaguar. When Britain entered Europe foreign cars came in much faster, and Leyland's prospects quickly worsened: they borrowed more money while the share-values fell. The bankers worried, but never seriously interfered; the big shareholders, led by the Pru, held on and hoped that more investment would turn it round. But the oil crisis in late 1973 was the last straw, for Leyland as for so much else: car sales slumped, competition intensified, and Leyland went bankrupt with all its proud components crashing together.

None of the responsible actors emerged with much credit. The disaster revealed all the rifts between London and the provinces, between the City and industry, between bankers and engineers. They had all contributed to allowing the company to drift helplessly into debt and disorganisation, not daring to look too far into the can of worms, while the Press had obediently responded to the PR puffs.

Surveying the debris the government (having turned down an offer from the Shah of Iran) was compelled to nationalise the company. Leyland became part of the new National Enterprise Board under Lord Ryder, who made his own study concluding that Leyland would need £1.4 billion from the taxpayers. Lord Stokes retired and was succeeded by the former chairman of British American Tobacco, Sir Richard Dobson, who had to resign eighteen months later after making a speech about bribing wogs. Then Ryder brought in a total outsider, Michael Edwardes, to take over the nationalised shambles.

Edwardes looks, as he is, like a being from another world: a tiny, agile man with a small head and narrow eyes, who moves like a tree-creature which might drop on your shoulder. He was brought up in South Africa and remains coolly detached from British tribes, living in a brand-new house in Richmond which might be in an American suburb. He thinks his un-British upbringing makes it easier to by-pass class problems: 'When I talk to the unions, they can't sort me out.' He avoids cosy relationships with colleagues and fortifies himself by giving them psychological and intelligence tests, remembering their IQs (he claims) to the last decimal point.

Edwardes had experience of mergers as chairman of the Chloride Group which had bought successive companies but left them with their separate identities. 'It's centralisation,' he assured me in 1978, 'that has given mergers a bad name. Centralisation creates rebellion: if you want to get separate companies to work together, you have to respect their territorial imperative: once managers feel secure, they'll work together far more easily than if you force them together.' He blames bankers for many of the merger mistakes: 'The City has an incredible lack of knowledge of business organisation.'

'Little Michael', as the trade unionists called him, hacked into the undergrowth of Leyland which had entangled so many others, with an icy purpose: 'I don't mind spending a few years hitting my head against a brick wall,' he told me, 'but I'm not going to do it for ever.' He rejected the idea of un-merging Leyland altogether, for its component companies needed each others' research and parts; instead he split the giant back into three—Leyland buses, Jaguar-Rover-Triumph, and Austin-Morris—with separate managing directors but with central services.

Edwardes' only hope of turning round Leyland was to cut down the overmanning, and he had the advantage of starting with a bankrupt company. He persuaded the unions that only by cutting down some jobs could he save the rest, and he soon closed down some unprofitable plants such as Speke outside Liverpool (with the significant backing of union members of the NEB). But he was determined to be as tough with the top-heavy Leyland headquarters as with the workers: he knew that senior managers had a vested interest in large units and that their salaries were often related to the numbers of men under them. He sacked them by scores, and brought in some new managers from other industries and countries. He was much hated, but he did not need to be liked.

Little Michael knew that time was running out: by 1978 almost half the new cars in Britain were foreign; the name Leyland was notorious abroad for delays and faults, and strikes still continued. Many of the problems were common to other European car-makers in the West, as the discipline of the assembly line became unacceptable to workers. But while the German, French or Swedish factories employed Greeks, Turks, Portuguese and Africans in the factories, the British employed their own cheap labour. Yet their productivity was relatively so low that their cars were equally expensive.

After May 1979 Leyland looked like a test of whether the Tory government would stick to its philosophy of non-intervention; but after a ritual period of suspense they could not let the company collapse, and promised another billion pounds. Edwardes had some new successes; he cut back the workforce still further, faced down the union militants, fired the communist works convenor at Longbridge 'Red Robbo', and successfully launched a new small car, the Metro. But after the next oil crisis in 1979 and a new world recession, all the Western car companies were facing much more serious problems—even Fiat and Ford were in danger—and Leyland made a net loss of £530 million in 1981. Only Japanese cars were still making major inroads into the European markets, with their combination of low-cost production and highly organised planning and marketing, while other new countries were creeping up behind them.

The Japanese factories, with their teams running to and fro, working with their managers and robots with military precision, seemed to show a united sense of purpose to which no British tycoon could aspire. All the European companies were now beginning to call for more protection, yet protection within national borders would Balkanise the Continent still further in comparison to Japan, and weaken the Europeans' prospects for export. What looked like a purely British problem ten years earlier was now looking more like a European predicament. But the British would still get the worst of it, and the dynamic challenge from East Asia emphasised the British weakness still further.

25

Nationalised Industries: Custodians or Competitors?

By making the most fundamental of all industries a public service carried on in partnership between the state and the workers, it will call into operation motives of public spirit and professional zeal which are at present stifled by the subordination of the industry to the pursuit of private gain, and will raise the whole tone and quality of our industrial civilisation.

R. H. Tawney (on the nationalisation of the coal industry), 1919

IT was the nationalised industries, the unloved old drudges of industrial society, which became the chief battleground between ideologies, between the aggressive and the defensive instincts, between individual entrepreneurs and old institutions.

They each had their own faded memories of Britain's heroic industrial past, and their own hereditary loyalties to their own industry. Most of the oldest industries—beginning with coal, canals and railways—had fallen into the lap of the state as they had become too costly or uneconomic for private shareholders. Though most of them had been nationalised by Attlee's Labour government in the forties, the issue was never as dogmatic as politicians later suggested. The Sankey Commission of 1919 first proposed the nationalisation of coal; the Tory entrepreneur Lord McGowan considered nationalising electricity in 1936; the Conservatives created the British Overseas Airways Corporation in 1939. But all the nationalised industries became more politically controversial as the public sector grew and the economic problems worsened; and all their chairmen found themselves in the centre of the fray.

In the fifties most of them still behaved as if they were 'the high custodians of the public interest', as Herbert Morrison described them. Sir Brian Robertson presided over British Railways like an ex-general and Sir James Bowman ran the National Coal Board like an ex-miner, without much concern about competition or profitability. But already by 1961 a Conservative White Paper was insisting that the nationalised industries 'are not, and ought not to be regarded as social services absolved from economic and commercial justification'. Over the next twenty years the battles raged about their commercial or social objectives, while these huge corporations—with their armies larger than the army and turnovers greater than any private corporation—became the chief receptacles and scapegoats for an ageing industrial nation.

The Conservatives, long before they came to power in 1979, made plans with bankers to sell off some nationalised businesses, including airlines, aerospace, hotels, oil and gas showrooms. Once in government they sold off British Aerospace and part of Cable and Wireless; and they even sold off the National Freight Company, which nobody else wanted, for £53 million to its managers and employees with the help of loans from the banks. The Monopolies Commission began investigating nationalised industries, to increase their competitiveness and accountability, while the select committee in the Commons became more trenchant in its complaints. By October 1981 Mrs Thatcher was saying that she would 'never have thought we'd be able to make so much progress with denationalisation in those first two and a half years'.

Yet after two years of recession, which had knocked many private corporations sideways, most nationalised industries were still relatively untouched and overmanned. Mrs Thatcher was still complaining after two and a half years that 'private business is still being held to ransom by the giant nationalised monopolies'. The old industries were still the problem-children of the national inheritance. Were they the special responsibility of the state, with social as well as economic justifications? Or were they to compete without privileges in the domestic and world market-place? The questions still dogged the men who were trying to run them.

CHAIRMEN

The nationalised industries' chairmen were shown up in sharper profile than the heads of private corporations. They occupied the most exposed of all industrial peaks, with a long record of casualties and destroyed reputations. They had to face the full blast from governments, unions and consumers, while they tried to provide some continuity and security for their workers.

Once a month they lunch and talk together in their own Chairmen's Group, the NICG. It began when Lord Robens of the Coal Board started a club for his fellow chairmen, which soon became formalised, and there are now twenty-one members including such

MAJOR NATIONALISED INDUSTRY CHAIRMEN 1981–82

Corporation	Employees	Chairman	Education
National Coal Board	297,000	Sir Derek Ezra	Monmouth School; Cambridge
British Telecom	246,000	Sir George Jefferson	Dartford GS
British Railways Board	239,680	Sir Peter Parker	Bedford School; London, Oxford
British Steel Corporation	181,000	Ian MacGregor	George Watson's, Edinburgh; Glasgow University
Post Office	180,000	Ronald Deering	
Electricity Council (and Boards)	158,780	Austin Bunch	Christ's Hospital
British Leyland	157,460	Sir Michael Edwardes	St Andrew's School; Rhodes University, South Africa
British Gas Corporation	104,100	Sir Denis Rooke	Westminster City School; University College, London
British Airways	56,860	Sir John King	
Rolls Royce	58,800	Lord McFadzean	Glasgow University; LSE

lesser-known chairmen as Lord Shepherd of the National Bus Company, Roy Berridge of the South of Scotland Electricity Board and Norman Payne of the British Airports Authority. The group now has its own little staff, compares notes on financial frameworks and arranges annual lectures on industrial problems. They share a common sense of persecution by government; but they only took off as a group (as one of them explained) when they became a strike committee. Their resentment about their own pay compared to private chairmen soon fused them together—particularly after Harold Wilson held back their pay increase in 1974. While Sir Derek Ezra has been the senior chairman, Sir Denis Rooke has been the most militant, their 'shop steward' for pay demands.

Their jobs by their nature are full of contradictions. Governments in theory want strong men to run their industries, but then insist on obedience to their varying instructions. The chairmen have to pretend that they are decisively in charge, exercising their own rational choices; while behind the scenes they are constantly consulting and pleading with union leaders—to close down a pit, open a railway siding, or abolish a job. Above all they have to try to act like breakwaters, as one of them put it, to provide smoother seas for their employees as the political waves break round them.

BANKERS V. ENGINEERS

Governments have never known quite where to look for their chairmen—whether towards industrialists, engineers or bankers—but when in doubt they turn to bankers. While the industries were trying to build up their own hierarchies, City men were weaving in and out, bringing their own values and motives. Some of the more puzzling appointments could only be understood in terms of City networks. The most pervasive influence was that of the Hill Samuel Bank, the merger created by Sir Kenneth Keith in 1970, which soon extended its embrace; and when Lord Melchett, the head of the Samuel half of the merger, lost out to Keith he was given British Steel as a consolation prize.

Keith himself assembled a board of industrialists and ex-civil servants with close links with the Department of Trade, whose permanent secretary, Sir Peter Thornton, soon became a director of Hill Samuel. Keith was on the board of British Airways, and was later followed by his friend Frank McFadzean, the joint head of Shell who became chairman of British Airways, which he ran for two days a week from the Shell building—to the fury of the airline's professionals. At the same time Sir Charles Villiers, from Lord Kissin's bank Guinness Peat, was taking over British Steel in 1976 from Melchett. Sir Kenneth Keith in the meantime had taken on another nationalised industry, Rolls Royce, which he ran for eight years until 1980 when he was succeeded by (surprise!) Frank McFadzean, now Lord McFadzean. When the Conservative government planned to sell off British Airways the City was not surprised that the bankers chosen for the task should be . . . Hill Samuel.

Watching these bankers' gyrations, spectators might marvel at their confident adaptability; but the professionals inside the corporations, particularly the engineers who were crucial to most of them, felt continually demoralised by the entrances and exits at the top. And when the engineers did reach the top jobs, they found themselves immediately facing unfamiliar political cross-fire. Nowhere did the gulf between engineers and politicians, with their opposite educational backgrounds, loom wider than in the nationalised industries.

The electricity industry, which was outside the comprehension of most politicians, had a specially rough ride as energy came to the political forefront. When the Labour government chose the mechanical engineer Sir Francis Tombs in 1977 as chairman of the Electricity Council, the umbrella-body of the industry, they promised him that they would reorganise the industry; but they did not, and he resigned. The Conservatives then spent four months searching for a successor, only to turn to the sixty-two-year-old deputy, Austin Bunch, to act as caretaker chairman.

But it was the chairman of the Central Electricity Generating Board, responsible for all power stations, who was much more exposed to all the controversies between coal, oil and nuclear fuel. After the energy crisis of 1974 the previous chairman Arthur Hawkins came under heavy fire over the oil shortage, while the rows about nuclear power (see chapter 14) raged round his office. In 1977 he was succeeded by Glynn England, a Welsh engineer who was brought up 'in the shadow of a Rhondda pitheap', went to the LSE and worked his way up the electrical circuits. He was an outspoken man with his own ideas about the industry: he favoured small units and was sceptical of economies of scale; and he discreetly became a founder-member of the Social Democrats. He did not disguise his difference with Ministers of Energy who (as he put it to me) did not really understand the problems of motivation and enterprise in a big undertaking. When in 1981 the Monopolies Commission reported on the CEGB they found that it was basically well-organised, with its costs under control. The industry, England insisted, could have been more efficient if it had paid less attention to the politicians. His job, he said, was like playing a piano concerto while having to explain what he was doing: 'Sometimes it seems as if we are trying to explain to someone who hasn't even seen a piano.' But industrialists complained about Britain's high electricity prices compared to those on the Continent, and the CEGB was blamed for delays in building new power stations, which had been extended by the nuclear arguments. At the end of five years in 1982 the Energy Secretary, Nigel Lawson, replaced England with the irrepressible apostle of nuclear power, Walter Marshall (see chapter 14).

The Post Office and telephone system had an equally confused leadership. In 1977 the Labour government had appointed a new chairman of the post office, Sir William Barlow, an electrical engineer from Manchester who had risen to be chief executive of English Electric, under Weinstock. Barlow insisted that the telephone system needed to borrow £200 million from the City to modernise the ageing equipment; but the Thatcher government complained that this exceeded the cash limits, and Sir William resigned in disgust to join private industry: he is now chairman of Thorn-EMI. The telephones were then split off into a separate corporation, British Telecom, run by another engineer Sir George Jefferson, one of the few British bosses who has not been to university. (He taught himself mechanical engineering at night school at Woolwich Polytechnic—'It was a damn good education. I worked with my hands as well as my brains.') But Jefferson is on one of the most political frontiers of all, for telecommunications are now in the thick of the battle between nationalised and privatised industries. By February 1982 British Telecom faced new competition when the government gave a licence to the Mercury consortium, which included Cable and Wireless and BP, to establish an independent telecommunications system for business customers; while the government proposed to sell off half the shares of British Telecom itself to the public, as part of the plan to provide a new cable system throughout the country.

The British National Oil Corporation was relatively easy for the Conservatives to privatise. It had been set up by the Labour government in 1976 and first run by the ex-chairman of Courtaulds, Lord Kearton, to ensure that Britain could maintain some control over the North Sea and share its profits; by 1981 it was making pre-tax profits of £500 million. The Conservatives put it in the hands of an archetypal banker, Philip Shelbourne, a tax barrister (like so many new Tories) who had moved into Rothschilds Bank and later became chairman of Samuel Montagu. Shelbourne and the new Energy Secretary Nigel Lawson planned to split up BNOC into a publicly-owned trading organisation and a production and exploration company, which would be partly privately owned. The proposal brought angy complaints from the two trade union directors of BNOC, Clive Jenkins and Gavin Laird: 'If there was ever a birthright of the British people,' they said in the *Guardian*, 'it must be the huge riches of the United Kingdom continental shelf. It might well be that these revenues are and will continue to be the single most important component for restructuring our industy and renewing the physical fabric of these islands.'

A much lamer duck was British Airways, which had provided dispiriting problems for successive chairmen since the merger of its two components BOAC and BEA in 1972, when mergers were already becoming discredited. The two parts, once again, never really merged, and the staffs remained duplicated down the line, with far more extravagance than European airlines. By the time of the world recession in 1980 British Airways had too many planes as well as people, while its losses were increased by the hectic competition across the Atlantic. The political resentment against British Airways was heightened when Sir Freddie Laker, the folk-hero among the airlines, went bankrupt in 1982; for BA more obviously deserved to collapse, and was only kept going by continuing subsidies and loans from the government.

The Conservatives since 1979 had been pledged to sell off British Airways to private investors, but the proposition was manifestly unattractive, and in 1981 a new chairman was appointed with the specific object of preparing the corporation for sale. Sir John King is a thorough-going free-enterprise tycoon, who set up his own engineering company after the war and rose to become chairman and director of a string of companies, as well as a country gentleman and master of fox hounds; he now combines the chairmanship of Babcock and Wilcox with British Airways. He commissioned an exhaustive study of the huge airline, and decided it should be split back into two parts, with another part for air tours: one more merger story had come full circle. He planned to sell off more planes and to cut back the workforce from 43,000 to 35,000 in two years; but the airline was a long way from being saleable and he asked in the meantime for another £600 million from government. One of the newest industries, in one of the most competitive businesses, was in one of the worst messes of all.

COAL AND GAS

Where the Conservatives could not sell off corporations they were determined to shake them up with new competition and controls; and only the oldest industry remained relatively immune. Coal was still the most basic and indispensable, and it had become part of the nation's political geology. Over the post-war decades the miners had faced threats from successive alternative fuels—from the flood of oil, the rush of North Sea gas and the prospect of cheap nuclear energy. But in 1973 the miners, like many others, found a moment of truth: for the energy crisis and the higher oil price had made them more indispensable than ever. After they had brought down Ted Heath no subsequent government was in a hurry to take them on.

The National Coal Board since its creation in 1946 had always been uniquely close to its union, the National Union of Mineworkers; and the closeness was encouraged by having only two chairmen in two decades—Lord Robens and his former deputy Sir Derek Ezra. They ran the Coal Board in parallel with the union leaders, appointing the mine managers with their approval, while over ten years Ezra became the confident of Joe Gormley, the miners' president. The bargain was a hard one: the miners resisted closing down pits and mechanising too fast, so that they now produced too much coal too expensively compared to foreign imports. But Mrs Thatcher dared not risk repeating Heath's mistake and when the miners protested about closures she swiftly gave way. When the fire-brand Arthur Scargill (see chapter 4) succeeded Gormley in 1982 he poured scorn on Gormley's treacherous friendship with Ezra, but he soon discovered the limits of his miners' revolutionary zeal. The NCB and the NUM remained bound together, and the government were in no hurry to break them apart.

Other old industries were more vulnerable to de-nationalisation, and it was the old despised gas business, with its associations of smell and suicides, which put up the toughest fight. Sir Denis Rooke, chairman and deputy chairman for the last ten years, is a rugged and plain-speaking engineer with a heavy frame and large head who has been determined to run his own gas, and is regarded as the most combative of the chairmen. 'I've played a large part in building up this industry,' he told me in 1982. 'I'm determined to keep it going, that's all.' He went into gas just after it was nationalised and took part in the technical revolution which transformed it: gasifying oil, liquifying gas from the Sahara, exploiting new gas reserves from the North Sea. He was fiercely loyal to his industry and workers: 'Our unpopularity knit us together, and it's very much a family business: half the top managers are engineers.' He understood both engineering and finance, and he made the most of the North Sea windfall; after the Gas Corporation had repaid £2.5 billion in loans it actually began lending money back to the Treasury.

Rooke sees himself as a 'dedicated Morrisonian', believing with Herbert Morrison that public utilities must have a special character, subject to political oversight but at arm's length—which he insists is much more sensible than the American private utilities run by lawyers subject to constant regulation and investigation. But he is continually frustrated by seeing long-term plans reversed by the political see-saw: 'There's a natural disjunction in the time-scale: by the end of a ten-year project you've had at least two bloody parliaments.' With Tony Benn as Minister of Energy he reached a kind of armed truce: Benn demanded that gas should be a social service while Rooke said the law required him to make it profitable, so that Benn in fact interfered very little. But Rooke was much more threatened by the return of the Tories, particularly when the relentless Nigel Lawson moved into the Department of Energy in 1981, insisting on selling off the corporation's gas showrooms, its rich oil field in Dorset, and its North Sea holdings. 'Nationalised industries are treated as a political football,' Rooke told me. 'It will only make Britain's recovery more difficult. We've got too few resources to waste them on restructuring things: we must concentrate on making people feel that they're contributing to running the country.'

RAIL

The most articulate and intellectual chairman has been Sir Peter Parker, who has run British Rail since 1976 with the panache he has carried through several careers—as an actor at Oxford, a management expert, a company director, and now as a chairman-statesman, discussing larger issues and relationships. He came into British Rail when it had already been through successive changes of philosophy—Sir Brian Robertson ran it like the army, Lord Beeching ran it like ICI—and there had been fourteen ministers of transport in twenty-five years (while there had only been fourteen chief engineers in the Western Region, Parker assured me, since Brunel in 1836). But British Rail's losses were now becoming much more politically controversial. No railways in the West were paying their way and many (like the German) were losing proportionately much more. But the British, as the first railway builders, probably had the most complicated emotions towards their 'permanent way', with its half-empty expresses and tribal traditions of railwaymen defended by three rival unions.

Sir Peter wanted to bring logical management to the system, and to revive morale after his abrasive predecessor Sir Richard Marsh. But he was familiar with the ambiguities of the job, the filtering of everything through civil servants and the minister—who appoints all the directors after consulting with him, so that the board could be 'a cauldron bubbling with conflicting personalities'. When he first arrived as chairman he realised as he put it that 'For the first time I was in a job where no one could tell me what *winning* means,' and the Tories later added their own problems: 'Mrs Thatcher defines nationalisation as failure: if it's a success, she asks herself, what is it doing there? So she thinks the people who run it must be failures.' Parker wanted British Rail to be seen not as a loss-making outfit, but as the provider of a service for which government should pay with a fixed contract; but the Tories were determined to take more of British Rail into the private sector, beginning with the hotels. 'You get a sense of battle-weariness,' he told me. 'The problem is like silt at the mouth of a river: however much you clear it it still comes back. But the real problem is the relationship between governments and all industry; nationalised industry is only the sharp end of it.'

Sir Peter has become wary of the corporate state, having been involved over twenty years with planning and 'tripartism' between government, unions and industry; and he advocates a new constitutional machinery to bring all industry—not just nationalised—into closer relationship with politics and parliament. 'The main party political differences seem to be symbolic rather than real alternatives,' he said in 1977. 'As a result, industry has had the worst of both worlds: disruption due to heightened inter-party conflict, but also exasperating immobility, in which neither party has followed through its declared strategy or dismantled tidily the machinery created by its predecessors.'[1] Sir Peter argues that Britain is already a corporate society, which must be democratically controlled: 'Parliament is already by-passed and corporate powers are already engaged in a tangled sharing of responsibility with government.' He advocates setting up a 'Council of Industry' of two hundred people from both sides of industry who would advise on economic policy and safeguard the public's interests 'against the centralising and secretive tendencies of corporatism'.[2]

But Sir Peter's view of the role of the nationalised industries was basically challenged by the Thatcher government, and particularly by the prime minister's economic adviser, Alan Walters, who was an expert on transport costs. The Conservatives were determined to stir up competition to the railways by encouraging coaches, and their Centre of Policy Studies even advocated ripping up tracks to build motorways. Sir Peter was trying to cut down the losses, and losing as many as a thousand railwaymen a month; but the overmanning was still heavy and passenger numbers were going down. He faced a bitter blow to his conciliatory policies in early 1982, when the engine drivers' union ASLEF embarked on a strike which exasperated public opinion and increased BR's loss by about £100 million; for the first time he seemed publicly to lose his cool. The ASLEF strike looked like an act of self-destruction in an industry that was already losing its custom, and the Conservatives pressed the case against further subsidies. Yet British Rail, like every European system, remained part of the social structure which no government could wholly ignore; to try to undermine its morale would only complicate its problems. To make it work would always depend on some kind of agreement between its managers, its unions and the government.

STEEL

It was Ian McGregor, who took over British Steel at its lowest ebb in June 1980, who had the most impact of any nationalised chairman. The stately steel headquarters overlooking Buckingham Palace had seen contrasting bosses over the previous ten years, oscillating in the British style between bankers and engineers—Lord Melchett the banker, Monty Finniston the engineer, Sir Charles Villiers the banker—while the unhappy industry was afflicted not only by domestic indecision but by a world producing far too much steel. When McGregor took over, British steel was beating even Leyland's record and losing £2 million a day.

[1] University of London: 'A New Industrial Policy', Stamp Memorial Lecture, London, 1977.
[2] *Ibid.*

McGregor was already a legend: a tough old Scots-American of sixty-seven with thin lips and a deadpan face like a block of granite, his funereal style seemed appropriate to the state of the industry. He was not only tough: he was both banker *and* engineer. He became a metallurgist at Edinburgh and later made a fortune as an industrialist and banker in America, until Sir Keith Joseph after much wooing persuaded him to come back to run British Steel. He and his partners in Lazards Bank in New York exacted a reward from the government which could earn him £2 million, a bargain which amazed American bankers as well as British politicians by its ruthlessness. The deal caused an uproar, but McGregor insists: 'It was a seven-day wonder. You need dedication and total personal sacrifice and you have to pay for results. I told my workers I was on a bonus system, and they felt they were getting a valuable property—like a centre-forward.'

McGregor moved into British Steel just after a strike had further worsened its international prospects (see chapter 4). As he described it to me at 8.15 one morning:

> The great secret was timing. The whole concern knew that something had to be done. I wouldn't have come here if I hadn't thought it could be turned round. I did some research and made an educated guess. When I came, I got rid of 80,000 people in one year. There was a lot of arm-waving and excitement, but we made sure we discussed it at the local level. The trouble about a hierarchical labour structure is that people at the top have a vested interest in amplifying the problem. So we had to get it back down where it belongs.

McGregor is a loner with no respect for hierarchies, and like Michael Edwardes at Leyland he has no English hang-ups about confronting the workers: 'When I arrived here I didn't belong to any group, I guess.' He works harder than any of his workers, identifying himself totally with the company and starting work before anyone else arrives. 'The difference between him and the bankers,' as one employee put it, 'is that we'd follow him over the top.' 'To run a business,' he explained to me, 'you must be the first out of the trenches and stand up to be counted. You've got to be thick-skinned and have stamina. I tell young men that it's a nice deal that we can all work together in harmony; but the world goes to people with a sense of individual competition.'

He was determined to by-pass top management and communicate directly: 'The trouble with hierarchies is that they amplify the problems as they go up ... I wear out a lot of shoe leather having seances and debates with the workers.' He quickly cut down the ponderous headquarters structure: 'I pushed management out of this building, de-centralising it into specialised markets. We're mov-

ing to Brixton with only 170 people at HQ. Arnold Weinstock's way
is the only way to run a business. You must give them a policy matrix
and expect them to develop their own solution.'

He had scarcely more respect for government, and having made
sure that he was allowed to perform drastic surgery he largely
ignored them: 'Governments aren't qualified to run any business
including their own. They can't produce a prompt decision-making
mechanism. The key to survival nowadays is to be able to adapt
immediately. But I don't get much interference from government. I
was lucky because steel was such a bad case that not too many people
in government wanted to be associated with it. And I don't have too
much trouble with the unions. When I warned that British Steel
could go bankrupt, they pointed out that the Steel Act made it
impossible. I said thanks for pointing it out, and changed the rules.
Now we *can* go bust.'

McGregor saw the world as a whole, and he was distressed by the
British insularity and backwardness: 'British Steel is now in good
shape with some wonderful people but it's tragic to use so much
unskilled labour: their Japanese equivalents are high school graduates. We have got to look for sophisticated solutions with new
technology and high wage patterns, like the Japanese. The British
trouble is that they can't weld together people with industrial
experience and with understanding of world financial markets.
We're not organised to run a sophisticated industrial competition.
People can't see the problems coming down the 'pike. Capital will
flow round the world from East to West, going back to the
East—where they make the effort to compete. Here we sit on our duff
and expect someone to bring things to us.'

McGregor had undoubtedly transformed the British steel industry, increasing its productivity and cutting its losses—though the
future still looked bleak in a world which still produced too much
steel. His version of state capitalism was more ruthless than that of
many private capitalists, but he could claim that there was no
alternative for an industry exposed to world competition. With his
elemental leadership he managed to keep the loyalty of his workers
even after sacking tens of thousands of them, and he had made the
connections between practical management and global markets
which few British industrialists had achieved. But his view of his role
had no room for the wider social responsibilities, and he left in his
wake long dole queues and desolate steel towns. It was a long way
from the old high custodians.

26

Multinational Corporations: the Global Market

For business purposes the boundaries that separate one nation from another are no more real than the equator.

Jacques Maisonrouge of IBM

NEARLY all British companies, whether private or nationalised, have found themselves operating in a more international context over the past decades, facing up to a new scale and pace of competition. But many of the most advanced industries are now in the hands of multinational corporations, whose vast resources have challenged not only local companies but national governments and institutions.

It was the American business invasion of Europe in the fifties and sixties which first raised these spectres. While the separate nations were tentatively trying to forge their European Community, the American companies from Cincinatti, Detroit or Armonk were selling and making their products as if frontiers did not exist, as if Europe were just like America, while instant communications enabled them to control and monitor their offshoots far more effectively than in earlier invasions. They created their own version of a Europe bound together by detergents, computers or cars.

Many Europeans began to fear that the success of the American multinationals—as they began to be called in the sixties—would lead to a new kind of technological hegemony as Jean-Jacques Servan-Schreiber warned in his book in 1967 *The American Challenge*. But the challenge was already producing a European response, as companies extended into the United States and elsewhere. By the seventies nearly all big British companies had acquired a base within the United States, and the contest between multinationals was part of the competition between the continents, including Japan.

Politicians were slow to perceive the significance of this global extension of corporate power, and during the sixties only a few economists and political scientists began to study it. Professor Ray Vernon of Harvard gave warning in 1967 that there would be a 'long and stormy period of transition' in relations between corporations and countries; and others discussed the 'global reach' and the 'coming clash' between these corporations and the old nation-state. Some heads of corporations began to see themselves as belonging to no nation or region: 'I have long dreamed of buying an island owned by no nation,' said Carl Gerstacker, chairman of Dow Chemicals, 'and of establishing the world headquarters of the Dow company on the truly neutral ground of such an island, beholden to no nation or society.' 'The international corporation,' said the American economist Charles Kindleberger, 'has no country to which it owes more loyalty than any other, nor any country where it feels completely at home.' Many corporations depicted themselves as by-passing the old national barriers that had caused wars and destruction, connecting up their workers and customers with a common interest in trade and prosperity.

But this rapid extension of business through the world—like the nineteenth-century extension through the continents—produced an inevitable reaction of national and local resentment. As the long boom and spectacular growth of the sixties subsided, followed by higher inflation and unemployment, so multinationals became bogies or scapegoats to the left all over Europe. In Britain the new left attacked them as unaccountable monsters, manipulating their prices and profits, evading taxation, running their own foreign policy or exploiting the Third World. Tony Benn saw the multinationals, together with the International Monetary Fund, as the instruments of the new imperialism: his experience as minister, he insists, 'convinced me of the colonial status which the multinationals have succeeded in imposing upon Britain'.[1]

The reaction was not just an irrational explosion, or part of Marxist dogma. It was based on a widespread resentment and fear that the nation was losing control over its destiny and that the levers of power were disappearing out of sight. The conflict between corporations and nations was a necessary one, for it was absurd for multinational executives to suggest that they could take over the role of running societies. But the angry national reactions throughout Europe produced many simplistic solutions. The global market-place could not easily be avoided by localised movements; and any effective countervailing power, to tame these new forces, would have to come from nations co-operating more closely with each other. The multinationals, with their global overview, their need to play coun-

[1] Tony Benn: *op cit*, p. 10.

tries against each other and their international expertise in tax-evasion, revealed all the limitations of national politicians trying to keep up with the scale of the world.

INDIVIDUALISM AND PERMANENCE

Have the great corporations become permanent world institutions, more permanent than some nations themselves? Many of them have achieved their centenaries over the past decade, and it was in 1870 that John D. Rockefeller set up his Standard Oil Company which was the prototype of many business bureaucracies that followed. 'The day of combination is here to stay,' he warned with brutal frankness. 'The age of individualism has gone, never to return.' And Rockefeller's company, after it was split up in 1911, produced offspring which now include three oil companies—Exxon (Esso), Mobil and Socal (Chevron)— which are among the biggest corporations in the world. Many nineteenth-century adventurers, such as Samuel Courtauld, Henri Deterding of Shell or William Lever of Unilever, built up very personal and often eccentric empires which later turned into impersonal institutions run by committees of managers. When Lever visited the Hebrides, he tried to help the Scots fishermen by setting up the company which became MacFisheries: the fish shops developed into a chain of supermarkets which soon sold almost everything except fish. These anonymous institutions with their hierarchies of managers and hundreds of thousands of shareholders seemed to run on their own momentum, like perpetual clocks, marking the victory of the managerial revolution against autocratic bosses and shareholders' control.

Many economists and historians now assumed that they had become permanent; and while the Third Reich and the Japanese Empire were liquidated, the corporations such as Krupp and Mitsubishi re-formed themselves from the ashes of war. 'Longevity is of the essence of corporations,' writes W. J. Reader, the historian of British multinationals, in his brief history of Unilever in 1980, 'and Unilever has the stuff of longevity in it. The East India companies of England and the Netherlands lasted a couple of centuries. There seems to be no reason, barring universal catastrophe, why Unilever, given competent management, should not last as long or a good deal longer.' [2] The same historian concludes his history of ICI: 'There is no reason inherent either in the economic system at large or in the nature of ICI itself why ICI, along with other large corporations, should not last for centuries. Indeed the probability is that

[2] W. J. Reader: *Fifty Years of Unilever*, Heinemann, London, 1980, p. 140.

it—and they—will, for the survival power of large and wealthy organisations, given moderately competent management, is great.' [3]

Certainly many of the giant corporations, as we will see, have shown themselves able to withstand the shocks of the last few years better than smaller and more national companies. The oil companies thrived on the price-increases which shattered many others, and Unilever comfortably survived the recession which killed off many smaller traders and shops. But the concept of permanence looks more questionable after the storms of the early eighties, as ICI and Courtaulds are still reeling from their ordeals: they will survive, but in a very different shape from that of five years ago. And the concept of the anonymous corporation now looks less convincing, whether in Britain or in America, as entrepreneurial drive reasserts itself inside corporations as well as outside, and as decentralised companies give more scope to individual leaders. Rockefeller's old prophecy—individualism has gone, never to return—has not yet been wholly fulfilled. Individual tycoons can still rapidly build up and dominate some of the biggest corporations, while once the tycoons leave them they can soon crumble apart. Some of the wonder-companies of the sixties were already disintegrating in the late seventies.

The most spectacular example had been the American multinational conglomerate, the International Telephone and Telegraphy Corporation (ITT) which under the despotic Harold Geneen had bought scores of other companies including Sheraton hotels, Avis cars and Levitt Houses, employing 400,000 people in 400 companies in eighty countries including Britain, where it owns the biggest telephone-makers (Standard Telephones and Cables). By 1972 ITT was the eighth biggest American company, and Geneen's inquisitorial methods were influencing many others. But the company's success was very fragile, depending on hectic juggling between its components: 'The ITT empire will prove impossible to hold together,' I wrote in a study of ITT in 1973, when the company was at its peak, 'without the drive and iron control of the master.'[4] Since then its performance has rapidly declined, and the present chief executive, Rand Araskog, has struggled to make sense of his intricate inheritance. By 1981 its return on capital was well below the average, and ITT had 'become an object of scorn and derision among Wall Street's analysts'.[5] The scattered provinces were increasingly difficult to control: 'If we are not having problems in Portugal,' said

[3] W. J. Reader: *Imperial Chemical Industries, A History*, vol 2, Oxford University Press, 1975, p. 472.

[4] Anthony Sampson: *The Sovereign State*, Hodder and Stoughton, London, 1973.

[5] John Thackray in *Management Today*, July 1981.

Araskog, 'we are in Brazil. And if it's not Brazil it's Spain. and if it's not Spain it's in insurance . . . we are too big to be understood: we operate in too many countries, we are too many businesses to be comprehended easily. I just don't think the analysts see us as an exciting company.' The crumbling empire gave its own warning of the dangers of over-concentration: 'Just how many other corporate structures and systems,' asked John Thackray, 'allegedly rational and rationalised, are in reality as whimsical and autocratic as ITT's?' [6]

The biggest thirty companies in Britain (see page 343) include five subsidiaries of foreign multinationals including the two oil giants, Exxon and Texaco controlled from New York, and the Ford company controlled from Detroit. They also include several British-owned multinationals with large interests abroad, including the tobacco companies Bats and Imps (see chapter 21). But the most practised multinationals over the last fifty years have been the famous trio of British Petroleum, Shell and Unilever, which have been competing for international markets across frontiers.

BP AND SHELL

The two giant oil companies, BP and Shell, tower above all other British corporations, whether rated by turnover, capital or profits; and they have provoked the most controversy about the nature of their multinational power. The global oil corporations—the 'Seven Sisters' whose history I have written elsewhere[7]—were virtually the first of the multinationals, as they stretched across the world in the early twentieth century providing the new fuel for cars, ships, and industry. In the United States the Rockefeller monopoly provided an early target for populist attacks. But the British companies which found their oil overseas were at first much less politically exposed, and they adopted the style of a junior (though richer) foreign service as if they were hardly interested in vulgar profits.

It was not until the seventies that they were more obviously in conflict with British governments and more politically vulnerable, through three separate developments—the discovery of oil in the North Sea, the energy crisis of 1973, and the evasion of oil sanctions against Rhodesia. The higher oil price and the North Sea bonanza added to the wealth of the oil companies compared to other industries, and the gap was widened by the recession.

It was the world oil shortage precipitated by the Arab embargo in 1973 which suddenly illuminated the divergence of interests between

[6] *Management Today*, July 1981.
[7] Anthony Sampson: *The Seven Sisters*, Hodder and Stoughton, London, 1975.

the companies and governments—more dramatically in Britain than elsewhere. Ted Heath, who was already faced with a coal miners' strike, was determined that Britain should not suffer from the embargo and summoned the heads of the two companies, Frank McFadzean of Shell and Sir Eric Drake of BP, to a stormy encounter at Chequers. Heath insisted that they must not cut their supplies to Britain, but both oilmen replied that they would risk expropriation abroad if they did not treat all their customers equally fairly. Heath reminded Sir Eric that BP was half-owned by the British government, but BP had already taken legal advice and Sir Eric asked for written instructions specifying which foreign countries should suffer. Heath had to give way and the oil companies had made their point: whoever owned them, they were engaged in a multinational trade where all their customers in a crisis must suffer 'equal misery'.[8]

The defiance of Heath showed one aspect of the oil companies' supranational role; the defiance of oil sanctions to Rhodesia showed up the darker side, throwing a sidelight on the relationships between oil executives and British civil servants. Harold Wilson announced sanctions against the white rebels in Rhodesia in 1965 with his own element of half-heartedness; but the oil companies had no intention of obeying. The then British head of Shell, Sir Frank McFadzean (now Lord McFadzean) was a right-wing conservative who was pressing for better relations with South Africa, including the resumption of arms sales. Like other multinationals, Shell could appear at one moment as a centralised colossus, the next moment as a loose group of local companies; and it now looked its loosest, with its Mozambique company smuggling oil to Rhodesia while the British navy was imposing an oil blockade. Oil executives, civil servants and ministers connived to deceive parliament and the public about the 'swap' with the French company Total which was frustrating sanctions, and the companies were invaluable allies to both Rhodesia and South Africa, which was being threatened by OPEC sanctions. 'There can be no greater blessing for South Africa,' the Johannesburg *Financial Mail* explained in 1973, 'apart from the fact that Iran is well disposed, than that the oil business is still largely in the hands of international companies with no discernible leanings of excessive patriotism.'

BP, half-owned by the government, showed no closer concern for British policy than Shell; its two 'government directors' had no wish to investigate until Tom Jackson of the Post Office union, who took his duty more seriously, was appointed in 1975. BP in South Africa still concealed a 'swap' arrangement to let oil into Rhodesia; when the *Sunday Times* revealed in October 1978 that BP, in spite of

[8] *Ibid*, p.263.

previous promises, was *still* letting oil get through, BP's chairman Sir David Steel immediately denied it as 'offensive and defamatory', before sending out investigators who confirmed that the allegations were true.

It was only after years of patient investigation by two freelance reporters, Martin Bailey and Bernard Rivers, that the government commissioned a full-scale enquiry by the QC Thomas Bingham (now the judge, Sir Thomas Bingham), whose subsequent report was able—partly helped by the accidental discovery of secret papers—to confirm the allegations in detail.[9] The 'oilgate' scandal revealed not only the companies' lack of patriotic or moral scruples, but a capacity for consistent deception which, like a clock striking thirteen, made them harder to believe on other questions.

The discovery of North Sea oil caused more commercial tensions between companies and the government. The exploration was a triumph for the geologists and engineers, but the companies were at least as skilled in evading taxes as in discovering oil, and they were all playing a long poker game with the government for high stakes, as they belittled the extent of the North Sea reserves and threatened to take their drillers elsewhere. Britain was now on the receiving end of the kind of rough treatment which had embittered the Arabs in earlier decades, and the Labour government eventually set up its own British National Oil Corporation to monitor the companies and their profits. The companies were still paying very low taxes: in 1979 Lord Kearton, then chairman of BNOC, revealed that BP had made a profit of a billion pounds on one oil-field alone, on which they paid taxes of only 18 per cent. The oil companies, he warned, 'don't like having an informed government'. They were making these huge profits while most other British companies were struggling to export in the gathering recession—and when the pound was being driven up by Britain's oil. But since then the tax-take has rapidly gone up, while the oil-price has fluctuated uncertainly.

The two giants in the meantime had undergone their own internal transformations. BP was now barely recognisable as a half-nationalised company: the monster had escaped from its Frankenstein, and abroad it played down the fact that the initials stood for *British* Petroleum. It had lost valuable concessions in Iran and Nigeria, but it had found oil in Alaska and had bought the American company Sohio to distribute it. BP had become more flexible and pragmatic since the days of its commercial imperialists such as the first Lord Strathalmond and Sir Eric Drake. Its new chairman in 1981, Peter Walters, is an unpretentious technocrat with a down-to-earth style who took a commercial degree at Birmingham Uni-

[9] See Martin Bailey: *Oilgate*, Coronet, London, 1979.

versity and who sees himself as one of a new professional generation of players after the generations of gentlemen. He is well aware that BP is politically vulnerable, as a rich corporation with inherited wealth surrounded by ailing industries, and he has developed his political antennae. He wanted to extend BP into other kinds of energy and other industries, as they did in 1980 when they bought up the huge mining company, Selection Trust. But by 1982, faced with a lower oil-price and higher British taxes, he was having to cut back and sell off subsidiaries to make a leaner company.

Shell was always more thoroughly multinational than BP, with an Anglo-Dutch ownership and polyglot shareholders which made it the most globally-minded of all the Sisters. The Rhodesia scandal had shown how little respect it could show for governments when they got in its way: 'Arrogantly asserting power,' (as Harold Wilson complained), 'with scant regard for responsibility.' [10] Its corporate history had helped to give it a split personality. Its formative years were dominated by a brigand of genius Sir Henri Deterding, a Dutch bookkeeper from the East Indies who turned the little 'Royal Dutch' company into the dominating partner with the English Shell. But Deterding ended up a megalomaniac and a convinced Nazi, and the company now tries to bury his memory: no biography has been written, no records revealed. Shell was determined to appear totally respectable, run by committees of Oxbridge graduates and Dutch engineers, with a dignified style as if it were part of Whitehall. But Deterding's ghost still flits through the corridors, to remind it of its old entrepreneurial past, and as Shell now becomes more competitive its profit-motive looms larger.

Shell is now run by a committee of eight managing directors —three British, three Dutch, one American and one French— who divide the oil world between them. The British vice-chairman, Sir Peter Baxendell, is a petroleum engineer from Liverpool who, like most of Shell's top men, has become internationalised by his postings round the world, including Egypt, Venezuela and Nigeria, giving him an instinctive awareness of the political hazards of oil. The Eight Men of Shell have relinquished much of their centralised control over their separate operating companies in each country, including Shell UK which is run from Shell-Mex House and which has control over North Sea oil: people in Shell UK talk about Shell Centre across the river as if it were a distant foreign power. 'The political strains became more serious after 1973,' Baxendell explained to me, 'when energy became so much more politically sensitive: we couldn't tell the heads of the operating companies that they had to take Saudi crude oil from Saudi Arabia; they had to

[10] Hansard, November 7, 1978.

buy from where they wanted, to be able to look their own governments in the eye. So what's left at the centre? Partly we're a kind of
friendly merchant bank—we try to be friendly—but we've also got
the expertise on tap for any Shell company that wants it.'

UNILEVER

Unilever, the third of the multinational trio, was a bilingual child,
with Anglo-Dutch parents, and with the same kind of strains and
jealousies. It too lives in the shadow of a dominant founder, the great
soap-seller William Lever who realised the crucial role of advertising
which the company could never forget (on which they now spend
£350 million a year). But Unilever could never be as self-important
as the oil companies in its homely business as the world's grocers
—selling products from Surf to Wall's Ice Cream, from Birds Eye
frozen foods to Stork margarine. Their business depends on both
innovation and marketing, operating between the consumer and the
laboratory; and their chairmen have oscillated between traders and
scientists. Lord Cole the trader was succeeded by Ernest Woodroofe
the scientist, succeeded by Sir David Orr the trader and then in 1982
by Kenneth Durham the scientist.

Unilever has suffered its own shocks of identity in the world
market-place. It had always prided itself on being sensitive to the
diversity of European national tastes; but in the sixties the American
company Procter and Gamble from Cincinnatti began sweeping
through Europe with their victorious army led by the wonder-
detergent Daz. Procter's hardly noticed the European diversity but
they had dynamic salesmen with shrewd marketing methods who
soon sliced off a chunk of the European markets. Painfully and
discreetly Unilever had to respond by centralising their national
managements with 'co-ordinators' who were really headquarters
bosses. They fought back with new products and tougher salesmanship, taking the battle on to the Americans' home ground; in 1978
they advanced further into the United States, when they bought the
National Starch company for $485 million (a facsimile of the cheque
decorates the drawing-room of the financial director Cob Stenham).
But the European Community is still the company's main
battlefield, accounting for 60 per cent of its turnover: it used to be
known as the 'seventh member' of the Common Market, and it
remains a large influence in any negotiation about food.

With its range of essential household products and foods, Unilever
has suffered less from the recession than most; but like nearly every
other big corporation it has become more ruthless in cutting down its
staff; and the current chairman of its British end, Kenneth

Durham, made his reputation as an axe-man. He is a physicist who came up by the Redbrick route, through grammar school at Black-burn and Manchester University, to become a researcher in Unilever laboratories; but he showed his business toughness when he merged two subsidiaries making animal feeds, thus offloading many staff: 'You can't expect to be loved if you hack away a group by a factor of two.' [11] He soon showed his value in cutting the workforce, and four years ago joined the 'special committee' which rules Unilever. His colleagues see him as a more intellectual and colder man than his Irish predecessor Sir David Orr, and he promises to dispose of subsidiaries which cannot be made profitable. But as a scientist he is determined to improve Unilever's record for innova-tion, and to penetrate further into the American markets which offer the real future prize. As with so many British companies, the scope for increasing profits and jobs within Britain is very limited.

THE NEW NOMADS

Do the multinational managers have any real nationality? Cer-tainly many of them have been caught up in a restless global mobility which was unimagined thirty years ago, flying between continents and spending only a few days or even hours in one capital after another. Many of the senior men will change their home base from one country to another every few years; for 'One cannot run a multinational corporation,' as Sir David Orr said, 'with managers all of whose experience has been in a single country.' Every am-bitious executive knows that his road will be a spiral, circling round the world as he climbs.

The nomadic existence is a constant source of airport jokes: IBM, they say, stands for 'I've Been Moved'; ITT means 'International Travel and Talk'. They compete with stories about their instant mobility: flying from London to New York and back in a day, just for a lunch; having a conference in Rome airport, without bothering to go into the city; keeping a spare wardrobe in Rotterdam; having a watch which shows both London and New York time. The briefcase, passport and credit cards are the symbols of *machismo*, a constant threat to wives who can make no confident plans. The multinational milieu remains defiantly male; and the drive depends, like that of a regiment, on separating men from their families.

The Shellocrats, IBM-ers or Unilever people might well seem more devoted to their company than their country, and much of their habitat seems to belong to no nation. The Intercontinentals, Hiltons or Inns on the Park appear interchangeable; the company country

[11] *Financial Times*, May 26, 1982.

clubs or conference centres are neatly segregated from the real countryside; Brussels, the headquarters for so many multinationals, remains a city without a country. As these Flying Dutchmen encircle the globe, they seem to become more closely bound to the company which holds them together, as they are met by the company chauffeur with a company car, taken to the company club for company talks. The cards which officials hold up at the airports to greet their visitors, proclaiming IBM, BOC or BP in the midst of the incomprehensible local script, are the cards of identity which make their world safe. Are they becoming company men first, fellow-countrymen second? 'You can already envision a time,' promises Roy Amara, the president of the Institute of the Future, 'when allegiance to the company may be more important than to the state.'

Certainly during two world wars the nationality of these corporations has been very uncertain. In 1942 ITT's German subsidiary was making Focke-Wulf bombers while its American and British companies were working for the allies; Exxon in New York maintained an agreement with the IG Farben company in Germany which Harry Truman (then a Senator) branded as treason. But in the contemporary European scene these corporations can claim that their lack of a single patriotism confers great benefits, as they bring together nationalities in a common peaceful purpose, helping to build a world society in which frontiers are no longer relevant and wars are unthinkable. Many of their executives and allies have seen themselves overcoming the primitive forces of nationalism and petty squabbles of parliaments, as they forge a more rational context for global prosperity and behaviour. Cabinet ministers are glad to see the heads of corporations, and may even look forward to joining their boards when they lose office; and the great chairmen such as Clifton Garvin of Exxon will expect to be received at Ten Downing Street. 'What strikes me about politicians,' said the head of one British oil company, 'is their irrelevance. They talk as if they were responsible for higher standards of living, and as if they can deal with the recession, and they end up believing their own rhetoric.'

Certainly these corporate groups are more cosmopolitan and integrated than most comparable European professions—whether university dons, scientists or politicians. The process of *engrenage* or intermeshing, which Jean Monnet saw as so crucial to 'making Europe', is more evident in company headquarters than in parliaments or the Council of Ministers; and as the executives speak the same Americanised and Germanised English and management jargon, it is hard to tell which is Italian, German or Swedish. The foreign-based corporations are constantly undermining the old concepts of commercial patriotism, as they buy up British firms, or lure

British salesmen to sell Japanese cameras or German cars. Perhaps the pursuit of corporate profits has provided more incentive to integrate nationalities than the higher ideals of a unified Europe. Certainly many executives would claim that their ambitions, generating trade, technology and a higher living standard, were much more peaceful and constructive than those of national politicians, and some would go much further: 'The larger corporations,' said Harold Geneen, the former head of ITT, 'have become the custodians of making our entire system work.'

But the obsequies for the nation-state have been premature; for whatever benefits the corporations confer they can never provide the security, welfare and stable environment which governments and communities offer. The more dynamic and adaptable the corporation, the less it can promise ultimate security for its employees—still less when it is forced to cut down in the face of a recession. The faster the executives are whirled round the world, the more they seek a firm base to give them a centre: however cosmopolitan they may seem in foreign capitals, most of them have few doubts as to which country they will choose to retire in. So long as the nation remains the dispenser of welfare, the guarantor of defence and the collector of taxes, it is likely to be indispensable to its citizens and their sense of identity. The conflict will continue between the interests of the nation and of the multinational—between the protective and the aggressive, the secure and the insecure, the social and commercial.

Behind their global rhetoric most corporations remain much more nationally based than they like to pretend. The Nestlé chocolate-and-food company looks British in Britain, American in America, German in Germany; but at its headquarters in Vevey only the Swiss can hold the controlling shares. IBM World Trade has a polyglot international board, headed by a thoroughly Americanised Frenchman, Jacques Maisonrouge; but at Armonk—the white palace outside New York which controls the corporation—there is no nonsense about foreigners being in control. There are only a few cases, such as Shell or Unilever, of very big companies which divide effective control between two or more nationalities; and they need their home governments more than they like to admit. The big British corporations such as BP and Imperial Chemicals play down the patriotism which is implicit in their names; but they are headed by British chairmen and British directors and they depend on their government's support in their critical negotiations.

Fifteen years ago, in the high tide of expansion, many experts predicted that the global corporations would become increasingly internationalised and detached from any single country. Some enthusiasts were putting forward proposals for a new supranational law which would mean, as George Ball put it, 'that world corporations would quite literally become citizens of the world'. Professor Howard Perlmutter, the prophet of multinationals in Geneva, was predicting that by 1988 three hundred giant companies would dominate world business, and that it would be the 'geocentric' corporations, such as Shell or IBM, which could ignore frontiers to become increasingly mobile and stateless, which would prosper more than the 'ethnocentric' corporations such as airlines or steel companies.[12] It is true that the gap has widened between the global giants—particularly the oil companies—and the more earthbound companies making steel, cars or food. But in the more competitive and perilous world of the eighties, as Western manufacturers try to fight back against the competition from the Far East, the triumph of the geocentric corporations seems much less certain; for as companies seek protection and special support they look once again towards their national homes, while the governments which looked largely irrelevant in good times begin to look less dispensable in bad.

[12] See Anthony Sampson: *The New Europeans*, Hodder and Stoughton, London, 1978, pp. 85–6.

27

The Press: the World and the Street

Seven multinational companies or wealthy families own all the mass
circulation newspapers in Britain. Generally speaking, they use their
papers to campaign single-mindedly in defence of their commercial
interests and the political policies which will protect them.

Tony Benn, 1981 [1]

WHAT was the British public to make of the scale and intensity of the
world competition which was hitting so many institutions, and
undermining so many communities and jobs? It had not only transformed the character of companies and services; it had changed the
whole context of Britain's challenge. The stage was no longer just
Britain or Europe but most of the world, as Japan and the Far East
set the new pace in advanced industries as well as traditional ones.

In the earlier expansions in the nineteenth century, when Britain
was still the dominant industrial nation, British workers or even
managers had found it hard enough to comprehend the widening
context; but now, when strange new nations were competing with
devastating results, it was much more difficult to grasp. Whole
factories and districts were being closed down as a result of competition from Korean textiles or Japanese electronics while British workers did not realise what had hit them. Britain had slowly become
accustomed to the threat of cut-price imports produced by cheap
labour in the Far East; now the British were the cheap labour in
out-of-date plants, compared to the Japanese working in the
advanced industries of the future. Yet Japan remained the unknown
'upside-down' country, better known as the home of Madam But-
terfly, the Mikado or grinning little soldiers than as the pioneer of
information technology and video recorders.[2]

The public could only become aware of these forces through the

---

[1] Tony Benn: *Arguments for Democracy*, Jonathan Cape, London, 1981, p. 103.
[2] For a historical study of Japanese stereotypes see Endymion Wilkinson: *Misunderstanding*,
Chuokoran-Shan, Tokyo, 1981.

media, which served as their focus for the changing world. But for all their variety and pervasiveness the media had their own kinds of myopia. British newspapers had long taken pride in their diversity and outspokenness, but they were themselves now becoming deeply intermeshed in the process of concentration, commercialisation and conglomeration. As they became interlocked with other industries they had growing doubts about their true role.

Was the Press just another competitive industry giving the consumer what he wanted, selling papers instead of soap or computers? Was it an extension of parliament and the political scene? Was it a receptacle for advertising, providing just enough news and entertainment to make the advertisements credible? Or was it a hidden annexe to other industries, a means of political pressure and manipulation of public opinion, concealed behind traditional façades? The questions became more worrying to many journalists, including this one, as they found themselves with new kinds of owners whose motives and ambitions were very unclear, while their task of honestly explaining the world became increasingly difficult.

But newspapers also had their own ways of frustrating big business. For in Fleet Street the tangible success of money and manufacture collides with the more nebulous values of politics, prestige, entertainment or fame. Vain entrepreneurs are confronted by intransigent newspapers, and money can be turned into either status or humiliation. Most national newspapers have long ceased to be profitable, but they have each set themselves up as spokesmen for the people and as part of the social fabric, each with their own stately mystique or cheeky irreverence, with Gothic headings or standardised shrieks. They still attracted rich men to buy them in search of recognition, amusement or political influence.

Twenty years ago British newspapers could still look like fixed institutions with stable if eccentric hereditary owners. The biggest popular groups were controlled by Lord Northcliffe's rival nephews, Cecil King and Lord Rothermere, and by Lord Beaverbrook and his son. *The Times* and the *Observer* were owned by Astor cousins; the *Telegraph* was controlled by the Berry family; the *Financial Times* by the Pearsons; the *News of the World* by the Carrs. Most of them seemed to belong to the political stage more than the commercial market-place, and only the *Sunday Times* had acquired (in 1959) a more single-minded money-maker, Roy Thomson. But Fleet Street today is much more obviously insecure; several of its newspapers have changed owners once or twice in two decades, and few can be confident about who will own them in ten years' time. Overleaf are the ten national daily newspapers and the seven Sunday newspapers with their chairmen or owners.

NATIONAL NEWSPAPERS IN 1961 AND 1981

(average circulations, July–December)

Daily	1981	1961
Sun (Rupert Murdoch)	4,136,927	1,394,919 (Herald)
Daily Mirror (Reed International)	3,413,785	4,561,876
Daily Express (Lord Matthews)	2,126,248	4,328,524
Daily Mail (Lord Rothermere)	1,887,051	2,610,487
Daily Star (Lord Matthews)	1,508,000	—
Daily Sketch (Lord Rothermere)	—	981,698
Daily Telegraph (Lord Hartwell)	1,342,007	1,248,961
The Guardian (Guardian Trust)	397,708	245,046
The Times (Rupert Murdoch)	297,787	253,441
Financial Times (Pearson Group)	197,742	132,928

Sunday		
News of the World (Rupert Murdoch)	4,236,715	6,643,287
Sunday Mirror (Reed International)	3,786,454	5,306,246
The People (Reed International)	3,629,687	5,450,727
Sunday Express (Lord Matthews)	2,993,763	4,457,528
Sunday Times (Rupert Murdoch)	1,363,640	994,459
Sunday Telegraph (Lord Hartwell)	916,644	700,000
The Observer (Tiny Rowland)	886,985	725,835
Reynolds News (Co-operative Press)	—	310,369

The costs of running a national newspaper were now beyond the resources of even the richest families, and their machine-rooms had become caricatures of Britain's industrial problems: the unions were more anarchic, the owners more flamboyant and the employees more defiant. Earlier Press barons in their haste to overtake each other had given their printers and casual workers virtual control over the presses, winking at 'old Spanish customs' and 'ghost workers'. The printers who belonged to the oldest industry were also the most resistant to change, and while newspapers in North America or the Far East were being tapped out on video-screens and made up photographically, Fleet Street was still full of clanking linotype machines and hot metal. Newspapers became much less profitable, and in 1981 the total turnover of £900 million produced profits of only £8 million—which were more than accounted for by a single newspaper, the *Sun*.

Yet in spite of huge losses and frustrations London only lost one morning and one evening paper (the *Sketch* and the *Evening News*) over twenty years and gained one (the *Daily Star*): it lost one Sunday paper (the *Sunday Citizen*, formerly *Reynolds News*) and gained one (the *Mail on Sunday*). Newspapers changed less drastically than the contrasts of owners might suggest, and Britain still had a variety of competing papers which few countries could rival. (American papers could claim to be classless and to cater for all groups, but they had local monopolies, like British provincial papers: Fleet Street reflected different classes and tastes, and offered more extremes from top to bottom.) The unions often seemed intent on bleeding British newspapers to death, but they always stopped short of taking the fatal last drop; while a rich new owner might still appear at the last moment to rescue a dying paper.

Had they become institutions like country estates which kept values and customs of their own as proprietors came and went? Were they taking part in an extravagant national folly, a last fling at a casino which was going out of business? Or were they pawns in a different kind of global political game which they themselves could only dimly understand? It was true, as Tony Benn said, that the British Press was owned by seven multinationals and rich families; but the effects of ownership were more complicated and interesting than promoting a 'single-minded campaign'.

THE POPULARS

It is the mass newspapers which have produced the huge financial prizes in the past, providing challenges to outsiders who can capture readers by breaking through the tribal taboos. Ever since the brilliant Irishman Alfred Harmsworth first invented the popular press with the *Daily Mail*, Fleet Street has seen successive replays of an old comedy: a newspaper owner makes a fortune from popular journalism, and then becomes more interested in politics or a peerage than in his readers; then a new intruder undercuts his forerunner with new sensationalism, only to follow the same course himself. Thus Lord Beaverbrook undermined Northcliffe's heir Lord Rothermere; thus Cecil King outflanked Beaverbrook; thus Murdoch undermined Cudlipp; and thus Matthews now challenges Murdoch. Each new challenger revealed that British readers were less literate and sophisticated than his predecessor reckoned. 'No one ever lost money,' said the American journalist H. L. Mencken, 'by underestimating the intelligence of the American public.' British mass-newspaper owners took an even lower view of their readers than Americans, without losing money.

The *Daily Mail* remains remarkably stable, in the middle of the market; the paper which Harmsworth (later Lord Northcliffe) founded in 1900 is still owned by his great-nephew Lord Rothermere. 'The policies of the *Daily Mail*,' he said in 1974, 'have remained unchanged for seventy years . . . our newspaper has been consistently to the right of centre and liberal conservative for all of its existence.' It is now part of a corporation which includes property, North Sea oil and Australian television and its policies are not visibly influenced by its owner. For the last eleven years it has kept the same editor, David English, who has kept up a provocative style, including union-bashing and sporadic jingoism, which has helped to maintain its circulation.

But the supremacy of its old rival the *Daily Express* came and went with its dominating owner Lord Beaverbrook: when his son Max Aitken could not maintain it the trustees sold it in 1977 to Trafalgar House, the property company built up by Nigel Broackes which had earlier bought Cunard and later the Ritz. ('I bought the *Express*,' Broackes told me, 'because the institutions wanted me to buy *something* after I had failed to get Bowater.') Broackes was assumed to be hoping for prestige and a peerage, but it was his cockney henchman Victor Matthews who moved into Fleet Street. Matthews was appalled by the extravagance and hostility inside the black glass building, and by the lack of respect for the boss: 'I love publishing less now than when I first came into it,' he said a year later, 'because I can see the unrealities.' But he saw the chance to use his Manchester presses to produce a new downmarket tabloid, the *Daily Star* (not to be confused with the communist *Morning Star*), which soon began seriously threatening Murdoch's *Sun*. Broackes still felt frustrated by his newspapers: 'I haven't lost money but I haven't made much,' he told me in 1982. 'There's an absence of gratification.' And he could not even prevent them from attacking his friends. By 1982 he had put the newspapers into a separate company, and was expected to sell them off. It was Matthews, not Broackes, who collected the traditional owner's reward: in the 1979 election the *Express* and *Sunday Express* were unswerving in their support for Margaret Thatcher, and soon afterwards (with unprecedented speed) Mr Matthews was Lord Matthews.

THE MIRROR

It was the *Daily Mirror* which showed the dangers of overestimating the public's intelligence. In the early sixties the tabloid seemed unassailable, with a circulation which went over five million (the world's biggest outside Russia and Japan). Its editors, led by Hugh Cudlipp, became closely involved in the Labour party, rewarded by the creation of four Mirror peerages (Cudlipp, Jacobson, Ardwick and Birk—although the chairman Cecil King refused one). But they were losing their magic touch with their readers, and began adding educational features and long editorials addressed to the government. When in 1964 Cudlipp launched the new *Sun* out of the ashes of the old *Daily Herald*, he looked forward to a new classless readership who would enjoy political columnists and highbrow reviewers rather than sex scandals and showbiz. But the *Sun* never rose very high, and the *Mirror* editors were too engrossed in their own politics and ambitions to perceive a new danger.

It was only in 1968 that the Australian invader Rupert Murdoch at the age of thirty-seven first gained a tenuous foothold in Britain, through an ironic turn of events. The owners of the salacious *News of the World*, the golf-playing Carrs, were appalled when the Czech-born tycoon Robert Maxwell (see chapter 22) tried to buy a large block of shares, and were determined to preserve its national character, 'as British as roast beef', as their editor called it. To forestall the dreaded foreigner they welcomed Murdoch as a co-owner. But they had invited the fox into the chicken coop. Within a year Murdoch had got rid of the chairman, sacked the editor and put up the paper's circulation by eight hundred thousand.

Murdoch had all the uninhibited drive of the aggressive invader. He was not really an outsider: his father, Sir Keith, was an Australian newspaper editor and his mother, Dame Elisabeth, who still lives in Australia, is a patron of the Melbourne Art Gallery and a children's hospital. But Rupert was not born rich, and with his limitless aggression he was determined not just to edit papers but control them. At Oxford he learnt enough about Britain's snobberies and flabbiness, and in Australia he discovered how to sell papers with sex and scandal. Having jazzed up the *News of the World* he saw an amazing new chance when the Mirror Group was foolishly trying to sell its sinking *Sun*, whose sales had dropped to below a million. Murdoch bought it, made a tough deal with the unions, turned it speedily into a sexy tabloid and doubled its sales in eighteen months, quickly threatening the group which had sold it to him. The *Mirror* belatedly fought back with more pin-ups but Murdoch was much more resourceful: by the mid-seventies the *Sun* had Britain's biggest daily circulation, while the Mirror Group faced continuing financial problems. Already by 1970 it had to merge with the Reed paper group, as part of a conglomerate including newsprint, paints, wallpapers and property, and the *Mirror* would never be so confident again.

Murdoch never stayed long in London, and he realised that his simple secret, of never overestimating the public taste, was applicable elsewhere. In 1973 he bought two papers in Texas and the next year launched an American scandal sheet, the *National Star*. Then he bought the *New York Post,* driving it downmarket in a deadly battle with the *Daily News*, and followed by capturing *New York* magazine.

He flew between three continents, hiring and firing editors, salesmen or photographers, cheerfully giving ultimata to union leaders. He had, he said, newspapers in his blood; but he soon had other business in his blood which excited him as much. He could use his papers to further his political and commercial ambitions, extending his Australian interests to casinos, television, airlines and oil, supporting both Reagan in America and Thatcher in Britain. He knew how to make the connections between (for instance) supporting a president in Washington and getting subsidies for aircraft in Australia.

But his success in Britain was now being challenged by a new outsider. When in 1978 Victor Matthews of the *Express* first launched his northern tabloid the *Star* it was selling less than a million, and hardly bothered the *Sun*; but in late 1980 the *Star* hit on a brilliant new promotion, linking the paper to bingo with weekly prizes going up to £30,000. By June 1981 it was putting on 100,000 sales a month and threatening the *Sun* which was already worried by a revival of the *Mirror*. Murdoch swiftly responded by cutting the *Sun*'s price and launching his own bingo; the *Mirror* followed suit and even the *Mail* started its own upmarket version called Casino. The popular papers were now competing in a war of attrition which was eating into all their profits, and Murdoch was seeing the dangers of exploring the bottom of the market: that there were always new depths to be found.

But the *Sun* was now on its mettle, and as other Murdoch properties in three continents were losing millions the viability of the whole empire rested on this single absurd newspaper. When the Falklands crisis broke on Britain in April 1982 the *Sun* soon discovered a new bottom. It quickly turned from bingo to jingo, outbidding every paper in the crudity of its war fever and contempt for the 'Argies': it sponsored a missile, on which its reporter with the task force wrote 'Up Yours, Galtieri'; when the Argentine cruiser the *General Belgrano* was sunk it carried the headline 'GOTCHA!' followed by 'UP YOUR JUNTA!' After Mrs Thatcher complained about newspapers being too sympathetic to Argentina the *Sun* took up its own campaign against the *Guardian* and still more the *Mirror*: 'What is it but treason for this timorous, whining publication to plead day after day for appeasing the Argentine dictators because they do not believe the British people have the stomach for a fight and are instead prepared to trade peace for honour?'

It was finally too much for the *Mirror*, which burst out into its own diatribe against the *Sun*. 'There have been lying newspapers before. But in the past month it has broken all records. It has long been a tawdry newspaper. But since the Falklands it has fallen from the gutter to the sewer . . . the *Daily Mirror* does not believe that patriotism had to be proved in blood. Especially someone else's blood . . . the *Sun* is the harlot of Fleet Street.'

THE QUALITIES

The gap between the top and bottom was getting wider and newspapers were both reflecting and magnifying British class distinctions. In the fifties the *Express* and the *Mail* seemed to be spanning part of the gulf, but by the seventies the *Mail* was almost the last bridge. The contrasts between newspapers are more extreme than between clothes or shops, with the *Sun* as defiantly proletarian as the *Telegraph* is middle-class—though the Sunday 'qualipops' offer more social mobility. The class distinction is hardened by advertisers who discriminate strictly (as they cannot on television) between 'AB' readers who might go to Harrods and 'CDE' readers who go to Tesco; and there is no newspaper equivalent to classless shops such as Sainsbury. It was true that over twenty years, as the chart shows, all the popular papers except the *Sun* had lost huge numbers of readers, while all the quality papers had added some, but the extra three million readers of the *Sun* had their own message. Fleet Street puts up its own barriers, and tabloid journalists mock the lofty pomposities of the 'unpopulars', while 'posh' journalists blame tabloids for their readers' tastes.

Three serious papers have maintained their independent ownership with the help of well-defined readers. The *Daily Telegraph* is still privately owned by Lord Hartwell and his family, and sticks to the staid tradition which his father Lord Camrose (the son of an estate agent in Merthyr Tydfil) bought in 1928. It still purveys foreign despatches and sex scandals in the same deadpan style, and still scarcely wavers in its Tory loyalty. Its circulation has remained fairly steady over twenty years, and it makes enough profits to carry the losses of the *Sunday Telegraph*. Its success remains a monument to the continuing conservatism of the British middle-class.

Another secure peak is occupied by the *Financial Times*, the bankers' paper which is only one branch of the widely-spread conglomerate controlled by the Pearson family, who also own Lazards Bank (see chapter 18) and half the *Economist*. The pink pages of the *FT* give a wider view of the world than its American rival the *Wall Street Journal*, including civilised articles about arts, gardening or wine. But with its banking connections it is more reluctant than the *WSJ* to reveal the seamier side of finance and has never taken the lead in exposing crooked financiers: it reflects the defensiveness as well as the leisureliness of the City compared to Wall Street. Its virtual monopoly of financial readers has given it a special hold on advertisers, which makes it more secure than its broader rivals.

The *Guardian* has the most heroic continuity as a less commercially motivated paper still owned by the trust set up by the Scott family who first established it in Manchester. Its character has remained unmistakable, with a strong emphasis on liberal causes, women's problems and the Third World, and a tendency towards prolixity and complacency, while its loyal readers and contributors reinforce its clubbiness. It staved off financial crises, and a threatened merger with *The Times*, by cutting salaries and costs and it is more economically run than the papers owned by tycoons; by 1982 its circulation of around 400,000 was ahead of *The Times* by 100,000. It has just survived with the help of its profitable sister the *Manchester Evening News*, but it remains vulnerable to competition from richer rivals. It still represents a formidable British tradition of dissent, linked both to old Liberals and new Social Democrats, for whom it provides a kind of house-magazine.

These three newspapers still remained relatively stable, consistent and British-owned. But the other quality papers were making losses which left them much more vulnerable: and any new owner had both to be very rich, and to have motives other than pure money-making. In the old days Press barons were attacked for making large profits out of their newspapers. Today there is more suspicion about owners who are prepared to take heavy losses.

THE TIMES

The Times had long ago provided an elegant booby-trap for unwary millionaires, to devour their money while frustrating their ambitions. Lord Northcliffe who bought it in 1908 was exasperated by the 'Black Friars' as he called its portentous leader writers, and suggested writing over the entrance: 'Abandon Scope All You Who Enter Here'. The Astor family who bought it from Northcliffe were able to make a small profit from it until competition became fiercer, but by 1966 *The Times* was losing £250,000 a year: the Astors sold it to Lord Thomson, the Canadian intruder who had already built up a profitable British empire, progressing from the *Scotsman* to Scottish TV to the *Sunday Times*. The Monopolies Commission investigated the sale, but concluded there was no real alternative.

Thomson was quite prepared to spend millions to make it profitable: he appointed a stately editor William Rees-Mogg while aiming to double its circulation with bolder stories and high-pressure salesmanship. The circulation went up, but the advertising lagged behind and the paper was losing its authority: *The Times* reverted to its staider style, still losing millions. Far from being pulled up by the *Sunday Times* (as the Monopolies Commission had hoped) it was now dragging it down, and the new building which they shared became a thicket of union restrictions imposed by printers who were becoming expert in the art of milking millionaires.

When the first Lord Thomson died in 1976 his organisation was already a multinational corporation run by accountants and lawyers, and included North Sea oil, package tours, book publishers, yellow pages, North American newspapers and Canadian department stores. His son Kenneth proved far less emotionally involved in newspapers: he preferred Toronto to London and resented the plummy and expensive style of *The Times* pundits. By 1979 the Thomson managers were exasperated by the printers' refusal to allow new technology, and when they resisted a new package of reforms they shut *The Times* down. But the printers who could pick up jobs elsewhere could out-stare the managers and when *The Times* reappeared after a year the managers had gained no real concessions and lost another £40 million. When *The Times* journalists went on strike for more pay it was the last straw for Thomson, who soon announced that he would sell the papers. The printers were amazed—such was the managers' failure to communicate—that the owner they had bled for so long had finally had enough.

There was again no great rush to buy this extravagant status symbol, and Thomson eventually sold *The Times* and *Sunday Times*, complete with building, supplements and presses, for the knock-down price of £12 million. They went to the only man who seemed seriously prepared to take them on—Rupert Murdoch. He would now have two Sunday papers and two dailies, at the top and bottom of the market; but the *Sun* and *News of the World* had enthusiastically supported Mrs Thatcher in the election and she had no desire to obstruct her benefactor by referring him to the Monopolies Commission. The Australian who had found his first foothold in Britain twelve years earlier was now its most powerful newspaper owner since Northcliffe. *The Times* solemnly welcomed him as 'The Fifth Proprietor', while its journalists quietly dreaded the consequences. Murdoch was no more ruthless than Northcliffe, who had failed to subjugate *The Times* seventy years earlier, but his interests were much more widespread and shifting, and newspapers were only part of them.

What did Murdoch really want to do with *The Times*? As he chewed his spectacles through meetings no one could really make out. He chose as editor Harry Evans, the much-admired crusader from the north who had built up the *Sunday Times*' reputation for fearless investigation, while he put the *Sunday Times* in the hands of its former deputy-editor Frank Giles, an urbane ex-diplomat known to old friends as Cravate Noire. Evans moved into *The Times* with a group of highly-paid feature-writers, but was given no budget or brief: by the end of a year the sales had gone up 25,000 but the *Guardian* was moving further ahead, advertising was falling and the year's losses reached £13 million. The old guard at *The Times* deeply resented Evans and his group and began to rally round the deputy editor Charles Douglas-Home who was now threatening to resign. Murdoch, appalled by the losses, suddenly struck, fired Evans, appointed Douglas-Home, and made hundreds of clerical workers redundant. He vowed to push up the circulation to 400,000 in three years, and eventually to 750,000—defying the warnings that it was a tribal newspaper. He scorned the idea of a small circulation 'for bishops and professors', and would keep *The Times* at 20 pence to undercut his rivals.

Whatever Murdoch wanted, the old *Times* had apparently reasserted itself. The new editor Douglas-Home was an Old Etonian, an intrepid foxhunter and ex-Guards officer, a nephew of the Tory ex-prime minister; he showed old-fashioned form in thundering editorials about the Falklands beginning with 'We are All Falklanders Now', while the paper reverted to a more subdued and respectful style. Yet through all its upheavals *The Times* had retained its own kind of continuity: even when it was not published for a year its rivals scarcely trespassed on its tribal territory, while its readers patiently waited for its return. It still gave the impression of belonging to its readers more than to anyone. While American, Canadian or Australian owners came and went, losing fortunes while collecting their peerages the traditional readers still wrote their letters to the editor, and announced their marriages, social engagements and deaths as if nothing had happened, still apparently secure in this garden of privilege.

It might seem odd that the irreverent Murdoch should now find as editors two conservative Englishmen from a class to which he seemed so antipathetic (both Giles and Douglas-Home had begun their careers as aides to colonial governors). But Murdoch's ambitions were now heavily interlocked with political opportunities, and in every country he knew the importance of playing along with the ruling powers. And his relationships with editors were much more temporary than those of his predecessors, as he had already shown to the many ex-editors of his earlier serious newspaper the *Australian*: they were not really meant to be permanent arbiters.

THE OBSERVER

The *Observer* in the meantime, the long-time rival of the *Sunday*

Times, looked even more like a pawn in an obscure game of global finance. For twenty-five years it seemed apparently stable under a single editor, David Astor, whose American grandfather Lord Astor bought it (along with his mansion at Cliveden and his title) as part of his integration into British life. David Astor made the most of his independence, championing liberal causes and taking the side of black leaders in Africa against their British rulers, while for two decades the circulation steadily went up. But after the arrival of Roy Thomson the Sunday competition became more intense and expensive, with magazines and growing over-manning, until the costs were too high even for Astors. By 1975 David Astor had retired as editor and was looking round for a new owner: he was desperately trying to fend off Rupert Murdoch when a new saviour appeared in the form of Robert O. Anderson, the chairman of the Californian oil company Atlantic Richfield.

Anderson seemed too good to be true, with his pixie smile under his ten-gallon hat. He saw himself as a world patron and statesman, advising political leaders and presiding over the Aspen Institute in Colorado which reconciled big business with culture. He seemed quite prepared to lose millions on the *Observer* without interfering with its policies, and his vanity was apparently satisfied by elaborate flattery, banquets for the famous and visits to Ascot and Downing Street. But he was still at heart a nomadic oilman who prided himself on impulsive personal decisions. He admired Mrs Thatcher and was cross when the *Observer* supported Callaghan in 1979; he became less interested as the newspaper's losses went up to £4 million a year and its printers resisted the new technology. He may also have hoped for more success in oil concessions in the North Sea. He played his cards, like a true oilman, close to his chest, but his attitude to the paper was becoming more whimsical: first he wanted to appoint the daughter of the Mexican ambassador in Washington to the board, then he wanted his close friend Kenneth Harris to become vice-chairman. When the other directors including Astor refused, he was piqued. The next day he announced that he had sold the paper—to another international entrepreneur, Tiny Rowland. Overnight Anderson's image changed from the high-minded patron to the cynical wheeler-dealer.

Rowland (see chapter 22) had more evident reasons than Anderson for wanting the *Observer*: he had extensive interests in black Africa where the *Observer* had special influence, and it was known that he was now especially interested (together with Anderson and Daniel Ludwig, the American shipping billionaire) in oil in Angola, which was in a critical state of political flux. He also wanted more political clout in Britain, and the *Observer* would give him easier access to Mrs Thatcher and her ministers. But his deeper motives were as usual shrouded in mystery.

David Astor was appalled that Anderson had secretly sold his old paper, with all the African goodwill he had built up, to a man whose chief concern was with his commercial ventures in black states. The editor Donald Trelford, supported by senior staff, bravely insisted that the deal was 'unacceptable', and the Secretary for Trade John Biffen was reluctantly pressed to refer the sale to the Monopolies Commission, while an alternative syndicate was waiting in the wings to bid for the paper. The Commission's chairman Sir Godfray Le Quesne (see chapter 21) now faced an embarrassing test case: would the sale (in the words of the Fair Trading Act) affect 'the accurate presentation of news and free expression of opinion'? The Commission were given copious evidence of Rowland's commercial motives and ambitions in Africa, Mexico and elsewhere. They conceded that he 'would be closely interested in some of the contents of the paper', and they even agreed that the sale 'might operate against the public interest'. But they could avert this danger, they decided, by insisting on independent directors who would safeguard the editor's freedom. Only one member dissented, Dr R. G. Marshall from the Co-op, who insisted that 'the crucial relationship between editor and chief officer is too close, subtle and continuous to be subject to control by third parties', and recommended against the take-over.

The report was received very sceptically by the Press: the *Guardian* called it 'muddleheaded and potentially dangerous' and the *Observer* itself called its safeguards 'illiberal, unworkable, unacceptable'. But John Biffen still believed (see chapter 21) that he needed a very good reason to stop any take-over: he swiftly approved the deal and agreed to the safeguard of five independent directors on the pattern of *The Times*. The journalists did their best to settle down with their unpredictable new owner, wondering which of his far-flung interests would show themselves first: would it be the rehabilitation of Jonas Savimbi in Angola, or of Milton Obote in Uganda? Support for Holmes a'Court, the Australian entrepreneur? The softening-up for a new assault on Harrods in London? The denigration of rival financiers? It was part of the tension that a few lines in a newspaper might be worth a few million pounds to an international entrepreneur; while a few lines omitted could be worth even more.

OWNERS AND EDITORS

What did any owner want from his newspaper? Twenty years ago Fleet Street could offer both profits and power: now it looked like providing both losses and impotence, as editors and journalists became more resistant to pressure. In all Western countries newspaper owners—whether of the *Washington Post*, *Die Zeit* or *Le Figaro*—were finding it harder to influence their own papers' policies. But most American or German owners could console themselves with profits, and American papers with their local monopolies were among the most profitable industrial investments of all. Fleet Street had more hectic competition and more entrenched unions, which could easily sabotage any profits. So why did rich men still buy them? As often in Britain there was no obvious economic answer. Many of the rewards—whether in terms of social acceptance, amusement, flattery or political influence—could never be measured.

The influence of contemporary newspaper owners is much less straightforward than that of the old Press barons. 'I run the paper,' Lord Beaverbrook told the Press Commission in 1948 with only some exaggeration, 'for the purpose of making propaganda and with no other purpose.' His propaganda, with all his vendettas, black lists and disinformation, though often counterproductive, was very open; and his dominating interests were British newspapers and politics. But many of the new proprietors have shifting international interests which are much harder to tie down. They may want the appearance of power more than the power itself—like showing the bulge of an unloaded gun under their jacket. They may be prepared to spend millions on refurbishing their own image; or they may have a project in another part of the world which could be advanced by the prestige of a newspaper. Like nineteenth-century railways, newspapers may not provide profits, but the access to profits elsewhere; and as the information industry becomes more complex and valuable newspapers will inevitably become more interlocked with other global businesses.

A contemporary editor may appear more independent than his predecessors and his owner will no longer bark commands into the dictaphone like Lord Beaverbrook. But ownership is a pervasive and encircling influence whereby priorities gradually change, assumptions develop, and newspapers slowly change direction. Even the most independent journalists are inclined to write for someone, whether a strong editor or a strong owner, and they need a context in which to communicate. The relationship between an editor and an owner becomes more subtly interlocked like a marital relationship in which neither side is sure who has won.

All editors become caught up in their own internal constraints (the more since all papers apart from the *Economist* have abandoned anonymity except in editorials, giving more scope to feature writers and columnists). And newspapers have become more like supermarkets offering a choice of opinions and styles. Yet readers still expect their newspapers, like their friends, to have definite characters even when they disagree with them—characters which only a strong editor can set. The confident diversity of the Press must always depend on the independence and security of editors, which can easily be undermined by the short-term interests of proprietors.

The journalists in the meantime have developed, like other professions, their own communal rituals. Inside their 'newspaper cathedrals' (as Simon Jenkins has called them), with their own priesthoods, sermons and incantations, they can easily protect themselves against outside realities; and their own closed shop has helped to insulate them further. Since they began straightforward personal letters to readers, newspapers have developed their own coded headlines, stylised columns and sob-stories. Reporters become fascinated by the parliamentary ding-dong or the rhetoric of party conferences, and slow to notice ground-swells of public opinion north of Watford Gap. The business pages are kept even more separate from political pages than the Treasury from the Foreign Office, while culture is kept insulated from both. Foreign news is kept at a distance and Britain's trading interdependence with Europe, the global trends of inflation, recession or unemployment, are hardly reflected in general reporting.

Television has added to the insecurity of journalists: would they become like piano-players after the silent movies gave way to talkies? The camera-teams made newspapers more restless in their foreign coverage as they followed them from crisis to crisis, so that the traditional foreign correspondent is now a rarity. Journalists have become more caught up in the demand for daily or hourly news, speculating like sports writers with a rash of subjunctive journalism—full of mays, coulds, and mights—which becomes outdated the next day, while the concept of the 'journal of record' becomes more uncertain. Bankers and businessmen look more to their own specialised sources and newsletters for international information, and Reuters, which had begun as a bankers' service before it expanded into a public news agency, is now again making most of its profits from private economic information. The general reader who wants to know how the world works is apt to be left out in the cold.

The ownership by multinational corporations has not made newspapers any more multinational in their outlook: perhaps less so. A global oil company has no desire to encourage investigation into its world markets; it is much more interested in improving its local political relations. The resources of newspapers are tiny compared to those of the big companies and banks, and the more editors fight for readers the more they are likely to be preoccupied with the national ⸱ dramas and rituals which provide their daily competition, while the rest of the world takes second place. And in the meantime the influence of newspapers has been overshadowed by the effects of the pervasive new electronic medium which was subject from its beginnings to more fundamental controls.

28

Television:
the End of Paternalism?

Newspapers were born free but television was born in chains, a monopoly created by the state, dependent on the state and in every country
regulated by the state.

Sir William Rees-Mogg

TELEVISION has brought together big business, government and
communications in a more critical battleground. Behind that small
screen all kinds of old British conflicts are at work: the competition
between private and public finance; the influence of big money on
images and ideas; the extension of the old parliamentary ding-dong;
and above all the old argument between the two political
philosophies, between paternalism and free competition, which has
shown itself more clearly in television than anywhere.

Every country has imposed its own national characteristics on the
new medium, which has always been more circumscribed and regulated than newspapers, books or films; and British television soon
began to reflect the traditions of its people. It could claim to provide
the best programmes in the world in terms of democratic argument,
serious documentaries and above all drama; it provided a new kind
of stage for the British theatrical tradition which had already lasted
four centuries. It brought great acting, Olympic sport, opera and
exploration into millions of homes which would never otherwise
have seen them, without the debasement of taste and the extreme
intrusions of advertising on the American screens; and it could
appeal across classes, whether with comedy series or with political
documentaries, as newspapers had never done.

But British television—particularly colour television—could also
encourage even more than the Press the national nostalgia about a
glorious past, constantly escaping from contemporary problems to
retreat down memory lane, whether to the British Empire or *Dad's
Army*. And its news and current affairs concentrated much more than
did other European TV on national events, personalities and views,

keeping away from foreigners who did not speak English. Who could believe, watching the nightly news of British strikes, debates or human interest stories, that this was a country which had been part of the European Community for ten years, dependent on it for its trade and sharing most of its problems, including recession, unemployment and inflation?

It was thirty years ago that British television became the battleground between the paternalism of the old BBC and the free enterprise of the proposed new commercial companies. The year 1955, which brought commercial advertising to the screen, appeared for years afterwards as a social milestone which changed the patterns of politics and consumption as well as the style of entertainment and news. Before it, when the BBC monopoly was unchallenged, television commentators observed formal and respectful relationships with governments and politicians, humbly inviting them to give their views of the world, while they could not discuss topics which were coming before parliament within fourteen days. The BBC appeared like a licensed annexe to Westminster and Whitehall.

The sudden commercial invasion, with showbiz producers constantly watching their ratings, undermined that relationship. Politicians were bombarded and rudely interrupted, and came back for more. The fourteen-day rule was forgotten and television interviews often became more important than parliamentary speeches. The top TV performers moved between the two channels, and the BBC was now no longer called Auntie, but the Beeb. The competition was so exhilarating that most of the past critics dropped their objections to advertising. The duopoly between the public and private systems seemed to work rather better than other versions of the mixed economy such as the mixture of state and independent schools, or of state and private medicine.

Yet the liberation of television was never as complete as it looked. Both systems, whether consciously or unconsciously, still played the familiar political football, thriving on the adversary style and neatly balancing government with opposition. The commentators established their own rituals, while the cameras gave a new power to old ceremonials. The narrow choice of channels, each discreetly controlled by the state, ensured a measure of paternalism, by which a small group of programme controllers decided what the public should or should not see.

THE BBC

The liberation of the BBC from its old fatherly style was epitomised by the daily programme *Tonight* which in 1957 intensified the counter-revolution against commercial TV, releasing new talents and egos. It ran for eight years. Its editor, Donald Baverstock, the hard-drinking Welshman who called everyone 'boy', insisted that television must be on the side of the viewer, against any Establishment. And he was backed up by Grace Wyndham-Goldie, the influential producer who had already invented *Panorama* with Richard Dimbleby two years earlier, and who now encouraged her young men to speak their minds. With its calypsos, cheeky interviews and inquisitive rambles round Britain *Tonight* opened up the new medium, taking over where magazines such as *Picture Post* had left off. In their chaotic offices in Shepherd's Bush the mixture of writers, musicians, actors and producers reinforced each other's revolt against the pomposities of the past with their war-cry of 'Bor-ring'. '*Tonight* never became an institution,' one of them reminisced. 'It was just a group of people who came together.' Many of them went on to pioneer other BBC innovations such as the series on the Great War and *That Was The Week That Was*. The old paternalistic, didactic BBC was never the same again.

Was there a small baby that went out with all the old bathwater? In their determination not to be reverential or preachy the young Turks dreaded the old role of the teacher. The word educational was death to a programme, and the task of explaining the world was secondary to the dramatic or political impact. On television the BBC news which on radio had earned the admiration of the world became more parochial and flippant than its commercial competitor, Independent Television News. Film was the key to all coverage, so that dictatorships which did not admit cameras were scarcely mentioned, and it was left to BBC radio, particularly the World Service, to continue the great tradition. The television symbol of the turning globe, or the slogan 'The Window on the World', represented only a partial truth, a window on a very limited world.

Twenty-five years after the first showing of *Tonight* its former editor Alasdair Milne presided over a reunion in 1982 to watch some early programmes. Some of its old boys such as Donald Baverstock, Alan Whicker or John Morgan had made money from commercial television; some such as Milne were now at the top of the BBC; some were established writers or film directors such as Bernard Levin, John Schlesinger or Jack Gold. Nearly all had been part of that cultural explosion of the sixties. At the reunion they looked back at their youth, marvelling at the freshness and directness. 'We had a blank page to print on,' said Milne. 'It looked so innocent then,' said the Scots reporter Fyfe Robertson, 'as if we were joining the family in the drawing room.' The old programmes looked as individual and intimate compared to standardised contemporary programmes such as *Nationwide* as personal letters compared to newspaper columns. Had audiences become more demanding? Had the medium itself become stale? Or was the BBC now too bureaucratic and cautious? 'The day that *Tonight* closed down,' Alan Whicker lamented, 'the circus left town.'

In two decades the young Turks had grown middle-aged while the BBC had first rapidly expanded and then retrenched. Its huge bureaucracy of 28,000—more than the entire Falklands task force— provides a kind of see-through version of other bureaucracies, always visible for inspection and criticism, dealing not with oil or chemicals but the more fragile commodity of truth (the BBC was, so Malcolm Muggeridge assures us, the model of George Orwell's 'Ministry of Truth'). In middle age, with a bulging corporate paunch, the BBC had naturally become more cautious and self-sufficient: its staff were offered employment for life with annual increments like civil servants, while outside contributions were discouraged by small fees. The sprawling BBC suburb round Shepherd's Bush had become still more self-contained, while the power of the medium could still bring politicians running to the studios from distant constituencies. At the top, the BBC's intricate hierarchies were hardly ever penetrated by outsiders, so the staff could play musical chairs with each other, adding chairs rather than taking them away.

The caution of advancing years was encouraged by the political pressures, as each government tried to use the licence-fee—which had to be upped with each inflationary rise—as a means to discipline and control the BBC. Offences against politicians—such as the portrayal of 'Yesterday's Men' in 1971 or of the Falklands crisis in *Panorama* in 1982—were met with swift retribution. With its shortage of funds the BBC had become less bold in cultural experiments, and economised with long hours of snooker and darts. The BBC had become the kind of conformist institution that its young Turks would have enjoyed mocking twenty years earlier, and there was not much sign of a new generation breaking through to overturn the old order. The younger producers had been brought up within the medium, with all the constraints of committees and camera-crews: they had to submit to what they called the 'Byzantine system of planning and control', in which artistic as well as financial control 'moved further and further away from themselves'.[1] They would never have the same scope as their forerunners twenty years earlier.

The centralised power of the BBC came under heavy fire when Roy Jenkins, the Home Secretary in 1974, appointed Lord Annan to head a committee on the future of broadcasting, which included a

[1] Report of the Committee on the Future of Broadcasting: Command 6753, HMSO, London, 1977, p. 102.

BBC man Antony Jay and an MP from television Phillip Whitehead. The committee members could not conceal their impatience with the BBC's limitations and complacency. They were more critical of the Corporation than of the commercial companies partly no doubt because, like other critics, they expected more of it. They found that the BBC's current affairs and news were inferior to those of their commercial rivals, that they covered industry very inadequately and that they lacked investigative reporting and criticism of British institutions. They all agreed that on BBC television 'the quality of individual programmes was patchy, sometimes dull and, on occasions, superficial to the point of banality'. They were impressed by the criticism voiced by Peter Jay and John Birt that TV on all channels failed to put news into a proper context, and encouraged a 'bias against understanding'; and they thought television news could learn much more from American practice.[2]

The Annan Committee were all persuaded of the importance of pluralism, and concerned that the media, including newspapers, were being controlled by too few people: 'All of us perceive that a diminishing number of independent sources of news, comment and opinion is a danger to any democracy . . .' They were worried about the BBC's 'institutional malaise' and its unitary control, not because of any conspiracy to manipulate public opinion, but because of the opposite: 'The BBC management is scrupulous to the point of paranoia about fairness, balance and impartiality.'

Some of the committee, including Jay and Whitehead, were convinced that the BBC's unitary control was excessive. In an eloquent dissent they warned about the dangers of its concentrated editorial authority and the tendency towards 'corporate osmosis' which spread the same views through all channels, and they concluded that the BBC should be split up between radio and television. There was certainly much evidence of serious overweight. 'We believe that the BBC is too large,' the Association of Directors and Producers told the committee, 'too unwieldy and far too top-heavy with non-creative and non-productive staff. The creative excellence which was the hallmark of the BBC for so many years, right up to the sixties when creative vigour reached its peak, has now been submerged under the weight of a vast bureaucracy. We believe, sadly, that the time has now come for this great monolithic sacred cow to be dismembered.'[3] But Lord Annan and the majority still concluded that the size of the BBC, with all its drawbacks, had the critical advantage of reinforcing its political independence and giving its chairman the weight and authority to stand up to the government.

[2] *Ibid*, p. 284.
[3] *Ibid*, p. 99.

After Annan's complaints the BBC was soon growing still bigger. The economic crisis which followed, and the Thatcher government's postponement of a higher licence-fee, compelled some slimming-down of the great apparatus. But like town halls and Whitehall departments the BBC managers are more willing to cut services to the public, such as orchestras, than to eat into their own bureaucracy; and they are now determined to compete in every potential new area of broadcasting. The BBC has a beadier eye on the future, as well as greater resources, than its commercial rivals, and since the trauma of losing its monopoly it has built up an elaborate lobby and PR machine. It has expanded into local radio, to compete with commercial local radio; it will have two satellites, when the commercial stations have none; and it will probably be one of the main investors in cable television. It intends to compete strongly in break-fast television, against the new commercial company (AM-TV) run by the former ambassador to Washington, Peter Jay. (The contest will provide a new challenge for more intelligent news presentation. For Jay remains determined to avoid the traditional obsession with film and to put news into a serious context, challenging the more superficial treatment of the BBC; and he likes to depict it as a personal battle with Alasdair Milne, the head of the BBC: 'between two generations of Wykehamists'.)

The promise of further expansion and the higher licence-fee, has restored much of the BBC's confidence, which exasperates its critics still more. Should this great bureaucracy be allowed to control still more air-time? Should the public's licence-fees be spent on massive and risky new investments? And who is responsible and accountable for the machine? The ultimate responsibility is held by the Board of Governors, made up of nine men and three women (including one black) who are selected by the Home Office and vetted by Downing Street, to serve for five years:

George Howard (Chairman)	landowner
William Rees-Mogg (Vice-Chairman)	ex-editor of *The Times*
Roger Young (Scotland)	headmaster
Alwyn Roberts (Wales)	Bangor University
Lady Faulkner (Northern Ireland)	widow of former PM
Lord Allen	former General Secretary USDAW
Lady Serota	former Labour minister
Sir John Johnston	ex-diplomat
Christopher Longuet-Higgins	scientist, Sussex University
Jocelyn Barrow	former Secretary Campaign against Racial Discrimination
Peter Moores	director, Littlewoods
Stuart Young	chartered accountant

The collaboration between chairman and director-general provides the classic British contrast between amateur and professional, outsider and insider. 'The relationship is always changing,' the present chairman says, 'because it depends on the people. It works if both sides want it to work.' Lord Normanbrook, the former Secretary to the Cabinet, was probably the most interventionist chairman in his years from 1964 to 1967, though the angriest explosion came when Harold Wilson appointed Lord Hill to restrain the very independent director-general Sir Hugh Greene. The present chairman George Howard was appointed in 1980, to succeed the zoologist Sir Michael Swann, by his old friend Willie Whitelaw, the Tory Home Secretary, and he soon made the most of it. 'I deliberately keep a high profile,' he told me, 'unlike my predecessor: if I'm going to carry the can I might as well be recognised.'

Howard's profile is not hard to recognise: he emphasises his enormous girth with flowered shirts or a caftan, and he seems in scale with his vast country house, Castle Howard, built for his ancestor the Earl of Carlisle and made famous by the Granada TV series *Brideshead Revisited*. As an old Etonian who went to Balliol and became president of the Country Landowners' Association, he seemed a fitting symbol of the new conservatism in broadcasting, but some BBC people complain that his emphatic style is misleading: 'The trouble with George' (as one of them said) 'is that he's really rather lightweight.' He visibly enjoys his new position—'He runs it like a wing of Castle Howard,' one governor complained—and he sees himself as a kind of constitutional monarch. 'Legally the governors don't *have* to have a director-general at all,' Howard told me. 'There's nothing in the charter about it. But of course I don't *run* the BBC: only the professionals can do that. It's a unique organisation because the initiatives come from below. I don't look at programmes beforehand: we're not purely regulatory like the IBA.'

The BBC governors in early 1982 did not cover a very wide range: the chairman, his deputy Rees-Mogg, and the retiring director-general, Sir Ian Trethowan, were all Conservatives, with a Labour politician and a trade unionist as partial counter-weights. The Tory chiefs were sitting ducks for left-wing critics who depicted the BBC as the instrument of the old feudal powers; but it was the Tories who were most furious with the BBC when they presented Argentinian views during the Falklands crisis. Most of the real direction of the corporation depends on the board of management and the director-general, and there was special expectation about the new appointment in 1982. 'We were looking,' said Howard, 'for someone to prepare the BBC for the nineties, when the real crunch will come.' And they chose Alasdair Milne, the man who was considered the toughest and most resourceful.

Milne is the first director-general to be an unalloyed TV man, having joined the BBC after Winchester (where he was head boy) and Oxford; he made his name as deputy editor of *Tonight*, as a stabiliser for Baverstock, and showed a command and decisiveness which gave him quick promotion, after a brief interval in commercial TV. He can be outspoken and irreverent, with an impish grin and a Scottish detachment, but he remains totally loyal to the BBC: 'We think we're the Guards—we're the best in the world—twice as efficient as ITV. It has to be big.' His reputation has been built on his administrative skills rather than on his creativity and intellectual range, and he remains rather puritanical and austere in his tastes. 'He's got the military skills which television needs,' one colleague explained: 'decisive, split-second timing, mastery of logistics. He knows how to control cameras like artillery, and how to maintain discipline. He's not at all interested in ideas.' But the huge operation now calls for organisational skills above all others. 'We consider the position of the director-general is an impossible one,' said the minority of five in the Annan Report. 'Editor-in-chief and resident theologian, pope and emperor in one, interpreting and executing one indivisible corporation.'[4]

COMMERCIAL TELEVISION

Less than thirty years ago television was opened up to a small group of entrepreneurs who within a few years established both new fortunes and new institutions. There had been no comparable sudden new wealth since the arrival of the South African gold millionaires in the early twentieth century. Like them the new television tycoons were mostly from immigrant families—such as the Bernsteins of Granada, the Grades of ATV or Paul Adorian of Rediffusion—who projected a new show-biz dynamism and brought the kind of instinctive feel for the mass taste, like the early Hollywood moguls, which the BBC lacked. Commercial television is sometimes represented as an extension of the power of the old aristocracy: 'Much of British television has long been run by companies with peers of the realm hovering in the background,' reports James Bellini.[5] But the big money and influence went to people right outside the old tradition, who got peerages as a result of the new wealth.

They were old-fashioned capitalists, taking risks which seemed high at the time, which most of the City and the old rich would not

[4] Command 6753, p. 110.
[5] James Bellini: *Rule Britannia*, Jonathan Cape, London, 1981, p. 208.

touch. For its first months in 1955 commercial television made disastrous losses: ATV lost £600,000 in seven months, and Lord Rothermere of the *Daily Mail*, who then owned a third of Associated Rediffusion, sold his shares to Harley Drayton of British Electric Traction. It was only after a perilous year that the advertising began to roll in, and the franchises became what Roy Thomson called a 'licence to print money'.

Most of the original TV companies have now been cut back or transplanted. Of the first two London stations, Associated Television (which became part of ACC, see below) was shunted to the Midlands with a half-share of Central TV. Associated Rediffusion was abolished outright, but its biggest shareholder, the conglomerate British Electric Traction, was allowed a half-share in the current weekday company Thames Television (whose other half is owned by another conglomerate, EMI-Thorn, whose products include records, electronics and weapons). 'Thames has the biggest revenues of any company, but the worst owners,' as one member of the IBA complained; and its relentless pursuit of short-term profits has exasperated creative executives who have left in disgust. The other London franchise was taken over in 1969 by London Weekend (LWT) which was partly owned by showbiz shareholders including David Frost, who offered high hopes of more creative programming. But LWT soon went through a crisis that almost finished it, after some of its shares went to Rupert Murdoch, until the IBA belatedly intervened. It was not until John Freeman, the ex-ambassador to Washington, was brought in as chairman that it was set back on its feet.

Granada has been the most enduring, the most profitable and also the most creative—an odd combination. Its first chairman Sidney Bernstein, who had built up the Granada cinema chain, came into television with more political sophistication than the others, and more interest in current affairs. He thought that BBC journalism was a joke, and brought in newspaper men (such as Barry Heads, David Plowright and Tim Hewitt) to apply Fleet Street standards to interpret current affairs. Granada also saw an opportunity from its Manchester base to encourage working-class drama, and it started *Coronation Street* in 1960, which has continued twice-a-week ever since, still among the Top Ten.

Granada has since diversified widely—into publishing, motorway cafes, bingo halls, nightclubs—and television now provides only 16 per cent of the income of the Granada group, whose chairman is now Alex Berstein, Sidney's nephew. But the television side is still important, strong on current affairs and prepared to defend its journalists; and it is still dominated by the Bernsteins and their nominee Sir Denis Forman, with some of the atmosphere of a family firm. It is still very profitable, though part of its territory was taken away in 1968 to create Yorkshire Television, which now has its own aggressive reputation dominated by its autocratic boss Paul Fox.

THE FALL OF GRADE

The last and most famous of the old impresarios was Lew Grade, the original co-chairman of Associated Television, the 'Palladium of the Air' which had translated showbiz on to the screen, and which had launched early TV triumphs such as *Emergency Ward Ten*. At his peak in the early seventies Grade ruled over an entertainment empire including theatres, cinemas, songs and records, linked with the EMI complex, which looked like monopolising most of show business. Grade had to resign the chairmanship of ATV at seventy, but he remained head of the parent company ACC (which now controls Central Television in the Midlands) dominating it by the force of his personality; he promised to retire in the year 2000. But Grade became ambitious to make expensive feature films, still confident of his instinct for the public taste. Only one film, the *Muppet Movie*, had a major financial success; his last big film, *Raise the Titanic*, lost over £15 million. ('It would have been cheaper,' Grade complained, 'to lower the Atlantic.')

By the end of 1981, ACC was living largely off its property and the rights of the Lennon-McCartney songs, and it was on the brink of financial catastrophe. Grade was determined to maintain his control, and saw himself threatened by his accountant-lieutenant Jack Gill, who had strengthened his position by setting up a financial strategy committee with two other powerful directors, Bill Michael and Ellis Birk. Before a board meeting in August 1981, when Birk was on holiday, Grade summoned each director in turn and told them that Gill was to be sacked, trying to placate each with other concessions. A historic board meeting ensued: Gill defied Grade, and threatened to reveal embarrassing facts. Lord Matthews (of the *Express*) warned that the company could not survive with two rivals at the top; others tried to postpone the decision until Birk returned. But Grade pushed it to a vote, and the majority dared not defy him.

Then Grade, to placate him, offered Gill a golden handshake of five times his salary—over £500,000—with an option to buy his company house for £100,000 below its market value. It was the last straw for those usually secretive shareholders, the pension funds, who had already been watching their ACC shares dropping fast. Some (such as the M & G funds) had already sold out, but those that remained were flexing their muscles and the huge handout to Jack Gill gave them their pretext. Ralph Quartano, the intrepid manager of Posfund (see chapter 19) led a group of ten big investors (including the Electricity Council's pension fund and the Sun Alliance and Eagle Star insurance companies) who owned 12 per cent of the shares, and took the company to the High Court to block the payment to Gill.

In the meantime a shadowy financier living 9,000 miles away had also been carefully watching the falling shares of ACC—and buying them up. Robert Holmes a'Court is a cold but stylish Western Australian, distantly related to Lord Heytesbury, and once described as 'Murdoch without the compassion'. He met and charmed Lew Grade, went to America with him and persuaded him to sell him his personal shares in ACC, promising him that he could still make films. A'Court then became chairman of ACC, and bid £36 million for the whole company. The IBA was embarrassed because a'Court was not a British resident and therefore an undesirable owner of a TV station; but the company was virtually bankrupt and the IBA separated the question of control over Central TV. Then a rival candidate, Gerry Ronson of the Heron Group, bid £46 million, which a'Court soon matched; Ronson went up to £49 million, a'Court replied with £60 million; after legal wrangles and resignations from two directors, Ronson finally opted out, and a'Court won control over ACC in April 1982. The company that had once dominated showbusiness had been juggled between the continents and was now controlled (like *The Times* and the *Sun*) from the other side of the world. And Lew Grade, the last tycoon of television, departed in a storm of recriminations about his company's extravagant perks and handshakes.

THE IBA

All such scenes are observed anxiously by the watchdog of commercial television, the Independent Broadcasting Authority (IBA), like a netball referee umpiring American football. From its beginning in 1953 the IBA, by allocating or taking away franchises, had the power to make or break fortunes. 'There's been nothing like it,' as Lord Goodman once said, 'since Charles II doled out patents for soap.'

Every six years or more the IBA requires the companies to justify their continued existence. 'The Authority has one moment of supreme and lasting influence over its programmes' (the first director of the IBA Sir Robert Fraser explained), 'when it decides who will make them and who will not.' The allocations are odd conjunctions between private enterprise and public control. For months before the day of judgment the companies polish up their image, by building new studios or making expensive cultural programmes, until they finally send documents to the IBA describing their achievements, aspirations and beliefs. In the meantime new rivals have prepared their own consortia of investors, judiciously mixing up aristocracy, money, show business and local interests to show their regional concerns. The old and new companies are then summoned by the directors of the IBA for brief and bewildering interviews. At last they are called in to receive a brown envelope, in which their fate is sealed, with no reasons given.

The IBA is a committee of carefully-balanced worthies, less prominent than the BBC governors but with the same kind of mix, including the statutory trade unionist, a black woman, a Scotsman and an Ulsterwoman. 'They're not very effective,' one of them explained, 'unless they concentrate on achieving one thing which they really know about. If they don't know what they want, they're helpless.' These were they in 1982:

Lord Thomson of Monifieth (Chairman)	Labour ex-cabinet minister, ex-commissioner of EEC
Sir John Riddell (Deputy Chairman)	Banker
Rev William Morris	Minister, Glasgow Cathedral
Sir Denis Hamilton	Former editor-in-chief, Times Newspapers
Jill McIvor	Barrister, Northern Ireland
George Russell	Assistant MD, Alcan Aluminium
Anthony Christopher	General Secretary, Inland Revenue Staff Federation
Juliet Jowitt	Conservative Councillor, Ripon
Paula Ridley	Project Co-ordinator, New Enterprise Workshops, Toxteth
Yvonne Connolly	Member of Inner London Education Authority
Alexander Cullen	Professor of electronic engineering, London University

Like the BBC, the IBA is headed by a part-time chairman and a full-time director-general, but their responsibility is quite different; for their job is to regulate the commercial companies, not to run them. The chairman's commitment has varied widely: the last incumbent, Lady Plowden, promoted and demoted syndicates with all the confidence of a committee-woman. The present chairman, Lord Thomson, is a well-liked ex-Labour minister from Dundee, who gained some experience of commercial pressures as the head of the

Advertising Standards Authority, to which he added some teeth. He has his own views about television standards—particularly about the awfulness of Saturday nights—and he wants to show that he can stand up to the lobby.

But his most important task has been to choose a new director-general after the long reign of Sir Brian Young, the former headmaster who (the TV tycoons often complained) was inclined to treat the companies as his schoolboys. Thomson and his deputy-chairman Sir John Riddell—a banker with cultural interests—were determined to look outside their own outfit for a new director, and they made a bold choice: John Whitney, who was running the most successful commercial radio station, Capitol. Whitney is that rare bird, a home-grown entrepreneur: the son of an inventor, he left school early and by twenty-one had his own radio production company with a staff of thirty. He was later involved in producing TV series, including *Upstairs, Downstairs*, but his great challenge came when he was asked to run Capitol Radio, to which he gave both commercial success and some social purpose—so that its Euston headquarters now provides a job-finding service as well as a pop music centre. Whitney is expected to be a more interventionist director of the IBA than Young, but he will also preside over a new era, when new kinds of television will emerge and when (some board members believe) the regulation will begin to wither away as competition provides its own counterweights.

The commercial TV companies were meant from the start to have strong regional characters, with both local shareholders and local coverage; but like other attempts at decentralisation these aims were frustrated. In 1981 the IBA deprived Southern TV (based on Southampton) of its franchise, partly because its distant owners, including Rank, Associated Newspapers and D. C. Thomson, were too little interested in Hampshire or Sussex. But at the same time the IBA awarded the new Midlands franchise, Central TV, whose shares were soon picked up by very non-regional investors including D. C. Thomson and Ladbrokes the bookmakers (who had just lost their casino licence). The regionalism of ITV was never very convincing, and the areas are not defined by traditional communities but by the range of transmission; where TV companies *are* owned by local business interests, they can sometimes exploit them for their commercial ends. Local news services are the most popular regional programmes, but the companies were also expected to provide a focus and patronage for regional culture, including actors, writers and musicians, and the record of most of them has been wretched. They have done little to help the struggling provincial theatres and art centres, and only Granada in Manchester has made much use of local writers and settings. It has been left to commercial radio stations to provide a more authentic local participation and patronage.

The battles between the regions are fought out in the Network Committee, where representatives of the fifteen companies work out what programmes to share, when to show them, and who buys what from whom. The Big Five (Granada, Yorkshire, Central, Thames and London Weekend) still dominate the network; but others such as Anglia or TVS have begun pushing to get more programmes on the network. The accountants in the 'little ten' find it cheaper to buy other people's programmes, while their producers demand more opportunity to show their work; but the quintopoly of the big five has come increasingly under fire.

Television also has a much less publicised controller: the unions. The wealth of the television tycoons was quickly followed (as in Hollywood) by spectacular wage-claims, particularly from the powerful Association of Cinematograph, Television and Allied Technicians (ACTT). Their secretary for the last thirteen years, Alan Sapper (see chapter 3), is a playwright and former botanist who has learnt how to divert profits towards his technicians. The unions can insist on a crew of ten to film features which could be filmed by three; on first-class air travel and luxury hotels; on long lunch hours in expensive restaurants; and on high wages for routine jobs such as videotape editing. Huge expenses abroad became the subject of apocryphal jokes (when one ITN reporter sent a vast expense claim back from Vietnam, his editor cabled back: YOUR JOB REPORT VIETNAM NOT BUY IT). The union's demands and restrictions encouraged further bureaucracy and cut off the TV teams from spontaneous human contacts: 'The cost of feeding and watering a camera crew,' complained one ITV chairman, 'is a greater impediment to good programmes than any of the early technical difficulties.' But no TV channel and few newspapers dared to criticise the unions.

The ultimate control of the commercial companies, through the IBA, is held by the Home Office, that Whitehall scapegoat which is always concerned with stopping things happening; and its permanent secretary periodically expresses complaints to the director of the IBA (including such details as the time-slot for *Charlie's Angels*). The commercial companies are always aware of the pressure of politicians on contentious subjects, and the government comes closest to direct censorship over Ulster, where they warn both the BBC and the IBA not to broadcast anything likely to induce sympathy for the IRA. Much of the political pressure on the IBA works through the old boy network—a quiet word about a forthcoming programme

Company	Region	Population coverage (thousands)	Chairman	Main voting shareholders
Thames	London	12,724	H. S. L. Dundas	BET (50%) EMI (50%)
London Weekend	London		John Freeman	Pearl Assurance (11.77%) News International (11.77%) Robert Clark (11.77%) *Daily Telegraph* (11.01%) Sableknight (11.01%) ITC pension fund (10.1%)
Central	Midlands	9,635	Sir Gordon Hobday	ACC (51%) D. C. Thomson (15%) Ladbrokes (10%)
Granada Yorkshire	Lancashire Yorkshire	7,702 6,847	Sir Denis Forman Sir Richard Graham	Granada Group Pearson-Longman (25%) Bass Charrington (25%) Trident Television (15%) Yorkshire Post Newspapers (10%)
TVS	South of England	6,162	Lord Boston of Faversham	European Ferries (20%) London Trust Company (20%)

HTV	Wales, West of England	4,605	Lord Harlech	(No shareholding of more than 5%)
Anglia	East of England	4,349	Marquess Townshend	The *Guardian* (24.2%) May Gurney Holdings (12.0%) Eastern Counties Newspapers (9%)
Scottish	Central Scotland	3,942	Sir Campbell Fraser	Sir Campbell Fraser (10.7%) William Brown (10.7%)
Tyne-Tees	North-east of England	2,572	Sir Ralph Carr-Ellison	Trident Television (20%) Vaux Breweries (20%) ICFC (15%)
TSW	South	1,724	Sir John Colfox	Phicom (15.05%) British and Commonwealth Shipping Co (11.92%) Britannia Arrow (11.32%) ICFC (11.32%)
Grampian	North-east of Scotland	1,191	Iain Tennant	Iain Tennant (6%) Lord Forbes (6%) Neil Paterson (6%)
Border	Scottish Border	617	Sir John Burgess	Cumbrian Newspapers (23.8%) Outram Newspapers (13.9%)
Channel	Channel Islands	115	E. D. Collas	Guernsey Press Ltd (14%) Harold Fielding (Continental) Ltd (11%)

which could discomfort top people, a quiet drink to suggest that a blockbuster might be postponed. The IBA regard their own role (as one ITV chairman put it) as 'seeing that established order is not too dented or shocked'. But ITV producers still find it easier than BBC producers to be contentious, and their executives do not need to keep one eye on their licence fee.

It is 'balance' which is the most limiting control over both the BBC and the companies. Every argument is assumed to have two sides—and no more—which must receive equal air-time. If the public hears the minister, they must hear the shadow minister; if a shop steward attacks the managing director, the latter must be allowed to justify himself. The concern for fair play leads easily to the stereotyped ritual, in which politicians or employers from the usual 'repertory company' of tame public figures appear as familiar adversaries forcefully putting forward opposite sets of expected views, like a school debating society; while they both agree, joking in the hospitality room after the show, that the real problem is in a quite different context. In political television, as in parliament, participants prefer to battle publicly with each other, than to look for solutions. Television, like football, has grown up with two sides taking turns and an umpire ensuring fair play, and the presentation of 'balance' can give the audience a benign feeling that the answer lies somewhere between the two sides. The whole game is spoilt if a new idea or a third party arrives on the field.

FOURTH CHANNEL

It was Lord Annan's report in 1977, with its concern for cultural and social pluralism, which gave more concrete form to a new kind of Fourth Channel to offset the conformism of the other three. The companies naturally wanted a second commercial channel, but Annan tentatively proposed a new Open Broadcasting Authority, which would collect its own revenue and commission its own programmes, encouraging independent producers. The companies lobbied relentlessly against it, and eventually the 'Whitelaw Compromise' was reached by the Home Secretary: the Fourth Channel would come under the IBA and be financed by the ITV companies who would collect the advertising revenue; but it would have its own Controller who would include programmes from independent producers.

The Controller of Channel Four, Jeremy Isaacs, is thus given a unique opportunity to broaden the medium. He is an articulate and committed television man, who has produced for the BBC and for Thames, which he left after a row with its very commercial managing director Bryan Cowgill—'something between resignation and the sack'. He genuinely wanted to encourage smaller producers, and he soon found that they made programmes more cheaply: in spite of union restrictions, they still have much lower overheads than the big companies, so that instead of the expected 15 per cent the Fourth Channel was commissioning more like 50 per cent from the independents.

Isaacs presides over Channel Four's exhilarating new offices in north Soho, with wooden trellises around a cluster of secretaries in the centre of a huge space, and with offices behind plate glass. He insists that his channel will not think of the viewers 'as identical mass-production model families with 2.4 children'; he specifically wants viewers to 'visit' Channel Four when they really want to watch something. He wants to give a boost to the independent producers who have shown the energy and enterprise to leave existing institutions, and he has been encouraged by their quick response to the challenge in 'the cultural ether'. He insists that the IBA must not apply the same sanctions to Channel Four as to the ITV companies: 'There will be a bust-up unless they recognise our distinctiveness.' And he wants to give young viewers the same kind of variety on the screen that they can get from reading matter.

TECHNOLOGY V PATERNALISM

In the meantime all kinds of new technological devices—such as video-cassettes, video-discs, cables and satellites—have been threatening to undermine the hold of all the channels. Brian Wenham, the Controller of BBC 2, depicts the history of broadcasting in three ages: the first age, dominated by radio, came to an end when the coronation in 1953 showed the full power of television. The second age was dominated by television, but 'deliberately and delicately regulated by parliament, through the aegis of the BBC and the IBA'. The third age, beginning in the eighties will see a weakening of regulation in all three key fields—production, distribution and exchange.[6]

The weakening is already visible. Video recorders have multiplied faster than TV companies expected; video-cassette shops are mushrooming and production companies are making educational films and magazine programmes specially for cassettes. But the recorders are still too costly to detract seriously from the broadcast programmes and video discs will at first be more expensive. Only a few thousand people so far can watch cable television, paying a subscription to receive two or three feature films on cable channels, which are less obviously attractive than in America where cables

[6] The *Observer*, March 21, 1982.

give much better reception than ordinary broadcasts. But new channels will be able to cater like magazines for specialist markets and to include for instance (as in America) a channel devoted entirely to news.

Satellite television looks a closer prospect. Britain is joining a joint European plan to launch a satellite in 1984, which could be picked up by subscribers through a 'dish' in each area or even in a back garden. The BBC is hoping to use the satellites to extend their own channels, but many people dread that satellites will also spread 'commercial crap', enabling advertisers from Luxembourg to sell liquor or cigarettes without controls across the continent, undermining the revenue of the existing channels.

While the controllers of the four British channels still dominate the air-waves, they wait anxiously to see where the new technology will first seriously break through. Will governments eventually be unable to control or censor what comes into their countries—as they could never (not even Hitler) altogether censor radio from abroad? Will television, which grew up as the most circumscribed and national of all media, be liberated into a new anarchy of the ether, as advertisers, pornographers and soap-opera merchants sell their wares across the globe? Will the richer and choosier viewers turn to cassettes and cables for their culture or information, leaving the main channels to the admass? Will these last three decades—when all classes watched the same serials, comedies and news—be only a temporary phase before television becomes as class-conscious and segregated as newspapers?

The debate about television technologies brings back in a topical form the arguments between paternalism and free competition which have run through this book. The BBC now presents the prospect of uncontrolled television from satellites and cables as a danger to both morality and equality. Brian Wenham warns that the rights to sporting events will be bought up by satellite or cable contractors, and relayed only to people who pay to watch them: 'Broadcasting's third age,' he says, 'could see deepening divisions between those who have access to the new and those who have no such access. It is a fair bet that this new division will once again lie along the basic south-east versus non-south-east economic fault that already disfigures the country.'[7] 'If cable in Britain were opened up to free market forces,' asks Alasdair Milne, 'what's to prevent major foreign operators like Warner-Amex buying into it, running *Dallas* every night and simply whittling away at the public service principles on which British broadcasting has been established?'[8]

[7] *Ibid.*
[8] The *Guardian*, March 18, 1982.

Yet the insularity and protectiveness of British television at its worst presents an equal danger: that viewers can be encouraged to take an isolated and nostalgic view of themselves, with still more serials about life in old country houses, histories of empire and Edwardian dramas, while the swirling tides of international change pass them by. The paternalism of the BBC is less easy to justify when it ceases to adopt an educative role, and opts out of explaining the world to its viewers, while it still carries the old danger of becoming an organ of national self-congratulation. Television still has a huge power to show people the larger context of their lives; and if the British do not face up to their problems the controllers of the screen must take part of the blame.

Conclusion

The Post-Imperial Trap

The characteristic danger of great nations, like the Roman, or the English, which have a long history of continuous creation, is that they may at last fail from not comprehending the great institutions they have created.

Walter Bagehot

My dear young man, there is a good deal of ruin in a country.
The dying Adam Smith to Sir
John Sinclair (who said that
Britain would be ruined), 1790

In this book I have tried not to impose any single theme or thesis on all these very different British spheres, to let people and facts speak for themselves, and only occasionally to pick up threads and clues which have run through the maze. But I have asked myself a recurring question, as I did twenty years ago: how far have Britain's institutions and rulers stood up to their historic challenge to revive and modernise a nation which carries a heavy weight from the past and faces a highly competitive future? Has Britain survived the classic fate of so many ex-imperial nations, from Egypt to Spain, of becoming trapped in bureaucracies and attitudes which are too inflexible to adjust to new problems? The question becomes more insistent in the face of bleaker winds of world competition, recession and unemployment.

INSTITUTIONS

Twenty years ago Britain was already full of reforming zeal and determined to modernise her institutions—even before Harold Wilson proclaimed his own white-hot revolution to transform whole areas of administration, from schools to scientists to civil servants. How seriously the politicians pursued many of those reforms is open to question. Certainly their failures gave much ammunition to true conservatives who insisted that all change was for the worse, and who believed in those pessimistic laws which explain that changes achieve the opposite of what they intend, that more means worse, and that if something can go wrong, it will go wrong.

The move to democratise education succeeded in strengthening the fee-paying schools and abolishing most grammar schools, the traditional poor boy's ladder to the top. The huge spending to apply science to industry succeeded in making scientists still more academic. The attempts to open up Whitehall and the Foreign Office made the mandarins more embattled and relatively secure. The failed reforms, in contrast to the successful Victorian reforms a century earlier, gave a special poignancy to Bagehot's warning in the mid-nineteenth century; for those 'great institutions', reinforced by their own trade unions and professional pride, had shown how effectively they could close ranks against change. As Sir Monty Finniston found when he tried to reform the engineering profession, Machiavelli's warning was still valid: 'The innovator has for enemies all those who have done well under the old conditions.'

Inside its own castle each profession can present its defences as part of a great tradition of autonomy and freedom, and everyone else's as selfish greed. Lawyers complain about trade union mono-polies, while they fortify their own monopoly; dons talk about academic freedom and journalists about the freedom of the Press, when they often mean their own freedom from reform. The huge extension of white-collar trade unionism in the sixties, which was expected to moderate the trade union movement, soon made it more extreme; and the TUC became more unpopular as each union refused to see beyond its own claims. But union attitudes were still less attractive when they spread to Whitehall. Many younger public servants would privately criticise their institutions as much as any outsider, but once attacked from outside they would close ranks to defend their overmanned offices or index-linked pensions, in a kind of reversal of Voltaire's principle: 'I agree with everything you say, but I will fight to the end to prevent it happening.'

It is much too early to assess the full consequences of many reforms of the sixties: long after the Victorians reformed education, the army or the civil service, conservative critics were mocking their democratic zeal. Any changes which depend on shifting attitudes will have a long time-lag; twenty years after Macmillan integrated the Ministry of Defence the armed forces are only beginning to adopt a 'tri-service outlook'. The effects of comprehensive schooling—the most fundamental of Labour's changes—will only become clearer after a new generation has grown up in that context. But the faith in 'social engineering' which marked much radical thinking in the fifties and sixties, whether in Britain or the United States, is now less evident, as old patterns of behaviour and institutions reassert themselves below the political surface. Disraeli's view in 1881 remains relevant: 'it is a very difficult country to move'.

In all their attempted reforms governments and commissions were reluctant to interfere with the traditional autonomy of professions or groups. They liked to assume that civil servants, scientists or teachers would co-operate in reforms from within; they shied away from statutory changes or imposing their own direction, and when they failed they preferred to conceal their frustration. The institutions remained largely immune in their autonomy while they had become increasingly separated from the centre or from each other. The overlapping circles which are portrayed on the endpapers of this book give my own rough impression of the relationships between Britain's institutions. The conspiratorial notions of a single 'Establishment' which holds them all together is all too untrue. The obstacles to Britain's reform have lain in the lack of effective co-ordination and control, and the circles are always threatening to pull themselves further apart.

The civil service which influences so many other bureaucracies remains basically unreformed. The criticisms of the early sixties—about its amateurism, unaccountability and lack of experience of industry and technology—remain almost as valid as ever. The scandal of the Crown Agents, the civil servants who in 1974 had squandered £180 million in irresponsible investments, provided a kind of caricature of Whitehall amateurism and separatism which the fiercest critics could not have imagined. The senior Crown Agent, Sir Claude Hayes, was a man who (as the Report of the Tribunal concluded in 1982) should never have been appointed, who never felt himself answerable to anyone and who 'was never able to exercise any effective supervision'. The Director of Finance Mr Challis had no experience of how to control his banking operations, and 'no one seriously tried to exercise any control over him'. The Crown Agents began speculating in investments with none of the necessary skills: 'For what they were now attempting they were on the whole no more than amateurs.' The Ministry of Overseas Development, the Treasury and the Bank of England all knew that something was going wrong, but shuffled papers between each other: 'The situation cried out for someone to use some common sense, show some initiative, and grapple with the problem. But nobody took the lead.' It was a story which illustrated all the worst fears of an overblown bureaucracy; arrogantly and secretly conducting its own operations with public money without anyone taking the ultimate responsibility.

Of all the legacies of empire the most dangerous is surely an immobile bureaucracy which can perpetuate its own interests and values, like those ancient hierarchies which presided over declining civilisations: the Pharaonic bureaucracy which still casts its spell over the chaos of contemporary Egypt; or the Byzantine bureaucracy which grew up in the Ottoman Empire; or the court of Imperial Spain which could not face the new challenges of the sixteenth century: 'Heirs to a society which had over-invested in an empire, and surrounded by the increasingly shabby remnants of a dwindling inheritance, they could not bring themselves at a moment of crisis to surrender their memories and alter the antique pattern of their lives.'[1] As the British mandarins reinforce their defences, awarding each other old imperial honours, do they hear any echoes from Castile or Byzantium?

BIGNESS AND CENTRALISATION

In the first post-war decades the decline of British power was mitigated by two special circumstances. The first was the Anglo-American relationship, which could conceal many of the humiliations—at least for those at the top—in the appearance of a common transatlantic identity, so that the British (as Macmillan put it) could be 'Greeks in their Roman Empire'. The second was the long Western boom, which allowed the British in spite of their industrial weakness to double their standard of living in a decade, and to expand as they never could during those pre-war decades when half the globe was still coloured red. Britain was never so rich as when she had offloaded her empire.

In this expansive mood the British embarked on many of their ambitious reforms: building new universities, hospitals or motorways, planning new towns, tower blocks and civic centres. At the same time the pursuit of bigness became a cult, encouraged by prosperity and American precedents: skyscrapers and neckties, tower blocks and television sets, hospitals and cars—they all got bigger and supposedly better. British institutions enlarged themselves without much questioning from economists, sociologists or politicians. Governments and civil servants enthusiastically merged ministries, counties or airlines.

But already by the early seventies the failure of many mergers—whether of companies or Whitehall departments—was becoming clear. After twenty years expansion was succeeded by contraction, optimism by pessimism and mergers by de-mergers. In Whitehall whole armies of civil servants had marched up the hill and down again. The Departments of Trade, Industry, Transport or Energy re-emerged as separate entities from their monster ministries; the Tory Secretary for Social Services tried to remove the extra tier

[1] J. H. Elliott: *Imperial Spain 1469–1716* (paperback edition), Penguin, London, 1970, p. 382.

which his Tory predecessor had added; British Airways planned to split up again into Overseas and European airlines. The Treasury survived its rivals, the Department of Economic Affairs and the Civil Service Department, and was once again the sole arbiter of national priorities.

But the age of expansion and bigness in the sixties had left many relics which could not easily be dismantled, like the great tower blocks in the cities which were symbols of the past arrogance of planners. The bigger bureaucracies had added to Britain's inflexibility, when she needed to be more flexible than ever: the town halls and county headquarters, the extensions of Whitehall, the irremovable dons in contracting universities, the middle-aged army of the BBC, were all reminders that yesterday's experiments had become today's heavy commitments. While private companies were compelled to lose some of their fat, public institutions were much harder to reduce; and the gap widened between the security inside them and the insecurity in the cold world outside. The great bureaucracies were like pie-crusts which had risen with the rising prosperity, and were now left as high superstructures while the rest of the pie had subsided.

Within government there had been a relentless trend towards the centre, and the spiders' webs of the Treasury and the Cabinet Office were now still more centralised. The countervailing powers of local government had been eaten away, the plans for regional devolution had been shelved and the private sector was far weaker. The Treasury model and the Treasury's control of public spending, with all its vagaries and missing billions, dominated a larger sector of the economy, while the Treasury itself was more tightly held by a group of Conservative ministers.

The combination of bureaucracy and centralisation in the metropolis had marked many declining empires, whose hopes for revival lay in provinces which were less demoralised by extravagance and overmanning. But the flow of power towards Whitehall and the Treasury has increased over recent years as local authorities, lacking their own proper accountability, have lost still more of their autonomy. Each mistake at the centre has been reflected round the periphery. When the Treasury retrenches, every university, school and local council has to retrench: the centre can only keep all these overlapping circles in check by the crudest yardsticks of money. Banks, industrial corporations, insurance companies and newspapers have followed the centralising trend, draining more of the decisions from Edinburgh, Manchester or Liverpool; while the London concentration has increased the preoccupation with control rather than opportunities.

Both the old political parties while promising decentralisation have taken more power to the centre, and only the Social Democrats and Liberals are now seriously promising to increase the powers of the regions. While Germany has a much more decentralised political system and France is now genuinely trying to delegate power from Paris, the British system has become still more concentrated on Whitehall and Westminster. Yet only by creating stronger regional powers with proper accountability and powers of taxation (as in Germany or in America) will the British be able to escape from the dead hand of the centre.

While many businessmen blamed governments for this accretion of centralised power, the private sector had created its own extravagant concentrations. Many of the company directors who pressed through mergers showed little sign of thinking seriously about who should run them, or how; they often expected them to produce their own logic and disciplines. They argued that larger units were essential to the new global scale, which was true for many high-technology and heavy industries, but the mergers which swept up breweries, service industries and entertainment into new conglomerates showed few benefits to the consumers; and the original mergers had more to do with unexploited assets and the stockmarket than with serious economies of scale. With relatively easy profits and without effective shareholders' control the companies could build up their armies of executives and workers, and when they merged, ostensibly to produce economies, they often (like British Leyland or British Airways) kept both staffs intact. (It was another echo of Imperial Spain, where aristocratic households grew still larger because of the Castilian custom that when a nobleman bought an estate he kept on all the predecessor's household, while adding his own. It was the numbers of workers which gave him his status, rather than their effectiveness.[2])

Politicians on both sides of the House were inclined to prefer bigger companies which seemed to make planning and negotiations easier at the top; Whitehall liked to deal with big companies and big unions while the TUC and the CBI agreed about the advantages of a merger which increased the monopoly power on both sides. The meetings of Neddy at the peak of the triangle began to look like Adam Smith's picture of men of business conspiring against the public. It was the consumer who paid the price for many of the mergers, but he was left out of the picture.

What lay behind the obsession with bigness and mergers in the sixties? Certainly the expansion often suited the ambitions of chairmen and directors, whose status and salaries were related to the

[2] J. H. Elliott: *op cit*, p. 315.

numbers under them. Certainly the example of American models, such as ITT or LTV, could be used to justify the British mergers—though the American background was quite different, and many of the American giants also came unstuck. But many of the British mergers in hindsight look very like an evasion of real responsibility—an attempt to escape from the problems of one business by merging it with another, hoping vaguely that mistakes would come out in the wash. Diversification often meant simply diversion; and the fashionable idea of the master-manager who could wear a different hat every day—a brewer on Monday, a builder on Tuesday, a hotel-keeper on Wednesday—could easily mean a manager who understood no business properly.

In the boom years the giants could conceal their irresponsibility and flabbiness, often by becoming still bigger; but the gales of the recession, first in 1974 and then from 1979 onwards, blew through their rickety structures. Blue-chip companies turned from profits to losses and nationalised industries, led by cars and steel, showed themselves helpless to compete on world markets. Chairmen could no longer evade the question of who was really responsible. Hiring was easy, but firing required hard decisions.

By the early eighties British attitudes to big business had fundamentally changed. The companies which survived the recession most successfully knew their own business inside-out and stuck to it, like Sainsbury and Marks and Spencer; while many new conglomerates like Imps or Bats now looked thoroughly muddled. The small company came back into favour as the provider of jobs, while the family firm which had so frequently been ridiculed now often showed more sense of identity, and of planning ahead, than anonymous managers. The entrepreneur, the old villain of the left, came back as the predator, swooping down on dying companies, picking them up, shaking them, dropping them elsewhere; and the global market-place gave new scope to operators with no fixed abode or nationality.

But the entrepreneurial spirit had also come back into the board-rooms of many big corporations. Directors could no longer act as committees shuffling decisions between them and in the midst of the storm they had to choose chairmen (such as Hogg of Courtaulds, Harvey-Jones of ICI or Durham of Unilever) who would take a bold lead, make unpopular decisions and stand up and be counted. Compared to Britain in the sixties the business leadership was much more obviously personal; no one had much doubt about where the buck stopped, and de-personalised management systems were swept away in the gales. Nationalised industries with their tradition of 'high custodians' now acquired some of the most ruthless chairmen of all competing over the numbers of people they had fired. Who among the original nationalisers could have foreseen the Age of McGregor and Edwardes? What will future historians make of a period whose rulers so rapidly changed their whole attitude to jobs, and allowed three million unemployed to become like ghosts outside the economic system?

THE PIT AND THE PENDULUM

Many of the mistakes and mergers were shared by both parties. It was Ted Heath who pressed for new monster-ministries and Sir Keith Joseph who complicated the social services. Both parties welcomed the merging of counties which extended and entrenched the local government bureaucracy. Giant trade unions and national-ised industries were mirrored by the gigantism of private corpora-tions. The swings of the political pendulum added an extra irrespon-sibility to the years of decline, for they allowed each side to blame the other for the national predicament, while each new government felt committed to its rash promises made in opposition.

The discontinuity influenced nearly every department of govern-ment, but it was the frontier between government, industry and technology which witnessed the most casualties, unsuccessful sorties and evacuated positions. Labour governments tried vainly to institutionalise the future, while Conservatives tried to stop inter-vening in industry until they were forced into reverse. The alphabet of institutions (with which hapless observers had to grapple over twenty years) from the IRC and the DEA and the CSD in the sixties, to the CPRS and NEB in the seventies, to the DTG and the merger between NRB and the NEDC in the eighties, reflected all the uncer-tainties of governments, as Britain looked sometimes towards America, sometimes towards France as her models for her future: lacking the incentives of the first, and the direction of the second.

Only Neddy, which Macmillan invented twenty years ago, neighed its way through every government, alternately welcomed as the only national meeting-place, and denigrated as the packhorse of corporat-ism and arch-appeaser of unions. The industrial horror-stories of the sixties, such as Leyland and Rolls Royce, provided their own warn-ings of the dangers of leaving crucial companies to themselves. But after all the political turnabouts and buffetings of recessions, the government in the eighties was not much closer to working out how to provide technological support for the key industries of the future, or the people to run them; and they demoted the most promising new institution, the NEB, which had salvaged and revived some of the industrial wreckage of the early seventies.

It was the lack of long-term planning for industry, the key to Britain's survival, which showed up most glaringly the absence of common purpose. Governments and industrialists had been alternately brought together and separated, with 'hands on' one year and 'hands off' the next. The chops and changes between parties had frustrated industrial plans that would outlive two or three governments, and these failures provided a damaging case against the two-party system. By the early seventies the political swings were becoming more extreme, as the static standard of living and the low growth-rate made the left more disillusioned with the mixed economy, while the right became more determined to weaken the unions and reinvigorate the private sector.

What was the most critical period in the break-up of the middle ground? Was it 1973, which ushered in a harsher economic era all over the West? Was it 1968, when student revolts helped to alienate a new age-group of intellectuals? Was it the very expansion of the sixties which, followed by contraction, ensured a more discontented generation? Whatever the turning-points, Harold Wilson's first government already showed clear signs that the mixed economy would not provide the kind of benefits forecast in Crosland's *Future of Socialism*; and many younger Labour intellectuals and trade unionists could not share the hopes of their elders.

The arrival of Thatcher undoubtedly marked a more complete break than the arrival of Heath ten years before, while the world recession, together with a high pound and high interest rates, provided a shock to British industry and a rapid increase in unemployment which exaggerated Thatcher's own severity. No one concerned by the inertia and irresponsibility of institutions could totally withhold admiration for Mrs Thatcher, who insisted on the responsibility of the individual and who tried much harder than her predecessors to cut down the Whitehall bureaucracy and stimulate competition. No institution looked quite the same after she had cast her beady eye over it.

But there was always a huge gap between her individualist philosophy and the effects of her policies. The first results of her tax changes, for all the talk of incentives and investment, was to make the rich richer; and the rich meant predominantly the old rich who were mostly not much interested in new incentives or new investment within Britain. While she was pledged to cut back the monopolies of trade unions and nationalised industries, she was much less interested in limiting the power of private concentrations of corporate power. Her government did little to prevent a new rush of mergers, including newspaper mergers, which were reducing the freedom of choice and the scope of individuals. And she presided over a new wave of centralisation towards London and the Treasury.

Much more serious, she had virtually abdicated the responsibility for mitigating unemployment which both parties had recognised since the end of the Second World War. The processions of tens of thousands from corporations to the dole may have been inevitable to enable companies to compete in the world; and the armies of jobless were growing all over Europe. But the huge increase in British unemployed within a highly centralised nation could only be tolerable if it were accompanied by imaginative policies from the centre. To unleash the forces of capitalism and concentration without protection and counter-action from the state was to revert to an earlier stage of British civilisation.

A government which made no serious attempt to cushion the effects with job creation and regional aid could only store up huge troubles for the future, and Thatcher's policy would swell the numbers of people who felt excluded and provoked by the Westminster system. The Conservatives had virtually lost the paternalist instinct which had enabled them to come to terms with so many working-class revolts in the past; or as one cabinet minister lamented to me: 'We are digging a pit which the party will take years to get out of.' Many industrialists as well as politicians were worried that an industrial revival could not command long-term confidence unless it were underpinned by political stability and reasonable relations with unions.

The pendulum had swung across a wider arc, and both the big parties were now more closely associated with specific class interests. The old battles between nationalisation and denationalisation, between nuclear armament and disarmament, were surging up again as they had in the late fifties. Each party's policies were linked to national attitudes, yet over twenty years the problems of both industry and defence had become more interlocked in a European or transatlantic context. Steel and cars would face the same harsh competition whether state-owned or privately owned, and unilateral disarmament made no long-term sense without European disarmament.

The parliamentary ding-dong could too easily conceal the real argument elsewhere. The Alliance between the Social Democrats and Liberals (I believe) should allow the British to face problems more realistically; to by-pass the outdated deadlocks between the two sides of industry; to escape from the corporate pressures of big unions and companies; to see Britain's predicament in a European dimension; and to begin the effective decentralisation of the powers of Whitehall and Westminster. But an innovating party faces all the entrenched attitudes of an adversary system which has become embedded in parliament and the media, and all the opposition of the corporate interests on both sides.

Behind all the swings and changes of the last decades was there any meaning left in the old idea of the Establishment, which had cast such a spell over the Macmillan years? Certainly the political leadership now shows little connection with that many-branched family tree of the Devonshires and the Salisburys which spread out to many of the key emplacements of power in the early sixties. Certainly school and university backgrounds have lost some of their significance in parliament. In the Labour party Michael Foot and Tony Benn (however disguised) both come from the old Oxford and public-school tradition; but as the party has moved to the left it has broken most of its links with the patrician or Fabian tradition, and new leaders such as Eric Heffer, Neil Kinnock or Eric Varley have come up from proletarian backgrounds.

The Conservatives have broken with their aristocratic leadership since they chose the Earl of Home, and Margaret Thatcher sees herself as owing no debts or loyalties to the old guard, and appealing directly to the people. After her reshuffle the Tory cabinet in 1982 was much more in her own mould, with two of her closest supporters—Cecil Parkinson as Tory chairman and Norman Tebbit as Secretary for Employment—both from modest backgrounds. Outside parliament, too, there is now less aristocratic influence; the Governor and the Deputy Governor of the Bank of England both come from outside the 'charmed circle'; the chairman and director-general of the IBA are both outsiders; nearly all chairmen of big corporations, scientists and vice-chancellors come from grammar schools; and none of the leading entrepreneurs have been to university at all.

Yet alongside this new meritocracy there still remains a remarkable educational elite which has maintained its continuity and influence through all the political upheavals. Few people in the early Wilson years would have predicted that in 1982 the chairman of the BBC, the editor of *The Times*, the Foreign Secretary, the heads of both foreign and civil services and half the chairmen of the big four banks would all be Old Etonians, while the Home Secretary, the Chancellor, the director-general of the BBC, a bevy of judges and the other two bank chairmen would come from the rival foundation, Winchester. Such a lasting duopoly must surely have some significance in Britain's anatomy.

Of course it was never likely that two medieval institutions which had survived King Henry VIII, Cromwell, Victorian reformers and two world wars would lightly surrender their influence to Harold Wilson or Anthony Crosland. But far from retreating, they have advanced into new areas of influence; and their success is more marked than in Macmillan's time or (as far as I can trace) than in any earlier time. The Victorian professions were full of self-made men who worked their way up to the top, and several schools prepared the way to power. Macmillan's Britain included outsiders such as William Haley editing *The Times* or Sir Norman Brook running the civil service.

But since then the products of these two ancient schools have reasserted all their old ability to climb the ladders of power, with a continuity which has no parallel in other industrial countries. 'Eton and Winchester sometimes seem to be conspiracies rather than educational establishments,' wrote Anthony Hartley twenty years ago; and today their pervasiveness looks still more remarkable, as other schools appear less preoccupied with power.

The success of Etonians does not represent a straightforward defence of the landed interest, or a reactionary response to social change. Many of the present crop are not rich or aristocratic; and three Old Etonians in Thatcher's previous cabinet—Gilmour, Soames, and Thorneycroft—were sacked for being too 'wet'. Etonians nowadays are servants as much as masters, and it was Thatcher who appointed Pym to the Foreign Office, and Armstrong to run the civil service. It is their political skill, their confidence and flexibility, which accounts for their rise much more than their wealth or family connections, and which equips them to serve as the power-brokers who can be so useful to any government. The old schools may retain their role as a new generation becomes more academically competitive, combining the drive of a meritocracy with the advantages of privilege. They have extended their earlier roles, when they provided clever boys to climb up through the Church and the law, and they have retained their preoccupation with power and worldly success long after it became less attractive to many others. In the last decades—while the empire has vanished, the world of culture and leisure has beckoned, and administration has become more specialised and exacting—many schoolboys have found the traditional 'glittering prizes' less glittering: the field-marshal's baton, the judge's wig or the governor's plumes have lost much of their glory. These old schools however have retained all their dedication to the power game, competing with their contemporaries all the way to the top; and it is power which remains their métier.

The traditional elites have also retained their own communication system which still gives them a special tribal role in the midst of contemporary Britain. As society becomes more complex and the circles pull apart, so the people who can make connections between them become more useful as the fixers, the lubricants or brokers between one sphere and another. In the world of finance, which depends on quick communications and trust, the Old Boy Net still plays a special part; and the disasters of 1974 only underlined the dangers of newcomers. And in the City the continuity of old traditions seems to merge with deeper tribal patterns of trust.

The foreigners who come up against the strange behaviour inside the square mile perhaps see more clearly its anthropological and tribal roots. 'Is complex society more rational than simple society?' asks a Japanese academic, Kazunori Oshima, observing the rituals of 'top-hatters' and the stylised conversations of City insiders, 'held together,' as he puts it, 'by a complex body of customs that are to an outsider as esoteric and bizarre as those in any preindustrial culture.' Oshima compares the City tribalism with the Black Muslims in America and concludes that 'the archaic behaviour of City men and the distinctive patterns of action of the Black Muslims are not unlike the symbolic pattern of behaviour of tribes in the simplest societies'.[3]

Is there a price to pay for these 'bizarre customs'? In the City, which is surrounded by risks, the rituals of trust have their obvious advantages. But in the wider context of Britain the rule of the Eton and Winchester tribes seems to reflect a degree of regression: a fear of disruptive forces and a preoccupation with controlling and containing new people from the centre. It is not very plausible that such a narrow elite could effectively represent the diversity of people with such different backgrounds from theirs; and their success lies more in restraint than in adventure. These traditional British nurseries of power remain very cut off from the world of technologists and industrial managers who offer the most promising hopes for Britain's future; while the old cross-purposes between engineers and administrators remain as extreme as ever. When the British need bold industrial leadership which combines technical mastery with political confidence they often have to look right outside their own class system—to the South African Edwardes in Leyland, the Scots-American McGregor in British Steel, or the American Giordano in British Oxygen.

Every advanced country, of course, includes very separate elites: New York bankers are cut off from Detroit industrialists, *Inspecteurs des Finances* in Paris from manufacturers in Lille. But the traditional British elite, fortified by their ancient schools and Oxbridge colleges, have maintained their edge over others—at some cost to the country.

[3] Doshisha Studies in English, 27: Doshisha University, 1981.

Their values are less closely related to technology and industry than to pre-industrial activities such as banking and the army, and their influence reached its apogee in the administration of the empire. Britain achieved the dismantling of the empire with remarkably little political revolt, but found it much harder to change her social structure to ensure her commercial survival.

THE QUIXOTE COMPLEX

It was the public response to the Falklands expedition—twenty-five years after Suez, forty years after the Second World War—which suggested most clearly that the older British values and attitudes were still lurking close to the surface, as if the war and the empire had happened only yesterday. Was the national consciousness, like the human brain, divided between the fore-brain which can calculate and reason, and the primitive hind-brain which reacts only to simple stimuli and dangers? If so, the Falklands brought the old brain back to the forefront. As the armada set sail so the language of politicians and the Press seemed to have reverted back four decades as they exchanged war-cries against the new-found enemies, the Argies.

The admirals and generals who had been off-stage for so long reappeared with all their confidence intact; the armada's prompt-ness and efficiency seemed out of character with other British nationalised industries; everyone knew his place in the structured class system of the army and navy. Parliament debated the Falk-lands with more passion and interest than they ever gave to technol-ogy and exports, and for a few weeks the British seemed to discover a national purpose and unity which they never brought to the prob-lems of economic survival. The resounding echoes from the Second World War were another reminder that advanced societies can still have a primitive basis. The sense of returning to old values and relationships was heightened when the Pope arrived in the midst of the war, visiting the Queen and the Archbishop of Canterbury as if to complete the medieval backcloth to the pageant.

Was Britain's surge of military pride another sign, as Dean Ache-son warned us twenty years ago, that Britain had lost an empire but not yet found a new role? Or was it—as Thatcher suggested—a renewal of the spirit of national confidence and self-respect, infusing all its other activities and relationships? 'We have proved ourselves to ourselves,' she said in July 1982. 'The faltering and self-doubt have given way to achievement and pride.'

Certainly the British response to the Argentinian invasion involved a genuine element of high principle which would have been humiliating to ignore. But that principle was rapidly overlaid by the war fever and military momentum; and Britain's allies were soon more alarmed by her intransigence than impressed by her honour. It seemed to some of them like a quixotic enterprise, in the literal sense; for Don Quixote—as Cervantes created him in the twilight of the Spanish empire—was fascinated by the romances and past glories of Imperial Spain, embarking on his excursions of honour and principle to rescue damsels or tilt at windmills, with a romanticism which baffled the rest of the world.

Britain's preoccupation with the Falklands, which gave her no economic or diplomatic advantage, likewise baffled her allies. The general British condition already had some worrying resemblances to the symptoms of decline in Imperial Spain—the preoccupation with the past and academic pursuits, the obsession with honours, the contempt for workaday trade. The enthusiasm over the Falklands War seemed to follow the same pattern. But in Argentina Britain found an enemy which was even more quixotic, with her inheritance of Spanish pride; and Argentina like Britain had found a unity in a military enterprise which had eluded her in the commercial competition of peacetime. The sense of purpose which Britain had shown in the Falklands expedition had no lasting value unless it could be transferred to the more critical industrial and social challenges at home, to foster unity rather than confrontation.

THE WORLD AND THE NATION

Was there a cure for Britain's post-imperial malaise? Many politicians since the Second World War had worried about it, with the spectres of Spain or Portugal lurking in their minds. Many Conservatives including Macmillan, Macleod and Heath had prescribed Europe as part of the cure, an opening-up on to a larger stage on which Britain would face up to the commercial challenges of the future. There was always no doubt an element of escapism in the vision of leaving behind Britain's problems on the way to Brussels. But the European Community during the long boom of the fifties and sixties did provide a kind of political magic, as the competition across frontiers and the growing standard of living gave the nations a sense of common identity. It was, I still believe, a major political tragedy that Britain did not take part in this European experience when it was most valuable and politically creative.

By the time Britain entered the Community in 1972 the European prospects were already less attractive and the nationalist reaction of de Gaulle had already weakened the spirit of unity. The climacteric year of 1973 soon had traumatic effects as each European nation panicked over its oil supplies and scrambled to make its own deals with OPEC powers, while the high oil-price helped to turn the boom into a recession. Many British Europeans (including myself) were reluctant to face up to the disillusion that followed. The British public began to associate Europe with higher food prices, with its own uncontrollable bureaucracy and powerless parliament; and while Britain had to pay large subsidies to European agriculture, the years of recession and low growth deprived her of the compensating regional subsidies which she had expected. Nationalism was reviving in Germany and Italy as well as France, and Jean Monnet himself became less confident in his last years that free trade could in itself integrate nations.

By the end of the first decade of Britain-in-Europe in 1982 most past enthusiasts had to admit that Britain had joined the Community either too late or too soon. The Common Market once again aroused bitter divisiveness within Britain as politicians blamed it for the gales of world competition, the mounting unemployment and the high cost of food. The cold shower which Macmillan had promised twenty years earlier turned out to be an icy pool which submerged many of the swimmers. The old Macmillan exhortations such as 'exporting is fun' or 'it's exciting living on the edge of bankruptcy' sounded less jolly to chief executives who had to close down whole towns in order to keep their corporate heads above water.

But the context of competition had now widened again. It was no longer just Mercedes and Fiat, Grundig and Olivetti, who were Britain's challengers; it was Datsun, Sony and Mitsubishi; cameras from Singapore, TV sets from Korea. The Japanese successes throughout Europe, on top of the American challenge, had changed the whole dimension: and to compete in high technology the Europeans would have to collaborate more closely, whether in common defence contracts, common production, or closer co-operation with governments. The old commercial battles between Leyland, Renault and Volkswagen began to look like Balkan rivalries compared to the threat from Japanese cars, electronics and information technology which were hitting Americans as well as Europeans.

Perhaps Europe's predicament could only be seen clearly from outside the continent. Viewed from Tokyo or even from Seoul or Singapore, it was not just Britain that looked a quaint out-of-date nation with a romantic history ('Is it true,' one Korean asked me, 'that Britain used to have an empire on which the sun never set?'); it was all Europe that looked increasingly old-fashioned, and rooted in the past. The Pacific Basin, with its islands, peninsulas and ambitious nations trading hectically with each other, began to look like a re-creation of nineteenth-century Europe, with the same zest for innovation and awareness of world markets as Victorian Britain or Wilhelmine Germany, and with a commercial patriotism which could bring together industrialists, ministers and scientists with a common interest in national survival.

As they faced this commercial bombardment, from the other end of the world as well as from Europe, the British were not surprisingly tempted to start putting up the shutters to protect their own industries more thoroughly. If they kept their windows open they would have to undertake a more drastic 'adjustment'—as economists euphemistically called closing down industries and opening up new ones—than other Europeans. Yet protection could offer no long-term solutions for a country which could never be self-sufficient and whose temporary new asset, its oil, would soon start to run out. Cutting back Britain's imports would inevitably lead to reprisals against Britain's exports. A country which depended so heavily on its exports would always have to compete in world markets.

It was easy to blame British workers and trade unionists for turning away from the facts, for insisting on pulling out of the European Community even though it accounted for 60 per cent of Britain's trade, and for obstructing technological change in their distrust of the future. But Britain's rulers and managers had not done very much to comprehend or explain the real predicament. Few industrialists dared to confront their employees candidly with the extent of their global challenge. The bankers, who knew most about the world economy, saw it in terms of impersonal numbers. The diplomats still preferred to see themselves on a loftier plane than mere trade. The Press and television were still largely circumscribed in a national context. The politicians themselves, engrossed in their parliamentary games, hated to admit that much that they said or did was largely irrelevant in this global drama. Was it surprising if workers still dreamt of retreating into a national Utopia where they could build socialism untainted by foreigners?

What does the notion of patriotism amount to in a complex and interdependent world? What is the relevance of ancient British traditions in a world of superpowers and high-technology nations? The questions loom larger at a time when the forces of nationalism appear to be reviving all over the world. The economists' assumptions in the sixties that the nation-states would be eroded by multinational corporations and global free trade now look much less convincing. The nation is still the chief focus for people's identity, the source of much of their security and confidence: the more uncertain the world climate, the more important the nation will seem. The Falklands crisis was a reminder of how rapidly patriotic emotions can be re-awakened.

Yet the sense of national resolve against aggression does not in itself solve any other British problems, which depend on patient and mature co-operation. The lasting historical achievement of British institutions has been to hold people together in peace with a sense of identity and mutual respect, to accommodate social change and to provide the political stability on which everything else rests. It was this which has been the basis of Britain's reputation abroad, which has provided the background of past industrial achievements and which has kept the City as a financial centre for five hundred years. It was the balance between political stability and economic drive which was the secret of Victorian Britain—for without the one the other could quickly collapse. And it is the British ability to resolve social conflicts through peaceful political solutions which remains the most valuable element in their patriotism.

Any cure to the British post-imperial malaise must begin with the opening-up to wider horizons and facing the real global challenges of the future. It will not be achieved by trying to recapture the self-confidence and arrogance of imperial Britain, which was based on a military power and industrial supremacy which can never return. It will depend on new opportunities, new kinds of people outside the old classes, who are aware of new opportunities, innovations and new markets abroad. Only if the British people are confronted by their real predicament, without the concealments of politicians and the obstacles of defensive institutions, can they be expected to respond to the challenge.

INDEX

Index

Compiled by Douglas Matthews

Ludwig, Daniel, 331, 393
Lusaka Conference (1979), 7
Lyons, J. (company), 289, 313
Lyons, Roger, 349

M

M & D Technology, 296
M & G Funds, 407
MI5, 240, 242
MI6, 240–2, 244
Macadam, Sir Peter, 343
McAlpine, Lord, 29
McAlpine, Malcolm, 341
McCarthy, Lord, 64
Macaulay, Thomas Babington,
    Lord, 164
McCrum, Michael, 126
MacDonald, Ramsay, 94
McDonnell Douglas, aircraft
    company, 284
McFadden Law (USA), 275
McFadzean, Frank, Lord, 359–60,
    374
MacFisheries, 371
McGahey, Mick, 82
McGarvey, Dan, 62
McGowan, Lord, 344, 357
McGregor, Ian, 67, 359, 366–8, 425,
    430
Machiavelli, N., 48, 213, 419
McIntosh, Ian, 284
McIver, Jill, 409
McKay, Alexander, 222
Mackworth-Young, William, 280
McLennan, Gordon, 82
Macleod, Iain, 35–6, 432
McMahon, Kit, 266–7
Macmillan, Harold
    antagonises Bill Rodgers, 101
    appointments, 428–9
    and aristocracy, 25, 28, 35, 126
    cabinet changes, 45, 51, 162
    and civil service, 173
    creates life peerages, 25
    and Defence Ministry, 247, 419
    and EEC, 35–6, 48, 233, 432–3

sets up NEDC, 61, 192, 425
    premiership, 35–7, 47, 79
    and science, 213
    on Thatcher shadow cabinet, 44
    on Thatcher government, 48
    and trade unions, 56, 61
    on US relationship, 421
    and university expansion, 129
McNaughton, Sir George, 222
McNee, Sir David, 208
Magdalen College School,
    Northamptonshire, 116
Magistrates (Justice of the Peace),
    154–5
Mail on Sunday, 385
Maisonrouge, Jacques, 369, 380
Maitland, Sir Donald, 179
Makins, Sir Roger, 232
Maland, David, 115, 120
Management, managers (*see also*
    Corporations), 317–18, 336–7,
    342, 434
Manchester
    banks, 273
    riots, 51, 211
Manchester Evening News, 390
Manchester Grammar School,
    119–20
Manchester University, 130, 142
    Institute of Science and
        Technology (UMIST),
        133–4, 142, 216
Manley, Norman, 143
Margaret, Princess, 8, 233
Margulies, E. S., 343
Marine Midland Bank (New York),
    276
Marjolin, Robert, 38
Mark, Sir Robert, 206–9, 212
Marks and Spencer Ltd, 12, 319–20,
    347–8, 424
Marlborough School, 122–3, 159
Marlborough, Duke of, 28
Marquand, David, 99, 103, 135
Marris, Robin, 136
Marsh, Keith, 116
Marsh, Sir Richard, 365
Marshall, R. G., 394

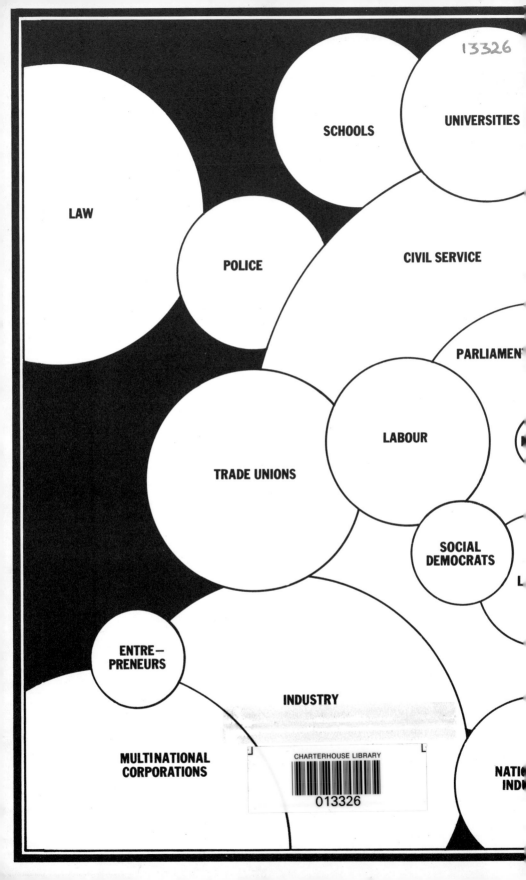

13326

SCHOOLS

UNIVERSITIES

LAW

POLICE

CIVIL SERVICE

PARLIAMEN

LABOUR

TRADE UNIONS

SOCIAL
DEMOCRATS

L

ENTRE—
PRENEURS

INDUSTRY

NATI
INDU